Maastricht Sc... ...l Management

Managing Cultural Diversity

Maastricht School of Management Series in Intercultural and Global Management

MANAGING CULTURAL DIVERSITY

Edited by:
Silvio De Bono
Stephanie Jones
Beatrice Van der Heijden

Meyer & Meyer Media

Maastricht School of Management Series in Intercultural and Global Management
Series Editors: Ronald Tuninga & Fred Phillips

British Library Cataloguing in Publication Data
A catalogue record for this book is available from the British Library

De Bono, Jones & Van der Heijden
Managing Cultural Diversity
Maidenhead: Meyer & Meyer (UK) Ltd., 2008
ISBN: 978-1-84126-239-0

© 2008 by Meyer & Meyer (UK) Ltd.
Adelaide, Auckland, Budapest, Cape Town, Graz, Indianapolis,
Maidenhead, New York, Olten (CH), Singapore, Toronto
Cover Design: Mana co, The Netherlands
Printed and bound in the Netherlands by: Koninklijke Wöhrmann bv, Zutphen
ISBN: 978-1-84126-239-0
E-Mail: verlag@m-m-sports.com
www.m-m-sports.com

CONTENTS

Introduction to the Series 6

Chapter 1   Defining Teams 8
Stephanie Jones and Silvio De Bono

Chapter 2   Leading Teams 27
Stephanie Jones

Chapter 3   Communicating in Teams 48
Silvio De Bono and Stephanie Jones

Chapter 4   Fostering Teams 72
Stephanie Jones and Silvio De Bono

Chapter 5   Conflict in Teams 91
Stephanie Jones and Silvio De Bono

Chapter 6   Introducing Strategic Human Resource Management 112
Silvio De Bono

Chapter 7   Recruiting Talent 130
Silvio De Bono

Chapter 8   Training and Development 145
Silvio De Bono

Chapter 9   Managing and Rewarding Performance 166
Silvio De Bono

Chapter 10   International Human Resource Management 183
Stephanie Jones and Silvio De Bono

Chapter 11   Defining Culture 203
Stephanie Jones

Chapter 12   Organizational Culture 222
Stephanie Jones

Chapter 13   National Culture 239
Stephanie Jones

Chapter 14   Developing Cultural Awareness 257
Stephanie Jones

Chapter 15   Conclusion 275
Silvio De Bono and Stephanie Jones

5

MAASTRICHT SCHOOL OF MANAGEMENT

Series in Intercultural and Global Management

Series Editors Ronald Tuninga and Fred Phillips

Volumes To Date

Stephanie Jones, Khaled Wahba, and Beatrice Van der Heijden
How To Write Your MBA Thesis: A Comprehensive Guide for All Masters' Students Required to Write a Research-Based Thesis or Dissertation (2007)

Joop Remmé, Stephanie Jones, Beatrice Van der Heijden, and Silvio De Bono (Eds.)
Leadership, Change and Responsibility (2008)

Silvio De Bono, Stephanie Jones and Beatrice Van der Heijden (Eds.)
Managing Cultural Diversity (2008)

In Press

Fred Phillips
Managing Innovation, Technology, and Entrepreneurship (2009)

Introduction to the Series

This series makes excellent, affordable textbooks available to students in emerging and developing countries. By emphasizing the international, multicultural, sustainability, and social responsibility dimensions of management, and by giving special attention to change issues in transitional economies, these volumes aim to define the way management subjects can be taught to multicultural audiences. Our goal as editors is to have the series seen as the imprimatur of the best textbooks in the field, and thereby influence the future of teaching international business.

Targeted readers include MBA students in Maastricht School of Management (MSM) overseas outreach programs, students enrolled in other universities, and practicing managers in many countries. Our authors write for readers who wish to be world-class managers, whether in their home countries or abroad, whether for indigenous companies or for multi-nationals.

We nonetheless believe it is not fair to such readers to frame all content in terms of problems and persons representing only business in the OECD nations. Volumes in the series therefore depict business situations drawn from many of the countries where MSM is active. We have chosen authors with broad experience on multiple continents, and specifically in emerging economies and developing countries.

We do not assume readers have access to the books, periodicals, databases, research journals, and fast reliable Internet connections that are taken for granted by MBA students in the OECD countries. Thus, each textbook in the series is a self-contained course on its topic. Each book is suitable for a condensed course format, but also allows teachers the flexibility to use the book for online or face-to-face courses in other formats.

For more than a half century Maastricht School of Management has focused on international cooperation. As a key player in the global education field, MSM is one of the few management schools that systematically combine education, technical assistance and research in its professional services. Offering high-quality management degree programs (MSc, MBA, DBA and PhD) and executive programs, MSM also implements management development research and international projects. With more than 2000 students graduating each year in nearly thirty countries, MSM is the largest and most international business school of the Netherlands.

MSM has worked for years at the interface of public- and private-sector management of transition processes in culturally diverse environments. Our guiding principle is the enhancement of performance of the private and public sectors to support balanced economic development. MSM provides technical assistance and specific training to government agencies, semi-government agencies, NGOs, post-secondary education institutions and the private sector, including small and medium enterprises. MSM offers graduate programs at campuses in Albania, China, Egypt, Germany, Ghana, Indonesia, Jordan, Kazakhstan, Kenya, Kuwait, Malawi, Malaysia, Mongolia, Russia, Namibia, the Netherlands, Peru, Rwanda, Saudi Arabia, Suriname, Tanzania, Uganda, Vietnam, Yemen, Zambia, and Zimbabwe.

Ronald Tuninga and Fred Phillips

CHAPTER 1

DEFINING TEAMS
STEPHANIE JONES AND SILVIO DE BONO

OPENING CASE:

Ranpak is a small, focused and innovative packaging company based in the Netherlands. It may be seen as an unlikely candidate for achieving the quadrupling of the return on investment of its American owners (First Atlantic Capital, New York), yet its earnings before interest, tax, depreciation and amortization (EBITDA) rose significantly in just four years. Now, the firm's prestigious clients – based in Europe, the USA and Asia – include Porsche, Roche, Motorola, UPS, Siemens, Toshiba, Audi, Grohe, Daewoo, IBM and Hilti. The story of how this was achieved is all about teams – how marshalling and mobilizing his teams enabled CEO Joost Dijkstra to turn around the business-to-business packaging firm in a dramatic way, creating a positive team climate and gearing the teams towards change. This involved promoting team-based communication, building team effectiveness, involving the teams in decision-making, and handling the inevitable conflicts in the teams. Joost Dijkstra's own leadership role also played a significant part in defining the work and inspiring the efforts of the teams responsible for Ranpak's success.

With the end of family ownership and the move to new acquirers, Ranpak ("Random Packaging") faced new objectives and profit targets. So, in 2002, the CEO announced the changes about to happen to the employee team. Joost Dijkstra called the labor force into the canteen, and shared with them the news and its implications. He started with himself: as a European he had to get used to an American style of management. Although he had studied for his MBA in the USA and had lived there for several years, this involved a big personal transition. His style was one of coaching his teams and delegating functional responsibility, but the Americans required a concentrated level of detailed hands-on focus, personal control and daily monitoring to provide precise evidence of what was going on in every aspect of the business. This was all quite new to him. He had to learn fast, and so did his teams. The new focus was on value creation – something quite revolutionary. He had to manage expectations – and exceed them. He had to show he could change quickly – and so must everyone else – otherwise the change process would overtake them all.

The way that Joost Dijkstra empowered his teams was so simple it could be summarized on one piece of paper. It was his "value matrix" whereby each team knew very clearly the target it needed to achieve which, added to the whole, would produce the overall revenues needed, on a monthly basis. And the CEO couldn't wait till the end of the month to see if his teams were on track. With the American bosses liable to call up at any minute any day asking to know minute details of the packaging machines installed, the packaging materials produced, the new orders signed up and the new client prospects targeted (even to the extent of the number of pallets leaving the warehouse), each team leader had to have his finger on the pulse, and keep the boss informed. The aim was to "achieve dynamic and lasting competitive strength through innovation, marketing and sales." There would be no easy life for anyone anymore.

At every step of the way, the value of the business and its processes had to be maximized, waste minimized and costs reduced. Non-value-adding activities had to be abandoned, as soon as possible. This involved change, innovation, re-engineering – whatever was needed to make the profit targets happen. And team leaders – and team members – were encouraged to keep thinking of new ideas to keep making things happen. Success breeds success – everyone wants to work for a successful company – and team members discovered reserves of ideas, energy and commitment which they didn't realize they had. They found new opportunities for products and segments, and new ways of making existing businesses more efficient. The lessons he shared with his teams? "Be in the lead of change or be part of change yourself. Never fight change. Accept it. Want change even faster than it is expected of you! Be eager for your own personal change plan, and inspire the involvement of others. Be accountable. Measure your outcomes regularly," explained Joost Dijkstra, reflecting on the process to a business school MBA class.

The assumptions he made about the people in the firm and their teams were honest and straightforward. "They have talents and expectations. They want to be able to learn and be rewarded. They need clarity in goals and direction. They want to be inspired and challenged. They ask for an honest chance to earn respect", he considers.

Inevitably, Joost Dijkstra – like all CEOs in the midst of rapid change – had to overcome hostility and discomfort with the rate of change among his team members. He had been through it himself before taking his teams through this process, which helped. There were certain principles on which he insisted. Firstly, the background against which everyone worked operated with the assumption that all activities brought the firm closer to achieving its goals, confirmed and developed relationships, and took place within a fair and equitable working environment. Secondly, all his team members would have just one boss – so they would not be confused and possibly derailed by others chipping in and telling them what to do. Thirdly, they helped to set their own targets so that they all made their own contribution to the organization's success – and everyone made his or her own unique contribution. It was teamwork, and no-one was more important than anyone else. Fourthly, they were all in this together, and everyone would reap the rewards.

So, in 2006, when the business achieved its targets for its American owners and Joost Dijkstra decided to move on, he awarded everyone in the company a 3,000 Euro bonus. It may not have been so much for the bosses, but it was a lot for the workers, and they deserved it. And despite massive change, he carried nearly all of them with him. Many team members moved to different departments and units within a massive reorganization process – but only a few moved out of Ranpak altogether. The achievements were impressive: in the two years between 2003 and 2005, revenue growth was up 25%, margin growth up 27%, SG&A (selling, general and administration costs) was up only 16%, EBITDA was up 37%, whilst capital expenditure on new investments was up only 7%. The firm is still flourishing, and the teams know more than ever how to add value.

Questions on the opening case: What are the main differences between the European and American management styles, according to the CEO and his team members? What were the most important elements of team empowerment? Why does having only one boss for team members make such a difference? In what ways can you imagine the team climate changing at Ranpak? What, in your opinion, might have been some of the areas for team member resistance and why? What would happen in your own organization if these changes had been implemented? Could this level of daily monitoring and control work in your own organization? Could teams in your workplace embrace this kind of urgency of goal achievement?

LEARNING OBJECTIVES FOR THIS CHAPTER

In this introductory chapter, 'Defining Teams', we look at the role that teams can play in developing individuals and the achievement of organizational goals. After establishing the importance of teams, we look at some definitions of groups and teams. How can individuals gain from working in teams? What can the team gain from individuals? How can we define the "climate" of our team? What is the involvement of teams in the change process? How can we define effectiveness in team communications? How about team effectiveness generally? What happens in team meetings and how could these be improved? What part can teams play in organizational decision-making? What is the impact of leadership on the progress of the team? How can teams survive conflict? Why are there such different attitudes towards teams in different cultures? This chapter also helps to introduce you to the other chapters in this section: Leading Teams, Communicating in Teams, Fostering Teams and Conflict in Teams.

THE IMPORTANCE OF TEAMS

The effective use of human resources is essential for any manager trying to achieve the goals of the project at stake, assuming these are part of the strategic goals of the firm. People are the primary resource of an organization and learning how to manage them is essential for a team leader. How a team member can participate in a team is also of top priority amongst people who live together and not in isolation (probably nearly all of us). Understanding how and why people behave the way they do, having the necessary knowledge to see through their behavior, and possessing the skill to influence their performance will help any leader (and any other member of the team, for that matter) enter into his/her role and face the others with confidence and commitment. Self-actualization of individuals, and the achievement of organizational goals, nearly always requires the input of teams.

A VERY IMPORTANT KIND OF TEAM – A FOOTBALL TEAM

Football used to be a hobby and a sport, of interest to a certain section of society in some countries once or twice a week. Now it's big business, an obsession for millions, and the job of managing and leading a football team has become of the greatest leadership and management tasks of the late twentieth and early twenty-first centuries. Why are some teams successful, and others complete failures? Even when they have the same players/members? Julian Birkinshaw and Stuart Crainer (2003:27) tried to answer this and other questions in their book *"Leadership the Sven-Goran Eriksson Way."* For example:

> 'Can't pass, can't keep possession, can't carry out instructions and give the ball away too much', reflected Kevin Keegan [the England captain] of the England team after they had been knocked out of the European championships by Romania in June 2000. He was right. England was awful. Yet, just over a year later the English team was able to pass, retain possession and carry out their instructions.
>
> 'The English team which beat Germany 5-1 away from home [in 2001] in one of the most dramatic victories in English football history included the core of the team – Seaman, Neville, Beckham, Scholes, Owen and Barmby – which had surrendered lamely the previous autumn to Germany at Wembley.
>
> If much of the team remains the same, the difference lies not in the make-up of the team but in the performance of the team and in the identity of the manager' (Birkinshaw & Crainer, 2003: 27)

If good teamwork used to be a mysterious phenomenon which sometimes worked and sometimes did not, this is not the case any more. Teamwork is now subject to scientific principles and active investigation. In the case of football – and for most organizations – teamwork is too critical to leave to chance. There are too many dollars at stake, for the organizations and the livelihoods of all the people involved.

Exercise: Consider any sports team of your choice (and you might also look at a drama group or even a group of students in class). Explain the difference between success and failure for this particular team or group. Contrast times when the team has performed well, and badly. What have been some of the reasons for this? Also mention the implications of both kinds of performance – financially and in other respects.

DEFINITIONS

A group can be any number of people who share goals, explain Hellriegel & Slocum (2004) quoting Homans (1959), and who often communicate with each other over time. A group is relatively small: it cannot be so many that they cannot communicate face-to-face individually. Most textbooks on the subject of teams define a number of different groups based on their membership and functions: friendship groups, task groups, and informal groups. They can be effective if, according to Yarbrough (2002) quoted in Hellriegel & Slocum (2004: 196) they:

- "Know why the group exists and have shared goals;
- Support agreed-upon guidelines or procedures for making decisions;
- Communicate freely among themselves;
- Receive help from one another and give help to one another;
- Deal with conflict within the group;
- Diagnose individual and group processes and improve their own and the group's functioning."

Teams, explained the authors of the same textbook, are usually made up of a small number of employees with complimentary competencies (abilities, skills and knowledge) who are committed to common performance goals and working relationships for which they hold themselves mutually accountable, according to LaFasto and Larsen (2001), quoted by Hellriegel and Slocum. Types of teams can include functional teams, problem-solving teams, cross-functional teams, self-managed teams, research and development teams and virtual teams.

George and Jones (2002) quote Shaw (1981) in describing a group as mutually interacting, so that a person's actions influence and can be influenced by another person's actions. Mills (1967) observed that group members perceive a potential for mutual goal accomplishment. That is, group members think that by belonging to a group, they will be able to accomplish certain goals or meet certain needs. George and Jones (2002) add more group types to the list: command groups, interest groups and informal work groups; the first-named report to the same supervisor.

By contrast to the definition of groups, this textbook defines teams (as opposed to groups) as more formal work-oriented groups with a high level of interaction among group members who work together to achieve a common goal . The key to the difference between groups and teams, George and Jones(2002) argue, is the intensity and focus of the interaction. A team is more formal, proactive, and purposeful. The main distinctive features is that teams generally go in the same direction, at the same speed and at the same time.

INDIVIDUALS AND TEAMS

Individuals are defined by the way they are, the way they behave, and the way they react with others. Whatever you do as an individual will inevitably influence others around you; you will inevitably add a new dimension to the team to which you belong (which can be positive or negative). Each member of the team is not just a numeric addition to the sum of the others. Put two persons together in a team and what you will get is not just "two" but a product of their relationship. This synergy can be worth more than the product of those two persons' independent work, if they did it on their own – or less. How can we measure and quantify this synergy? Do we think about this enough?

The benefits individuals gain from working in a team depend on certain factors. Whenever there is a change in the team, be it a new member or a new policy, each existing member of that team will have an opinion on that change. Arguably, the team can be more effective if each individual agrees on the change and accepts it. The individual needs to 'fit' into a team, and whatever the team activity, this 'fit' is one of the crucial factors which determines the effectiveness of the team dynamic. The individual needs to be viewed both as a person and as a member of the team. There is an overall tendency for individuals to put themselves first and the team second. It depends on levels of cohesiveness, conformity, diversity and conflict in teams – to be discussed below.

For you to add value as a member of a team, you have to know yourself (your skills, experience, attributes) enough to know what you can add to the team. You may need to modify your own behavior in order to make yourself a better team member. And how can the team add value to you? This depends on the extent to which you are prepared to accept and take on board the feedback you will receive. The following chapter – and the section as a whole – is designed to help you understand how teams can operate, and how you can add to the process, and realize the contribution of the team to your effectiveness.

TEAM CLIMATE

The *climate* of the team of which you are a member of (or even, more especially, a leader) determines the ways in which you choose to operate or participate. The climate can be assessed by observing the behavior and understanding the members' actions. The assessment would include observing:

- The means of communication;
- The roles and agendas of each member;
- The effectiveness of meetings;
- The clarity of goals;
- The avoidance of role conflict; and
- The opportunities for team problem-solving.

In order to develop an effective team climate, members of a team (especially in the workplace) must:

- clearly know their place in the team (from the organizational structure);
- understand what is expected of them (from their job description, for example);
- receive explicit and detailed feedback on their performance, both positive and constructive negative;
- appreciate the opportunities for personal self development within the team (from appraisal exercises);
- understand the opportunities and challenges for collective ventures (the team's operational plans).

Arguably, an appropriate team climate for successful individual and team development is one that allows each individual to fulfill his/her potential, and there is also the need for alignment with the goals of the organization. A positive organizational climate will enable individuals:

- to be at ease with each other;
- to build rewarding and positive relationships that are caring and stable;
- to take up challenges, to create and innovate;
- to identify clear and worthwhile individual and organizational goals; and
- to implement collectively those goals into products and/or services.

Exercise: How about your own team climate, in terms of the team in which you work most of the time – which might be your department? How would you rate it according to the assessment areas above? In looking at the paragraphs on the individual and the team above, *how do you feel about your contribution? How do you define and assess your role in the team in which you work? What could you do to improve your value to the team? What could your team do to improve? Do the other team members feel the same way? In the rest of this chapter and section, you will be able to put your thoughts and comments into a clearer framework, but it is useful at the start to define your attitude to yourself and your team. This attitude might be the result of the culture of your organization, or of the national culture in which you operate.*

TEAM BEHAVIORS, ACTIVITIES AND ROLES

Studies of teams confirm that a team can achieve more together as a group of people than its members can in working individually. Participating in a team is more powerful than individual isolated working and learning situations. When people pool their efforts and ideas together an added dimension is created. Each member is both a resource providing expertise, and a recipient of the expertise of others. Sharing ideas, values, feelings, knowledge, attitudes and thoughts can be highly productive in dealing with tasks, handling innovation and change. Meanwhile, heightened self-knowledge is acquired through teams. Each team member receives feedback about contributions made and therefore, individuals are able to appraise themselves more accurately through these interactions.

This introductory chapter, gives a taste of how team dynamics work by explaining vital factors of a team, the roles of members, leaders and organizers (or employers or bosses) of a team towards the team's performance.

Teams are complex in character because many things are going on at the same time in a typical team's activities and tasks. Primarily, teams are involved and are impacted by the following issues:

- teams and change;
- team development (explained more in Chapter 2);
- teams and communication (explained more in Chapter 3);
- team effectiveness (explained more in Chapter 4);
- meetings;
- decisions;
- leadership roles (explained more in Chapter 2);
- conflict (explained more in Chapter 5).

TEAMS AND CHANGE

Many departments, organizations and teams of people working together are in active, dynamic situations with people wanting to put forward new and better ideas and suggestions of how things should be done. At the same time (almost paradoxically) many people like stability and often, in some way, oppose changes made in the work they have been doing for years. How do we personally respond to changes proposed in our teams?

Consider the anger, tension and even perhaps bitterness that can evolve within members of a given team when they are not involved in the decisions impacting on a change taking place. Many in-house programs on organizational development make the mistake of basing themselves on one of the oldest work-myths that exist: You as the manager sit down with the rest of the management team, agree on policies, aims, strategies and so on, and pass them down for others to implement. Even with extensive staff training for others down below, this often does not work, because there is no taking into account what those down below think, and already know about the organization, its products, customers, etc. This top-down approach does not take into account their different personalities, attitudes and the effects of their involvement in the process of change. Contrast this approach (which is very common) with the approach taken at Ranpak, in our opening case.

For example, let us consider an organization that is working on its self-image (with the general public in a marketing campaign). Members of the team may feel anxious, may feel they lack status and identity and are confused during the whole public relations (PR) exercise – and these feelings need to be taken into account. They may not approve of the new PR image being created, and feel that it does not reflect the values of the organization – which they know better than the consultants! The involvement of the team is vital, because it is through the attitudes of (and need for acceptance from) each member of the team, that the success or failure of that self-image campaign is decided. It would be the same for other campaigns and objectives.

Exercise: Consider a time of substantial, definable change in your organization. How did your organization cope with the change process? Did everyone buy in to the need for change, or was there resistance? To what extent were you personally involved in the change process? Did you feel that it was consultative, or autocratic? Was training provided to help you and your team to manage the change? Was it designed to get you involved, or just tell you what to do? How did top management communicate the change to the teams? Reflect on the subsequent outcome of the change and the impact on your team.

TEAM DEVELOPMENT

Here we are looking at how teams evolve and undergo important stages on the way to performing in an optimal way. The theory of team development, especially that explained by Tuckman and Jensen (1977) is explained in more detail in a case quoted in Chapter 2. When teams are formed and team members get together, they tend to go through a process of storming and conflict as a way of sorting out their roles and priorities. Sometimes the team breaks up at this point; at other times it continues, in an improved way. The phenomenon of norming then occurs, when the team members decide on their acceptable behaviors and rituals. Again, failure can ensue, but if it does not, the team can progress towards performing, and may carry on performing for a sustained time. At any point it can collapse and fall apart – teams can be delicate things.

TEAM COMMUNICATION

As will be discussed more in Chapter 3, the type of consultation (involvement, support, asking for advice and other strategies) required by teams facing change can ease the process of change. In other words, change needs honesty, empathy and genuine communication. All members of the team need to develop effective communication channels with their colleagues so that support may be sought when needed, given when sought, and that regular feedback on progress and achievements may be provided – in both directions.

Summed up in a series of brief points, effective communication in a team entails:

- talking about the action rather than the actor;
- being specific and clear rather than generic and vague;
- directing the communication towards something that the receiver can do something about;
- being well-timed, ready for any contribution on the communication as welcome feedback; and
- asking and consulting rather than imposing or forcing.

TEAM EFFECTIVENESS

As explained more in Chapter 4, there are many factors that help teams to work effectively. This can include the following three points:

- Philosophy   - members sharing common ideas and values;
- Work   - members working and achieving things together;
- Relationship - members relating well to each other.

If one of these three vital elements is missing, the team is less likely to achieve much (or to last long as a team). A team that works well achieves its overall purpose within its value frame, gets the job done and makes its members feel good about being involved. In other works, the team accomplishes the *task* and looks after its *people*. It is both relationship- and task-oriented.

As recognized in our opening case about Ranpak, it is well known that people in teams like to be:

- Accepted and appreciated;
- Feel they are useful;
- Ready to use their talents;
- Recognized and respected;
- Valued;
- Clearly having a role to play;
- Credited with their ideas;
- Seen to be making an effort;
- Achievers in what they do.

Since the work of McGregor (1960) in discussing the differences between X and Y style management, it is frequently suggested that these needs are part of human nature and can encourage people to do their best in the workplace in a team environment.

Arguably, teams exist so that people can combine and use their talents - and the end result is better. Teams can provide individuals with opportunities to work together for the common good. It should be appreciated that all the people coming to the team have different personalities, different backgrounds and experiences, and different hopes and fears. This can be an asset or a hindrance to the team, and this depends on how much the team can harness and integrate all those differences to the best advantage of the team and for the end result.

To consider in more detail the theoretical framework, team effectiveness can depend on **context**, or the external conditions affecting a team, such as technology, physical working conditions, and the way that team members are compensated. **Team goals** also make a difference to effectiveness, and these can be a mix of being task or relationship-related. **Team size** is another issue. The smaller the team, the lower the demands on the leader, the need for direction by the leader, the lower the member tolerance of direction provided by the leader, member inhibition, use of rules and procedures, and time taken to reach a decision. Lencioni (2002) considers that in larger teams the reverse happens, with high demands on the leader, high member inhibition, etc.

Other writers discuss the tendency for 'social loafing' or that less effort tends to be made when groups and teams are larger (Latane, 1986). Shaw (1981) confirms that an increase in 'social loafing' can take place when larger numbers of people in a group make I more difficult to identify individual performance. **Team member roles** inevitably vary, between being task-oriented, relations-oriented and self-oriented (Lustig, 1987).

George and Jones (2002) also talk about the importance of group composition in team effectiveness – being homogenous or heterogeneous. The former like and get along well, share information, have low levels of conflict and few co-ordination problems; the latter can have stronger decision-making effectiveness because of their diversity, and can perform at a high level because of its varied resources, experience and skills.

Exercise: If you are a leader (or organizer) of a team, it will help you to put yourself in someone else's position who is a member of that team. Ask yourself:

- *How would I like to be treated and how would I like things to work out?*
- *Are people welcoming me at the first impressions stage?*
- *How am I in terms of punctuality... do I start meetings and projects on time... and finish them on time?*
- *Do I make an effort in trying to get to know the members of the team?*
- *Do I know why am I there leading this particular team?*
- *Do I try to make everyone get involved in all the team's activities?*
- *Do I take everyone in account when I talk to the team?*
- *What kind of attitudes do I have towards each single member of the team?*

Consider the checklists above and how you and your teammates would respond to them and about you and your attitude. Are you specific and clear about the action needed in your team? Do you really share goals and values? Are you open in your communications? Do you all feel you are playing an important part in the team? Are you achievement-oriented? Is your attitude shared by the others?

TEAM MEETINGS

This team activity is of critical importance in coordinating effort and effecting change. It is a very important tool in the leader's hands and his/her role is to ensure that the meetings are vehicles for communication and action rather than for confusion and frustration. Yet, this is exactly the feeling felt by many attending meetings. A worthwhile experience is to spend some time during the actual meeting asking people to pool in and share their experiences about meetings. This must be carried out in the context of the elements of an effective team discussed above, such as context, size, roles, etc.

Some of the reasons why many meetings go wrong are outlined below:

- times of meeting are set when people are rushed, tired and/or unavailable;
- meetings never start punctually, so those coming early waste time;
- meetings take too long;
- meetings seem out of control and pointless;
- the same members during the meetings just talk on and on;
- people do not listen to each other (they are interested in what they will say when the other has finished);
- it is all talk with no time to reflect and think;
- it is all talk with no action;
- the agenda is drawn only by one or two members;
- not everyone has the chance to say what the team should be doing;
- no link exists between one meeting and the other;
- there are no strategies, no plans, no objectives, no targets;
- when decisions are taken, few are followed up;;
- the place where the meetings take place is uncomfortable and inconvenient to most;
- some members are difficult and behave uncooperatively;
- some members do not accept criticism.

Complaints are important. They are clues about what needs attention. If complaints are ignored then the people making them will feel 'put down' or unimportant. As a result they will either drop out of the team, or become obstructive, or just give up trying. Rather than putting down a member's complaint, a leader or manager who raises it up in a meeting and gives it attention will take that leader or manager a long way towards keeping people involved and committed. Each of us needs to feel that what he/she says will make a difference in the meeting and in the outcome of the team's work.

According to a number of authorities of managing meetings, the key criteria for judging a meeting's effectiveness are three:

- Did the outcome of the meeting justify the time spent on it collectively?
- Could there have been a better outcome for the same resources spent?
- Will the outcome be acted on? And if yes, how, who, when... and so on?

There are various measures, tasks, and exercises to test the effectiveness of your team's meetings. The most important is on the team's performance and its results. They are either there, or they are not.

TEAM DECISIONS: MAKING THINGS HAPPEN

Teams need to achieve and feel that they are succeeding both on a short-term and on a long-term basis. People need a sense of purpose and progress to maintain their commitment. Achieving sound decisions requires the reflection-action sequence. The sequence is vital and the two parts inseparable. If either is missing the other is poorer. So the reflection finds expression in action, and action takes direction and energy from the reflection that precedes it. The cycle consists of:

- setting clear objectives for the team;
- reviewing these objectives and seeing how feasible they are;
- setting the team's priorities;
- making good action plans and targets;
- implementing the team's decisions;
- evaluating the success of the team's decisions.

This is done by using S.M.A.R.T. (Specific, Measurable, Attainable or Agreed, Reachable or Results-Oriented and Timely) objectives all through the cycle.

A number of issues impact on decision-making in teams, particularly those of **norms** and **cohesiveness**. What is normal behavior in team decision-making, in terms of the processes usually adopted? Is it a team norm to consult each member separately outside of a meeting and then come together to make a decision? Or is there active discussion from scratch on the matter in the meeting? Norms help to make team behaviors more predictable and help to make team members feel more comfortable. Feldman (1984) gives the examples of not discussing salaries, social and romantic attachments and not visiting each others' homes as possible group norms, to prevent embarrassment or feelings of inequity (quoted in Hellriegel & Slocum, 2004).

Cohesiveness is often misunderstood. It is not the same as conformity. Cohesiveness is defined as wanting to remain in the team; conformity is about everyone thinking the same way. Highly cohesive groups, with high member commitment, can also encourage and benefit from high levels of debate and discussion. But when decision-making teams are both conforming and cohesive, the result can be **groupthink**, where members agree with each other at any cost, which can result in ineffective decision-making which, in its turn, fails to make good use of the talents and experience of the team (Janis, 1989).

Cohesiveness must be aligned with organizational goals to be most effective, although there are disadvantages in being too cohesive, suggest George and Jones (2002). When there is a high level of participation and communication within the group, the group members can be more likely to perform behaviors necessary for the group and organization to achieve goals. Information flows quickly around the group, and staff turnover may be low. On the other hand, group members may waste time socializing and chatting about non-work matters. When there is high conformity, the group is able to control members' behavior to achieve group goals, but excessive conformity can produce resistance to change and failure to discard dysfunctional norms.

Exercise: How are decisions made in your team? Are they effective or do they result in running around in circles and getting no-where? Do you evaluate the results of your decisions? Do you consciously learn from mistakes? Do you make good use of all the talents (skills, experience and knowledge) of your team members? Reflect on the levels of cohesiveness and conformity in your team, and the incidence of groupthink. To what extent is this present or absent? Give examples of the norms established by members of your team and of your team's behavior as a result.

TEAM LEADERSHIP

As discussed in more detail in Chapter 2, it is clear that the role of the leader (or team organizer) is a crucial one. John Adair (2002) defined leadership as the control and integration of three elements:
- Accomplishing the task (task needs);
- Building the team (team maintenance needs);
- Developing the individual (individual needs).

The role of the leader is generally seen as there to motivate the individuals to work within a team to complete the task. The point is that effective leadership is at its best if all of these factors are considered seriously; if not, one factor will undoubtedly adversely affect the other two.

Leading a team can take various styles depending on a number of internal and external factors. The major ones have been outlined in this summary of the work of several leadership authors, and other approaches are discussed in Chapter 2.

- **Dictatorial**   (autocratic)
  The most important factor is the high value placed on safety;
  The ultimate aim is the task, regardless of the cost in relationship terms;
  The leader will consider his/her obligations and challenges, and think less about the people;
  The leader will work towards ab solute power, requiring total obedience.

- **Paternalistic**   (good-hearted dictator)
  Like the father, or the teacher, this leader teaches the truth;
  "I am the one who knows what's good for you";
  Obedience and respect of the members is vital;
  This leadership style is good for people who are dependent
  on being led;
  Knowing all, this type of leader can't stand criticism;
  The leader will listen to the members with respect, but their
  comments would be valid only if they agree with what
  he/she is thinking.

- **Administrator**   (bureaucratic, keen on effectiveness and results)
  The emphasis in this style of leadership is work, productivity
  and results;
  Formal structures, procedures and rules are vital - human
  personality and relationships less so;
  The members of the team have total loyalty towards this leader –
  and how structured, ruled and regulated work will proceed.

- **Laissez Faire**   (French for 'let it be')
  Authority is something that only the leader feels. He/she cannot
  (and is not able to) pass it on to any of the members;
  Values independence, sharing and total trust;
  Of priority here are interpersonal skills that people feel they need
  to develop;
  Unclear direction is given; and structure is spontaneous and loose;
  The leader often finds it difficult to take a decision and to
  be assertive;
  The sharing of emotions is given importance;
  The leader is ready to listen, facilitate and weigh options without
  confrontation.

- **Democratic**   (everyone counts)
  The human ability and contribution towards the progress of the
  team is vital here;
  An environment is created where the structure creates space for
  self-actualization while work is being conducted;
  A democratic leader is full of enthusiasm, initiative and creativity;
  Although sympathizing and understanding, confrontation is also
  used where and when necessary

- **Servant**   (here to serve)
  The main characteristics are interdependency, responsibility,
  collectivity, creativity, and relationships;
  Decisions are taken in a team, and collective agreements are very
  important - more than the individual opinion;

Apart from the team's objectives, the aim is that everyone is working towards the common good;

The leader sees that everyone is working, and his intervention and confrontation is minimal - to the extent that the members feel they are all doing their work and making their own contributions.

Members of a team have different needs and preferences of leadership. All leadership styles are important and necessary at the right time; there is no ideal way of leading a team. One answer to the question 'Which is the best type?' is: 'It's according to the situation (that is, according to the task, the team, the individuals)'. Chapter 2 discusses this important issue in more detail.

TEAM CONFLICT

As explained more in Chapter 5, the 'I win - you win' results are important if the team is to survive conflict situations. It is obvious that disagreements emerge as teams develop and implement their objectives. Each one of us will have (and will think he/she has) right, fair, important or essential ideas to contribute. The most important factor or consideration here is to accept that:

- disagreements are normal if people share their ideas honestly and speak out about what they feel;
- differences in themselves are not a problem, but a sign of richness and valuable diversity;
- conflict is caused not by differences, but by the way we deal with them; and
- accepting – and appreciating the possible improvements – when one person's idea is turned upside down by another idea from someone else.

What should be done when there are conflicts amongst team members?

- Listen – carefully to each other and do not just insist on giving your own views. When others are expressing their ideas, DO NOT think about what your idea is, and mentally formulate what you will be saying in the moment when they finish; think about what they are saying now.

- Raise questions – only to understand what is being said; rather than asking questions to object, pinpoint failures in structure or to identify short-comings. Give time to explain first.

- Avoid attacks – on personality features. It is essential to try and separate differences in the ideas from feeling about the members personally. If disagreements spill over towards criticisms of other members' behavior, character, personal integrity, and so on, the way is open for a lack of respect, which destroys team cohesion.

- Be prepared – to concede some things, compromise your ideas, in exchange for others – especially when consensus prevails.

- Look for – similarities between two diverging opinions. Look for 'win-win' results. Find a way for each person to feel that they have been listened to and have got some of what is important for them. If necessary go back to your primary objective of the discussion – it is essential that everyone is clear as to what is being discussed.

- Keep cool – Serious disagreements require a cool head. Do not allow aspects of your personality (be it extra calm or a tendency to be nervous) to interfere with the nature of the conflict. Sort out the issue at hand, for the benefit of all concerned.

CLOSING CASE

Dr Harrington's Mouse Story – about the American and the Japanese Mice – is described as an "adult fairy tale" by its author, H. James Harrington, an international quality advisor with global audit firm Ernst and Young. Resonant with some of the ideas included in Kenneth Blanchard's *"Who Moved My Cheese?,"* this short fable describes an experiment with three mice in a maze – on both sides of the Pacific. Of course, this is rather over-simplified and exaggerated, as all fairy tales might be! Reality is much less black and white than this, but this simple story might add to your ideas about teamwork…

The American mice, normally well-fed and comfortable, are competitive and non-co-operative, running around individually in the maze until they find their cheese – or not, as the case may be. As a result, each mouse spends a number of cheeseless days, when they get more and more hungry and get lost repeatedly in the maze. One has more success than the others, but not to a large degree. They are all three spending at least two days without cheese for each day when they get fed. Of a total of 120 days of the experiment, mouse #1 was not fed 70% of the time; mouse #2 was not fed 64% of the time and mouse #3 was cheeseless 66% of the time.

By contrast, the Japanese mice – who enjoyed none of the advantages of the American mice in terms of comfort and normal availability of food - spent the first couple of days planning their strategy to crack the puzzle of the maze. Sniffing and squeaking, they held meetings to discuss the situation. Working as a team and climbing on each other's shoulders, they surveyed the maze, making a map of how to get to the cheese. They try out their map and it works. The investment in planning and mapping pays off, as the mice are then able to all reach the cheese every day, using their jointly-prepared map. After three days of planning and strategizing, they rushed through the maze directly to the cheese, which they repeated every day for the remainder of the 120 days. They even brought their sake with them and geisha girls to serve them!

The American mice, believing they are in a dog-eat-dog (or mice-eat-mice) world, do not consider co-operation and teamwork. As a result, most of the time, the American mice missed out on the cheese, whereas the Japanese mice enjoyed their cheese every day. In reality there was enough cheese for all, but the American mice did not realize this.

Characteristics of American and Japanese Mice

American Mice	Japanese Mice
High stress level	Relaxed and not worried
Tough competition	Situation planned
Survive or starve	Future guaranteed
Error-prone	Did it right every time
Trying harder and rushing faster	Process right so kept improving it
Becoming more and more frustrated	Satisfying and enjoyable
Non-co-operative	High level of co-operation
Other mice are the enemy	Each mouse dependent on the other
If they get fed, you go hungry	All benefiting from the process
Untrusting, suspicious	High level of trust
Fear of other mice cheating	All the mice working in harmony
Low morale	High morale
Everyone is against me	We enjoy working together
I must keep my guard up	We relax together
Everyone is against me	We support each other
No-one cares about me	We all care about each other
Displeased with the system	We adjust to the system
Must try to find ways around it	We have made the system work for us

Questions on the closing case: To what extent does this case illustrate your own competitive situation within your own team? Are you competing with the others, or co-operating? What are the results? Could you co-operate more? Are you losing anything if you do not compete? Is it better to compete together as a team, and how can you do this? How do you feel about the other team members? Is there stress, mistakes, a lack of co-operation, little trust, low morale and criticism of the system and what is happening? Or is your team more like the Japanese mice – relaxed, competent, co-operating, with trust, with high morale and confidence in the system in which you work?

CONCLUSION

In this chapter we have looked in an introductory way at the relationship between teams and their organizations, the mechanisms of team operations, and the perceptions of people about their teams and their role in their teams. Briefly, we have considered the 'climate' of our team, and the factors impacting on this. How does our team perform in the change process? Do we feel that our team is ready for change? We have also looked at effectiveness in the ways teams communicate, and team effectiveness generally, asking ourselves if we rate ourselves positively here – or not. Team meetings are another issue in measuring how we feel about our team performance – if they are valuable, or a waste of time and space. In terms of organizational decision-making, our team can play its part, or sit on the side-lines. We also need to consider the impact of leadership on the progress of the team, and if the leadership of our team contributes to its failure or success. A further test is the ability of our teams to survive conflict. We also need to consider the extent to which the attitude to teamwork differs in different cultures. Basically, do we consider good teamwork, and wanting to be in a team, as a weakness or as a strength? Are we motivated towards competition or co-operation?

REFERENCES

Adair, J. (2002) *Effective Strategic Leadership.* London: Macmillan.

Birkinshaw, J. & Crainer, S. (2003) *Leadership the Sven-Goran* Eriksson Way. London: Capstone Books.

Dijkstra, J., seminar presented to Maastricht School of Management MBA class, March 2007.

George, J.M. & Jones G.R. (2002) *Organizational Behavior.* 3rd. ed. Upper Saddle River, New Jersey: Prentice Hall.

Harrington, H. J. (1992) *Dr Harrington's Mouse Story: an adult fairy tale.* USA: Ernst & Young.

Hellriegel, D. & Slocum, J.W. (2004) *Organizational Behavior.* Mason, Ohio: Thomson/South Western.

Homans, G.C. (1959) *The Human Group.* New York: Harcourt Brace.

Anis, L.L. (1982) *Groupthink.* 2nd ed. Boston: Houghton Miflin.

LaFasto F. & Larsen, C.E. (2001) *When Teams Work Best.* Thousand Oaks, CA: Sage.

Latane, B. (1986) 'Responsibility and Effort in Organizations', in P.S. Goodman, ed. (1986) *Designing Effective Work Groups.* San Francisco: Jossey-Bass.

Lencioni, P. (2002) *The Five Dysfunctions of a Team: a leadership fable.* San Francisco: Jossey-Bass.

Lustig, M.W. (1987) 'Bales interpersonal rating forms; reliability and dimensionality', *Small Group Behavior, 18:* 99-107

McGregor, D. (1960) *The Human Side of Enterprise.* New York: McGraw-Hill.

Mills, T.M. (1967) *The Sociology of Small Groups.* Upper Saddle River, New Jersey: Prentice Hall.

Shaw, M.E. (1981) *Group Dynamics.* 3rd ed. New York: McGraw Hill.

Tuckman, B.W. & Jensen, M.A.C. (1977) 'Stages of small-group development revisited', *Groups and Organization Studies, 2,* 419-442

Yarbrough, B.T. (2002) *Leading Groups and Teams.* Mason, Ohio: South-Western/Thomson.

RECOMMENDED FURTHER READING

Ackroyd, S. & Thompson, P. (1999) *Oranizational Misbehaviour.* Thousand Oaks, CA: Sage.

Andres, T. D. (1992) *Team building and creating effective work systems: A manual.* Quezon City, Philippines: New Day Publishers.

Belbin, R.M. (2000) *Beyond the team.* Oxford: Butterworth Heinemann.

Belbin, R.M. (2004) *Management teams: why they succeed or fail.* Oxford: Elsevier/Butterworth Heinemann.

Blitt, B. (1997) 'The seven sins of deadly meetings', in *Handbook of the Business Revolution,* Fast Company, Boston, 27-31

Dumane, B. (1994) *'The trouble with teams',* Fortune, 5 September, 86-92

Feldman, D.C. (1984) 'The development and enforcement of group norms', *Academy of Management Review, 9:* 47-53

Gersick, C.J.G. (1988) 'Time and transition in work teams: toward a new model of group development', *Academy of Management Journal 31*: 9-41

Kirkman B.L. & Rosen, B. (1999) 'Beyond self-management: antecedents and consequences of team empowerment', *Academy of Management Journal, 42*: 58-74

Levi, D. (2001) Group Dynamics for Teams. Thousand Oaks, CA: Sage

Mendenhall, M., Punnet, B.J., & Ricks, D. (1995) *Global Management.* Oxford: Blackwell.

Nelson, B. (1997) *1001 ways to energize employees.* Workman Publishing, New York.

O'Connor, M. P., & Erickson, B. (1996) 'Team Building: A strategic advantage', (online). Available:http://www.oconnor.ie/cos/advantage.html.

Purser R. & Cabana, S. (1999) *The Self-Managing Organization: how leading companies are transforming the work of teams for real impact.* New York: Free Press

Turniansky, B. & Hare, A.P. (1999) *Individuals and Groups in Organizations.* Thousand Oaks, CA: Sage.

Van der Heijden, B. (2005) 'No-one has ever promised you a rose garden. On shared responsibility and employability enhancing practices throughout careers', *Inaugural lecture, Maastricht School of Management/Open University of the Netherlands.* Van Gorcum: Assen.

CHAPTER 2

LEADING TEAMS
STEPHANIE JONES

OPENING CASE:

"We few, we happy few, we band of brothers;
For he today that sheds his blood with me
Shall be my brother; be he ne'er so vile,
This day shall gentle his condition.
And gentlemen in England, now abed,
Shall think themselves accursed they were not here;
And hold their manhood cheap whiles any speaks
That fought with us upon Saint Crispin's day." -
William Shakespeare, Henry V, (IV. iii. 60-67)

"I had the happiness to command a Band of Brothers"
- Admiral Lord Nelson

Admiral Lord Nelson, widely regarded as one of the most celebrated leaders in English history and a pioneer of team leadership, left England for the last time on the 29th September 1805, his 47th birthday. Less that a month later, his fleet achieved one of the greatest victories at sea of all time against the ships of Napoleon, the Emperor of France. But it was to cost him his life.

Nelson had received a rapturous farewell from England, the pressing crowds controlled by a military escort. In a typical winning-hearts gesture, he took a letter from a mother for a seaman in the fleet, asking her to kiss it so he could carry the kiss to her son too. An observer wrote: "a crowd collected, pressing forward to obtain a sight of his face – many were in tears and many knelt down before him as he passed. All knew that his heart was as humane as it was fearless... that with perfect and entire devotion he served his country with all his heart and with all his soul and with all his strength" (Jones & Gosling. 2005, :183).

His welcome from the seamen in the fleet and freely-expressed popularity with captains and officers set the scene for an unprecedented victory ahead, especially in contrast with low morale, confusion and conflict in the enemy fleets of France and Spain: "Lord Nelson is arrived, and a sort of general joy is the consequence."

Nelson commanded a new naval force assembling off Cadiz in Southern Spain, where the Combined Fleet had taken refuge. Back in England for a little over three weeks, he spent the time in a fever of detailed planning and lobbying for the resources he needed for the campaign. His job now was to prepare this force of 20 – 30 ships (the number varied as some went for supplies and others joined the fleet off Cape Trafalgar, near Cadiz) for battle. Two thirds of the captains were new to Nelson – including his Third in Command. Alongside the routine administration of the fleet, Nelson worked on molding this new team into a 'band of brothers.'

The first thing Nelson did to build his team of captains was to invite them aboard the flagship for dinner. Nelson liked to deliver letters to his captains personally and they rowed over to the 'Victory' in a state of excitement. One wrote home to his wife "he received me in an easy, polite manner, and on giving me your letter said that being entrusted with it by a lady, he made a point of delivering it himself. I have no fear of obtaining his goodwill by the conduct of my ship; because I shall do my best to deserve it, and he is a man well able to appreciate my endeavors." Another of Nelson's captains knew that his wife was about to deliver a baby, and Nelson asked him "if he would have a girl or a boy. I answered, the former, when he put the letter into my hand and told me to be satisfied". It was a girl. Nelson then delighted him by "telling me that he should give me my old station, which is his second in the line of battle. This is very gratifying to me, as it puts me in a very prominent situation in the order of battle, and a very convenient and pleasant one in the order of sailing" (Jones & Gosling, 2005: 184).

So dinner on the 29th was very special, the junior admirals and senior captains gathering at the large mahogany table in the great cabin, with gleaming silverware and cut glass, good food and wines and convivial company. This was vastly superior to life on their own ships. There were captains from Nelson's previous battles, as well as men Nelson had never met before. The old 'band of brothers' soon brought the newcomers into the fold. Nelson shared with them his plans for the battle and his expectations of the enemy's approach, inviting a full and open discussion. Meanwhile, he did his best to sort out personal problems and make everyone feel comfortable. One was worrying about his son (for whom Nelson had arranged his lieutenant's examination and first commission), who had deserted his frigate and run off with an opera dancer in Malta. Nelson sympathized – but alerted his contacts in Italy to find him, settle his debts, and persuade him to return to sea. As he wrote to his old friend Alexander Ball, now Governor of Malta, "I am not come forth to find difficulties, but to remove them" (Jones & Gosling, 2005: 185)

Dinner the next day, on the 30th, was "for all of us who did not dine on board the Victory [the flagship] yesterday," as a captain wrote home. "What our late chief [the former admiral, who was comparatively unsociable] will think of this I don't know; but I well know what the fleet will think of the difference; and even you, our good wives, will allow the superiority of Lord Nelson in all these social arrangements which bind his captains to their admiral" (Jones & Gosling, 2005: 185).

The captains' pleasure at Nelson's return was partly because in only three weeks they had become fed up with his deputy. The latter's style serves to highlight why Nelson was so unusual and so popular. He was dour, depressive and unfriendly, "a selfish old bear. That he was a brave, stubborn, persevering and determined officer everyone acknowledged, but he had few, if any, friends and no admirers. In body and mind he was iron, and very cold iron" (Jones & Gosling, 2005: 185).

Nelson's predecessor detested entertaining, discouraged the captains entertaining each other – they came to see a court martial as a good enough excuse for a get-together – and forbade the innocuous and popular tradition of allowing provision boats to enter the fleet so that officers and men could buy small treats and luxuries for themselves. When Nelson returned to the fleet, "the signal is made that boats may be hoisted out to buy fresh fruit... or anything coming into the fleet" (Jones & Gosling, 2005: 186).

Nelson, by contrast, took every chance to entertain his officers and captains, never eating a meal alone (in any case he needed help cutting up his meat, as he had lost his right arm in battle) whilst inviting them in rotation, getting to know them one by one, and gladly sharing all the details of his plans for the upcoming battle. Thus one captain, who had never met Nelson before, wrote "he is so good and pleasant a man that we all like to do what he likes without any kind of orders. He is the pleasantest admiral I ever served under" (Jones & Gosling, 2005: 186).

The rest of the story is well-known. On 21 October 1805, Nelson and his "band of brothers" won the most devastating and strategic naval battle in British history, which ensured supremacy of the seas for a hundred years. And it was won with the simple instruction that "no captain can do wrong if he places his ship next to that of the enemy." No other instructions were necessary, as all the captains knew what they had to do.

Sir John Harvey-Jones, author of leadership and corporate turnaround studies, regards Nelson "as the founder of participative leadership." Harvey-Jones, a widely respected and internationally recognized business leader known for his keen interest in motivation and teamwork, explained that "my own leadership style has been based very much on Nelson. He has been a lifelong hero of mine." All Boards of Directors, Chairmen and CEOs should be like Nelson and his 'Band of Brothers', claims Harvey-Jones, "knowing and trusting each others' hearts and minds" (Jones & Gosling, 2005: 123-4).

> "When I changed my career from the Navy to industry the lessons seemed even more applicable", Harvey Jones feels. "While a leader has to provide the framework, he has to give away the leadership when actually going into battle, so to speak", he explains, referring to the way that Nelson, with his 'Band of Brothers' built loyalty, based on trust, honesty and mutual understanding so that each knew what the other was thinking and could act for each other, without being told what to do. Loyalty to the team was the most important thing.

> "People will do what they themselves are committed to. Getting commitment is a matter of talking and reasoning until everyone is totally clear what the objective is", Harvey Jones adds. "Endless detailed command is enormously expensive and ineffective because it switches people off. People need to understand what the whole enterprise is about. Leadership is about getting people to buy into the same ideal. Thus Nelson explained everything, and then trusted his people to get on with it".

Harvey Jones feels that there has been much scope for the leadership lessons he learned from Nelson at the beginning of his career. "In the public sector [in the UK], I soon realized that there is so little trust, people are checked on, micro-managed all the time – the antithesis of what Nelson believed in", he noticed. "Trust is contagious. Trust is something that is communicated immediately – you can instantly see if people trust their leader", Harvey Jones argues.

"Leadership has to be by personal example, believing in it totally, and exemplifying it", Harvey Jones points out, describing how Nelson walked the talk, led from the front, and didn't expect men to do things that he wasn't prepared to do himself. Nelson listened to his captains, won their confidence and trust, understood their problems, and tried to help. And he communicated with passion. "If you don't care, this communicates immediately. Leadership has to be felt as much as understood. The presentation of your ideas has to be a seamless whole, and reflected in all your actions. You have to believe in your ideas and demonstrate them with action."

Nelson's loyalty to his officers and men was a significant part of his legacy, Harvey Jones feels. "Most leaders have the wish to leave behind them something worthwhile. People get to the top by ambition, and when they get to the top their ambition stretches beyond that – but the longevity of your legacy depends on what you believe and what you leave in the beliefs of those you lead", Harvey Jones considers. Nelson's legacy of loyalty, teamwork and participative leadership lives on.

Harvey Jones points out that loyalty is not easy to build. "It takes a lot of courage to trust the people you lead – but it's not something you can command. Nelson won the loyalty he enjoyed. Loyalty is something you give your people, you share with them, and you'll get it back in return" (Jones & Gosling, 2005: 123-4).

Questions on the opening case: *What did Nelson do to bring the new captains into the team? Why was he seen as such a committed leader? What do you think is the importance of loyalty and trust in teamwork? What examples of 'small things' did Nelson do which made a difference? Do you know any leaders in your own context who operate like this? Would you be (or are you) like this in your own team in your workplace? Is being a team player a natural or unnatural way of operating for a leader?*

LEARNING OBJECTIVES FOR THIS CHAPTER

Here, we will be looking at the challenges and problems of leading a team. How can we get to know our team members and build trust and support for ourselves as their leader? What are the benefits of making an effort to be a team leader? What are the variables that can influence team leadership, such as personality, attitudes, perception and attribution, attitude to learning and motivation to be a leader? How do leaders go about the job of leading a team? What is the preferred team role of the team leader? How does the leadership style of the leader affect the team? What about the subordinates' styles?

In this chapter, we will also look at how the process of leading a team can change over time, with the growing seniority and maturity of the leader. He or she can become a different style of leader, showing a different preferred team role, making an impact on his or her subordinates. Finally, we look at the stages of team development, the role of the leader in the different stages, and how this changes and evolves. The aim is to help you grasp the practical issues of managing a team, and understand as well some of the theoretical framework of this vitally important subject.

Before we look in detail at how to lead a team, it is important to realize that **individual behavior and team dynamics** have a strong relationship, in which personality plays an important part. Different personality styles affect the way the leader leads his or her team. Let's take, for example, the Myers Briggs Type Inventory personality types and how these affect team leadership. The extrovert type will find communicating with the team easier than the introvert type, if only because he or she sees interacting with others as a source (rather than drain upon) energy reserves. The sensing leader will be looking for the following of rules and regulations, of searching for all the pertinent facts and figures. By contrast, an intuitive leader is likely to be more trusting if he or she gets the right impression of a subordinate. If he or she has a hunch or feeling that something is right, then the plan can go ahead. A thinking leader makes decisions with his head, and shows a certain amount of logic and task-orientation. Meanwhile, a feeling leader is very focused on relationships, and is concerned with the team members being comfortable within themselves about their roles and duties.

The attitudes of individual leaders make a difference too, especially in terms of positives and negatives. Do they trust people easily, having faith and confidence, or do they assume the worst, thinking that they must experience the behavior of their team at first hand before they can make a judgment? Is their glass half full or half empty?

Perception and attribution are another issue – the way a leader perceives his or her team members and the characteristics he or she sees them as possessing. He or she may make quick judgments on behaviors and appearance, and may attribute aspects of them to a person's personality or ability. They can be right or wrong, but sometimes the judgments persist, and affect the leader's decisions to delegate to each team member – or not to delegate.

Learning is for every leader and every person – do they evolve over time? This issue is discussed in our case below – how do leaders change in their leadership style and the way they manage their teams, after a space of some years? Is the learning from their experience in the organization, or is it from life experiences?

Motivation to be a leader of a team is crucial. Let's look at the context of the Maslow model – people want to be leaders of a team to achieve self-actualization, or to gain status and self-esteem – it makes a big difference to the specifics of what motivates them. And, based on the McClelland model – are they driven by power – the need to control – or by achievement, the need to get things done? Or maybe it's because of affiliation. They may want to work with other people as a main driver of motivation. But this can be less common, because sometimes as a team leader you need to place yourself apart from the rest of the team, especially if you used to be one of them and you have recently been promoted. This is a tough one, which not everyone can handle.

HOW LEADERS LEAD THEIR TEAMS, AND THEIR APPROACH TO LEADERSHIP

Team roles: how can we develop an understanding of the roles and relationships underpinning effective teamwork? This is based on the needs of the individual team member, and their own personality type and motivators. There is also the issue of meaningful involvement – does the team member think that he or she is doing a worthwhile job? Do they feel that they are 'in on things' or left out of what is going on? Or is the team just going through the motions and the team leader making all the decisions? What is the degree of equality in the team? To each according to his abilities and merits, or according to his or her relationship with the boss? What are the informal roles in the team – spy for the boss, hardest worker, team pet? And the formal roles, such as deputy, public relations person, best salesperson? The team leader himself or herself can also vary, in terms of their informal 'emergent' status and their formal 'appointed' status. There may be no formal leader at all – as in a self-managed work team – but one seems to be looked to as the leader. Otherwise the leader may have a confirmed role in the organization structure. One has power without authority, and the other has authority but may not have the power, in terms of the respect and acceptance of the team.

THE CHARACTERISTICS OF THE TEAM LEADER

What are leader behaviors and what impact do they have on the team? The leader can be playing one or more of these roles, based on the Belbin Team Types Belbin, (2000, 2004), a useful concept and related psychometric instrument, which identifies and defines nine types:

- The Co-ordinator
- The Sharper
- The Imlementer
- The Team worker
- The Resource-Investigator
- The Monitor-Evaluator-Critic
- The Completer-Finisher
- The Specialist
- The Plant

Team Roles measure how a person is likely to interact with colleagues in a team situation, and their general propensity for a particular team role orientation. Different team roles may be adopted according to the demands of the situation. Any study of team roles draws heavily off the work of Belbin (2000, 2004).

The **Co-ordinator** is seen as typically calm, self-confident, controlled and mature, good at utilizing contributions, clarifying goals and objectives and delegating, but can appear manipulative, and is not known for intellectual or creative ability.

As a leader he or she has advantages with this focus on the outcomes, but other team members may come through in stronger leadership roles, such as that of the **Shaper**, who is usually outgoing and dynamic, with the drive to overcome obstacles and challenge complacency, but can be impatient and irritable.

The **Implementer**, mostly conservative, dutiful, efficient and predictable, has good organizing ability, common sense, and turns ideas into practical actions, but can be inflexible and fail to respond to new ideas. A leader of this type is doing busy doing the work himself or herself to be focused on being the leader.

The **Team worker** is often socially-oriented, perceptive and a good listener, able to avert friction and respond to people and situations to promote team spirit, although may be overly sensitive to criticism and be indecisive in a crisis, so as a leader of a team they have certain drawbacks.

The **Resource-Investigator** is known for being extrovert, for enthusiasm and good communication skills, contacting people and exploring new opportunities, but may lose interest once an initial fascination has passed. Their effectiveness in leading can come and go – one minute inspirational, the other bored and reluctant to have the responsibility.

The **Monitor-Evaluator-Critic** is typically unemotional, prudent and discerning, displaying accurate judgment and hard-headedness but lacking in inspiration, ability or drive to inspire and motivate others. Thus, he or she may not be the kind of leader that many subordinates want.

The **Completer-Finisher** is often painstaking, conscientious and perfectionist, following-through and delivering on time, but prone to worrying about small things and reluctant to delegate. As a leader, they tend to keep everything to themselves, and may not trust others to reach their standard.

The **Specialist** contributes on a narrow, specialist area only, and few of these types become leaders. If they do, they carry on with their expert areas of interest and are not particularly interested in their team leader roles.

Finally, the **Plant** is creative, innovatory, individualistic, self-starting, with knowledge and imagination and good at solving problems and generating new ideas, but can be too narrow and impractical to be very successful as a team leader (Belbin 2000 and 2004).

Exercise: Considering the nine team roles, think about which one most sums up your role in your team. Think about your personality, behaviors and motivators as well as the job you officially hold in your workplace. The role of Shaper is most commonly connected with leadership, but there are many effective leaders exhibiting other roles, either singly or in combination.

Once you have decided on the one (or two or three) roles which most accurately describes you – you should then attempt a '360 degree' appraisal of yourself. If you feel in a position to do so, ask your immediate boss, a colleague at the same level, and a subordinate or someone you supervise to give their opinion, preferably with reasons and an example. Then consider the extent to which their answers vary and what might be the reasons for this. Who do you think gives the truest picture? Do you like what you hear, or does this worry you?

ORGANIZATIONAL DESIGN AND TEAM DYNAMICS

Looking at different types of organizational designs, can teams reinforce these styles, or are the teams themselves reinforced by them? Hierarchical designs with many different layers can force teams to remain in a narrow band, not roaming outside of them. Flat organizations can encourage teams to evolve and develop. The circular organization also encourages team flexibility, as does the network-based organization. Teams form and reform as required. The variable system organization also favors teams with different experts and specialists to contribute on a wide front.

LEADERSHIP STYLES AND THE WAY THEY INFLUENCE THE TEAM

What are the broad types of leaders and their attitudes to 'subordinates' and how can this impact on 'team members'?

- Directive
- Delegative
- Participative
- Consultative
- Negotiative

The Bernard M. Bass (1994, 1996) model of **Leadership Styles,** which describes this classification, aims to "describe the range of styles" a person is most likely to adopt. This may be of relevance to a variety of situations where there is a requirement to manage others. As with most personality characteristics, the profile only describes one's most likely styles and not performance" (Stogdill, 1974: 386-392).

Directive leaders have "firm views about how and when things should be done... they leave little leeway for subordinates to display independence ...having a high goal-orientation and being particularly concerned with results, the Directive leader will tend to closely monitor the behavior and performance of others...they will lead by their own opinions rather than inviting others to contribute their ideas... leading to the ideas of others being excluded" (Stogdill, 1974: 386-392).

Bass and Stogdill further explain the ramifications of directive leadership in referring to the leader playing an active role in problem-solving and expecting group members to be guided by his/her decision. They mention error-avoidance being greatest under directive leaders, yet suggest that the quality and quantity of productivity can be enhanced by directive leaders. Groups performed more effectively under directive leaders when in a highly structured task-environment, but non-directive leadership resulted in more effective problem-solving for tasks of low and medium structure.

The **Delegative** leader, by contrast, operates by "delegating work to subordinates... their style is not strongly democratic... so may not involve consultation... subordinates will be assigned work rather than have active input into how projects should be conducted. However, once the work has been assigned only little direction will be provided and subordinates will largely be expected to work with the minimum of supervision" (Stogdill, 1974: 386-392).

According to Bass and Stogdill (1974: 348-349, 352, and 374), increases in subordinate responsibility and authority are positively linked to delegative leadership. When superiors are high in responsibility and authority, subordinates tend to delegate and accept delegation less freely, perhaps due to the greater demands for co-ordination and control made upon the subordinates of these kinds of superiors. Full delegation (permissiveness) results in solutions of better quality and higher satisfaction than a more restrictive form of leadership. Delegative leadership has been related to theory Y and directive to theory X. However, group productivity, satisfaction or cohesiveness is not necessarily higher under delegative styles.

Participative leaders, further down the hierarchy of subordinate involvement, "are primarily concerned with getting the best out of a team as a whole... they believe in pooling ideas and coming to a consensus view... they are unlikely to impress their own wishes and opinions onto the other members of the group but see their role as an overseer of the democratic process... ensuring each member of the group is given an equal opportunity to express their opinion" (Stogdill, 1974: 386-392).

Bass, quoted in Stogdill (1974: 386-392) discusses how the participative leader "permits or encourages group members to participate actively in discussion, problem-solving and decision-making" and that "job satisfaction is related to participative leadership... group cohesiveness is also positively related" and seen as more effective in changing group opinions.

The **Consultative** leader "combines elements of both democratic and directive leadership orientations... they tend to encourage contributions from the separate members of the team... however *Consultative* leaders typically make the final decision as to which of the varying proposals should be accepted... the effectiveness of this leadership style will be dependent upon the individual's ability to weigh the value of the ideas produced by the group and their capacity to encourage them to accept a final decision that may not necessarily be that favored by the majority" (Stogdill, 1974: 386-392).

Negotiative leaders "motivate subordinates by encouraging them, through incentives, to work towards common objectives... to arrive at some mutually equitable arrangement with the other members of the team... *Negotiative* leaders tend to rely on their skills of persuasion to achieve their stated goals... many have well-developed image management skills... coupled with a desire to achieve, can mean that sometimes they adopt unconventional methods to achieve their desired objectives" (Stogdill, 1974: 386-392).

Bernard M. Bass' work also provides a framework for **Subordinate Style** preferences, which also focus on a range of five possibilities, also ranging on a hierarchy, this time from maximum accommodation of leader demands to maximum autonomy and independence of idea generation. This study of preferences aims to "describe the range of subordinate styles one is most likely to adopt. This may be of relevance to a variety of situations where a particular management style is in place. As with most personality characteristics, the profile only describes the style of management to which the subordinate is most likely to respond and does not describe effectiveness or performance" (Stogdill, 1974: 386-392).

Fiedler (1967: 18-32) categorizes Bass' subordinate styles into three groups, with receptive and informative seen as part of the interacting group; reciprocating and collaborative as in the co-acting group; and self-reliant and collaborative as in the counteracting group.

Receptive subordinates "are typically accommodating individuals" keen to finish their work "according to pre-specified procedures" and tend to be conservative. They "typically leave the generation of innovative ideas to other team members" and will take the position that their job is to carry out others' ideas (Fiedler, 1967: 18-32).

In comparison, **Self-Reliant** subordinates are most effective in environments where they can "freely express their ideas... they are innovative and concerned with achieving results but their ideas... are tailored to solving the particular problem in question" and there can be trouble if they have to follow existing procedures and methods. "They then feel that their individuality is being stifled, becoming discontented and irritable. It would therefore be inappropriate for these subordinates to be managed with a directive style as this will invariably result in a mismatch of approaches (Fiedler, 1967:18-32).

Also by contrast, **Collaborative** subordinates "believe that the problem-solving power of the team is more than that of the individual members included within that team". They want to be sure that the team achieves its objectives. They enjoy group discussions and often have innovative ideas of their own. They also like to discuss the ideas of others. "They show little reluctance to point out weaknesses... and usually accept the criticisms of others... they are most effective when working under managers who share their ideas about group participation... and not directive leaders" (Fiedler, 1967: 18-32).

Informative subordinates are usually approached by managers because their ideas and opinions tend to be sound and informed, and they are good at hinking of creative ideas and innovative solutions. They are also quite critical of all new ideas so "their proposed solutions rarely have any major flaws". *Consultative* leaders tend to value such people in their teams, seeing them as reliable sources of information (Fiedler, 1967: 18-32).

At the end of the scale, Reciprocating subordinates "tend to be individuals with an emotionally mature outlook, who rarely become upset by criticism or setbacks". They are happy to promote their own ideas and negotiate with managers concerning the best approach to specific projects. They can work well with a Negotiative leader and, "given that Reciprocating subordinates usually have strong views of their own, any exchanges between subordinate and manager will typically be productive" (Fiedler, 1967: 18-32).

Bass began his research in the 1950s looking at nine original categories of leadership and subordinate styles. These included consideration, direction, production emphasis, decision participation, work facilitation, autonomy of delegation, conflict management, interaction facilitation and positive reinforcement (Hunt & Larsen, 1979:169, 186, 195). His early questionnaires focused on direction, consultation, participation, delegation and manipulation. Bass has been criticized by other writers for tending to view leader behaviors as entirely separate rather than as a mix of styles. He later addressed these issues by attempting to bridge the gap between academics and practitioners with further modification of his questionnaires, as well as the development of the famous transformational and transactional dimensions.

Exercise: most of us are both leaders and followers, but how do we see ourselves in these roles? Which of the above do you feel describes you most accurately in terms of both leader and follower? Are they contradictory, i.e. would you not want to be your own boss, or would you not want a follower like yourself? What are your strengths and weaknesses in these roles? Can you think of a number of examples which illustrate your natural leadership and followership preferences? In which ways do these behaviors advance, or hold back, your career in business and management?

CASE: LEADING TEAMS IN A BANK IN THE UNITED ARAB EMIRATES

This case contrasts two groups – 41 newly-hired school leavers and 39 experienced and high-performing executives – at a major local bank in the United Arab Emirates. What are the differences in leadership, subordinate and team styles between the two groups? What factors affect first-level entry recruits just starting their jobs? How can we see the evolution of their leadership, subordinate and team styles in people who have been working for several years? Can we see the results of training inputs? Or are changes the result of experience and maturity, of work and of life?

On investigating the profiles of a sample from both groups, significant differences were discovered. This suggests that there are important predictors of success of this specific group of new hires and young managers, in terms of being team members and team leaders. This is of particular interest to a study of localization. These UAE nationals in the banking sector have been prioritized in the UAE government's localization campaign – every year the bank must hire a larger and larger number of locals and reduce the number of expatriates.

Given that the fresh recruits were selected from a large population after rigorous selection processes, and that the experienced executives had been identified for a high-level personal development planning initiative, the findings are of consequence to managers and human resource and training staff seeking to comply with localization targets, yet maintain leadership quality in the bank.

All of these respondents are members of a fairly homogenous group of UAE nationals, working in their home country in which they form only a small percentage of the workforce, and all employees of this major local bank in the Emirates (which boasts a larger than average proportion of Nationals of over 30%). The bank is predominantly privately-owned, but with a substantial government holding.

A detailed study of leadership, subordinate and team styles between the two groups suggests that the bank typically does not focus strongly on developing its potential senior management cadre of UAE nationals, or that it has only started doing this recently, or that its efforts are not having a tangible effect on personal managerial and leadership attributes. It may be that this is true of many organizations, despite the efforts they think they make towards creating team leaders and leadership development. It seems likely that, given the relatively small differences between the two groups, the corporate culture of the Bank (conservative, prudent, risk-averse, highly-structured and process-oriented) and the typical national culture characteristics of the Arab world (high power-distance, uncertainty-avoiding, diffuse and synchronic) have a stronger impact on the behaviors of the sample groups than their individual personal attributes.

In the case of both groups, it would seem that the nature of their work at the bank, and the pressures of society, may have served to reinforce their natural styles of operating. They are a relatively homogenous group, feeling the impact of the dramatic economic and infrastructural development of the UAE over the last thirty years, which has far outstripped any social and political advances in this small country. As mentioned, this national grouping forms only a small minority of the population, even in their own country. They are substantially influenced by their traditions of "tribal-kinship influences and orientations towards centralization, rigid rules, clear divisions of labor, low tolerance for ambiguity and autonomy" (Mendenhall, Punnett & Ricks 1995, p. 575). Meanwhile, the nature of the Islamic religion, "where both the material and spiritual spheres of life are considered its appropriate domain" has its own impact. Paradoxically, "taking Islamic precepts… at their face value, one would expect… teamwork, consultative, participative, egalitarian management styles in Muslim organizations" points out researcher Monir Tayeb (1997: 352-364); but, she then explains, 'this is far from being the case" discussing in particular the attitude to consultation in the Arab countries of the Middle East as "an information gathering mechanism [only]… a few selected people are merely consulted, and the selected few are determined by the circumstances. Moreover, although consultation can occur, decisions are never made jointly and are not delegated down the hierarchy" (Tayeb, 1997: 52-364).

The HR department and other recruiters in the Bank are facing a major dilemma: they are under pressure to recruit more and more UAE nationals every year to replace expatriates to achieve the Government's quota of an extra four per cent per year, reaching to 40% by 2010, but there is a major contradiction between the leadership styles, subordinate styles and team roles of the UAE nationals they are recruiting.

Whilst predominantly directive in their leadership style preference for themselves, many of them have a tendency towards subordinate styles that clash with their own leadership style. Therefore, as subordinates, many of them will be uncomfortable with their directive bosses and, when they become leaders themselves, their subordinates will be unhappy working for them. With the majority of UAE national respondents in both of our groups exhibiting self-reliant and reciprocating subordinate styles, they are clearly keen on expressing and promoting their own strongly-held views and ideas and are resistant to environments which require strict adherence to existing procedures. This is the exact opposite of the only subordinate style happy to be working with directives – the receptives or 'empty vessels.'

Similarly, with team roles predominantly showing up as Monitor-Evaluator-Critics and Shapers, they are also by this measure at odds with directive leaders, who are not interested in inviting the ideas of others and accepting criticism and who themselves operate as somewhat undemocratic leaders, prone to irritation and impatience with subordinates.

In predicting and encouraging certain leadership styles for the future, the bank could do well to identify, select and encourage collaborative subordinates who could develop into participative and negotiative leaders, rather than directive leaders – depending, of course, on the characteristics seen as desirable by the bank. If, indeed, directive leadership is not encouraged as an ideal leadership style, the bank could highlight the specific subordinate and team styles seen to encourage and support more 'democratic' styles of leadership encouraging more subordinate empowerment.

So, if we can identify what the bank is looking for in future leaders, we might be well-advised to suggest focusing on the subordinate and team role styles of new young recruits, emphasizing the value of self-reliant and collaborative subordinates and team builders, who are less likely to produce directive leaders in the future. If we want to encourage negotiative and participative leaders (seen as particularly appealing, especially to college-educated individuals, discussed Campbell, Bommer & Yeo, 1993, and more supportive of improved quality, see Politis 2003: 181-193), we need to attract reciprocating and collaborative subordinates. Training programs and job and task design initiatives could be created to further promote teamwork ability, independent idea-generation and creativity, influencing and impact skills, an aptitude for negotiating, and the development of critical thinking and analytical skills.

Questions on the case: What are the differences in leadership, subordinate and teamwork styles between the two groups of staff members? Why is this study important to the bank and its development plans, given its drive for localization? What are the national and religious factors impacting on their leadership, subordinate and teamwork styles, and what is the result of these factors? What is the nature of the contradiction between the leadership style and the subordinate style in the case of many of the respondents? Why could this be a problem? What are the most common team roles of these respondents, and what problems could be caused as a result of this focus on team role behaviors?

HOW DO WE BUILD A TEAM SO THAT WE CAN LEAD IT EFFECTIVELY? WHAT ARE TEAMS, TYPES OF TEAMS, AND HOW DO THEY EMERGE AND DEVELOP?

Building a team is not an easy task, but is important whenever the task requires more than one person. At least two people or more have to be organized, be cooperative with each other, be coordinated, and collaborate in their activities in order to attain the organizational goals. Therefore "team building may be thought of in terms of combining and integrating the talents, skills and energy of individual employees to solve problems and accomplish goals and objectives that may be difficult or impossible to achieve by management or other individual efforts alone" (O'Connor & Erickson, 1996: 1). 'The best results are obtained, when members of the team are committed to one another and to the organization as well' (Andres, 1992: 6).

In answering the questions what is a team, and what is a group, and are they different, we have to distinguish between the meanings of the words 'team' and 'group.' "A team is a small number of employees with competencies (abilities, skills and knowledge) who are committed to common performance, goals and working relationships for which they had themselves mutually accountable" (Hellriegel & Slocum 2004: 194), whereas a group is defined by "any number of people who share goals, often communicate with one another over period of time, and are few enough so that each individual may communicate with all the others, person to person" (Hellriegel & Slocum 2004: 194).

A successful team achieves *synergy*, which "occurs when people together create new alternatives and solutions that are better than their individual efforts. The greatest chance for achieving synergy is when people don't see things the same way" (Hellriegel & Slocum 2004: 281), noted as "the whole is greater than the sum of its part" (Kreitner 1992). Most textbooks define **five types of teams:** Functional, problem-solving, cross-functional, self-managed, and virtual.

CLOSING CASE: FORMING A TEAM

Here we will look at a team under the heading of **problem-solving** that "focuses on specific issues in our areas of responsibilities, developing potential solutions and often are empowered to take action within defined limits" (Hellriegel & Slocum, 2004: 197). The example is the 'kill fish problem' which happened in Hong Kong in the summer of 2002, and the need to find solutions for this problem. Fish were dead all along the shoreline. The top management of local Institute for Scientific Research had to form a team of highly skilled and specialized people in the area of analytical chemistry, environment and marine biology/fishery. The team consisted of three managers in environment studies, in fishery, in the laboratories in marine studies, and in analytical chemistry.

In the words of the analytical chemistry manager, "We knew and worked with each other previously. Every one of us knew our duties and what was expected from us , but we had to pass these messages to our sub-teams. Our team in analytical chemistry (four of us) had to meet every week or whenever needed to discuss what we have done and to prepare a final report for the top management. For us as a team, we had a few conflicts and arguments with each other, as we had to agree on how to handle the samples and schedule time for delivering and picking them up. Sometimes we had problems because the technician would drop off samples at around 2:00 pm instead of early morning, which meant we would finish the analysis around midnight if not later, and come to work very early the next morning. The excuses for not delivering the samples on time included that the technician was busy doing some other duties, or the pilot of the boat was not around and could not be located. We had to take this problem to the top management to give it a top priority for sample collections. In the process of working together, we found ourselves going through the five stages to develop a team."

This five-stages concept is based on a well-known theory by Bruce Tuckman (1977).

1) Forming Stage: Individual behavior is often driven by a desire to be accepted by the others, and to avoid controversy or conflict. "The sub-team in analytical chemistry, consisting of four people, showed themselves as hard workers and willing to participate in setting our goals. They were told about the problems that we were facing, and were asked to think about it for a few days before the next meeting would take place. By that time, with this chance to think about their tasks, how do they feel about it? If they have any concerns regarding their feelings or anything else, they could like to bring it up in the meetings." In the meeting, the team leader defined and specified the goals and made it clear to them in order to get them committed and do more than their best".

The team leader followed the principle of setting SMART goals which means:

- **S**pecific, samples have to be prepared if necessary and analyzed for heavy metals [Mercury (Hg), Lead (Pb), and Cadmium (Cd)].

- **M**easurable, samples have to be measured against standard reference material from World Health Organization (WHO) using chemical equipment. Samples with low concentrations must be analyzed by Graphite Furnace Atomic Absorption Spectrometry (GFAAS) whereas samples with high concentration must be analyzed by inductively Coupled Argon Plasma Atomic Emission (ICP-AES).

- **A**chievable, that the goals could be achieved because the team had the tools to work with and the skills to use them in solving this problem and making things happen. It was not a difficult task to achieve, but it was a challenging one, "and we had agreed that we do more than our best to get things right (effective) and get the right things right (efficient)".

- **R**ealistic, that it is not far-fetched, it is possible and it could be done, once we set our mind into it.

- **T**ime-framed or according to a duration of time was very crucial. Each patch of shoreline had to be completed within a week's time (for solid sample), and within a day or 2 for water samples.

By setting SMART goals every member in the sub-team knew exactly what to do and how to do it and when to do it. They knew their responsibilities and duties and understood them very well. "Every morning we discussed what we had done the previous day. We looked at the results, checked, and rechecked and double checked with other methods of analysis and finally wrote down my report for batches we had received. For the main team, we did not have to meet everyday but we informed the overall team leader of the results of the sub-team, and if she needed more explanation or she thought our meeting is a must then we all (the three senior members) would meet. The schedule was to meet at the start of each week only if necessary".

2) Storming Stage: "This stage was shortened or even avoided in this case because the sub-team in analytical chemistry had been working with each other for years, and they did not have to get acquainted with each other. They got along with each other and worked their differences and conflicts previously. Now they were in the comfort zone where they accept each other the way they are. They were warned that on this project they could be working 7 days a week and more than 12 hours a day, depending on the batches of samples the team were receiving. This issue raised conflict about working hours for the weekends, but the team leader sorted it out by having two shifts, married ones would work from 7:30 AM to 3:30 PM with half hour to one hour lunch break, whereas single ones would work from 3:30 PM until 12:00 midnight with half to one hour dinner break, but I would be working with them both shifts." The manager put in their minds that when "people are working together, 2+2 equals more than 4. People achieve more than they would on their own as part of a cohesive and effective team, capitalizing on each other's skills, experience and strength."

The manager of analytical chemistry had an argument with the top management when the Director Manager (DG) asked her to fly with the helicopter pilot to collect water samples from different locations. "I told him that this is not my job. This is the job of environment team. They would know where to pick the water samples from the assigned location. The environment team would have the local map with locations where the water should be tested. Just because they could not find anyone from the team on a weekend and I was available at that time, they pressured me to do it. I told them that I do not mind doing the job, I would be happy to do it, if the pilot knows which locations to fly, to get the samples. Unfortunately I could not help, as I was leading the team, not coordinating the sample gathering. Because of that, samples were delivered late to us and we had to work longer than what we had anticipated."

3) Norming Stage: At this stage conflicts between the team members are usually resolved. Harmony between team members can then take place because they can now manage their time and their work quality with growing competences, confidence, and independence. It is commonly thought that if a team leader is faced with conflict at this stage, he or she should actively try to manage it, and not suppress it or withdraw from it. According to the manager in this case, "The following were our own norms of behavior (my sub-team) that were established and agreed upon and this was the way how we applied them:

- Meetings start on time. People coming late should not interrupt the meeting by asking questions that had already been discussed.
- Everyone was encouraged to speak what's on their mind. To do so I as a team leader spoke my mind first about certain issues, and that encouraged some of the team members to come forward.

- Everyone had to respect each other's opinion (there were no silly ideas when it came to brainstorming to help in getting problems solved).
- Meeting should not last more than one hour. I was a chair person and in 45 minutes I let them know that we had to finish in 15 minutes. Because some times we had discussions that if I did not interfere it would have taken more than one hour.
- Agenda of the meeting would be sent every Monday before the meeting on Wednesday, so that the team members would be prepared for the meeting and can add to the agenda, what they would like to discuss further.
- Meeting notes would be sent to the team members on the next day of the meeting. Because in the past people came to the next meeting without knowing what had happened in the previous meeting, that caused us to waste time explaining and going through previously discussed issues.
- Reporting on the completed tasks and discussing the ones on progress. This meant needing techniques and tools to help the team plan objectives, making use of communication, co-operation and collaboration.
- The manager continues: "Because my sub-team members valued their membership in cohesive groups, they were willing to adjust their behaviors and attitudes to group standards that we agreed upon in our own norms."

4) Performing Stage: In this phase, team members typically help each other, conflict is de-personalized, problems are solved and successive goals are achieved and exceeded. "Team members show how effectively and efficiently they can achieve results together during the performing stage" (Hellriegel & Slocum, 2004: 205) because "everyone knows each other well enough to be able to work together and trust each other enough to allow independent activity."

According to the manager, all the team members were in their comfort zone and all their energies were directed toward completing the tasks that they had in their hands. Satisfaction and pride become dominant emotions in this phase. The team takes pride in their work, pride in the accomplishments, and pride in their team members. "My sub-team performed very well because we concentrated on solving the problem of the fish kill and completed our tasks that were assigned to us. We were effective (doing the right thing) and efficient (doing things right). Once we received the batch (water samples) each day, we analyzed them right away and had the report ready by the end of the day. Solid samples needed 5 days to be completely analyzed, and reports issued. For analysis we had to use certified standard reference materials to validate our methods to be confident in our results. My sub-team knew when they had to work independently. A batch of 20-25 samples was assigned to everyone. They helped each other when we had a batch of 100 samples or more. They helped each other by washing flasks, preparing standards, diluting samples if needed, calibrating the equipment before starting the analysis."

She continues: "After the analysis, we evaluated our results; observed if there were any alarming signs, such as a high concentration of toxic elements such as Mercury (Hg), Lead (Pb), and Cadmium (Cd). All the results showed that all the concentrations were below the standards of World Health Organization (WHO). So we had to think more into details about the problem of the fish kill. From so many meetings and discussions of our results, we eliminated the possibilities that caused the fish kill. The possibilities that we thought that might had to do with the problem were the following:

- Hospital wastes were dumped to the sea before treatment.
- Accordingly we analyzed for hydrogen sulfide (H2S).
- Untreated water was dumped from the water plant. Therefore chlorine analysis was performed.
- Petroleum products were leaking into the sea before treatment. Therefore lead, mercury, and cadmium elements were analyzed.
- The heat wave that we had that summer had caused the temperature of the water to rise, to an extent that the fish could not bear it. Therefore water temperature was measured and it was normal.
- The last possibility was The RED TIDE. More algae used more dissolved oxygen in the sea near the shore, that caused a decline in the level of oxygen, and eventually the fish did not have enough oxygen to survive. Therefore the dissolved oxygen in the seawater was analyzed and it was at the normal levels."

As she then explained "I had to write a report of the findings that my sub-team found, that nothing was alarming, and we couldn't find the reason for the problem, although we tried everything we could think of. I discussed the report with my team. I suggested to them that we must look into something deeper than chemical analysis. After studying these possibilities thoroughly, and because of my sub-team's cohesiveness that we worked together and had a united effort to accomplish our goals and objectives, we came to the conclusion that we had to divert our attention to fish diseases. I would say my sub-team had good team chemistry, and successfully went through all the phases of team-building. With the team that I was in, we had diversity, three of us were from different departments working on different tasks, and we operated as a unified group. I am really proud of myself and my sub-team to be able to assist in solving the fish kill problem, even though we didn't find the reason in the end."

5) Adjourning Stage: This is the stage of completion and disengagement from both the tasks and the group members. "At this stage every member was proud to be part of this enjoyable group (even though we worked very hard) and happy to have achieved so much. I was pulled off from the task and so was my sub-team, because the issue transferred to fishery's team. My sub-team carried on working together on different tasks. We all were happy because united we stand, divided we fall 'and' all for one and one for all became mottoes for us. Because of this, we could accomplish our goals. It was nice to see the team members getting get along very well with each other, but I also emphasized on their productivity must not be jeopardized by their social interactions and once we understood each other, the work went smoothly. We were proud to be part of this team that we could help in solving an important local problem and to give a positive image to our institute."

Questions on the case: This team saw itself as problem-solving – do you think any other type of team might apply? What were the characteristics of the forming stage of this team? Why was the use of SMART goals relevant here? Why was the storming stage minimal here? What typically happens with other teams in this stage? Why is it necessary? Discuss the creation of group norms. List norms for a group in which you currently work or study. Are there cultural issues in the norming process, such as organizational or national cultural issues? (See later chapters if necessary.) How can the performing stage be defined? Do you think this team performed, even though they did not find the immediate answer? How did the role of the leader – the narrator of this case – change over time? Were her behaviors impacted by the stage of team development?

CONCLUSION

This chapter has focused on team leadership in the context of the leader behaviors towards the team members. Are these positive, supportive and trusting, or is the leader reticent, stand-offish and reluctant to get involved? What are the most important variables influencing the relationship between the leader and his or her team? In this chapter we have focused on introducing the range of possible leadership styles and subordinate styles – and how they work (or do not work) together. We have also looked at team roles – especially the impact of the leader's team role on the rest of the team. Our case studies have provided more insights on how these roles change over time, especially based on the stage of team development. Our next chapter looks at communicating within teams, based on this framework.

REFERENCES

Andres, T.D. (1992) *Team building and creating effective work systems: A manual*. Quezon City, Philippines: New Day Publishers.

Awamleh, R. & Dmour, H. (2004) 'The impact of Transactional Leadership Styles on Employee Satisfaction and Performance in Jordanian Banks', *The International Business & Economics Research Journal*, November

Bass, B.M. (1996) 'Is there universality in the full range model of leadership?' *International Journal of Public Administration, 19*: 6, 731-61

Bass, B.M. & Avolio, B.J. (1994) *Improving Organisational Effectiveness Through Transformational Leadership*. Thousand Oaks, CA: Sage.

Belbin, R.M. (2000) *Beyond the team*. Oxford: Butterworth Heinemann.

Belbin, R.M. (2004) *Management teams: why they succeed or fail*. Oxford: Elsevier/Butterworth Heinemann.

Campbell, D.J., Bommer, W. & Yeo., E. (1993) 'Perceptions of appropriate leadership style: participation versus consultation across two cultures', Asia Pacific *Journal of Management, 10*: 1, 1-19

Fiedler, F.E. (1967) *A theory of leadership effectiveness*. New York: McGraw Hill.

Hellriegel, D. & Slocum, J.W. (2004) *Organizational Behavior*, 10th Ed., Mason, Ohio: Thomson South Western.

Hofstede, G. (1984) *Culture's Consequences: International Differences in Work-Related Values*. Beverley Hills, CA: Sage.

Hunt, J. & Larsen, L.H. (1979) *Cross-Currents in Leadership*. Illinois: Southern Illinois University Press.

Jones, S. & Gosling, J. (2005) *Nelson's Way: leadership lessons from the great commander*. London: Nicholas Brealey.

Jones, S., Singleton, M., & Awamleh, R. (2004) 'The Impact of Socio-Political Context on the Efficacy of Customer Service Training: a UAE Case Study', *The Australasian Journal for Business and Social Inquiry, 2*: 3

Kreitner, R. (1992) *Management*. Boston: Houghton Mifflin.

Mendenhall, M., Punnet, B.J., & Ricks, D. (1995) *Global Management*. Oxford: Blackwell.

O'Connor, M.P., & Erickson, B. (1996) 'Team Building: A strategic advantage', (online). Available:http://www.oconnor.ie/cos/advantage.html.

Politis, J.D. (2003) 'QFD: the role of various leadership styles', *Leadership & Organization Development Journal, 24:* 4, 181-193

Stodgill, R.M. (1974) *The handbook of leadership: a survey of theory and research*. New York: Collier Macmillan/Free Press.

Tayeb, M. (1997) 'Islamic revival in Asia and human resource management', *Employee Relations, 19*: 4, 352-364

Tuckman, B.W. & Jensen, M.A.C. (1977) 'Stages of small-group development revisited', *Groups and Organization Studies, 2*: 419-442

RECOMMENDED FURTHER READING

Atwater et. al. (1999) 'A longitudinal study of the leadership development process: individual preferences predicting leader effectiveness', *Human Relations, 52*: 12, 1543-1562

Chimaera Consulting Limited, (2001) 'Famous Models, Stages of Group Development'. Available: http//www.chimaeraconsulting.com/tuckman.htm

E-Learning for Personal & Management Devt (2006). Forming an Effective team. Available:http://www.shef.ac.uk/stdu/elearning/pmd/teamworking/forming.

Gastil, J. (1994) 'A definition and illustration of democratic leadership', *Human Relations, 47*: 8, 953-976

Jones, S. (2003). Reasons for failure in UAE recruitment, *Human Assets Middle East Summer 2003: 3,* 18-19

Keller, T. & Dansereau, F. (1995) 'Leadership and empowerment: a social exchange', *Human Relations, 48*: 2, 127-147

Lejk, M. & Deeks, D. (2002) *An introduction to system analyst techniques.* Pearson Education Limited, London.

Levi, D. (2001) *Group Dynamics for Teams.* Thousand Oaks, CA: Sage.

Muczyk, J.P. & Reimann, B.C. (1987) 'The case for directive leadership', *The Academy of Management Executive, 1:* 3, 301-311

Nelson, B. (1997) *1001 ways to energize employees.* New York: Workman Publishing.

Ozaralli, N. (2003) 'Effects of transformational leadership on empowerment and team effectiveness', *Leadership & Organization Development Journal, 24*: 6, 335-344

Richards, T. & Moger, S. (2004) 'Creative leadership processes in project team development: an alternative to Tuckman's stage model', *British Journal of Management, 4:* 273-283

Sarros, J.C., Tanewski, G.A., Winter, R.P., Santora, J.C. & Densten, I.L. (2002) 'Work alienation and organizational leadership', *British Journal of Management, 13*: 285-304

Stages of Team Development. "Self Directed Work Teams Develop in Stages" accessed on August 7th 2006, available:http//www.strategosinc.com/work_team_3.htm.

Trompenaars, F. & Hampden-Turner, C. (1997) *Riding the waves of culture: understanding cultural diversity in business*. London: Nicholas Brealey.

Turniansky, B. & Hare, A.P. (1999) *Individuals and Groups in Organizations*. Thousand Oaks, CA: Sage.

Yarbrough, B.T. (2002) *Leading Groups and Teams*. Mason, Ohio: South-Western/Thomson.

Yousef, D.A. (1998) 'Correlates of perceived leadership style in a culturally mixed environment', *Leadership & Organization Development Journal, 19*: 5, 275-284

CHAPTER 3

COMMUNICATING IN TEAMS
SILVIO DE BONO AND STEPHANIE JONES

OPENING CASE:

The attitude of the CEO of Cisco Systems – John Chambers – and how he communicates with his team tells an observer a lot about how things are run there. Chambers believes in open communication among his team members, in a way which some find slightly scary. For example, Chambers was hosting an orientation for new staffers at the corporate head office in the USA, and during this event he approached a particularly young and nervous-looking new recruit. "How am I doing?" Chambers asked him. "How's my presentation so far?" "Am I doing a good job?" Terrified to suddenly be addressed by The Great Man, the rookie new Cisco employee mumbled, "Great. Fine. Excellent." Chambers then turned to him and said, "Would you tell me if I wasn't?" Dumbstruck, the new staffer admitted, "No, I wouldn't...Sir!" Having made his point, Chambers addressed the group: "That doesn't work around here. We all need feedback. Telling someone they are great is OK but it doesn't add that much. We all have to get better, all of us. Including me. Especially me." This is a vital part of the communication process between John Chambers of Cisco and his team. It involves asking questions, listening, encouraging the open discussion of ideas, and speaking the truth. It is challenging for some team members to cope with, but it shows that he cares about them, he wants his team to succeed, and that he treats them like 'family members.' "You must love the people you work with," he insists, "as if they are members of your family."

Questions on the opening case: How would you feel if your boss communicated with you and your team like this? Do you feel that there are dangers in adopting a communication style as open as this? Would people in the teams still respect the boss or respect him or her more? This is a USA-based example – do you think there are cultural issues here?

LEARNING OBJECTIVES FOR THIS CHAPTER

In 'Communicating in Teams,' we will look at the background of how communication actually works, to enable you to build awareness of communication as a process, and thus how teams communicate. This includes developing an understanding of the mechanics of communication and of the factors influencing our daily communication efforts. Then we consider the reasons why we communicate, and the role of language. Meanwhile, body language has become recognized as an increasingly important part of communication. And we communicate not just through what we say and show, but through touch and need for space, and even through our choice of color. We must also appreciate that communication must be at least two-way (especially in a team), so how are we at listening? For many of us, communication is how we build relationships, and we inevitably have a relationship between each person in our team. Yet we find some easier to work with than others – and how do we analyze this? Overall, communication is an essential part of the way teams operate in organizations. This process provides the team with objectives, and helps management and staff to work together, making use of different methods of communications. There are different lines of communications, to different functions in an organization, using different communications tools. Communications play a vital part in organizational creativity and innovation. Finally, miscommunication happens and can be disastrous for the individual or team concerned.

THE COMMUNICATION PROCESS

"Communication refers to the act, by one or more persons, of sending and receiving messages that are distorted by noise, occur within a context, have some effect and provide some opportunity for feedback." (Devito, 1985: p. 4)

In his masterwork entitled 'Human Communications', Joseph Devito (1985) presents his main model of communication. His model, which served as a basis for this chapter and which is widely quoted in academic work in this field, includes the following variables as main components of the communication process.

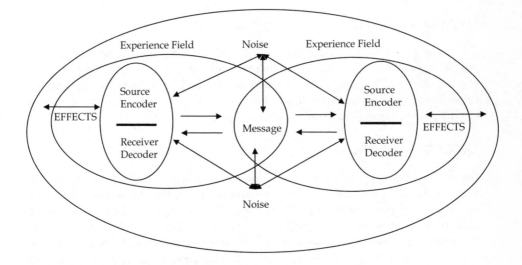

Diagram 3.1 The communication model

The Communication Model: Adopted from: Devito, J. (1985). Human Communications, The Basic Course, New York: Harper & Row Publishers Inc.: p. 4

In the course of the past years several authors in the field of communication have given their version of the communication model. A simpler way of looking at it might be to consider a longitudinal process, where a source passes a message through a system of encoding, using a channel, decoding and then reaching the receiver, who uses a system of feedback to check with the source that he or she is on the right track (Robbins, 2003). For a further discussion of communication theories and concepts, see Dwyer (2002) and Adler and Rodman (1988).

CONTEXT

The Communication Diagram attempts to show and explain the communication context. Communication always takes place within a particular and defined context. At times this context is subtle and unobtrusive; at other times, the context stands out boldly, and the ways in which it restricts or stimulates our communication are obvious.(Devito, 1985). Compare, for example, the differences in communicating in a funeral home, football stadium or in a formal restaurant. The context for communication can also be at work or at home, with members of the team or between just two people. The importance of context in understanding group or team effectiveness was introduced in Chapter 1 – many of these contextual issues relate to communications (Hellriegel & Slocum, 2004). The physical working environment – including the proximity of workers to each other – can make a difference.

SOURCES-RECEIVERS

Communication by definition demands that someone sends signals and someone else receive them. Within the team, some members are more likely to play the part of the sources, and others usually play the part of receivers. It is important in fostering communication that we hear from the receivers too. See more discussion of communication models and theories in Dwyer (2002).

ENCODING-DECODING

The act of producing messages - for example speaking or writing – is termed an encoding. By putting our ideas into sound waves we are putting these ideas into a code, hence *encoding*. By translating sound waves into ideas we are taking them out of the code they are in, hence *decoding*. Very often, the meaning gets lost in the process, or changed significantly, and ways have to be found to overcome this dangerous tendency which can affect the success of the team (Devito, 1985). For example, a message to carry out a task at some point can be decoded as needed now, and vice-versa, when there was no mention of prioritizing. Then the receiver might change the order of their tasks – something which the sender did not want!

MESSAGES

The messages that are sent and received in communication may be sent and received through any one or a combination of sensory organs. Although we think of communication messages as being verbal (including both oral and written), we also communicate non-verbally (body language and other signs). For example, the clothes we wear communicate something to other people. These signals are picked up and interpreted by team members, who then make judgments (being both positive and negative), as to how serious and professional we are, or how lazy and sloppy, for example. It can be difficult to separate the different parts of a message, as all these signals can be jumbled up.

FEEDBACK

The untrained person may not give feedback its due importance. Feedback may come from both the source as well as the receiver. By nature, feedback may take different forms. It can be both positive and negative. In certain isolated instances, feedback can also be neutral. Feedback also has a temporal dimension and as a result can be immediate or delayed. It is essential in communicating within a team-based environment; otherwise no progress can be made in team development (as discussed in the opening case). Many team members hesitate to give feedback (as in the case of the young Cisco recruit) and some treat feedback with hostility, but arguably you are not a team member if you cannot give and receive feedback. As we discussed in the first chapter, feedback from team members offers an individual a chance to gain personal development. Further advice in providing accurate and effective feedback in discussed in Hellriegel and Slocum (2004).

NOISE

Noise can be defined as that source which for a number of reasons (intended or unintended) distorts the original message. It is generally present in any communication system to the extent that the message sent differs from the message received. In the human communication process, noise takes a psychological dimension and would include biases and prejudices in senders and receivers that lead to distortions in the processing of information within the team (Devito, 1985).

EFFECT

Communication always has effect on one or more persons. This effect may vary from one person to another. For every communication act, there is some consequence. The effect may be felt by either of the participants or both. In a team-based situation, the first of these is among the most important, and is a crucial part of how teams operate (Devito, 1985).

Cognitive: Example - getting new information, such as how to evaluate
Affective: Example - love, passion
Psychomotor: Example - Mind and body work together – such as throwing a ball, moving a lever, driving a car, etc.

Exercise: Look at the diagram at the beginning of the chapter (incorporating context, sources-receivers, encoding-decoding, messages, feedback, noise and effect). For this exercise, take an example of a typical message passed around among your team members. An example might be something as important as the announcement of a new policy decision from the company, or as down to earth as when a person is going on holiday and needs to be covered by colleagues. Identify the sources and receivers and the process of encoding and decoding.

Explain the noise and the impact of the experience field, or what might have happened before which can impact on the receiving of the message – such as cynicism, disbelief, etc. In what ways is the message modified or adapted in the process? Does this have a positive or negative impact on the receiving of the message and the subsequent outcome?

WHY DO WE COMMUNICATE?

The reasons why people communicate are endless. In most cases, people communicate for a cause or a purpose which varies considerably. It must be pointed out that communication may also be conscious and/or subconscious. The need for faster communication has changed our lifestyles. We send and receive information through electronic mail, work at computer terminals and use mobile phones. For active teams, communication is increasingly conscious, deliberate and constrained by time. Communication can be part of an everyday process used by everyone, or specifically for business; see Dwyer (2002).

MODES OF COMMUNICATION: LANGUAGE

Verbal communication includes *language*, defined as a code, which is generally utilized in the construction of verbal messages. If it were not for the desire of one person to communicate a meaning to another person, language would probably not exist. Consequently, meaning must be placed at the centre of any attempt to explain language. We can differentiate between the 'First Level' versus the 'Second Level' of Meaning (Denotation versus Connotation). The denotative meaning of a word is more general or universal - that is most people agree with the denotative meanings of words that have similar definitions. Connotative meanings, however, are extremely personal, and few people would agree on the precise connotative meaning of a word. The denotative meaning of a term can be learned from a good dictionary. Connotative meaning, on the other hand, must be found in the person's reactions or associations to the word. Close team members understand each other's connotative meanings, and teams develop their own language: you have to be part of the team to understand it.

An example of connotative language can be seen in the everyday street talk developed by a small community of people living in Central London, who refer to themselves as 'Cockneys.' So that others (especially members of the authorities) cannot understand what they are talking about, the Cockneys have devised an elaborate connotative language of their own based on using words in English which rhyme with their meanings, such as:

Apples and pears: stairs
Whistle and flute: suit
Artful Dodger: lodger
Trouble and strife: wife
Barnet Fair: hair
Dog and bone: phone

They take the first word of the rhyming words and make a whole sentence, such as "The Artful just came down the apples with a new whistle. Meanwhile Trouble called on the dog to say she's having her Barnet done." This makes no sense at all to a non-Cockney person listening, but it is English, and each word can be found in a dictionary, in classic literature or on a map.

Exercise: Give examples of your own specialist form of language which you use in your organization, team and even between you and another close associate. How has this form of connotative language developed? Is it a form of technical jargon or does it have a highly individual meaning, just for you and your colleague? One way to do this would be to invite an outsider to visit your office and make a point of asking you about every word they do not understand. Ask them to make a glossary or dictionary with definitions. Students working in totally different jobs could exchange roles, in an attempt to understand the importance of language in communication.

USES OF LANGUAGE

Language can be used badly and in a way that confuses and wastes time. Dwyer (2002) quotes the following examples, amongst others:

Poor use	Better use
In the event that	If
Subsequent to	After
The majority of	Most
Despite the fact that	Although
Because of the fact that	Because
I personally	I

Clichés
The bottom line
At this point in time
The object of the exercise
The writing on the wall
At the end of the day
A spanner in the works
Firing on all cylinders
Bite the bullet

LANGUAGE AS PART OF DAILY LIFE

Language is a social institution that is designed, modified and extended to meet the ever-changing needs of the culture or subculture. As such, language differs greatly from one culture to another and equally important though perhaps less obvious, from one sub-culture to another. All sub-cultures (such as teams in organizations) develop their own sub-language to facilitate intra-group communication to identify members, to ensure communication privacy, and at times, to impress and confuse others (as in the case of the Cockney rhyming slang). This can become an important part of communication in teams.

PARALANGUAGE

In addition to stress or pitch, paralanguage includes such vocal characteristics as rate, volume, rhythm, as well as the vocalizations involved in crying, whispering, moaning, yawning, and yelling. The speaker who speaks quickly communicates something different from the one who speaks slowly. Even though the words might be the same, if the speed (or volume or rhythm or pitch) differs, the meanings we receive will also differ (Devito, 1995). On the basis of paralanguage (or paralinguistic cues) we make a number of judgments, including:

- Judgments about people – our fellow team members;
- Judgments about controversial turns in events;
- Judgments about believability, whether or not we are convinced.

Examples of paralanguage:

Are you going to see the boss?
Are *you* going to see the boss?
Are you going *to see* the boss?
Are you going to see *the boss*?

NON-VERBAL COMMUNICATION (BODY LANGUAGE)

This refers to one of the buzzwords of the decade – the messages that are communicated by body posture, eye movements, facial expressions, gestures, use of space, vocal volume and rate and even silences. Through the body movements, facial movements, and eye movements we communicate our thoughts and our feelings vividly, accurately and frequently. Generally, when we are listening to one another, we are not passive. Rather, we nod our heads, purse our lips, adjust our eye focus and make various paralinguistic sounds such as *mmm* or *tsk*. This is frequently noticed in team communications and gives positive or negative signals. Other team members make up their mind about you based on non-verbal communications as much as what you might say (Devito, 1985).

Facial expressions also communicate types of emotions. Although researchers are not unanimous in their agreement, most concur with Paul Ekman, Wallace V. Friesen and Phoebe Ellsworth (1982), who claim that facial messages may communicate at least the following emotions categories: happiness, surprise, fear, anger, sadness and disgust/contempt. Non-verbal communications researcher Dale Leathers (1997) has proposed that facial movements may also communicate bewilderment and determination.

Eye movements communicate messages varying by duration, direction and quality of the eye behavior. In every culture there are rather strict, though unstated rules for the appropriate duration for eye contact. In the Western culture the average length of gaze is 2.95 seconds and the average length of mutual gaze (to persons gazing at each other) is 1.18 seconds. When eye contact falls short of this amount we may think the person is uninterested, shy or preoccupied. When the amount of time is exceeded, we generally perceive this is indicating unusually high interest. Many researchers have noted four major functions of eye-to-eye communication:

- to seek feedback;
- to inform others to speak;
- to signal nature of the relationship;
- to compensate for increased physical distance.

Non-verbal communication is often seen classified as an aspect of interpersonal communication, together with oral communication and written communication (Robbins, 2003).

SPACE COMMUNICATION

Space speaks just as loudly as words and sentences. In addition, speakers who stand close to their listener and their eyes focused directly on those of the listener communicate something very different from the speaker who sits in a corner with arms folded and eyes on the floor. Similarity, the executive office suite on the top floor with huge windows, private bar and plush carpeting communicates something very different from the 6 by 6 cubicle occupied by the rest of the workers. The distance between the team and the leader is heightened and exaggerated. Eye contact and space can be culturally loaded, relating to cultural perceptions (Robbins, 2003). What is your own experience?

SPATIAL DISTANCE

According to Devito (1985) there are four situations that define types of relationships Each of these four has a close phase and a far phase, giving us a total of eight clearly identifiable distances. The four distances, corresponding to the four major types of relationships are:

- Intimate   (0 - 18 inches);
- Personal   (18 inches - 4 ft);
- Social   (4 ft -12 ft);
- Public   (12 ft - 25 ft or more).

A number of variables have been found to have a significant effect on our treatment of space communication situations:

- Status;
- Culture;
- Context;
- Subject Matter;
- Sex and Age;
- Positive and negative evaluation.

TOUCH COMMUNICATION

Touch is perhaps the most primitive form of communication. In terms of sense development, it is probably the first to be utilized; even in the womb the child is stimulated by touch. Touching as a form of communication can serve a number of important functions, communication-wise, in:

- Consolation;
- Support;
- Dominance.

Space communication, spatial distance and touch communication are widely seen as differentiators in different national cultures. Attitudes to comfort about space vary substantially between people in different countries (Hofstede, 1984; Trompenaars, 1997). For example, in Chinese cultures people don't seem to mind sitting on a beach in close proximity to others, whereas many northern Europeans, such as British people, prefer to find isolated beaches where they can be alone, even at considerable trouble to themselves and others. See also Dwyer (2002) and Samovar and Porter (1988) for their lengthy discussions about intercultural communication.

COLOR COMMUNICATION

Communication can be more than just words and actions. Have you ever thought of it in terms of colors? These are used frequently in communication, often subconsciously. When we are in debt we speak of being in the red; when we make a profit we speak of being in the black. When we are sad we are blue, and when we are healthy we are in the pink. To be a coward is to be yellow and to be inexperienced is to be green.

Some positive and negative messages given by the use of colors include those in this listing, which is by no means exhaustive:

Table 3.1 Color Communication Table

Color	Positive Meanings	Negative Meanings
Red	Warmth Passion Life Liberty Patriotism	Death War Revolution Devil Danger
Blue	Religious feeling Devotion Truth; justice	Doubt Discouragement

Yellow	Intuition	Cowardice
	Wisdom	Malevolence
	Divinity	Impure Love
Green	Nature	Envy
	Hope	Jealousy
	Freshness	Opposition
	Prosperity	Disgrace
Purple	Power	Mourning
	Royalty	Regret
	Love of truth	Penitence
	Nostalgia	Resignation

Adapted from Henry Dreyfuss (1971) Symbol Sourcebook. New York: McGraw Hill

Exercise: Using the concepts of body language, spatial communication, touch, eye contact and even color communication, describe an encounter with a colleague in which neither of you uses words. Explain your perception of your colleague based on these elements only. How revealing is this experience? How does it make you feel about the other person? Is it easy or difficult? How often do you find yourself doing this?

LISTENING SKILLS

If we measured the importance of communication approaches in terms of the time we spend in an activity, then listening would be our most important communication activity. As a member of a team, being an effective listener is a highly-regarded asset.

Suggestions to improve effective listening skills include making eye contact, using affirmative head nods and appropriate facial expressions, avoiding distracting actions or gestures, asking questions, paraphrasing, avoiding interrupting the speaker and not over-talking. (Robbins, 2003)

The following percentages developed by various "communicologists" (Devito, 1978) reflect the above assertion of the importance of listening in communication:

Speaking	16% - 30%
Reading	16% - 17%
Writing	9% - 14%
Listening	45% - 53%

Listening, which is generally done for a number of reasons including enjoyment, sharing information and to seek or ask for help, is an active process of receiving aural stimuli.

Contrary to popular conception, listening is an active rather than a passive process. Listening does not just happen but takes energy and commitment to be effective. Active listening among team members is a vital aspect of team communications. Listening involves receiving stimuli and is thus distinguished from hearing as a physiological process. There are three distinct levels of listening:

- The first is the level of non-hearing. Here the individual does not listen at all; rather he or she looks at the speaker and may even utter remarks that seem to imply attention such as "Ok", "Yes", "Mmmm", but there is really no listening. Nothing is getting through.

- The second level of listening is hearing. Here, the person hears what is being said and even remembers it, but does not allow any of the ideas to penetrate beyond the level of memory. The material is not being processed and thought through.

- The third is the level of thinking, where the listener not only hears what the speaker is saying, but also thinks about it. The listener here evaluates and analyses what is being said. It is the third level of listening-thinking that is most important, and needs to be actively practiced for effective teamwork.

Exercise: Explain your own attitude to listening, and the situations where you might use the three different levels of listening. When would you make a big effort to use the third level? Give examples of when you might use the different types of listening, with both positive and negative effects. How would you rate yourself as a listener? To what extent and how often do you feel that you should have listened more intently? Do you notice your listening skills, and sometimes find it hard to keep concentration? Do you have any aids to better listening, such as note-taking?

RELATIONSHIP DEVELOPMENT AS PART OF COMMUNICATIONS

Although this may not seem an obvious connection, communications play a vital role in the whole business of forming relationships. Teams often evolve naturally reflecting the need of people to work together. When other team members are absent for prolonged periods of time, often depression sets in for the remaining person or people, and self-doubt surfaces. Yet relationships are never easy. There are three significant characteristics of relationships. Devito (1985, 173) proposes the following stages:

- Relationships are established in stages

The five point stage diagram (below) describes some of the significant stages in the development of relationships. For each specific relationship, you might wish to modify and revise the basic model in various ways, according to your own experience within your particular team, as there may be some stages you have not yet reached, or may never reach:

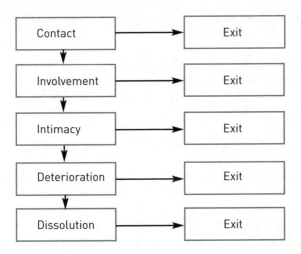

Diagram 3.2 Relationship development

The Communication Model: Adapted from: Devito. J. (1985). Human Communications, The Basic Course, New York: Harper & Row, p. 173.

Exercise: *Discuss your own ability to develop relationships, and the cycle through which your relationships tend to pass. Do your relationships deteriorate too quickly? Are you reluctant to reach the intimacy stage and tend to stick to a more limited involvement? Do you deliberately avoid commitment? For what reasons are you attracted to others? Is there a link between your attraction reasons and the usual cycle of your relationships? In what ways is this affecting your successes and failures in your business career?*

ORGANIZATIONAL COMMUNICATION

As we have seen, communication is any means by which a thought is transferred from one person to another. As business has become increasingly complex (and in many environments the size of typical organizations has increased) we have all tended to become specialists, either operating singly or in teams. When specialists communicate with others who have a similar background they talk a language of their own (what we have called connotative language, above). This technical jargon – which may not be looked up in an ordinary dictionary – has advantages because it saves a great deal of time. Yet the more specialized the nature of our work, the more we find ourselves unable to communicate with those who do not possess our specialized knowledge. Thus 'jargon' can become a barrier to communication, especially from a specialist within a team talking with other team members, or between a team of specialists and another team (or a senior management team). Sometimes technical experts cannot 'sell' their ideas to management as they cannot explain their ideas without this perplexing terminology.

It is always important to speak and write as clearly and concisely as possible, to get our ideas across effectively and avoid misunderstanding. A helpful process is to explain the meaning of 'jargon' words to an outsider, and thereby bring them into the fold. This must be handled sensitively – terms must be explained without the receiver thinking that the sender thinks he or she is 'stupid' or 'uneducated' or 'out of date.'

Remember that technical jargon can be departmental and company-wide. Members of one department may use highly-specific language that others in other departments cannot understand without explanation. But they all understand company-specific terms, which can be incomprehensible to outsiders.

Communications in organizations have often been categorized in terms of direction, as downward, upward and lateral. This refers to communication from bosses to subordinates and the other way around, and amongst peers in an organization at any level. As Robbins (2003, 116) points out, lateral communications can be both positive and negative. "Since strict adherence to the formal vertical structure for all communications can impede the efficient and accurate transfer of information, lateral communications can be beneficial. In such cases, they occur with the knowledge and support of superiors. But they can create dysfunctional conflicts when the formal vertical channels are breached, when members go above or around their superiors to get things done, or when bosses find out that actions have been taken or decisions made without their knowledge."

OBJECTIVES OF COMMUNICATION IN ORGANIZATIONS

One of the objectives of communication in a company is that everyone should be aware of what the organization wants to achieve. This end may be attained by the communication of the organization's common objective, purpose, aim or goal. The policies of the organization should offer guidance to the team members concerned in achieving outcomes related to these objectives.

Training ensures that there is a similarity of outlook in communications and thus a uniform method of attacking problems. Of particular importance is the training provided by an induction program which should have the purpose of communicating to the new employee about the background of the company, its mission, general organization, regulations, communication systems and its leading personalities. Further, it should seek to describe the highlights of the organization's achievements in providing products or services and thus its economic and social value to the community.

Organizational communication can include formal small-group networks, the grapevine, and computer-aided communication such as email, intranet and extranet links, videoconferencing, etc. Small-group networks can be especially valuable in passing information around in an organization. They are often categorized in terms of a chain (from one person to another); a wheel (around in a circle with several people communicating with the central person or hub of the wheel) and all-channel, with each person feeding back amongst themselves. In terms of speed, the wheel and all-channel communications can be fast, but the chain and wheel networks can be more accurate. A leader is most likely to emerge in the wheel arrangement, and member satisfaction is seen as highest in all-channel communication (Robbins, 2003: 119-120).

MANAGEMENT/STAFF COMMUNICATIONS

Communication is clearly a vast subject, but it is possible to resolve it into two main aspects in an organizational setting – the internal and external relationships of the organization. Of internal communications, there is the way in which information may be represented to management, staff and workers. There is also the upward movement of information, so that the feelings of staff and workers are made known to the management. Since communications are of joint interest to management and employees, in some companies the communications policy is wholly or partly written into the organization's rules. The advantage of having communications policy in writing is that all employees should understand that there is a formal procedure for dealing with grievances. There may also be a separate policy for external communications, such as talking with the press and members of the general public.

Management is often defined as the art of directing human activities so as to secure the greatest possible conformity with the policy of the organization. This requires constant communications. Employees, widely seen as an asset within each organization, need to relate with one another and discuss issues which do not only pertain directly to them. Employees are motivated or de-motivated by the amount of information which is made available to them – or not.

METHODS OF COMMUNICATION

Adaptability: It is sometimes a problem deciding which method of communication to use. This depends on several factors, such as the time available and the geographical location of the people who are to receive the message. Some managers insist that important policy statements should be made personally wherever possible. It is important to judge how the other person will react. Communication is a two-way process. A face-to-face oral contact or a telephone call will often produce immediate results whereas a letter will remain unanswered.

The means of communication used will depend upon a number of factors. As we discuss the methods in turn we shall see that our personal knowledge of the person we wish to contact, the time available, and the cost of communication are among the points we shall have to bear in mind when deciding to communicate or not to communicate. Thus adaptability in methods of passing on information is essential.

Visual methods: If information and figures are presented visually the meaning and implications are nearly always more readily understood. It is also important for management purposes to grasp the trends or rates of change at the earliest possible movement. Visual methods enable the trends to be presented to the manager much more easily than in any other way. Some visual methods which could help in any presentation include charts (Bar charts, Pictograms, Graphs, Z charts, Pert charts and Gantt charts); Maps; Film (Film strips, closed circuit television and video); Posters; etc. In this context, some organizations issue newsletters, whilst others would rely on senior management addressing group meetings of employees. See a more detailed explanation in Dwyer (2002).

Exercise: *Which methods of communications would you use for specific purposes? How flexible and adaptable are you in communications? Do you prefer verbal or visual communications? Give an example of a recent communication exercise within your team, and how you got your message across. In what ways was it effective? In what ways could it have been improved? Discuss the modes of communication in your organization which you find to be the most difficult and challenging.*

LINES OF COMMUNICATION

These are the channels through which information is transferred from one person to another. Communication is essentially a two-way process; information has not only to be sent but has also to be received and understood, and then acted upon. Some form of mechanism must be available through which there can be downward communication (from superior to subordinate), upward communication (from subordinate to superior), and horizontal communication (between people of comparable status and also between management and union). For a further discussion, see Fischer and Nothey (1993).

The lines of communication should not be too long. If they are, those people who have to take action on the information may not, in fact, receive the exact message intended. The lines of communication within organizations are usually formally structured and employees have to limit themselves to the tools and systems that they have available. Such formal structures are directly related to tightly coupled organizations such as the armed forces. There are other instances where informal structures, such as informal meetings and sports activities, enhance the communication process between different members of the same organization.

LINE MANAGEMENT AND COMMUNICATION

By line organization, we usually mean a vertical line organization where one rank is clearly below another to which it is directly related. There has been much discussion about functional and staff management, and some observers on communication have given the impression that the main techniques used to solve the difficulties which inevitably arise are joint consultation, suggestion schemes, company magazines and attitude surveys.

Many well-structured and clearly-defined organizations have experimented with a Management by Objectives approach. In brief, this is a systematic approach to management, which includes setting objectives for the organization and for the individual; control and review; and management development and appraisal. The introduction of an [MBO] may be part of a systematic approach to management training and development, and this kind of approach will require from management a carefully drawn action plan covering the following aspects:

1. The specific assignment of responsibility within the company for management development;
2. The analysis of managerial jobs;

3. The assessment of present and future needs;
4. Recruitment and selection;
5. Personal records and appraisal.

All these tasks require a strong emphasis on communication, and a lack of clear communication can undermine the achievement of an MBO system in an organization.

FUNCTIONAL MANAGEMENT AND COMMUNICATION

As organizations grow more complex it has become necessary for those who are operating at a high level to delegate some of their authority to others. The principle of the division of labor has therefore been applied to management. In this way people are made responsible for the specialized functions of management such as selling, production, finance or personnel relations. In turn these functions are further subdivided to enable people to take direct responsibility for a sub-strata of specialized jobs. This requires increasingly accurate and responsible communications. The most important aspect in this approach is to have clear and defined communication tools that enable you (wherever you may be in the organization) to understand clearly the message of your own manager and then be able to convey the same message to your subordinates. This is particularly vital in an MBO situation where objectives are cascaded down throughout the organization.

Staff appointment and communications: Of all the managerial positions, those who must be most skilled in communication hold designations such as Human Resource Manager/Personnel Manager, Training Adviser, Public Relations Adviser, Industrial Relations Officer, and so on. Almost all positions in the organization need communications skills. Although in many instances this person may not hold any decisional powers, he or she is very often held responsible towards the communication patterns and networks within the organization. Of course, people occupying this role are not always as adept in communication as their position requires.

Principle of authority and communication: One of the tried and tested principles of scientific management is the principle that the lines of authority should be clearly defined. Nobody should be accountable to more than one superior, who must be held responsible for the acts of those subordinate to him (as in the case of the Ranpak example in Chapter 1). Yet experiments are frequently tried with forms of organization which do not allow the conventional line management communication. A matrix structure of subject-specialist schools and degree-level divisions is common in colleges and is based on the assumption that a more effective service for students will result if course designers and supervisors are organized into schools, and teachers are organized into divisions based on disciplines and degree-level.

To organize itself into a structure to accomplish its goals, maintain itself good working order, and adapt to a changing world, a group or team must structure its communication. Meetings will be scheduled; reports from group members will be requested; conferences among members will be set up; summaries of group progress may be written and sent to all members. All these activities are structured communication opportunities. The communication network thus created determines the amount and type of information a group member will receive from the other members. The very nature of communication implies that communication is selective, that a communication network exists, that incentives to use it properly are present, and that members must use certain procedures for communicating with each other.

One-way communication, two-way communication and feedback: The procedures used within the formal communication networks of a group can be examined in several different ways; the approach most relevant to a discussion or authority of hierarchies focuses on three types: namely one-way communication, two-way communication, and feedback. In an authority hierarchy, a one-way communication procedure is characterized by a chairperson giving instructions or making announcements to other team members. These team members are not necessarily allowed to communicate back in return.

One-way communication with feedback is often called directive or coercive communication. In this communication procedure within an authority hierarchy, the chairperson presents a message and the team members give feedback on how well they understand it. The exchange is completed when the team members indicate to the chairperson that they have received the message correctly.

Two-way communication is a reciprocal process in which each member starts with sending messages and tries to understand the other members' messages. In a two-way communication procedure, the chairperson and the other team members freely exchange ideas and information in a productive discussion. Both sending and receiving skills are needed. All members are able to participate at will, and minority opinions are encouraged and more apt to be expressed. Feelings of resistance or doubt can be discussed and resolved at the time they are experienced so that they are not potential barriers to commitment. Two-way communication encourages open and candid member interaction, distributed participation and leadership consensual decision-making. Arguably this can be a highly effective way of communicating in teams.

Even when a two-way communication procedure is encouraged, the authority hierarchy will influence communication among team members. High authority members usually do most of the talking, and most of the messages are directed at them. Low authority members often do not communicate very much with each other during a meeting, preferring to address their remarks to high authority members. Because they generally fear evaluation by those with power, members without power can be expected to take few risks, speak inconsequentially, and avoid frankness in their remarks.

High authority members often hesitate to reveal any of their own limitations or vulnerability, a tendency that also decreases open and effective communication among members. Thus, several influences push the group's use of communication procedures towards practices that thwart the kind of discussion and problem-solving needed for it to function effectively. Thus the role of power in effective communications in teams is a highly significant one.

Feedback can be used to improve performance, one of the most vital communications skills used in organizations. How in particular? There is a need to focus on specific behaviors, by keeping feedback impersonal and goal-oriented. By making sure feedback is well-timed and well-understood this technique can be improved. Directing negative feedback toward behavior that is controllable by the recipient is also useful (Robbins, 2003). See also Leavitt and Mueller (1951) for a fuller discussion.

Exercise: Explain how lines of communication operate in your organization. To what extent are these formal or informal? Would you describe them as 'political'? In what ways are the efforts of the organization reduced and compromised by problems in communications? Is communication from your higher authority figures mostly one-way? Or is it more like the example in our opening case about Cisco? Consider the extent of the usage of one-way and two-way communication, and feedback in your organization.

COMMUNICATION TOOLS IN ORGANIZATIONS

Organization charts: These can show lines of authority and responsibility in a company, which can be a great assistance to management in improving the communication system. Some companies issue the organization chart to all staff, and some print pictures of the men (or occasionally, women) by the side of their names on the chart, thus stressing the personal aspect of management and communication. The task of preparing an organization chart enables every unit to be brought under review and the relationships of the units to one another is assessed. It ensures that the management considers the necessity of delegating to each employee the necessary authority (including the communication systems) to permit him/her to carry out the responsibilities.

Job descriptions: These are also considered as a major communication tool. The object of describing the job in detail is to establish clearly its work content and requirements for its satisfactory execution. This brings more certainty and clarity in the communications between team members.

Joint consultation: This has two meanings. In the first place it is used to cover the principle that workers should be notified of changes in policy, especially aspects of labor relations. Joint Consultation also refers to the framework of committees by which labor and management are brought together to discuss those matters of common concern which do not fall within the scope of the negotiating machinery. The various bodies which are used in joint consultation provide employees with an opportunity for expression, and thus they can fulfill a useful purpose in communication.

Suggestion schemes: These can be one of the chief ways of making sure that the bright ideas of all members of an organization are considered. They are used for office workers as well as for those whose employment is in factories. They can be most effective when encouraged with reward schemes.

Networking: When one-way communication procedures are used in a team, comprehension of messages is often so poor that team members turn to the informal communication network to clarify what has been communicated. Often certain team members will be better able to interpret messages from 'higher-ups' using this technique. In such cases other members will seek them out and ask them what the 'higher-ups' meant by the latest communication. Such members are called opinion leaders or gatekeepers because they have more influence over members' comprehension of messages than do the persons in higher authority positions who originated the messages.

There are two common types of opinion leaders:

- Information gatekeepers, who receive messages from superiors and outside sources or who read, listen, and reflect upon written reports and verbal messages to a greater extent than other team members;
- Technological gatekeepers, who read more of the theory and research literature in their field and consult more with outside sources than do the other team members.

Opinion leaders frequently serve as translators by taking messages from superiors and rephrasing them into more understandable form and into the specific meanings they have for different group members.

Such instances of networking to clarify communications are important because one-way communication creates three common barriers in organizational communication:

- Leveling, when the receiver tends to reduce the amount of information he or she receives by remembering much less of the message then was presented by the sender.
- Sharpening, when the receiver sharpens certain parts of the information so that a few high points are readily remembered while most of the message is forgotten.
- Assimilation, when the receiver takes much of the message into his/her own frame of reference and personality. Thus his/her interpretations and memories of what was heard are affected by the person's own thoughts and feelings. This process involves not only changing the unfamiliar to some context, but also leaving out material that seems irrelevant and submitting material that gives meaning in the person's own frame of reference.

Either way, these filters act as significant barriers to communication between senior management and the rest of the team. Barriers to communication can include not only filtering but selective perception, information overload, gender styles, emotions and language (Robbins, 2003).

Employees inevitably belong to different groups, even within the same organization. This can occur both formally and informally. This assumption applies to groups within and outside of the organization. The person who connects one group and another is referred to as the 'Liaison Officer.' The gap between the group members is referred to as the 'Bridge-link.' This informal networking can be an effective tool in the communication process, especially in an organization where the structure of communication is too tightly coupled, or highly structured. In some instances this form of informal communication process is important to reach those who isolate themselves and do not mix in groups.

IT: ANOTHER FORM OF COMMUNICATION

Data on its own does not make any sense. The process of interpretation of data is what makes sense in any dynamic organization since it adds value to the information available. In today's organizations, we have whole departments, working on the job of gathering all sorts of data. This is being done because we have realized its importance in the running of any organization.

Yet certain data should not be limited to those people at the top only. The transfer of data to other people would obviously help attain full understanding of organizational concepts, decisions and policy-making models. What type of data to make available? To whom should it be available? How to make it available? How to ensure full understanding of this data? There is no off-the-shelf answer to these questions. Therefore in such a situation one must consider a number of features. If I make this information available, will I enhance the communication process? If yes, I should make the information available. If I believe that the information should be made available, my next question would be to whom? In order to answer this question, I must ask myself if the person at the receiving end is interested to know for personal purposes or for the benefit of the organization. Another question of how to present the data requires a number of skills and understanding of those people who are at the receiving end. Employees at the shop-floor level may be interested to know why profits decreased but may not be interested in the detailed figures you have available.

THE PROCESS OF INNOVATION AND COMMUNICATION

Several organizations are passing through phases during which they have to make certain changes to keep themselves in the marketplace. The outcomes of these changes are directly related to the extent of effective communication processes. These usually start with some form of felt needs which may not only be personal. The phases in the process of innovation are the following:

1. Knowledge;
2. Persuasion;
3. Decision;
4. Implementation;
5. Confirmation.

It is very important to understand that at each and every phase a whole structure of communication is not only important but imperative. In order to facilitate communication during such phases, very often big organizations find people who assume the role of Change Agents, as discussed in later chapters. Such people who are well informed not only accept changes but also facilitate innovation. The strongest asset that such people must possess is communication skills. The Change Agents are the links between different phases of development and different people. They act toward highlighting the need for change and equip themselves with knowledge in order to be in a very good position to inform others. Another communication skill which is considered as an asset is the skill of empathy and understanding. Change Agents must be able to work through opinion leaders who are also communicators within organizations. These two communicators can together diagnose the organization in order to create the best structure and develop the right communication systems.

CLOSING CASE

Miscommunications are particularly common between people of different cultures and languages. This all goes to show that communication causes some of the most significant challenges in expatriation. As shown below, language problems are only part of the issue – it is also one of mindset. In China, such problems are especially frequent between Chinese and foreigners – here are three examples, quoted from *"Managing in China"* (although you may feel that these miscommunications can happen anywhere)...

A Western business person (WB) is talking with a Chinese hotel employee (CHE):

WB – Do you have cars for airport pick-ups?
CHE – Yes, we have cars.
WB – I need several cars to pick up incoming visitors tomorrow.
CHE – Yes.
WB – I need one car to pick up Director X coming in on the 9 o'clock flight from Hong Kong, one car to pick up Mr Y and Mr Z coming in at 12.20 from Bangkok, a seven-seater to pick up a group of six managers coming in at 3.1 from Singapore...don't you have a pencil?
CHE – I have a pencil.
WB – Why aren't you writing this down?
CHE – I do not need to write this down.
WB – Why not?
CHE – Because we have no cars.
WB – But you told me you have cars.
CHE – But we have no cars tomorrow.

A foreign resident (FR) wants to move house. He phones a company which rents vans and speaks with a staff member (SM):

FR – I'm moving house – do you have a van?
SM – Yes.
FR – I need it for Saturday.
SM – OK.
FR – How much would it cost?
SM – The same as the usual rate for a large taxi.
FR – OK, good. Here's my address (goes into extensive detail on the address of both the old flat and the new one).
SM – OK.
FR – Please arrange for the van to come to my old flat at 2PM on Saturday.
SM – But the van is hired out on Saturday afternoon.
FR – But I said Saturday and you said OK!

SM – Yes. Saturday morning at around 7AM is OK.

FR – That's too early for me!

SM – I'm sorry, that's the only time we can make.

FR – OK, I suppose I can make an early start. Please come at 7AM on Saturday to pick up my furniture and boxes.

SM – Oh, we can't carry furniture or boxes. The van is for people only – police regulation. Our van is licensed for people only.

A foreign visitor (FV) is ordering drinks from a Chinese waitress (CW) for herself and friends.

FV – I would like to order four cans of Coke, please.

CW – If you order one large bottle, it's cheaper than four cans, and will be enough for four people.

FV – What a good idea! Thank you very much. I'll order one large bottle of Coke. What a nice and helpful waitress!

CW – Sorry, we don't have any large bottles of Coke.

Questions on the closing case: Why did these particular miscommunications happen? What have these three cases have in common? How do they reflect the different ways of thinking between Westerners and Chinese? What would be your reaction if these miscommunications happened to you? How could you prevent these miscommunications from happening? Are there any lessons from our study of communications in this chapter which could help here?

CONCLUSION

Here, in this chapter, we have explored the character and mechanics of the communication process, to better understand how teams communicate. The factors affecting successful communication depend on us, others, and the context. We communicate for specific reasons, using a specific language, which can be a help or barrier. We communicate non-verbally too, and through touch and spatially. Listening is an ongoing challenge, as is the job of building relationships. Clearly, communication is an essential part of the way teams operate in organizations. But are the methods of communication used appropriate? Are the lines of communication working? Which communication tools are employed? How can we use communication more in organizational creativity and innovation? How can we avoid damaging and frustrating miscommunication? This chapter has opened a new perspective on how we operate.

We have not, however, included references to more strategic and ethical issues of communications, such as the credibility of the content of communications; the use of communications channels such as email to spread false information and rumors; the possibility of anonymity in such communications and the implications of this; and the use of communications channels to shift the responsibility for tasks from one co-worker to another. The reader is referred to our companion textbook, Leadership, Change and Responsibility.

REFERENCES

Adler, R.B. & Rodman, G. (1988) *Understanding Human Communication.* 3rd ed. , New York: Holt, Rhinehart and Winston.

Cockney Rhyming Slang – a short introductory text – tourist brochure

Davis, M. (1985) *Intimate Relations.* Harmondsworth: Penguin.

Devito, J.A. (1978) *Communicology: an introduction to the study of communication.* New York: Harper and Row.

Devito, J.A (1985) *Human Communication. The Basic Course.* New York: Harper & Row Publishers.

Drefus, H. (1971) *Symbol Sourcebook.* New York: McGraw Hill.

Dwyer, J. (2002) *Communication in Business: strategies and skills.* 2nd ed. Sydney: Prentice Hall.

Ekman, P., Friesen, W.V. & Ellsworth, P. (1982) *Emotion in the Human Face.* Harmondsworth: Penguin.

Fischer, A.B. & Nothey, M. (1993) *Impact: a guide to business communication.* Englewood Cliffs, New Jersey: Prentice Hall.

Hall, E.T. (1959) *The Silent Language.* New York: Doubleday.

Hellriegel, D. & Slocum, J.W. (2004) *Organizational Behavior*, 10th Ed., Mason, Ohio: Thomson South Western.

Hofstede, G. (1984) *Culture's Consequences: International Differences in Work-Related Values.* Beverley Hills, CA: Sage.

Jones, S. (2008) 'The Impact of Socio-Political Context on Preferred Conflict Mode Styles of Business Trainees: a UAE Case Study' *Employment Relations* January

Jones, S. (1997) *Managing in China.* Singapore: Butterworth Heinemann.

Leathers, D. (1997) *Successful Nonverbal Communication: principles and applications.* New York: Allyn and Bacon.

Leavitt, H. & Mueller, R. (1951) 'Some effects of feedback on communication', *Human Relations, 4:* 401-410.

McCarthy, T., *Leadership Seminar*, Kuwait, March 2007.

Robbins, S.P. (2003) *Essentials of Organizational Behavior.* New Jersey: Pearson Education, Upper Saddle River.

Samovar, L.A. & Porter, R.E. (1988) *Intercultural Communication: a reader.* 6th ed., London: Wadsworth.

Trompenaars, F. & Hampden-Turner, C. (1997) *Riding the waves of culture: understanding cultural diversity in business.* London: Nicholas Brealey.

RECOMMENDED FURTHER READING

Abrams, K.S (1986) *Communicating at work: listening, speaking, writing and reading.* New Jersey: Prentice Hall, Englewood Cliffs.

Bearner, L. & Varner, J. (2001) *Intercultural Communication in the Global Workplace.* Boston: McGraw Hill.

Chaney, L.H. & Martin, J.S. (2000) *Intercultural Business Communication.* Upper Saddle River, New Jersey: Prentice Hall,

Devito, J.A. (1989) *The Interpersonal Communication Book* 5th ed., New York: Harper and Row,

Fiske, J. (1990) *Introduction to Communication Studies.* 2nd. Ed. London: Methuen.

George, J.M. & Jones G.R. (2002) *Organizational Behavior.* 3rd. ed. New Jersey: Prentice Hall, Upper Saddle River.

Hall, E. (1969) *The Hidden Dimension.* New York: Doubleday.

Homans, G.C. (1959) *The Human Group.* New York: Harcourt Brace.

Johnson, D.W. (1993) *Reaching out: interpersonal effectiveness and self-actualization.* Englewood Cliffs, New Jersey: Prentice Hall.

Marchetti, M. (1996) *'Talking Body Language', Sales and Marketing Management, 148:* 10, 46

Myers, D.G. (1992) *Social Psychology.* 4th ed., Boston: McGraw Hill.

Trenholm, S. (1986) *Human Communication Theory.* Englewood Cliffs, New Jersey: Prentice Hall.

Turniansky, B. & Hare, A.P. (1999) *Individuals and Groups in Organizations.* Thousand Oaks, CA: Sage.

CHAPTER 4

FOSTERING TEAMS
STEPHANIE JONES AND SILVIO DE BONO

OPENING CASE:

The transformation of GE by Jack Welch is well-known – especially the changes in the product portfolio, the business performance and the financials. What is perhaps less clear for many observers is his impact on developing teams in the organization. Many would dispute this, focusing instead on the 'Neutron Jack' image – named after the bomb that kills people but leaves the buildings intact. Yet Jack Welch was keen on the forming of an 'A team' in each area of his business – getting the best people he could possibly attract in each business unit. "You must take the trouble to get an A person in each job", he would insist. "If you get C people, they end up costing you a lot, because they don't perform and then you have to make up for this."

Jack Welch also looked for 'A people' and 'A teams' who were also strongly committed to the company. "If you have people who are strong performers but who rubbish the company, it poisons other people," he explains. "Others take them seriously because they are strong performers. But even though we might miss their contribution short term, we are better off without them long term. It is better for us to develop our very loyal people into better performers than try to convert those strong performers who don't want to be with us."

Thus Jack Welch was building 'A teams' of dedicated people who had bought into the vision of GE, who understood his approach as CEO and really wanted the organization to succeed. But people who languished in the bottom quartile of the performance league table for more than a quarter [three months] were not tolerated, either. Loyalty was a start, but it was not enough – you had to perform, too.

Questions on the case: Why would 'C' performers probably end up costing the organization? Why did Jack Welch see loyalty and commitment as more important than performance, at least initially? How would he justify filtering out the bottom of the pile of his performers every quarter? How does this attitude compare with your own CEO and your own organization? Is this a typically American business culture approach, or is it unique to GE?

LEARNING OBJECTIVES FOR THIS CHAPTER

In 'Fostering Teams,' we look at how teams can be nurtured and developed, to add more value to their organizations, and to the individuals within them. Here, we will look at the stages of team development (based on Tuckman's 1977 model), adding to our introduction of this subject in Chapter 2. Then we will consider how feedback can be used as a mechanism in team development. We then look at a number of approaches to presenting feedback on team performance, which can be used especially in appraising teamwork skills. These approaches can be used for fostering team development in a professional and non-threatening way. This is followed by a few pointers about do's and don'ts of teamwork and team development. An introduction to the role of teams in negotiating and handling conflict leads into our next chapter, on Teams and Conflict. We finally look at a case on team development in China, based on the Belbin Team Types model (2000, 2004) to which we were introduced in Chapter 2.

WHAT STAGE IS YOUR TEAM IN?

A good way to start thinking about our own team, and the extent to which it may need fostering, is to ask what stage are we at right now in our team? The best idea is to ask all members of the team to complete the following exercise (based loosely on Tuckman's 1977 model – or at least you can consider your own experience. Is the current stage appropriate for where the team should be? Is it progressing well in achieving its targets, is it aligned with the organization, or is it getting bogged down in an early part of the team development cycle? The team discussed towards the end of Chapter 2 – handling the Hong Kong Kill Fish problem – was well on its way to maximizing its effectiveness, especially after its experiences. Yours may not be there yet. Review this exercise at the end of Chapter 2, to reacquaint yourself with the concept of team development and the definitions of the stages. Then, in the following exercise, choose the rating for your team. There is no right or wrong answers, but it offers a useful opportunity to reflect.

Exercise: For each of the following questions, consider where your team is on the following Likert scale: 1: Rarely; 2: Seldom; 3. Sometimes; 4. Often; and 5. Almost Always.

1. We attempt to set procedures to make sure things run smoothly (i.e. in meetings, make sure everyone has the opportunity to have his or her say).
2. We quickly get to the job at hand, without spending much time at the planning stage.
3. Our team members feel we are all in it together and we share the praise or blame for the team's success or failure.
4. We have clear procedures for agreeing on our goals and planning the way we will complete our tasks.
5. Team members are afraid and reluctant to ask others for help.
6. We take our team's goals seriously and assume a shared understanding.
7. The team leader tries to keep us in order and contributes to the task at hand.
8. We do not have fixed policies and procedures; we make them up as the job progresses.
9. We generate lots of ideas, but we don't use many of them because we don't listen carefully and often reject them without understanding them.
10. Team members do not always trust the other members and often closely monitor others who are working on a specific task.
11. The team leader or facilitator ensures that we follow the procedures, do not argue, do not interrupt the meetings, and keep to the point.
12. We enjoy working together; we have fun and we are a productive time.
13. We have accepted each other as members of the team in which we work.
14. The team leader is democratic and collaborative in approach.
15. We are trying to define our team's goals and what we need to accomplish.
16. Many of the team members have their own ideas about the team and its progress; many of them have their own personal agendas.

17. We fully accept each other's strengths and weaknesses and work around these.
18. We give clear roles to team members (team leader, facilitator, time keeper, note taker, etc.) in terms of action items.
19. We try to achieve harmony and peace by avoiding conflict.
20. The team's tasks are very different from what we first imagined and seem very difficult to accomplish.
21. There are many vague discussions of the concepts and issues; some members are impatient with these discussions.
22. We are able to work successfully through group problems.
23. We argue a lot, but in the end we agree on the real issues.
24. The team is often tempted to exceed the original scope of the project and get out of control.
25. We express criticism of others in the team in a constructive way.
26. There is a close attachment to the team by the members.
27. It often seems as if little is being accomplished towards the team's goals.
28. The goals we have established seem unrealistic and impossible.
29. Although we are not fully sure of the project's goals, we are excited and proud to be on the team.
30. We feel we can share personal problems with each other whenever we need to do so.
31. There is a lot of resistance to the tasks we are working on, such as quality improvement initiatives.
32. We get a lot of work done in the end.

Add up the scores for your team:

1.	2.	4.	3.
5.	7.	6.	8.
10.	9.	11.	12.
15.	16.	13.	14.
18.	20.	19.	17.
21.	23.	24.	22.
27.	28.	25.	26.
29.	31.	30.	32.
Forming	**Storming**	**Norming**	**Performing**

Scores can vary from 8 to 40 for each phase. If the highest score for your team is 32 or more in one category, this is a strong indicator of your belief that you have reached this stage in your team. If your lowest score is 16 or less, then you do not consider your team to be in this phase. You may be in a transitional phase between two stages. If you have the same score for two adjoining phases, it is possible that you are about to reach the most developed phase, i.e. nearest to Performing. Ideally, if you were able to ask a number of members of your team to complete the exercise, you can compare your scores, and discuss where there may be differences. This can be seen as a useful diagnostic exercise to evaluate the progress of your team.

Where are you in these stages of team development? Is this where you want to be? Why or why not? What might be stopping you from getting where you want or need to be? What is the role *of the team members, and of the organization as a whole, in the process of undergoing the team development phases?*

THE TEAM DEVELOPMENT STAGES

As mentioned above, this concept of the four stages of team development is based on Bruce Tuckman's model (1977). The forming stage describes the process of the team members coming together for the first time. The process of forming is inevitable, but if it's taking a long time, the team is not being very productive. The storming phase, rife with conflict, inevitably comes next, and in some cases the team does not survive this phase, but falls apart. Norming is a valuable stage of developing codes of accepted behavior, either consciously or unconsciously. The performing stage is where the team consolidates and really gets on with its work.

EFFECTIVE FEEDBACK IN TEAM DEVELOPMENT

The importance of feedback was touched upon in our previous chapter, and it plays an important role in fostering teams. In the work environment, objective feedback on team development and performance focuses on measures based on results which can be objectively analyzed, such as attendance records and sales figures, and which do not involve a substantial degree of human judgment. Subjective measures are more complex in nature, and include performance rating scales and observers' opinions. By definition this implies that subjective measurement, either intentionally or even unintentionally, is based on the individual's perception of that reality at that particular point in time. As a manager, you probably spend a good deal of time reviewing and measuring all kinds of information to understand the factors that affect your business. *Effective feedback* requires that you use the same attention to detail that you employ when analyzing business performance.

Creating and delivering a specific message based on observed performance is the key to effective feedback. You may have told a peer, a subordinate, or even your boss that this person is a good leader or that s/he communicates well. You may believe that such statements are helpful examples of feedback. But these statements only evaluate and or interpret, they don't describe specific behavior so that a person can learn and develop by repeating or avoiding that behavior. It is the same situation with analyzing teams.

Effective feedback should enable the receiver to walk away understanding exactly what the leader did and what impact it had on you. When feedback is this specific and this direct, there is a better chance that the person receiving the feedback will be motivated to continue, or stop behaviors that affect performance. Think about statements you might have made to your fellow workers, then ask yourself: What did the person do or say that made me think that he was a good communicator?

Giving feedback, especially constructive (negative turned to positive) feedback is one of the most difficult forms of communications there is. It is also one of the most needed. So many people and their teams have serious blind spots with which they never come to grips because no one knows how to give them feedback. People are too fearful of rupturing a relationship or of having their personal future compromised by 'taking on' their boss.

DEVELOPING EFFECTIVE FEEDBACK SKILLS

When establishing relationships within the team, the best way to give feedback is to describe yourself and your feelings, not the person to whom you are giving feedback. Describe your perceptions of what is happening rather than accusing, judging and labeling the person. This approach often causes the other person to become open to information about his or her blind spot without being so personally threatened. For further discussion of feedback giving and receiving feedback, see Hellriegel & Slocum (2004), George & Jones (2002), and Leavitt & Mueller (1951).

THE SBI MODEL

A technique aimed at simplifying the process of formal and informal feedback has been developed by the Centre for Creative Leadership (www.ccl.org). The Situation/Behavior/Impact (SBI) model gives a person giving feedback a framework for structuring the information and perceptions of another by breaking down an individual's performance into three areas. This model requires the person giving the feedback to describe the:

Situation	Specify where and when the specific behavior occurred.
Behavior	Indicate the characteristics, observable actions, verbal and non-verbal behaviors that need to be changed or improved.
Impact	Point out the consequences of the behavior on the person giving the feedback.

A PRACTICAL EXAMPLE OF THE SBI MODEL

Example of feedback provided based on the impact felt by the receiver:
During your presentation yesterday, you stopped several times and spoke so slowly and quietly that it was difficult for me to hear you. Then, towards the end of the presentation, when people asked questions, you spoke very fast. The way you presented made me feel like you weren't well prepared for the presentation. Furthermore, the way you spoke faster at the end made me feel like you were in a rush to get out of the room.

This way of giving feedback can aid the process of team members getting to know each other in a frank and sincere way, discussing 'shortcomings' or 'weaknesses' in such terms that the feedback receiver can appreciate, in a non-threatening way, the negative effects of his or her behavior on others. Note how the person giving feedback first notes the situation (the presentation yesterday), describes the behavior (the quiet and slow then fast delivery) and the impact or effect (that the person receiving feedback was giving the impression that he or she wanted to finish and leave). This is not judgmental – the listeners can draw their own conclusions for themselves.

FURTHER WAYS OF PROVIDING FEEDBACK

A number of other techniques have been developed for reducing perceptual errors and biases when giving feedback on team member performance. Two of these methods –

there are many others – are Behaviorally Anchored Rating Scales (BARS) and Behavioral Observation Scales (BOS).

BARS

Behaviorally Anchored Rating Scales are designed to reduce the rating errors and include a number of performance dimensions that give very specific behavioral examples of effective and ineffective performance in a team member. For more details, see Dessler (2005) and Ivancevich (1986). Appraisers rate each dimension on a scale as in the following example on 'Teamwork':

A   Often contributes new ideas and suggestions, and respects other people's points of view. Keeps everyone informed about own actions and is aware of what other team members are doing to support team objectives.

B   Takes part in team meetings, contributes frequently. Listens to colleagues and keeps them informed about own actions while knowing what they are doing.

C   Mentions opinions and suggestions at team meetings now and then but is not a major contributor to activities. Receptive to other people's ideas and willing to change, but does not always keep others informed or know what they are doing.

D   Tendency to comply with other people's suggestions. May withdraw at team meetings but sometimes can show personal antagonism to others. Not very interested in what others are doing or in keeping them informed.

E   Tendency to go own way very often without taking much account of the need to make a contribution to team activities. Sometimes uncooperative and unwilling to share information.

F   Mostly uncooperative. Goes own way, completely ignoring the wishes of other team members and taking no interest whatsoever in the achievement of team objectives.

Table 4.1: A typical ranking system used in Behaviorally Anchored Rating Scales

BOS

Behavioral Observation Scales consist of rating scales that indicate the frequency with which workers perform specific behaviors that are representative of the job dimensions critical to successful job performance (see Noe et al., 2003, and Latham & Wexley, 1994). This often makes use of a Likert Scale.

Exercise: Think about these three techniques for giving and receiving feedback – the SBI model and BARS. Try out these techniques for yourself and the other members of your team.

Carry out an SBI exercise on a fellow team member. Does the use of the SBI system help you to be more objective? How did the receiver feel about it?

Then consider the BARS exercise. Where are you at in terms of your attitude to your team, and contribution to its objectives? How about the other team members? How does this scale help you to make an assessment of your team development needs?

SOME DO'S AND DON'TS OF EFFECTIVE FEEDBACK IN TEAM DEVELOPMENT

Do:
1. Be specific when recalling the situation
2. Be specific when describing the behavior
3. Acknowledge the impact of the behavior on you
4. Judge the behavior
5. Pay attention to body language
6. Use verbatim quotes
7. Re-create the behavior, if appropriate
8. Give feedback in a timely manner
9. Give your feedback, then stop talking
10. Say "I felt" or "I was" to frame your impact statement
11. Focus on a single message
12. Be sensitive to the emotional impact of your feedback

Don't:
1. Assume
2. Be vague
3. Use accusations
4. Judge the person
5. Pass along vague feedback from others
6. Give advice unless asked
7. Psychoanalyze
8. Qualify your feedback by backing out of the description
9. Use examples from own experience
10. Generalize with words like 'always' or 'never'
11. Label your feedback as positive or negative
12. Use words in your feedback messages like 'but'

SUBORDINATE FEEDBACK CHECKLIST

Managers should consult this checklist regularly to remind them of the main elements involved when they give feedback to subordinates within their teams:

- Give feedback frequently.
- Make feedback timely. Don't wait too long after observing a subordinate's behavior
- Keep feedback simple

- If possible, provide a private, neutral setting when your feedback concerns behavior that must be corrected
- Focus on the situation you have observed
- Describe the subordinate's behavior without interpreting motives
- Communicate the impact of the subordinate's behavior on others
- Offer your subordinate's suggestions and support for making changes in their behavior
- Take your subordinate's information style into account and be prepared for unexpected information
- Leverage your subordinate's strengths
- Catch people "doing things right"

Exercise: Consider these do's and don'ts. Observe a colleague giving feedback to another colleague. Make a list of their positive and negative approaches. Discuss your comments with them. Then reverse roles and he or she can carry out the exercise using you as subject. Meet and reflect on your findings and the value of this exercise in fostering teamwork and developing the professionalism of your team. You may also wish to consider the subordinate checklist – and perhaps the word 'subordinate' here should be changed to team member!

NEGOTIATION AND CONFLICT

The purpose of studying negotiation in looking at fostering teamwork is to improve the performance of your team in this essential area. Teams spend a lot of time negotiating with other teams – to win business, to start new projects, to work together with other specialists, to create alliances. Negotiating in a team environment is very different from negotiating as an individual. Much of the rest of this chapter will focus on this important area. For additional insights, see Robbins (2006), Hellriegel & Slocum (2004), Daft (2003) and Whettan & Cameron (1998).

Negotiating skills are especially required in a team situation whenever there is some sort of conflict between team members within the team. These conflicts must be resolved before the team can progress to negotiate in a united way with other teams. Conflict is inevitable at some stage of team development – see the team development phases in the Tuckman (1977) model. Conflict within a team can come from one or more of the following cases:

Pseudo conflict – Where in fact no conflict exists but parties or one of the parties sees a possibility of conflict. Although some may think that this type of conflict is just a theoretical belief and perception, it can create considerable problems. This non-real conflict situation may bring about a certain amount of discomfort and frustration which can induce time-consuming negotiation sessions, which more than anything else are opportunities for clarifications for understanding. An example might be based on rumors such as the possibility of a merger between two companies and the creation of competition for jobs which may or may not exist.

Content conflict – This is usually in the form of disagreement about a subject matter or a point. Content conflict is probably the major source of conflict where negotiation sessions in teams are generally needed. Content conflict may be the result of new measures adopted by one of the parties concerned or a result of an outstanding issue between the two sides.

Value conflict – This is where parties disagree about some set of values or beliefs. Several studies in the field of team member communication have proved that this is a major source of conflict. Values and perception vary drastically from one individual to another.

Ego conflict – This is where one of the parties sees the opponent as a threat. Wherever there is some sort of conflict, it seems natural for the inexperienced team member to perceive the other party as an enemy. In this instance one party may go to the negotiation session well armed with facts and other relevant documents not only to prove his/her point but to diminish the personality of the other party. This is common in teams and can be highly unproductive.

CONFLICTING REALITIES

Problem 1
Conflict can be the result of group members working too closely together or too interdependently.

Solution
Smoothing conflicts implies – even before going to any negotiation session – the redefinition of the communication process. How should team members co-operate and communicate with each other?

Problem 2
Conflict can be the result of differences in the perception of skills requirements.

Solution
Preferably this type of conflict can be best dealt with before any employee is recruited. Whenever the team is looking for a new person, there must be a clear and defined description of what needs to be done by that particular person.

Problem 3
Conflict can be the result of a difference in needs and values.

Solution
It is recommended that this type of conflict be looked upon in a different manner than the normal conflict strategies. Conflict between different values can be detrimental to both the team and the individual. If such conflict arises the issues should be thoroughly discussed and brought out into the open.

Problem 4
Conflict can be the result of internal/external incidents which have a direct effect on the team.

Solution
First there is a need to define the conflict and seek facts to assure whether this has been internally or externally caused. Secondly, every party in the conflict should have their say about the issue, not just those who are complaining but also those who might have an indirect effect on the issue. Thirdly the team members should formulate their own opinions and convey it around the team.

CONTENT VERSUS PROCESS PREPARATION IN CONFLICT RESOLUTION

Negotiators from different backgrounds clearly indicate that a key ability of skilled negotiators is their ability to separate the negotiation 'process' from the negotiation 'content'. Not only are they able to distinguish these two important elements, but they also manage each quite consciously and purposefully, especially in dealing with a team-based disagreement.

Content   The facts or substance of the particular negotiation;
The 'what' you are negotiating about; the matter in hand.

Process   The method by which negotiations are conducted;
The 'how' you are managing the negotiation; the approach.

For example, consider that whenever you get deadlocked in a negotiation within your team, it is most likely to have happened because you have focused on the content, especially the things you think important, and not the process. Two people might want to do radically different things in their teams, and don't appreciate that if they work things out together, they might be able to accommodate both their areas of interest.

PHASES OF NEGOTIATION IN TEAMS

Negotiation sessions can be seen to be following an orderly step-by-step ritual. Certain clear patterns emerge, and four distinct phases can often be discerned. In order to achieve a satisfactory resolution to a negotiation, it is important that each phase is allowed to develop and be fully played out. This ensures that negotiators achieve the sense of actively being involved in the negotiation process.

Experienced negotiators are aware of these phases occurring in the negotiation sessions, and prepare for them as part of overall strategy. Identifying phases is particularly important when making decisions regarding the pacing of negotiation, and timing the introduction of tactics, making concessions, and final settlements' offers. These are all inevitably phases of the way in which a team and its members operate.

1. Introductory phase
- Take process control from the outset (and maintain the momentum)
- Settling-in (introductions, general small talk)
- Building common ground at both personal and team level
- Climate development (opening remarks to generate a positive opening response, if possible)

2. Differentiation phase
- Clarification of issues and testing of opening positions
- Establishment of the outer limits of the negotiation range
- Conflict management (showing a clear display of differences)
- Emotion (recognizing the need to express feelings about being upset)
- Keeping discussion of differences at a team level (not personal attacks)

- Separating conflict between parties from antagonism between people
- Deadlock-breaking (identification of underlying needs)
- (Making content concessions during this phase should be avoided)
- Stay in process control

3.   Integration phase
- Active reconnecting of the negotiation range (looking for common ground)
- Transition from an inter-party exchange of position stating to an inter-personal exchange of joint problem solving approaches
- Transition from an inter-party exchange of position stating to an inter-personal exchange of joint problem solving approaches
- A need to carefully monitor the negotiating style and climate variables
- A shift from a focus on the past to a focus on the future (and the need for long-term relationships)
- The use of general tactics (creating options and building common ground)
- The use of general tactics (creating options and building common ground)

4.   Settlement phase
- Summarizing, recapitulation of the common ground
- Final offers (must be credible, and show clear commitment)
- If the other negotiator is not the final authority, there is a need to get agreement in principle
- At this point, lock in the agreement at both the team and personal levels
- Consider the development of a disputes' settlement procedure

5.   Post settlement phase
- Implementation of agreement, and monitoring compliance
- Maintain other party's esteem, and building relationship for next time.

Exercise: In your own experiences of negotiating within your team, are you conscious of going through these phases? Which are the most challenging? Do you consider yourself as knowledgeable about negotiating? Is your team able to negotiate itself out of difficulties, or does it frequently encounter stalemate?

SYSTEMATIC PREPARATION STEPS

Preparation for negotiation means hard work. Intensive preparation will not guarantee success, but it is an essential step in the process. Preparation for negotiation can be viewed as following an orderly and structured process. It can be systematized and segmented into a series of logical steps, each of which inter-relates with others. Skilled negotiators distinguish between preparing the 'content' (i.e. what they are negotiating about, the substance) and preparing the Process (i.e. how they will manage the negotiation). See Bazerman and Neale (1992), Northcraft and Neale (1990), and Adler (1977) for further information.

Step 1 (Content): Ascertain the subject matter of the negotiation
Beware of preparing the wrong material due to misunderstanding the overall nature of the subject matter under negotiation.

- Clearly ascertain the broad subject matter.
- Identify the overall area of common purpose for both parties.
- Review similar prior negotiations in which you have both been involved.
- Check perceptions of the nature of gain (joint gain versus own gain). Anticipate the planned duration of the relationship and the overall commitment of both parties to the outcome.

Step 2 (Content): Establish objectives

Clearly state the aims of both and identify the needs that they are seeking to satisfy. For both parties prepare the negotiation range.

- List the maximum objectives, aspirations, ideals.
- List the minimum objectives, bottom line, and develop the 'best alternative elsewhere.'
- Consider realistic objectives (and if possible, order priorities in between).
- Combine your objectives and their objectives to give an indication of negotiation range. Where do they overlap (common ground)?
- Relate the available negotiation time frame to your and their objectives.
- Try not to be too rigid, and plan for flexibility.

Step 3 (Content): Test assumptions

Assumptions are a system of guesses we make based on probability. They come from direct observation and what we are told by others. As we are all prone to fall into set patterns, our assumptions tend to become 'facts' and part of our belief system – yet they may be wrong. Negotiation errors are often made due to misunderstandings caused by wrong assumptions.

- Anticipate the other party's assumptions. Are they to your advantage?
- Identify your assumptions. Check their source. Validate them.
- Carefully test your assumptions by making them explicit (to yourself).
- If ever you are surprised, it is often due to making a false assumption.
- What assumptions are the other party or you making about:
    - rules, constraints, norms, conventions, precedents, procedures;
    - rationality, reciprocity, equity, ethics, trust;
    - authorities, time frames, past and future relationships;
    - stereotypes (age, gender, race) and cultural variance;
    - the idea that there are no other options?

Step 4 (Content): Research Facts

Information is power, and a primary source of negotiating influence. The more dependable your information, the more options you can develop and the better your decisions will be. Any factual errors considerable reduce your credibility and negotiation power.

- Research in detail all facts, data, information, ground rules.
- Carefully check each item. Sift out inferences and opinions.
- Decide what these facts mean for their case/for your case.
- Review the strengths and weaknesses of both sides.
- Find out as much as possible about the other party.
- Consider the value of a pre-negotiation fact-finding meeting.

Step 5 (Content): Define the issues and identify the options

Any matter on which there is a choice may become a negotiation issue with arguments for and against, and therefore be available as a trade-off option.

- Analyze issues into:
    - Other party's issues (these may be different from yours).
    - Your issues (conditions as you see them).
    - Common issues (which affect both parties).
    - Hidden issues (which you may want to bring out).
    - False issues (even imaginary issues have trading value).
- Divide issues into categories that best suit your purpose.
- If seeking cooperation, state issues as discussion items rather than specific demands (a demand is only one solution to a problem).
- Plan a presentation of the issues. Set the agenda.

Step 6 (Content): Decide the positions and concessions

Only after the issues are clearly defined can you decide on your position. Your position is where you take your opening stand. In the course of negotiation, you may want to change your stated position. Accordingly, unless it is your final commitment, state your position in terms that conceal as well as reveal. From your stated opening position, prepared concession-making can then occur purposefully as part of your tactics.

- Anticipate the other party's opening position (on each issue).
- Decide your opening position (on each issue).
- Prepare counters.
- Plan concessions.
- Anticipate reciprocal deals.

The above completes the preparation of the content or the factual material, the 'what' you are in negotiation about. Skilled negotiators next systematically prepare the process – 'how' you will manage the negotiation.

Step 7 (Process): Reconsider the needs of the negotiation

We negotiate as a means to satisfy our needs. In order to decide the most influential negotiation strategy, we must know the other party's needs, both stated and 'hidden'.

- Ascertain the other's needs at both the team and the personal levels.
- Note that their real needs may be quite different from their demands.
- You may have to dig deep to bring the other party to awareness.
- Consider inventing needs and selling them to the other party (particularly if you are in a weak negotiating position).
- Review your own needs at both team and personal levels.
- Identify the potential common ground.

Step 8 (Process): Develop a negotiating strategy

The above process preparation step provides the means to develop your overall strategy – your total negotiation plan as to how you will conduct the negotiation and manage the overall process. Consider both sides and make appropriate decisions about:

Negotiation style
- What will be the other party's style tendency and how flexible will they be?
- What will be your overall style preference and how flexible will you be?
- If you or the other party is negotiating as a team, consider each member and the internal relationships.

Negotiation climate
- How will you manage the three climate variables of time, place and mood?

Negotiation tactics
- What tactics will the other party use and how can you counter these?
- What tactics can you develop and how do you expect them to be countered?

Negotiation phases
- How can you prepare yourself to manage the movement of the negotiation through the phases?

Step 9 (Process): Rehearse the options

Undertake a rehearsal of the possible options available for managing the process of the negotiation (as well as testing the content). Such rehearsals about options help develop negotiation competence and considerably enhance confidence in managing the overall process.
- Test 'what if...?' alternatives.
- Plan the mechanism for locking-in the other party's compliance.
- Review the implementation and monitoring procedures.
- Evaluate the need for an agreed disputes' settlement procedure.

Step 10 (Process): Negotiation: an ongoing preparation

Having completed your homework, and developed and rehearsed your overall plan, you are now ready to enter the negotiation. However, note the circularity of the systematic preparation process. Often during the negotiation you may have reason to reconsider any of these preparation steps again (in any order).

Exercise: This level of preparation for a negotiation may seem to be too much, but it should seriously be tried out by the different parties and can contribute to negotiating success. Chose an issue over which you and your team have negotiated at length, perhaps without any clear result. Does this system help make a difference to bring it to a conclusion? Have you ever tried separating content and process in this way?

CLOSING CASE: FORMING TEAMS – A CHALLENGE IN CHINA

In Chapter 2 we introduced the concept of the Belbin Team Types as a useful way of understanding the contribution of people with quite different characteristics to the success of the team as a whole. In forming successful teams to achieve specific objectives in the workplace, common use has been made of this exercise, as a well-known team-based psychological instrument developed by Dr Meredith Belbin in the UK

(2000, 2004). Recent work in analyzing the characteristics of Chinese staff working for multinationals and local companies in China has identified the following three types: Chuppies, or young Chinese up-and-coming urban professionals; Westernized Chinese, who have spent some years overseas and see themselves quite differently; and Traditionals, or (often) older Chinese who stick to their own customs and ways of operating. Arguably, there is some relationship between the Belbin types and the different types of Chinese identified in this study.

Firstly, in continuation of Chapter 2, here is a short summary of the team types:

Shapers – who are dynamic, outgoing, highly strung, challenging, pressurizing, finding ways around obstacles – but who are prone to provocation and short-lived bursts of temper.

Co-ordinators - who are mature, confident and trusting, good at being a chairperson, clarifies goals, promotes decision-making – but is not necessarily the most clever or creative member of the group.

Monitor Evaluator-Critics – who are sober, strategic, discerning, seeing all options, judges accurately – but lacks drive and ability to inspire others.

Team Players – who are social, mild, perceptive, accommodating, listening, averting friction – but who can be indecisive in crunch situations.

Plants and sometimes augmented by Specialists in some versions – who are creative, imaginative, unorthodox, solving difficult problems – but who can be weak in communicating with and managing ordinary people.

Implementors – who are disciplined, reliable, conservative and efficient, turning ideas into practical actions – but somewhat inflexible, slow to respond to possibilities.

Resource-Investigators – who are extrovert, enthusiastic, communicative, good at exploring opportunities and developing contacts – but lose interest once the initial enthusiasm has passed.

Completer-Finishers – who are painstaking, conscientious, anxious, searching out errors and omissions, delivering on time – but are inclined to worry unduly and reluctant to delegate.

Relating the different types of Chinese with the Belbin types: Chuppies can be good Plants – they can have a lot of ideas – and they tend to work well in teams, so they can be good Team Players. One of their strongest roles can be as Resource-Investigators, because they can be good at seeing the world outside the company, and networking amongst their other Chuppie friends and ex-classmates. They can lack the experience to be good Shapers and Co-ordinators, because Chuppies typically have more of a day-to-day outlook rather than being visionary and seeing the big picture.

Westernized Chinese like to be Shapers and Co-ordinators, and can be quite good at this, feeling that with their Western exposure they can be natural leaders. But they need the discipline of being good Monitor-Evaluators and Completer-Finishers in order to be most effective. Sometimes Westernized Chinese can be good at being Resource-Investigators, as they also use networking too, and this can be on a worldwide basis, including amongst Chinese living in the West.

Traditionals can be good Monitor-Evaluators, who can understand the viability of a project, because they typically have a tendency towards risk aversion and conservatism – this makes them more prudent in outlook. They can effective as Implementors – workers – who if given precise instructions, can settle down and get on with the job, and finish it, as capable Completer-Finishers. Networking is also their forte, like many Chinese, and this may include some useful government connections.

According to findings from the question "who would you describe as your three best friends in China?" we have put together an indication of the combination of types within teams which may work well together:

Chinese types in teams: Chuppies like to work with other Chuppies – they have similar backgrounds (young, university graduates, speaking English fluently, working in management level positions and ambitious to move up) – and they expect the same pace of work and enthusiasm – they would be happy working with young, localized foreigners who have a similar outlook but different experiences, and would be more comfortable with them than with Westernized Chinese (see below), and may be suspicious of foreigners who show signs of 'going local'. Chuppies can find it hard to work with very traditional Chinese – communication can be difficult as their outlooks and values are so different

Westernized Chinese would work well in a team with Westerners of all types and other Chinese who have spent time overseas – but they may not work well with Chuppies and traditional Chinese, who resent their (sometimes evident) attitude of superiority and privilege, based on their overseas experiences. They consider foreigners with a localized outlook to be rather on the strange side – why don't they behave like foreigners are expected to behave?

Traditional Chinese would choose to work with similar types, maybe friends from their city, who may have been friends since childhood, who they trust and like to help. These colleagues would have specific job responsibilities and duties which would tend to be demarcated clearly, rather than shared. They may be more comfortable with remote foreigners who keep distant and in leadership and expert roles, although the more open Traditional Chinese would appreciate the efforts of more localized foreigners to try to understand their language and their world. In terms of Chinese in their team, the Traditional Chinese don't like Chuppies very much – they are slightly intimidated by their education and insights, and Westernized Chinese can also make them feel uncomfortable.

Westernized Chuppies can work well in teams with Westerners of all types, and other Chuppies. They respect other sophisticated and well-travelled high-achievers such as themselves. They would probably not work so well with Traditional Chinese, who may find them impatient and not so respectful of traditional Chinese values.

Traditional/Westernized Chinese would work well with most foreigners – except the very localized, possibly – but would not be very comfortable with Chuppies, who would be too demanding and go-getting for them, and may pose a threat to the job security of this type. The people in this type are likely to be older than Westernized Chuppies, and would also espouse more Chinese traditional thinking, but with some Western values, often with more of a spiritual dimension. The lack of spiritual values of many Chuppies might frustrate this group.

Modern Traditionals can work effectively in teams with a mixture of Chuppies and some traditional Chinese. However, although they are also young and outgoing, but are less influenced by modern materialism than complete Chuppies, they may clash occasionally. As they are not so interested in Western trappings, and may have had little exposure to the West except through consumer products, they may not get on so well with Westernized Chinese or Westerners generally.

Multi-types – a mix of all the Chinese types identified – can work in teams including all kinds of Chinese and foreigners, including Chinese who have lived in the West, and those with traditional Chinese lifestyles. The multi-type Chinese would be able to get on with the widest range of people, and is the easiest person to work with in a team comprising a very mixed group.

This is a brief extract from a study of the complexity of dealing with Chinese staff working in teams in multinational and local companies in China. It is indicative of the challenges of putting together people from many different backgrounds into a team situation. Even though all these staff members are from the same country – China – they interpret the development of their country and how it has impacted on them quite differently. Thus developing and managing a team of such complexity has many challenges.

Questions on the closing case: How can we create teams based on putting together people with other people they like to work with, avoiding people they probably do not feel comfortable with, based on this example? Can we use these categories as comparing personalities with team types? How can we foster teams based on creating productive units which work well together? Or do you think that a level of diversity – and the conflict it can bring within the team – can be productive? How would you describe the diversity of your own team members? Do you also have issues of which ones tend to have specific team skills, and which ones are lacking in these? How would you categorize these different predispositions to teamwork?

CONCLUSION

In this chapter we have taken the concept of team development further, from looking at defining, communicating with and leading teams, to nurturing and developing teams for maximum performance, especially through constructive feedback in developing teamwork skills. We have looked at measuring the progress of our team through the development cycle, and ways in which its effectiveness can be constantly improved. In particular we have looked at performance ratings to check on progress, and how the work of a typical team – such as negotiating and conflict management – can be developed. This is vital within the work of the team externally, and resolving differences internally. Finally, we examined how teams and their essential constituent parts can be impacted by cultural perspectives. Different cultural types can adopt different team roles more comfortably than others. Fundamentally, we must appreciate that teamwork must be fostered and developed, and it does not happen just by chance. This chapter then leads into our final team-oriented topic, on teams and conflict.

REFERENCES

Adler, R.B. (1977) 'Satisfying personal needs: managing conflicts, making requests, and saying no', *Confidence in Communication*. New York: Holt, Rhinehart and Winston.

Bazerman, M.H. & Neale, M.A. (1992) *Negotiating rationally*. New York: Free Press.

Belbin, R.M. (2000) *Beyond the team*. Oxford: Butterworth Heinemann.

Belbin, R.M. (2004) *Management teams: why they succeed or fail*. Oxford: Elsevier/Butterworth Heinemann.

Centre for Creative Leadership, www.ccl.org See also eds. C. D. MacCauley, R. S. Moxley & E. Van Velsor (1988) *Handbook of Leadership Development*. San Francisco: Jossey Bass.

Dessler, G. (2005) *Human Resource Management*. International edition., Upper Saddle River, New Jersey: Pearson.

George, J.M. & Jones G.R. (2002) *Organizational Behavior*. 3rd. ed. Upper Saddle River, New Jersey: Prentice Hall.

Hellriegel, D. & Slocum, J.W. (2004) *Organizational Behavior*, 10th Ed., Mason Ohio: Thomson South Western.

Ivancevich, J. (1986) 'A longitudinal study of behavioral expectation scales: attitudes and performance', *Journal of Applied Psychology, 30*:3, 619-628

Jones, S. (2000) *Managing People in China*. Unpublished manuscript, with sections published in China Staff journal (see below).

Jones, S. (2000) Beyond the stereotypes: the changing face of China's workplace, *China Staff VI: 9*, 19-24.

Latham, G & Wexley, K. (1994) *Increasing Productivity through Performance Appraisal*. London: Addison Wesley/Longman.

Leavitt, H. & Mueller, R. (1951) 'Some effects of feedback on communication', *Human Relations, 4*: 401-410

Noe, R.A., Hollenbeck, J.R., Gerhart, B. & Wright, P. (2003) *Human Resource Management*. New York: McGraw Hill.

Northcraft, G. & Neale, M. (1994) *Organizational Behavior: a management challenge*. Chicago: Dryden Press.

Tuckman, B.W. & Jensen, M.A.C. (1977) 'Stages of small-group development revisited', *Groups and Organization Studies, 2*, 419-442

Welch, J. (2005) 'Speaker Series September 18, 2002'. Available from: http://mba.tuck.dartmouth.edu/cgl/downloads/JackWelch.pdf [Accessed 13 November 2006]

Welch, J. (2005) *Winning*, New York: HarperCollins.

Welch, J. (2006) Press release, book tour stop February 09, 2006. Available from: http://www.24-7pressrelease.com/pdf/2006/02/09/press_release_10871.pl

Whetten, D.A. & Cameron, K.S. (1998) *Developing Management Skills*. New York: Addison Wesley.

RECOMMENDED FURTHER READING

Ancona, D.G. & Caldwell, D. (1992) 'Bridging the boundary: external activity and performance in organizational teams', *Administrative Science Quarterly 27*:459-489

Dyer, W.G. (1987*) Team building: issues and alternatives*. Reading, Mass: Addison Wesley.

Foster, S.F., Heling, G.W.J.,Hackman, B. & Remme, J.H.M. (1996) *Teams in Intelligent Process Based Organizations*. Leiderdorp: Lansa.

Hackman, J.R. (1990) *Teams that work (and those that don't)*. San Francisco: Jossey-Bass.

Johnson, D.W. & Johnson, F.P. *Joining Together: group theory and group skills*. 5th ed., New York: Alyn and Bacon

Katzenbach, J.R. & Smith, D.K. (1993) *The wisdom of teams*. Boston: Harvard Business School Press.

Levi, D. (2001) *Group Dynamics for Teams*. Thousand Oaks, CA: Sage.

O'Connor, M. P., & Erickson, B. (1996) *'Team Building: A strategic advantage'*, (online). Available:http://www.oconnor.ie/cos/advantage.html.

Ozaralli, N. (2003) 'Effects of transformational leadership on empowerment and team effectiveness', *Leadership & Organization Development Journal, 24*: 6, 335-344

Richards, T. & Moger, S. (2004) 'Creative leadership processes in project team development: an alternative to Tuckman's stage model', *British Journal of Management, 4*: 273-283

Tuckman, B.W. (1965) 'Developmental sequence in small groups. *Psychological Bulletin 63*: 384-399

Turniansky, B. & Hare, A.P. (1999) *Individuals and Groups in Organizations*. Thousand Oaks, CA: Sage.

Yarbrough, B.T. (2002) *Leading Groups and Teams*. Mason, Ohio: South-Western/Thomson.

Wellins, R.S., Byman, W.C. & Wilson, J. M. (1991) *Empowered Teams*. San Francisco: Jossey-Bass.

CHAPTER 5

CONFLICT IN TEAMS
STEPHANIE JONES AND SILVIO DE BONO

OPENING CASE:

Back in the 1980s and 1990s, British Airways [BA] CEO Colin Marshall faced make-or-break problems with Britain's flag-carrying airline, revealing a series of conflicts between different teams of people working at the troubled corporation. Marshall was under pressure to prepare BA for privatization, to make the airline attractive to investors as a strong, state-of-the-art business, popular with its customers and therefore likely to be a sound investment. But there was an underlying conflict between this plan, and how the teams of people on the ground saw it, expressed here as a Force Field Analysis.

Driving Forces	Restraining Forces
Political pressure to privatize, raising profits/performance	Intense pride in the 'fly the flag' tradition at any cost
	Opposition from staff who fear job cuts/performance pressures
	Ideological opposition from labor unions
Need to cut costs to be profitable	Opposition from unions protecting jobs
	Fear of reduction in standards
	Change from British aircraft types to some USA brands – opposed for reasons of tradition, and protection of British aircraft manufacturing jobs
Need to become customer-focused	Unfamiliar with customer service concepts, need change approach
	Low staff morale
Need to improve industrial relations and have happy and productive staff	Still unresolved issues from merger of BOAC, BEA, BCal (other airlines in Britain at the time)
	A new culture for unified BA has not been set or communicated

Improve adherence to schedules	Power of unions at Heathrow, confrontational
Boost reputation worldwide to deserve the role of flag carrier	Residual imperialist attitude criticized
Meet competition from charter airlines and USA de-regulation	Perceive the airline in the public sector and themselves as civil servants (government. employees) unaccustomed to commercial competition
Need to rationalize the fleet of aircraft	Opposition from unions protecting jobs

The Force Field Analysis is a useful tool explained in several textbooks (see Hellriegel and Slocum, 2004). Here, through this perspective, we see several points of conflict, especially in the drive toward privatization and the protectionist attitude of the staff members, supported by their union. The airline was trying to become more service-oriented and more customer-focused, to attract and sustain a loyal customer base to drive up revenues, thereby attracting investors. Meanwhile the staff members were more interested in job preservation, and saw themselves as part of a high-status organization which was a national asset and should be supported as such. This force field analysis especially highlights the conflicts on the management and staff sides of the fence.

How were these conflicts resolved? Observers at the time considered that the result was achieved by a change of attitudes on both sides, and by sending out the right messages at the start. One of these was that members of the management – who were not usually seen on the planes at all – suddenly started appearing on early morning flights. In terms of effecting redundancies, far more of the management ranks were thinned out and experienced job losses than lower level staff. And suddenly customers were seen as people to serve, not just walking cargo to be loaded onto planes and taken from A to B.

The conflict began with the politically-inspired merger in the early 1970s between two state-owned airlines – British European and British Overseas Airways [BEA, BOAC] – with the result that the airline was grossly overstaffed, and employees from two contrasting cultures were forced into a marriage of convenience. Customer service declined as energies were focused on internal crises. At one point, there were 40 different industrial disputes in progress. Then an industry-wide recession brought about a financial crisis which threatened the airline's ability to survive.

Meanwhile there was a conflict between the need to keep upgrading aircraft and the lack of capital, exacerbated by inadequate profit levels. Borrowing then brought ever-increasing interest charges. Chairman Lord King was brought in to privatize the airline, but his first job was to save it from bankruptcy. Another conflict arose between the need to downsize staff and the union pressures to maintain secure employment. Staff numbers were cut by 40% or 23,000, of which 69% were managers. Yet then, the airline was freed from its burden of excess staff and could return to making money. Short-term financial disaster was averted, but to become competitive the airline has to focus on customers.

The main conflict here was that the the way many employees saw their job was that all they had to do was to lift people off the ground in one place and put them down again safely somewhere else, and this they did reasonably well. A high proportion of customers had to fly BA not because they wanted to (their organizations booked the flights for them), and lost no opportunity telling horror stories to their friends. Economizing and low morale led to poor service, dirty and uncared-for aircraft, broken trolleys and ovens.

Senior managers, used to sitting in their offices, were seen boarding planes at all times of the day and night to address customer complaints. As BA's cash flow improved, money was spent on basic equipment, carpets, catering equipment and ground vehicles. It was also spent on training to improve morale, providing insights into other people's jobs in BA to increase teamwork, and a new livery and uniforms. The training program "Putting People First" was rolled out throughout BA. The turnaround was seen, by CEO Colin Marshall, as the result of basic management qualities of clear thinking, common sense and leadership, guided by a clear picture of what he and the company wanted to achieve, with hard work on the implementation.

Questions on the opening case: What was the basis of the conflict between management and staff? Which moves by the management had the greatest impact on staff morale? Why would knowledge of another person's job improve inter-staff relations? Why might there be a conflict between the need for customer service and being a secure, status-oriented, state sector 'flag-carrier'? What kind of message was sent out when 69% of the 23,000 laid off were managers? Why would a merger of two companies produce conflict? Was it necessary to create a new image to consolidate the changes?

LEARNING OBJECTIVES FOR THIS CHAPTER

In this chapter 'Conflict in Teams' we focus in detail on how conflict in teams can emerge, and how it can be resolved. Building on our last chapter, we look at how conflict often starts – often because of personality clashes, different agendas, and different cultural standpoints. Sometimes different teams – such as management and staff, staff of two merged companies, and management and unions, in the BA case – are traditionally in conflict, and rarely in harmony. We look at the competencies of effective (and less effective) team members, in terms of how they work together in causing and then handling conflicts. We then look at the background of the origins of conflict in organizations, and then focus on conflict-handling styles in detail, and examine the impact of conflict mode preferences in an organization – a hotel operation in Singapore.

How do we handle conflict in a team? Which competencies in team members are especially relevant to team conflict-handling?

First of all, which are the attributes in a team member which are not helpful? How can we identify behaviors which are contrary to good teamwork? This helps us to identify positive behaviors, which can reflect strong teamwork skills, including being able to manage conflict:

Teamwork competencies: negative behavioral indicators – these can cause conflict in a team

- When a team member works on his/her own, and makes suggestions not discussed before in private with the team, in front of a customer/dealer/principal – how do the rest of the team feel about this?
- When a team member disagrees with team mates but does not express disagreement privately with the team – and focuses instead on expressing these in front of customer/dealer/principal, which undermines team mates.
- When he or she resents and criticizes negatively the inputs of other team members – wishes they were not around and he or she could handle projects alone.
- When a team member fails to support other team mates when they are being criticized by colleagues and especially by outsiders, such as a dealer/principal.
- When he or she avoids blame by passing mistakes onto team mates.
- When he or she interrupts other team mates when they are speaking.
- And changes the subject without asking permission of other team mates.
- And says "I" rather than "we" or "us".

By contrast, how should a team member behave to minimize conflict, and successfully handle it when it may emerge? How can we identify behaviors of team members who are genuinely trying to prevent conflict? Some indicators are mentioned below. Constructive team members tend:

Positive behavioral indicators
- Say "we" or "us" rather than "I";
- Support others when in difficulties in the meeting even when they do not fully agree with them;
- Seek solutions of overall value not just to help themselves individually;
- Listen, make notes, and do not try to speak more than others;
- Encourage weaker or less experienced members of the team to contribute;
- Refer to comments made by others when making a point;
- See the team winning as more important than their own views.

Exercise: consider these teamwork (and anti-teamwork) competencies. Think about your own behavior, and examples of when you behaved in certain ways. Ask a fellow team member for their views – do they see you as a good team player or not, according to these competencies? In the next step of the exercise, observe your team in an active situation, especially negotiating with customers, dealers, suppliers – outsiders of the organization. Without needing to name names, observe how often positive and negative team behaviors are being used. Most significantly, observe the impact of these behaviors – on the rest of the team and on the outsiders. Was the overall outcome of the meeting impacted by these behaviors? And in what way was it affected, i.e. positively or negatively?

WHICH ARE THE MOST POSITIVE BEHAVIORS IN TERMS OF BUILDING A TEAM-BASED CULTURE?

How can an organization create a culture of trust and honesty? How can it create employee commitment to each other? How can it encourage integrity? First of all, why would it want to? Research into 350 predominantly USA-based organizations by Human

Synergistics has shown a relationship between organizational culture and overall service quality. Organizations with the highest quality service showed 'constructive' styles. These promoted high quality service and products, attaining "excellent service by encouraging staff members to behave in self-actualizing, supportive and encouraging, achievement-oriented and affiliative ways". (www.human-synergistics.com).

What exactly does this mean? It means that staff members were 'constructive' and effective in teams when they believed that they were encouraged to "think in unique and independent ways" and to "maintain their personal integrity." Then, 'self-actualized', they felt disposed to "help others to grow and develop" and were generally "supportive of others" in their behavior, In this context, they were glad to "take on challenging tasks" and also spent more time "thinking ahead and planning". Further aspects of 'constructive' teams who were good at handling conflict included the sharing of "feelings and thoughts" and that they "co-operated with others" as a general rule.

By contrast, teams where conflict is a norm, and where service quality is lower, are described by Human Synergistics as 'aggressive defensive'. These behaviors – perfectionistic, obsessed with detail, controlling and authoritative, competitive and oppositional – have a neutral impact on service quality. These are predominantly task-oriented groups who are concerned with their own individual agendas.

Finally, the least effective teams according to this research are described as 'passive defensive'. Basically, they hide behind their team members waiting for others to act first. They are approval-seeking, dependent on others for their views and support, conventional and conservative, and risk and blame-avoiding. There are few conflicts in these groups, but nothing gets done, and there are always excuses for inaction. Conflict is rife in 'aggressive-defensive' teams, and is mainly negative, as a result of clashes in personalities seeking power and to be always right. Conflicts in 'constructive' teams happen, but people work them through. Self-actualizing staff members have no power and competition agendas, and achievers need other people to achieve their goals. Being generally supportive and encouraging of others, as well as affiliative, are seen as among the most useful techniques for managing conflict in a positive way.

CONFLICT STYLES IN TEAMS

To understand different conflict preferences and how these can impact on creating and handling conflict in teams, we need to look at these conflict styles and identify our own preferences. These determine how conflicts can arise: for example, if we are highly competitive (see below) and work with another person with the same inclination, conflicts will inevitably occur and it may be difficult for either party to step down. These conflict preferences have been identified and developed by several authors, and refined by Thomas and Kilmann (1974):

- Competing
- Accommodating
- Avoiding
- Compromising
- Collaborating

Exercise: Complete this exercise (broadly based on the work of Thomas and Kilmann) to identify your conflict handling preference scores. Choose A or B statements in each case, and select the option which best describes your usual behavior, especially in the workplace and especially when working as a team:

1. A-There are times when I allow other people to be responsible for solving a problem.
   B-I prefer not to focus on areas of disagreement, but try to emphasize things on which we both already agree.

2. A-I try to find a compromise solution to a problem.
   B-I try to deal with all of the concerns of others, and mine.

3. A-I am usually quite clear and determined in following my goals.
   B- I try to calm other people's feelings and maintain our relationship.

4. A-I try to find a compromise solution to a problem.
   B-I sometimes give up on what I want to please the other person.

5. A-I very often seek the help of others when trying to work out a solution.
   B-I try to do what is necessary to avoid tension in relationships when this is not necessary.

6. A-I try to avoid unpleasant and painful situations for myself.
   B-I try to win my position and get what I want.

7. A-I try to get more time to think about a difficult issue when I'm not sure what to do.
   B-I am willing to give up some things I want in exchange for other things.

8. A- A-I am usually quite clear and determined in following my goals.
   B-I attempt to get all issues immediately out in the open for discussion.

9. A-I feel that differences between us may not be worth worrying about.
   B-I make some effort to get what I want.

10. A-I am clear and determined in following my goals.
    B-I often try to find a compromise solution to a problem.

11. A-I attempt to get all issues immediately out in the open for discussion.
    B-I try to calm the feelings of others to keep our relationship.

12. A- I sometimes avoid taking a stand on something controversial which may cause me problems later.
    B-I will let others have what they want if they let me have some of my needs.

13. A-During a discussion with others I often suggest a middle ground between different points of view.
    B-I am anxious to make my points in an argument.

14. A-I tell other people about my ideas and suggestions and ask for theirs.
    B-I try to show others the advantages and benefits of my ideas.

15. A-I might try to calm the feelings of others and keep our relationship.
    B-I do what I can to avoid tensions in relationships.

16. A-I try not to hurt the feelings of others if I can do this.
    B-I try to convince the other person of the advantages of my arguments.

17. A-I am usually determined and persistent in pursuing my goals.
    B-I do what I can to avoid useless disputes, arguments and tensions.

18. A-If it makes other people happy, I don't argue against them unnecessarily.
    B-I will let other people have what they want, if they will let me have some of what I want.

19. A-I attempt to get all concerns immediately out in the open for discussion.
    B-I try to get more time to think it over difficult thngs.

20. A-I attempt to immediately work together to resolve our differences.
    B-I try to find a fair combination of gains and losses for both of us in a negotiation.

21. A-In approaching negotiations, I try to think about the other's needs and wishes.
    B-I always try to encourage a direct discussion of the problem.

22. A-I try to find a position that is half way between another person and mine.
    B-I assert my wishes and needs in discussions.

23. A-I am very often concerned with satisfying all our needs and wishes.
    B-There are times when I don't mind if others take responsibility for solving a problem.

24. A-If another person expresses something which seems very important, I would try to meet the needs being expressed.
    B-I try to get the other person to settle for a compromise between us.

25. A-I try to show the other person the advantages and logic of my suggestions.
    B-In approaching negotiations, I try to think of the other person's needs.

26. A-I propose a middle ground between myself and others.
    B-I am nearly always concerned with satisfying all our wishes and requirements.

27. A-I sometimes avoid taking positions that would create problems and raise controversial issues.
    B-If it makes others happy, I might let them say what they like in a discussion.

28. A-I am usually firm and determined in pursuing my goals.
    B-I usually seek the help of another person in working out a solution.

29. A-I propose a middle ground between the two of us.
    B-I feel that differences between people are not always to be concerned about.

30. A-I try not to hurt the feelings of others unnecessarily.
    B-I always share problems between us so that we can work it out.

On the chart on the opposite page, circle the letters which you chose on each item of the questionnaire, either A or B. It is important to choose A or B in each case, even if both sentences seem to apply to you, or neither. Add up the scores at the bottom of each vertical column to create a profile of your conflict mode preferences. Usually two or three preferences can be scored with high numbers, and two or three lower or low. Scores of nine to twelve are generally high, and scores of zero to three are seen as low, on each dimension.

CASE STUDY – A FIVE-STAR HOTEL IN SINGAPORE

Here, we look at the challenge of delivering corporate objectives when training employees in a cultural context at odds with the proposed training outcomes. We are using 'conflict mode preferences' – as discussed above – as a tool for measuring the progress in the training. As part of a typical training plan to create appropriate behaviors in a luxury hotel property, a training program was created to encourage collaborative and competitive styles in handling situations of conflict with prospective customers and guests. This research was initially carried out in the context of an Arab Gulf state (Jones, 2008), but was repeated in a hotel in Singapore (described below) with remarkably similar results.

A review of the literature on the subject of conflict in teams suggests that collaborative and competitive styles (among all the conflict mode preferences) can have a positive correlation with business performance, especially in the service sector, such as in a luxury hotel. Yet the overwhelming preference for compromising and avoiding styles found amongst trainees in this hotel showed that specific cultural context can significantly modify (and even negate) the desired outcomes of Western-style training programs. This study of 50 junior hotel group management trainees suggests that training initiatives aimed at developing collaborative (problem-solving) and competitive ('go-getting') attitudes can be significantly compromised by the cultural context within which that training takes place. In Singapore, high power-distance behaviors, low individualism and high uncertainty-avoidance attitudes are common. Most members of the population of Singapore are well-off and keen on developing themselves, but are comfortable and risk-avoiding.

Significant differences were discovered between the attitudes of our hotel group management trainee group and the conflict mode preferences described in an international benchmarking study of excellence and quality in customer service. This has important practical implications for training effectiveness in non-Western cultures, which rely heavily on Western training materials. Here, the conflict mode exercise is a useful

No	Competing (Forcing)	Collaborating (Problem solving)	Compromising (Sharing)	Avoiding (Withdrawal)	Accommodating (Smoothing)
1				A	B
2		B	A		
3	A				B
4			A		B
5		A		B	
6	B			A	
7			B	A	
8	A	B			
9	B			A	
10	A		B		
11		A			B
12			B	A	
13	B		A		
14	B	A			
15				B	A
16	B				A
17	A			B	
18			B		A
19		A		B	
20		A	B		
21		B			A
22	B		A		
23		A		B	
24			B		A
25	A				B
26		B	A		
27				A	B
28	A	B			
29			A	B	
30		B			A

Total number of item circled in each column:

Competing   *Collaborating*   *Compromising*   *Avoiding*   *Accommodating*

Review the outcome of the preferences shown in your results – which preference gains your highest score? It depends on the numbers of As and Bs circled under each preference, added up vertically. You may have a second and third preference with a score of seven or higher, and one or two with scores of three or less. Details on the implications of each preference, with definitions, are given in the case study below.

tool in measuring training outcomes, given that certain ways of handling conflict are being encouraged, and certain other ways positively discouraged.

So what is the impact of cultural context on conflict mode preference, and therefore the effectiveness of training of new recruits? Especially in basic business skills, including negotiating skills, conflict resolution and dealing with customers and guests generally? The findings of this case study suggest that business skill training outcomes based upon international standards and assumptions may be changed by culturally-specific beliefs and values. These can be revealed in terms of the predominant conflict modes adopted.

What are international standards in business skills training, particularly in negotiating and conflict resolution? Can these standards be identified, and have they been validated by previous research? What are international standards with regards to appropriate behaviors in conflict situations and the implications for business success? These definitions have been taken from sources originating in North America, Europe and Australia. However, yet they are being applied all over the world, largely ignoring cultural variations.

RESEARCH ON CONFLICT STYLES

The work of Thomas and Kilmann (1974) and Thomas (1979) and the creation of their measure of conflict, widely quoted in textbooks as well as in research papers (and the source of the exercise above), has been used to examine conflict mode preferences amongst our sample of 50 hotel group management trainees. The authors have defined five modes of conflict: *Competing, Accommodating, Collaborating, Compromising* and *Avoiding.* These five modes were adapted from Blake and Mouton (1964) that linked personality strategies to conflict resolution, first defined as *Forcing, Smoothing, Problem-solving, Sharing and Withdrawing.*

Each style has advantages and disadvantages in particular contexts. However, Lawrence and Lorsch (1967) observed that an integrating or collaborative style can be most effective for managing conflicts in organizations. This style is aimed at solving the problem, and collaborative behaviors respect the interests of both sides: collaboration is based on achieving a satisfactory outcome for both parties.

Most studies of conflict mode preferences and their impact on learning business skills and hence contributing to business success were developed in the West. Analysis of cultural context in conflict-mode preference is generally lacking in the copious literature on conflict management. However, internationally-operating trainers must be alerted to factors that could negate their efforts to achieve management and customer service objectives.

The cultural context of Singapore, as mentioned above, encourages an aversion to risk and modest ambition described as 'the three C's' – car, condominium [or flat or apartment] and certificate [e.g. an MBA degree]. In relationships with colleagues and customers, this manifests itself as an aversion to using discretionary workplace attitudes and behaviors, and following strict guidelines. This can compromise positive business outcomes for the hotel group (such as in making sales, solving guest problems, developing corporate customer relationships and building teamwork amongst colleagues).

Two authors in particular have had a major influence on understanding cross-cultural behavioral issues – Geert Hofstede (1984, 1994) and Fons Trompenaars (1997). Their work is discussed more in later chapters of this book. Especially Hofstede's work on cultural difference has been discussed widely. He recognizes four dimensions of culture (Hofstede 1984), described as individualism ('I' versus 'we' consciousness), power-distance (levels of equality or the importance of status), uncertainty-avoidance (the need for rules and regulations) and masculinity (attitudes towards achievement and the roles of men and women). Hofstede's research suggests that Singapore (and other cities and countries with a Chinese heritage, such as Hong Kong and Taiwan) score highly on both power-distance and uncertainty-avoidance (Hofstede 1994).

These 'cross-cultural management' studies argue that business attitudes and behaviors, including attitudes to negotiating and conflict, can be culturally-specific. So we could expect to find within the Chinese world attitudes and behaviors that reflect this. These can be seen in avoiding and compromising stances within customer and colleague relationships. Thus, international values in respect to handling conflict with customers and colleagues may be compromised in the face of these different cultural contextual values. This has implications for the design and delivery of training, and attempts by trainers to achieve corporate management objectives in areas like communications and customer service.

Conflict mode benchmarks: Conflict has been defined as a struggle over values, status, power or resources, in which the aims of the parties involved can also be aimed at damaging rivals (Losef, 1967, quoted in Porter and Taplin, 1987) The issue here is the positive use of conflict, especially for dealing with colleagues and customers and thus trying to improve business performance.

Thomas and Kilmann and their 'Conflict Mode Instrument,' identifying the *Competing, Compromising, Avoiding, Accommodating* and *Collaborating* modes, was used as part of the training approach in this case study of an intake of first-level hotel group management trainees at a major hotel group in Singapore. These concepts were matched to 'ideal' negotiating and conflict resolution styles as suggested in the literature.

The literature concludes that a *Collaborating* style can be generally effective in most organizational conflicts. This is especially the case where there are communication problems or a need to solve strategic problems linked to planning in organizations (Wood, 2004: 604). Research also shows that many managers believe that a compromising style hinders performance and goals achievement (Lawrence and Lorsch, 1967: 1-47).

Thomas and Kilmann (1974), although insisting that there are 'no universal right answers' in relation to their *Conflict Mode Instrument* and that effectiveness depends on the requirements of the situation and the skill in which the conflict mode is used, do mention that 'social skills' might lead certain individuals to 'rely upon some conflict behaviors more or less than necessary'. They list some warning signals for the over-use or under-use of each mode, described below.

Interpreting your conflict mode profile: A high score for the *Collaborative* mode can waste time in solving problems, and may fail to encourage collaborative behaviors in others (it takes two to effectively solve a conflict). Little use of this mode can mean a lack of appreciation of differences as opportunities to learn and solve problems, and can also mean lack of commitment to problem-solving outcomes.

Being too *Competing* can result in intimidating colleagues, who then do not want to share problems. Being low on this preference can mean feeling powerless and being unable to make firm decisions. *Accommodating* can be a sign of being too easy-going and creating lax discipline. However, not being accommodating suggests problems in building goodwill and a lack of recognition of knowing when we are wrong.

Too much *Compromising* can reflect a lack of appreciation and awareness of the important issues of the principles, values and long-term objectives of the organization. It also suggests bargaining and trading, gamesmanship, and undermining interpersonal trust. Too little reflects embarrassment over bargaining and refusal to make concessions.

Finally, too much *Avoiding* suggests a lack of co-ordination where people avoid discussions of issues, the use of too much energy spent on caution and the avoidance of issues, and the need for issues to be faced and resolved. Important decisions may be made by default, without adequate consultation. On the other hand, the under-use of Avoiding can result in the stirring up of hostilities and the feeling of being over-whelmed by too many issues.

Implications for behaviors in the workplace: A useful summary by the *Harvard Business Review (HBR)* confirms the literature emphasizing the importance of the *collaborative* or problem-solving approach to conflict. Overall, conflict is seen as healthy, as long as it produces productive and creative resolution of problems. For example, corporate harmony and individual initiative can be preserved when managers make an effort to understand the nature of differences (through *Collaborating*), whilst *Avoiding* tends to reduce creativity (Schmidt & Tannenbaum, 1960). Meanwhile, 'enriched problem solving' has the benefits of welcoming differences, promoting understanding; clarification regarding the nature of the conflict; a recognition and acceptance of feelings; the establishment of ground rules; the maintenance of relationships and the creation improved communications.

Another *HBR* article looks out two different approaches to problem-solving. These help in seeing issues from each others' point of view, and the forming of views about an ideal relationship between the two groups. It is suggested that *Co-operative* and *Collaborative* behaviors can be encouraged and mediated by neutral facilitators (Blake & Mouton, 1984).

Keiser (1988) suggests that confrontation (or *Competing/forcing* behaviors) 'will poison the water' and *Compromise* 'will rob you of your margin'. The solution is to 'lure your customer into a search for inventive answers to tough problems'. A further research study, which sees conflict-handing and the negotiating process as a corporate capability (Ertel, 1999), suggests that a common, yet ineffective, way of handling negotiation is to confuse the short-term deal with the broader relationship, offering concessions and *Compromises*, threatening to terminate the relationship (*Competing or forcing*), withholding information (*Avoiding*), being suspicious of each other, and ending up with a low-value deal. A better approach, Ertel (1999) suggests, is the separation of the short-term deal from the longer-term relationship, exchanging information and being more creative and *Collaborative* in discussions, improving mutual understanding, sharing information, improving trust and communication, expanding the scope of the discussions, and creating valuable options.

Other writers arguing for the creative and positive use of conflict and the role of active problem-solving include Pascale (1991) and Pascale, Millemann and Loija (2000) who look at the value of self- and company-renewal through the creating and breaking of paradigms. They argue that there will always be battles between the forces of tradition and the forces of transformation, and that these must be dealt with proactively and not *Avoided or Compromised.*

The famous author of books on thinking – de Bono – also enters this debate (1986) and argues against *Compromise* and consensus in his study subtitled 'a better way to handle conflicts'. With his life-long emphasis on the study of thinking, De Bono suggests that the way the human mind works can influence one's attitude toward conflict. People disagree because they see things differently, they want different things, their thinking style encourages them to act in a certain way, or because they feel they are supposed to do a certain thing. Thus conflict handling involving fighting (*Competing*) and negotiating and bargaining (*Compromising*) are not the answer, but there is a need to 'design a way out' to achieve 'de-confliction', based on understanding differing realities and working together to fully explore the issues, perhaps using the *Six Thinking Hats* technique (De Bono, 1985).

Avoiding is discussed in the conflict literature for its negative influence on conflict outcomes. It is used by conflict participants who do not see the conflict as important, who are not prepared to spend time on it, who procrastinate, who avoid emotional involvement and, as a result, indulge in 'gunny sacking' or the carrying around of grievances as if stored in a sack (Mayer 1990). *Avoiding* is described as 'exclusion, withdrawal and behavioral de-escalation' (Canary & Stafford, 1994), focusing on the status quo without the process of 'value-adding' to an existing relationship.

Additionally, some texts argue a cognitive development process linked to conflict handling with the moving away from *Competing* at an early age to the 'use of non-confrontation or *Avoidance*' strategies in adolescence (Canary & Stafford, 1994) followed by a problem-solving *Collaborating* approach in later life.

In general, this brief literature review suggests that *Collaborative* behaviors are related to positive outcomes in conflict with a positive impact on business. This positive impact is seen in terms of sales results and the building of customer relationships, together with improving teamwork in organizations. *Competitive* behaviors can be positive but not always of long-term benefit. *Accommodating* behavior is seen as having a neutral impact on customers and colleagues (sometimes positive, sometimes negative, depending on the scenario); and *Compromising* and *Avoiding* behavior is seen as generally having a negative affect on customers and colleagues.

This case study, of an intake of Singapore college graduates (who had reached Diploma level but not Bachelor degree level) joining a major local luxury hotel group as management trainees in the process of their orientation and training, looks at their exposure to business skills training which subscribes to the Western (i.e. North American, European and Australian) values. The aim of this training has been to prepare the new recruits for their subsequent placements in the hotel group's front-line customer interface – both with hotel guests and corporate clients. Their attitudes towards conflict handling in their teams, and with these customers and guests, has been an important part of the training.

At the conclusion of these five months of training, the hotel group management trainees were asked to complete a diagnostic instrument, the *Thomas Kilmann Mode of Conflict Inventory* (1974), which asks a series of questions (in pairs with the choice of 'A' or 'B' options) designed to identify conflict mode preferences between the possibilities of being predominantly competitive, collaborating, compromising, accommodating or avoiding. (This is the instrument that appeared as an exercise earlier in this chapter.) In completing this questionnaire, the trainees revealed their perception of customer and colleague relationships in conflict situations (interpreted as any instance of professional disagreement with differing opinions and agendas).

It should be noted that at the hotels in the group, customers and guests are relatively 'high-touch' and require a hands-on problem-solving approach to ensure customer satisfaction. They have high expectations of this luxury group which positions itself at the top of the market. Typical customer problems were identified – such as late or wrong delivery of food and beverages, disappointment over room allocation, delays over checking-in, confirming airline reservations and making restaurant bookings – all scenarios requiring a large degree of 'problem-solving freedom' and 'problem-solving complexity' given that the scenarios in the training exercises placed participants in a leading customer service role and did not assume the active presence of a higher corporate authority. The trainees were also required to develop productive and positive relationships between themselves in the daily execution of their duties, which were similarly challenging in this environment.

The new recruits, in four groups of around 12-15 participants, experienced this training in separate monthly batches over a five-month period. These new employees were given the scenario of the need to improve the occupancy (and hence profitability) and customer service quality ratings of their particular hotel property, primarily through improved selling skills, customer and guest relationships and inter-employee teamwork. Several conflict scenarios were explained and the participants examined strategies for successful outcomes that would lead to customer and guest retention, and at the same time enhancing teamwork. This exercise took place towards the end of their training, after they were involved in other business skill training activities, including presentations from managers across a range of divisions in the hotel group.

The scenario was outlined in which they were responsible for sales to new and existing customers in their hotel property, but where several damaging conflicts had emerged in their attempts to sell new and additional products and services. Conflicts had also broken out with fellow employees in the course of their daily work together in the hotel. These conflict situations were presented as neutrally as possible, but with the unspoken suggestion of potential opportunities for the hotel property in terms of developing new customers and expanding business with existing customers. Relationships with colleagues were presented as necessary for the on-going successful running of the hotel. In the scenarios, their particular property had performed less than satisfactorily, disappointing head office in terms of its track record of obtaining new customer business and repeat customer business (could be higher) and inter-colleague support and teamwork (could be better).

As a result of the scenarios, the participants were charged with the task of completing a questionnaire identifying how they would respond to a number of different situations involving customers and colleagues.

It was emphasized that the behaviors of customer service personnel had one of three different results on the customer in terms of achieving sales or at least ensuring customer retention: positive, neutral or negative. Competitive and collaborative behaviors had a positive impact; accommodating was neutral; and compromising and avoiding were potentially negative. The objective of the exercise was to maximize the positive impact on the customer base and higher sales for the hotel. These behaviors, identified by the training and consulting firm Human Synergistics, are explained above near the beginning of this chapter.

Analysis of the research findings showed differences between this group of hotel trainees and the findings of the literature review in negotiation and conflict resolution. The conclusions of the literature on ideal conflict handling behaviors provided an international benchmark for purposes of comparison to the results of this sample.

According to the literature, Collaborative and (to a lesser extent) Competitive behaviors had the most positive impact on sales and business performance; Accommodating behaviors (allowing the customers and colleagues to 'win' in the conflict situation) as neutral; and Compromising and Avoiding behaviors were the most negative, leading to lost sales, reduced margins, unprofitable customer relationships and hence declining business performance overall.

In contrast with these views, the participants from the bank chose a diametrically opposite series of preferences. Some participants worked individually and some worked as groups. However, there was little significant difference between the individual scores and the group scores. The reason here was that many of the participants, in order to clarify their understanding of the concepts, discussed most of the elements in the group before deciding their 'individual' score. Many were exhibiting risk-averse and uncertainty-avoidance behaviors during the exercise itself, seeking approval from others for their choices, depending on others for opinions, following the path of which was the most conventional approach, and avoiding making decisions at all.

In analyzing the highest and second-highest preferences of the five conflict modes of the participants, by far the highest scores were given to the preference for Compromising or

Avoiding. Only a small fraction of the participants did not record either compromising or avoiding as their top two preferences.

"Proposing a middle ground", "trying to find a position intermediate between his/hers and mine", "trying to get the other person to settle for a *Compromise*"' and "finding a combination of gains and losses for both of us" were listed by the vast majority of the participants as their first or second choice. According to international norms, this can be seen as a negative behavior in a conflict situation that, although expedient, produces a poor quality and only temporary solution to the conflict, does not lead to long-term profitable customer retention, or lasting and positive workplace relationships. Twenty-four participants chose compromising as their primary preference by a substantial margin over other preferences (Exercise quoted from Hellriegel & Slocum, 2004, p. 244-246.)

Second, "letting others take responsibility for solving the problem", "*Avoiding* unpleasantness for myself", "postponing the issue so I have time to think about it" and "thinking that differences are not worth worrying about" was recorded by over three-quarters of the participants as their first or second choice. Seventeen participants saw this as by far their preferred behavior in a conflict situation. According to field tests in the West, this mode ranks as the very lowest in modes designed to achieve a successful outcome in a conflict situation with a customer, leading to rapid customer account loss, increased customer dissatisfaction due to lack of conflict resolution, and diminishing colleague trust.

Third, *Competitive* behaviors – regarded as more positive in achieving successful customer conflict outcomes – were chosen by only a minority as reflecting their attitude to winning customer business. This preference is seen as less positive compared with the *Collaborating* preference, however. 'Win-win' is widely argued as preferable to 'win-lose' in sustaining long-term business performance.

Fourth, *Accommodating* behaviors – seen as neutral in international surveys of conflict handling and as being appropriate only in circumstances where the conflict was of little importance to the organization to build customer relationships through promoting harmony – were identified by another twelve participants as their first preference in customer or colleague conflict.

Lastly, *Collaborative* or 'win-win' attitudes to conflict were preferred by only seven of the participants as their first choice conflict handling mode.

Collaborative and *Competing* behaviors were chosen only in a small minority of cases. *Avoiding* and *Compromising* behaviors, seen as negative in the pursuit of successful sales, were the preferences of most participants. *Accommodating* behaviors, of neutral impact, were comparable with the fieldwork testing in the Western benchmarking exercise. The promotion of harmony and building on an existing relationship by giving concessions important to the customer but unimportant to the organization can be an occasional solution to customer conflict situations.

The sample group's more positive behaviors, especially collaborative and competing approaches, contrasted with the main findings of the literature review of conflict mode preferences and impact on successful conflict resolution. In each case, the behaviors regarded as having a positive impact on customer conflict handling and sales outcomes were present, especially the preferences for being accommodating and competing. However, they fell substantially short of the levels seen as required to produce effective conflict handling behaviors. In particular, the importance of collaborative behaviors, in poll position in the Thomas Kilmann findings, scored least among the conflict mode preferences of our sample group. It seems that 'problem-solving' and 'sharing', requiring a commitment to work together to solve a disagreement to the 100% satisfaction of both parties, involving considerable initiative, creative thinking and the taking of responsibility, was at odds with the 'uncertainty-avoidance' culture and the professed need for detailed instructions and guidance in order to avoid unnecessary risk-taking.

Implications of the findings: Clearly, the preferences for compromising and avoiding in conflict situations of this sample group reflect attitudes in contravention to those suggested by research in the West as the most constructive and positive in customer and collegial relationships. Arguably, the willingness to adopt avoiding behaviors by such a large majority of the trainees who will be placed in front line sales and customer service roles in their hotel property will soon become a major problem for this employer. Furthermore, it can be suggested that no customer, of any socio-political background, will tolerate delays and a lack of decision-making on their issues for long. Many customers exhibit frustration when faced with these attitudes and resultant behaviors and this might result in a negative impact on the competitive performance of the organization in question.

The choice of the avoiding preference reflects risk-aversion and high power-distance – that to do your job well, you should avoid making any mistakes, even if this means doing nothing. This also suggests a tendency towards convention, of trying not to 'screw up' and 'keeping your nose clean', and avoiding complaints at all costs. It implies a reluctance to think outside the box, when this might deal effectively with a customer or collegial conflict situation. This preference suggests a continuing concern over job security, a fear of loss of face, reluctance to take responsibility, and concern over what those in authority might do if the dreaded mistake was discovered and a victim had to be found. There is a complete lack of recognition of the value or appropriateness of admitting being wrong, and hence learning from it. It would seem to contradict the customer service dictum of 'the customer is always right', preferring 'the customer is always right if my boss says so'.

The compromising tendency, listed by the majority of the participants in the exercise as first or second choice , shows a pragmatic, bargaining attitude and lack of long-term, strategic thinking. This relates to the local traditions of customers and vendors in traditional market places where prices are rarely fixed and the outcome of a transaction depends on the bargaining ability of the participants. It also suggests a reluctance to learn new things and to take risks, and an avoidance of depending on others who know new things when you don't. Conflict resolution resulting in a long-term attitude to achieving a successful outcome for the benefit of both parties involves a scale of commitment at odds with the compromising preference.

These two preferences, of avoiding and compromising, imply a need to know what is going on, a lack of trust, and high power-distance. There may be an unwillingness to work harmoniously in teams, suspicion, and risk-avoidance. There may be a belief that 'knowledge is power' and lack of interest in sharing that powerful knowledge with others. There may be a perception by our sample group, as young employees entering the bank, of their duty being to 'fit in' and not 'make waves'. But this is at odds with the international context that emphasizes problem-solving skills and using personal initiative. However, there must be a high degree of trust and comfort before this can take place.

Training initiatives emphasizing delegation, teamwork, empowerment and non-threatening ways of sharing responsibility might help offset these dangerous avoiding and compromising tendencies. In this study, the training participants – although showing a lively interest in the training – were predominantly influenced by perceptions of how they should react in a conflict situation that are significantly mediated by their socio-political context.

The implications for the efficacy of a range of business skills training – especially sales, which always involves an element of conflict-handling and negotiating – are clearly substantial. The cultural issues identified here can reduce organizational performance and competitiveness, especially given the dependence on human assets in the service sector to achieve that competitiveness. Given these findings, it may be necessary to consider adjustments or modifications to business skills' training within certain socio-political contexts in order to achieve the desired training outcomes. In this particular scenario there is, firstly, a need for greater clarity about desired outcomes in sales and customer service scenarios, particularly in terms of areas of individual responsibility (to clarify when avoiding is desirable or not, and the impact of delays on a potential customer whilst a decision-maker is being sought), based more closely on the hotel group's customer service surveys.

Secondly, there may be a need here to deal with the possibly negative impact of compromising behaviors exhibited by participants. Which aspects of the hotel group's policy towards customers cannot, on any account, be compromised? What is the bottom-line in service standards? How can more proactive, collaborative behaviors, be encouraged? Furthermore, more emphasis by management on the importance of customer service to the bank could enhance the efficacy of its customer service training programs. Basically, training would need to be further institutionalized into the hotel group's corporate culture (Jones, 2004: 22-24). Also, for the training outcomes to be achieved, the goals of the training should be linked to a reward system in order to provide an incentive to the staff members to change customer service behaviors. Again, this use of incentives might counter-balance the pressures of the socio-political context.

Third, an organizational culture that supports constructive customer service behaviors in frontline staff should be encouraged. This would mean that supervisors, middle management and senior management would need to attend training sessions aimed at encouraging the development of supportive work environments. Such training would need to pre-date specific customer service training for frontline staff. Of course, there is a problem here: The supervisors and managers themselves are likely to display resistances similar to those suggested in this study – indicating a need for a carefully designed program, probably delivered over an extended period.

Questions on the case: Why was there a conflict between the preferences of the trainees and the focus on customer service and effective sales? Do you think that it is fair to say that there is such a thing as a universal standard of customer service? Is it possible that customers in Singapore, being of the same cultural background as the trainees, would find their behavior acceptable? Are the reactions of the trainees typical of young people in their first job, regardless of their national cultural norms? How useful is the concept of conflict preference in analyzing behavior?

ACHIEVING MEANINGFUL AGREEMENT ON OUTCOMES OF CONFLICTS

Related to the cases above (about British Airways and the hotel in Singapore) and generally, how can we explore ways of attaining meaningful outcomes to a team conflict, and what is their potential for success? Consider the possibilities below:

- Consensus – can be valuable if it includes detailed, collaborative and problem-solving discussion;
- Voting and averaging – less useful as it may involve not really addressing the most important issues, also too mechanical;
- Alignment – an objective which, if it can be achieved at the point of conflict resolution, might be extended to future ways of operating – this could be an ideal outcome;
- Seeking an accommodation – might be useful for one particular area of conflict, but does involve one party giving up their needs;
- Managing difference and disagreement – is the desired outcome, especially if a clear process can be developed;
- Surfacing and testing assumptions is essential in the conflict resolution process, not "brushing these under the carpet";
- Commitment and ownership are another desired outcome, on the particular issue involved, and ideally for the future;
- Outcomes from the means (rather than the ends as outcomes) can be useful, if the means were collaborating, brainstorming, listening and placing yourself "in another's shoes" as a way of empathizing. If "the means" meant that the participants were avoiding, compromising, accommodating too much and not really addressing the issues – just to get a result – this is less positive.

GUIDELINES FOR EFFECTIVE TEAMWORK

Finally, we need to consider some principles which underpin effective teamwork, encouraging positive rather than negative conflict within the team. Based on the teamwork competencies listed at the start of our chapter, we can summarize the **golden rules of working together as a team** as including the following:
- "We" or "us" rather than "I";
- Helping others in difficulties even when it doesn't help us;
- Seeking solutions of value to the team not just to us individually;
- Listening and not speaking more than others;
- Encouraging weaker or less experienced members of the team to contribute;
- Referring to comments made by others when making a point;
- Seeing the team's success as more important than promoting own views.

CONCLUSION

In this chapter we have examined the concept of conflict in detail, especially looking at the five conflict preferences, considering our own profiles, and examining them in the light of job and task requirements, such as in the cases, primarily concerned with organizations overcoming conflict to provide improved customer service. We looked at how the use of the 'force field analysis' can be used to highlight conflicts, by focusing on driving and restraining factors (in the British Airways case). We also examined positive and negative behavioral indicators of good teamwork practice, and hence the minimizing of conflict. We saw how constructive team behaviors, as opposed to aggressive defensive and passive defensive, can also reduce conflict in teams. We looked at how conflicts can be managed and handled, supported by following guidelines for effective teamwork. The case about the hotel in Singapore gave us some indicators of conflict preferences impacted by cultural issues. Conflicts will always be there wherever there are teams, but the reasons for these conflicts can be diagnosed and dealt with – if we understand why they arose in the first place.

REFERENCES

Blake, R. & Mouton, J. (1964). *The Managerial Grid.* Houston: Gulf Publishing.

Blake, R. & Mouton, J. (1984). 'Overcoming Group Warfare', *Harvard Business Review* November-December

Canary, D.J. & Stafford, L. (1994). *Communication and Relational Maintenance.* London: Academic Press.

De Bono, E. (1986). *Conflicts - a better way to resolve them.* Harmondsworth: Penguin.

Grugulis, I. & Wilkinson, A. (2001) *'British Airways – culture and structure' Working Paper*, Loughborough University Business School

Harvard Business Review (2000). *Harvard Business Review on Negotiation and Conflict Resolution.* Boston: Harvard Business Review Press.

Hellriegel, D. & Slocum, J.W. (2004) *Organizational Behavior.* Mason, Ohio: Thomson South Western.

Hofstede, G. (1984). *Culture's Consequences: International Differences in Work-Related Values*, Beverly Hills: Sage.

Hofstede, G. (1994). Management scientists are human, *Management Science 40*: 1, 4-13.

Human Synergistics Inc. www.human-synergistics.comJones, Stephanie (2004). The ABC, 123 of corporate culture, *Human Assets Middle East Winter* 2004: 5, 22-24.

Jones, S. (2008). Training and Cultural Context in the Arab Emirates: fighting a losing battle, *Employment Relations, 30*, 1, 48-62

Keiser, T.C. (1988). Negotiating with a Customer You Can't Afford to Lose, *Harvard Business Review* November-December.

Lawrence, P.R. & J.W. Lorsch (1967). Differentiation and integration in complex organizations, *Administrative Science Quarterly 12*: 1, 1-47

Pascale, R.T. (1991). *Managing on the Edge - how successful companies use conflict to stay ahead.* Harmondsworth: Penguin.

Pascale, R.T., Millemann M., et al. (2000). *Surfing the Edge of Chaos - the laws of nature and the new laws of business.* New York: Random House.

Porter, J.N. & Taplin, R. (1987). *Conflict and Conflict Resolution*, New York: University Press of America.

Schmidt, W.H. & Tannenbaum, R. (1960). Management of Differences, *Harvard Business Review* November-December.

Schneider, S.C. & Barsoux, J.-L. (1997). *Managing Across Cultures*. Harlow: Prentice Hall.

Thomas, K.W. & Kilmann, R.H. (1974). *The Thomas-Killmann Conflict Mode Instrument*, New York: Xicom.

Trompenaars, F. & Hampden-Turner, C. (1997). *Riding the Waves of Culture: Understanding Cultural Diversity in Business*, London: Nicholas Brealey.

Wood, J. et . al. (2204). *Organizational Behaviour*, Sydney: John Wiley.

RECOMMENDED FURTHER READING

Belbin, R.M. (2004) *Management teams: why they succeed or fail*, Oxford: Elsevier/Butterworth Heinemann.

Canary, D.J., Cupach, W.R. , et al. (1995), *Relationship Conflict*. Beverley Hills, CA: Sage.

Dumane, B. (1994) 'The trouble with teams', *Fortune*, 5 September, 86-92

Feldman, D.C. (1984) 'The development and enforcement of group norms', *Academy of Management Review, 9*, 47-53

George, J.M. & Jones, G.R. (2002) *Organizational Behavior*. 3rd. ed., Upper Saddle River, New Jersey: Prentice Hall.

Gersick, C.J.G. (1988) 'Time and transition in work teams: toward a new model of group development', *Academy of Management Journal 31*, 9-41

Hackman, J.R. (1990) *Teams that work (and those that don't)*. San Francisco: Jossey-Bass.

Johnson, D.W. & Johnson, F.P. *Joining Together: group theory and group skills*. 5th ed., New York: Alyn and Bacon.

Jones, S. (1991). *Working for the Japanese: Myths and Realities*, London: Macmillan.

Jones, S. (1992). *Psychometric Testing for Managers*, London: Piatkus.

Jones, S. (1997). *Managing in China*, Singapore: Butterworth Heinnemann.

Katzenbach, J.R. & Smith, D.K. (1993) *The wisdom of teams*. Boston: Harvard Business School.

Levi, D. (2001) *Group Dynamics for Teams*. Thousand Oaks, CA: Sage.LaFasto F. and Larsen, C.E. (2001) When Teams Work Best. Thousand Oaks, CA: Sage.

Latane, B. (1986) *'Responsibility and Effort in Organizations'*, in P.S. Goodman, ed. (1986) Designing Effective Work Groups, San Francisco: Jossey-Bass.

Mendenhall, M., Punnet, B.J., & Ricks, D. (1995) *Global Management*, New York: Blackwell.

Mills, H. (1999). *Artful Persuasion*, Auckland: MG Press.

Robbins, S.P. (2003) *Essentials of Organizational Behavior*, Upper Saddle River, New Jersey: Pearson Education.

Samovar, L.A. & Porter, R.E. (1988) *Intercultural Communication: a reader*. 6th d., London: Wadsworth.

Trompenaars, F. & Hampden-Turner, C. (1997) *Riding the waves of culture: understanding cultural diversity in business*, London: Nicholas Brealey.

CHAPTER 6

INTRODUCING STRATEGIC HUMAN RESOURCE MANAGEMENT
SILVIO DE BONO

OPENING CASE:

XYZ is a family-owned company established in 1983 in Dubai in the United Arab Emirates (UAE) in the Arabian Gulf as a pharmaceutical distributor with a goal to set up a multi-diversified distributor (wholesale) company and retail business in this area. The company has diversified its activities through acquisition and organic growth and now occupies a significant position in the local market (throughout the UAE) in the following lines of business:

- Pharmaceuticals & Health Care
- Consumer Products
- Environment Health
- Hospital & Laboratory Equipment & Supplies
- Sports Equipment and Apparel
- Stationery Products and Office Supplies
- Automotive Distribution (of Peugeot cars)
- Retail Pharmacies – operating 13 pharmacies in all over UAE
- Retail Sports Goods Outlets

The organization has a sales-dominated culture. The management is primarily oriented towards short-term thinking, and look toward monthly profitability figures as the main measures of success. The values of the organization can be summed up as entrepreneurial, yet mostly traditional and conservative. It has an aggressive sales approach, but in other respects is not so pro-active or dynamic. It has invested heavily in state-of-the-art IT equipment to manage its distribution business, but puts much less emphasis on people in the company. The company is run as an old-fashioned Arab family business, with some resistance to change, and the management is autocratic in style.

XYZ employs more than 300 employees in three locations, and the company is structured around six product divisions, serviced by four separate functional support divisions: Warehouse, Information Technology, Administration, and Accounts. Each product division has its own sales structure, which has evolved in a fairly random way from the different requirements of each industry sector. This structure varies considerably between each unit. For example, the pharmaceutical division has a sales team selling all products based on geographical area, such as Dubai, Abu Dhabi, and the other Emirates. By contrast, the stationery division has brand managers for each separate product in different locations all over UAE. There is little consistency in the running of the different divisions – and some of the managers are experimenting with different management styles according what seems to work.

However, each division has a fairly uniform structure with its own Sales Co-ordinators, and most divisions have Sales Supervisors with an average of 4 to 5 Sales

Representatives reporting to them in each case. The Sales Representatives are seen as the 'foot soldiers' or the 'grass roots' of the company. The support functions provide centralized services for all the product divisions, regardless of industry or location. The warehouse and IT functions are fairly advanced in terms of investment in new equipment.

There are 25 managers, 15 supervisors, 10 Sales Coordinators and 100 Sales Representatives. There is a high concentration of personnel in the Warehouse, which is run in a highly labor-intensive way in terms of support functions including drivers, helpers and unskilled laborers. This function has therefore the largest number of employees, except the sales force as a whole. The IT division has recently upgraded the state of-the-art ERP (Enterprise Resource Planning) Oracle Financial® and Retail Pur ® with highly skilled staff. However, there is no human resource management function in the company at all.

The Board of Directors consists of a father and his sons. Father has been leading and running the business since its inception. These are all UAE Nationals. The two sons are overseas educated in prestigious universities, but recently the more progressive son left the company and joined a world-class management consulting firm. He found that the family company was too conservative to make full use of his talents. The father, already in his early 60s, is very traditional in running the business. He is sorry that his son is no longer active in the family company, but hopes he will return.

The father, known as 'The Owner' makes most of the decisions in the company. He expects a high level of loyalty from his management team. Sometimes his demands are seen as unreasonable. For example, he tends to arrive at work around 1PM in the afternoon, and gives out urgent projects to staff members to complete during the later afternoon and early evening. However, these staff members are required to be on duty from 8.30AM and often find that they have to work long hours to complete these projects.

Other projects are started and staff members are put under pressure to complete them, and then the projects are delayed and put on hold for no apparent reason, when The Owner decides he no longer sees them as so urgent.

Although the company has expanded rapidly and is relatively successful in terms of profitability, and is modern and progressive in the IT sector, it has done so without emphasis on people. Also, even though the company is heavily dependent on sales people and its labor-intensive distribution system, it has neglected to develop people and does not place emphasis on the importance of people as an asset of the company.

Staff turnover is high. For example, the average time span of the typical manager with the company is 1 to 2 years only, and for Supervisors 4 to 5 years, but the owner believes that management turnover is not important, as long as the sales team is more stable. The Sales Representatives are often with the company a long time, up to over 15 years. But this has advantages and disadvantages. They provide good continuity with the customers and have good knowledge of their business, but they are reluctant to change and they are critical of young people entering the industry. They are not so interested in new products and learning any new sales techniques, because this involves extra work with no more pay, and can be risky.

This is one of the reasons why the company needs an HR function – because of its dependence on people, and to address issues such as high staff turnover which cause financial loss to the company, lack of continuity in the business and damage to the company's reputation in the market. Problems with the company's image in Dubai are affecting its ability to hire staff, its servicing of new and existing principals, and its customer relationships. The problems resulting from running the company without HR functions include:

1. High employee turnover;
2. Communication problems;
3. Lack of clarity of job tasks;
4. Lack of motivation of some of the staff members;
5. ack of clarity over the company's vision and long term plans;
6. Lack of training and development opportunities for staff;
7. Gap in integration and communication between different departments;
8. Lack of team work;
9. The company does not consider the personal life of the staff members;
10. Lack of empowerment of people in their jobs;
11. The company could do a better job in customer services .

The managers in the company feel that the existence of these problems is stopping the organization for being more successful. Although the company is profitable, it is being held back from being more profitable and fulfilling its potential. As a result, costs are increasing through high staff turnover, impacting the company's competitive positioning. Competitors are winning better business opportunities through better people. There is a duplication of some efforts and neglecting of some duties, due to confusion and error on job descriptions and clarity over objectives.

Arguments in favor of a HR function were initially rejected on the grounds that the line manager can carry out the majority of HR functions with the support of a Junior Personnel Officer, who could be recruited for the purpose. The Owner of the company believes that there is no need for a full-fledged HR department, because the company is not large enough (with 300 staff) to warrant this.

It was suggested that a modern HR Management function, led by an experienced and trained HR manager familiar with this environment, would address the following issues:

✔   A good HR Manager would set up recruitment functions to hire the right people in a cost-effective way either promoting from within or identifying and attracting people from the market to help the company gain competitive advantage, especially in a sales-driven company which depends heavily on having good people.

✔   This HR Manager can set up an effective performance appraisal system carrying out staff appraisals, implementing an effective reward system, improving productivity by providing rewards to those employees who are making outstanding contributions to the company.

✔ The HR Manager can implement a training needs analysis, identifying skills' shortages and developing an appropriate personal development plan for each staff member including the evaluation of training effectiveness. This would create a continuous training cycle. There is also a need for the design and implementation of induction training for new staff, as part of an ongoing system of training and development.

✔ A good HR Manager will have the experience to quickly understand the positioning of the company in terms of compensation and benefits and will ensure the company offers an attractive package to attract and retain staff. It would also be important to ensure internal equality to prevent any feeling ofunfairness amongst company staff.

✔ The HR Manager will help to prepare job descriptions and objectives for each staff member to achieve clarity of job role and to improve internal communications.

✔ Finally, this function can facilitate agreement on the company's vision and mission and will communicate this clearly throughout the organization. This can be aligned to the mission and vision expressed by the Marketing Department in promoting the company.

A strong HR function in XYZ could help create a company culture which would encourage a high level of staff commitment, increase productivity and thus improve profitability for a company as whole. This would also help the staff members to see the benefits of working together as a team in a spirit of equality and with merit-based rewards and promotion. This might not only improve XYZ internally, but make the company more attractive to new and existing principals and, most importantly, customers.

Questions on the opening case: For what reasons is there resistance to setting up a HR function in XYZ? What are the immediate drawbacks of this lack of Human Resource Management (HRM) for the company? And what could happen in the longer term? What are some of the problems associated with having different structures in different parts of the organization? Why do you think that the owner feels that if his sales team is stable, it doesn't matter about the rest of the work force? At what size do you think a company should consider investing in a HR function? Do you think that a company should recruit a HR manager as soon as it starts operating? What is the impact of national culture on the attitude to HRM here?

LEARNING OBJECTIVES FOR THIS CHAPTER

It is often said that if Human Resource Management and Development Strategies was the latest washing powder, the advertisers would say that it will wash our whites whiter and our colors brighter, is environmentally friendly and it will remove those stale odors that personnel managers left behind! For this reason many believe that 'Human Resource Management and Development Strategies' is simply a re-labeling and re-packaging of personnel management, promoted by personnel managers in search of enhanced status and power. Many progressive organizations today realize that Human Resource Management is not a new washing powder, but on the other hand it is a much desired necessity, one which can help create a convergence of organizational and individual requirements for success.

By the end of this chapter you should be able to:

- Understand how different management theories have developed over time and these now emphasize human resources as at the centre of the management equation;

- Appreciate how over the years, different scholars have given higher importance to the management of people and their individual needs;

- Realize how modern management theories place particular emphasis on human capital as the new dividends for investment.

We will start off by introducing early management theories and take you through the increasing emphasis on the humanistic approach, helping you to understand this evolution and how HRM has become of increasing strategic importance to organizations. Looking at both open and closed systems of HRM, we finally introduce you to the all-important need for an alignment between HRM strategy and the organization's strategy.

THE ORIGINS OF HR: EARLY MANAGEMENT THEORIES

The development of theories of management has been based on a process of interpretation and reinterpretation of experience of many people over many years. The initial step taken by Frederick Taylor (see Appleby, 1994) was to interpret the workings of organizations as the churning of a huge machine. Taylor's theory of scientific management imports ideas from the engineering field to that of organization management. Taylor knew that the efficiency of any machine depends on its initial design and the appropriateness of materials used. In order to keep the machines working efficiently the required fuel and lubricants must be supplied and all the parts must be kept under constant check so that any loosening or wear is spotted and checked immediately and thus no play is allowed to develop. Thus Taylor emphasizes the need for scientific design of work processes, the scientific selection of recruits to work in the organization, the tight control by a functional foreman, and production-related pay as the fuel for motivation. Taylor regarded the complexities of human behavior as the major hindrance for the smooth functioning of an organization and thus his objective was to eliminate as much of this human element as possible.

Classical theories of management continued in the same vein by seeking to eliminate human uncertainties through the careful design of organizational structures and management principles. The basic assumption of these theories was that humans by nature seek to avoid work and the task of management is to find ways to make workers comply with their orders and instructions.

Management's outlook started shifting as a result of the much quoted and debated Hawthorne Studies (Hellriegel & Slocum, 2004). Results yielded by these studies seemed anomalous to explanations and predictions of established management theories. The only way that these observations could be interpreted was by taking into account the emotions and relationships of the operators being studied. The result was that the human element had to be brought into the equation. This, however, was done very cautiously and only when there was enough evidence to show that ignoring it could jeopardize management's efforts to control and ensure compliance. Since this added 'cog' had to be integrated into the 'wheel' of the model, a new tool had to be forged with which to keep it in tune. Management realized that it had to undertake the added task of managing communication strategies in order to create and maintain the required social environment to optimize performance. The required communication strategies had to be designed to give workers a sense of belonging or participation.

Although the results of the Hawthorne Studies only led to an enlargement or a development of established theories, their shock waves were to have more serious repercussions further on down the line. The most significant novelty was that the prevalent assumptions on the motivation to work were naive or insufficient. The classical theories had assumed that the only need satisfied though work is the economic need. Now researchers wondered what motivational factors other then the newly found social needs could have gone unnoticed.

It was at this point that the paradigmatic change started taking shape as the likes of Maslow (Hellriegel & Slocum, 2004) and Douglas McGregor (Daft, 2003) suggested that there may be an array of human needs which drive people to work. These could be classified into deficiency needs; such as the needs for physical subsistence, safety, social recognition and self-esteem; and growth needs or the need for self-development and self-actualization. The change of paradigm here involved a reinterpretation of workers' nature. It was now not only possible to regard workers as people who needed recognition, and who had their own social agendas, desires and ambitions but also, for the first time, it was possible to start thinking about ways of integrating these facets of human nature into the management of organizations in a beneficial way.

If it is accepted that people seek self-actualization through work, then it starts making sense to inquire about what the benefits to the organization may be if opportunities are made available for these needs to be actualized. The change in paradigm thus brought about a shift in the main task of management - a shift from an outlook of regimentation and coercion to one of nurturing and development. The benefit or return for the organization was that management could now expect worker commitment to organization goals rather then mere compliance to rules. This shift made the development from personnel management to human resource development possible.

Exercise: Reflect on the evolution of these theories. Consider the progress of your own organization – what is the management's view of the staff? How much appreciation is shown by the human resources policies towards individual needs? Is this a cultural phenomenon, in so far that some countries are more disposed towards the nurturing and developing perspective, whilst others are more interested in regimentation and coercion? Consider Maslow and his definition of self-actualization – is making use of this need part of the management's philosophy in your organization?

PROGRESS TOWARDS HRM AND HRD AS A STRATEGY

The human resource management and development movement is based on the realization that self-fulfillment and self-actualization can be strong motivational forces. This has helped influence HR strategies, but there is no one clear definition of what we really mean by HR strategies. A number of valid definitions may be cited each with its own particular perspective and insight:

Keith Sisson, editor of the *Human Resource Management Journal*, defines Human Resource Management (HRM) to refer to policies, procedures and processes involved in the management of people in work organizations (Sisson, 1990, p.1). As such, the term embraces traditional subject areas like industrial relations, personnel management, organizational behavior and industrial sociology.

According to this author there are four main features which are increasingly associated with HRM. Primarily there is a stress on the integration of personnel policies both with one another and with business planning more generally. First HRM is not only a strategic activity in itself but is now central to the achievement of business objectives, the human resource is now recognized and utilized as the most valuable of all organizational resources.

Secondly, the locus of responsibility for personnel management no longer resides with specialist managers, but is now assumed by senior line management, in other words the personnel manager needs to give away responsibility for the human assets to senior line management. Thirdly, the focus shifts from management and trade union relations to management and employee relations, from collectivism to individualism – representing an overall shift from industrial relations to human relations.

Finally, according to Sisson, there is also a stress on commitment and the exercise of initiative with managers now taking on the role of enabler, 'empowerer', and facilitator. The creation and management of organizational culture is now given as much importance as the organization's work itself, with individuals offered the opportunity to realize their full potentials, ably assisted by line management – clearly this is an ideal situation.

Michael Poole, editor of the International *Journal of Human Resource Management*, offers a wider, macro approach to the subject matter. He argues that apart from the central aspect of HRM being the link with business policy and strategic management, the subject is perhaps best viewed as involving a synthesis of elements from international business, organizational behavior, personnel management and industrial relations (Poole, 1990: 1-2).

Human Resource Management and Human Resource Development inevitably require a central philosophy of the way people in any organization are managed. This needs personnel policies and practices to be integrated so that they make a coherent whole, and also that this whole is integrated with the business or organizational strategy. These themes of interpretation and central philosophy of people management have been drawn out by a number of writers, for example Handy et al. (1989) and Henry and Pettigrew (1986). Baird et al., as early as 1983, go one step beyond this and argue that there can be no organizational strategy without the inclusion of human resource issues.

Human resource strategy is generally behavior-based. In the traditional ideal model there would be an analysis of the types of behavior required to fulfill business objectives and then an identification of personnel policies and practices which would bring about and reinforce this behavior. Schuler and Jackson (1987) claim that the success of an organization depends on the degree of integration of employees and personnel policies with organizational structures and strategies.

In this model employees are seen as the key in the implementation of the declared organizational strategy, and human resource strategy is therefore designed to fit the requirements of organizational strategy. This emphasis on the alignment and integration of HR and the Organization strategy is evident in the early formal models of human resource strategy, particularly that proposed by Fombrun, Tichy and Devanna in 1984.

Later developments on this model introduced a skeptical view on whether or not it was possible to meet all organizational strategies and objectives through a systematic implementation of a series of HR strategy. The more critical Harvard model claims that people within every organization should be considered as the key to competitive advantage rather than just the way of implementing organizational strategy. Exponents of this model (Beer et al., 1984) claim that HRM involves all managerial personnel; it regards people as the most important single asset of the organizational; it is proactive in its relationship with people; and it seeks to enhance company performance, employee needs and societal well being.

The Harvard model is recognized as drawing its academic lineage from the Human Relations School of management thinking. It is developmental humanism in the tradition of the pluralist approach of management. In contrast, the Michigan school suggests a form of utilitarian-instrumentalist (Fombrun et. al., 1984; Hendrey & Pettigrew, 1990).

In Britain, a distinction has been drawn between soft and hard HRM, the former embracing the Human Resources Development concepts and the latter emphasizing Management issues (Storey, 1989). The soft Human Resource Development version is seen as tapping reserves of human resourcefulness by increasing employment commitment, participation and involvement. This is tackled through policies of training and development, and career development within a strategy for organizational development. The hard version of Human Resource Management is, on the other hand, a method of maximizing the economic return from labor resource by integrating Human Resource Management structures into business strategies (Keenoy, 1990, p. 3). This focuses on Management or Human Resource Planning rather than development. This aspect emphasizes the importance of recruitment and selection, training, reward management and succession planning.

A much more humanistic definition on the subject matter is offered to us by Guest (1987, 1989, 1990, 1991) who stresses the importance of four major key policy organizational goals: high commitment, high quality, flexibility, and strategic integration.

Human Resource Management here reflects an attempt to redefine both the meaning of work and the way individual employees relate to their employers. They are self-conscious attempts to change not merely social behavior, but to transform the norms and values guiding social behavior. Then, the agenda of HRM is significantly distinct from that of personnel management.

This major distinction is made clear by several theoretical works produced by Beer and Spector, (1985) and Guest, (1991) later developed further by Walton in (1985) and Torrington et al. (2005). From all definitions listed so far there seems to be an agreement toward the fact that the differences between Personnel Management and Human Resource Management can be characterized as follows:

Table 6.1 Difference between personnel management and HR management

Issue	Personnel Management	HR Management
Time & Planning Perspective	Short-term, reactive and 'ad hoc', marginal	Long-term, proactive, strategic and integrated
Psychological Contract	Compliance	Commitment
Control systems	External Records	Self-control
Employee Relations	Pluralist, collective, low trust	Monist, individual, high trust
Preferred Structures	Bureaucratic/mechanistic, centralized, formal and defined roles	Organic, developed, flexible roles
Roles	Specialist/professional	Largely integrated into line management
Evaluation criteria	Cost-minimization	Maximum utilization (human asset accounting)

Source: Torrington, Hall, and Taylor (2005) Human Resource Management, 6th ed. London: Prentice Hall.

In summarizing the above, it can be argued that:

"Personnel Management is most realistically seen as a series of activities enabling working man and his employing organization to reach agreement about the nature and objectives of the employment relationship between them, and then to fulfill those agreements." (Torrington and Chapman, 1979: 4)

"Human Resource Management is a series of activities which first enables the working people and the organization in using their skills to agree about the objectives and the nature of their working relationship and, secondly, ensures that the agreement is fulfilled." (Torrington, Hall and Taylor, 2002:13)

Exercise: *Explain the attitude towards HR in your organization, using this chart as a guideline. Does HR in your organization have short-term or long-term time horizons? Is it opportunistic* *or does it have a clear, published strategy? Is it looking for individual personal commitment from people, or does it just expect people to comply with the rules? Is it externally audited in any way – perhaps through HR quality award programs? Is there a lot of trust between employees? Is the organization structure formal or informal? Are people genuinely seen as the assets of the company and used in this way?*

HR, CORPORATE SURVIVAL, AND CULTURE-BUILDING

All organizations, if they are to survive, have to make an adjustment to the pressures on them from the external environment. That they do survive implies that the adjustment is to some extent satisfactory. The omnipresence and ever-increasing rhythm of change and competition means that many organizations seem more concerned with planning and survival rather than employee development. In fact, in contrast with the traditional approach of the personnel manager, the new Human Resource Manager starts not from the employees of the organization, but from the organization's needs for human resources: with the demand rather the supply (Torrington, 1989, p. 60).

In order to reach the high level of pro-activity required for survival of the organization, the new Human Resource Manager makes the best use of building awareness of all external pressures influencing the internal functions of the organization, and taking these into account. Therefore his or her concerns are with job flexibility, job enrichment and enlargement processes, decentralization and deployment, and performance-orientation toward job performance. HR now needs a high degree of quality consciousness and cooperative principles, reflecting the need to build team building strategies.

This means that the new Human Resource Manager perceives today's and tomorrow's organizations as unitary institutions, where all members within the organization parameters share common interests. The major elements of Human Resource strategy and functions can be related to organization culture in the form of a flow chart (see headers below):

Exercise: Consider your own organization's culture – explained in this next part of this textbook if you are not yet familiar with the concept– and think about the role of HR in your organization as a champion and custodian of this culture. To what extent is the culture strongly connected to the mission and vision? Does HR help define your culture, or has it been handed down to them? Are people recruited with a view to building and further developing the culture? Is this too much of an ideal, and can any corporation be so aligned and integrated – or is it just impossible?

OPEN AND CLOSED HR SYSTEMS

In meeting the new strategic HRM requirements which corporations are now under pressure to adopt, Poole (1990) and Beaumont (1993) have proposed that an integrated approach towards the managing of people demands an open approach.

This approach, which is seen in the diagram below, puts the employee at the heart and the centre of the organization. The employee becomes the central factor on which the organization activity circles. In such an open system, the corporate structure, organization culture and structure as well as the implementation of any HR systems and strategies generally keep the human factor in mind.

Table 6.2 The process of HR

Corporate mission and strategic plan
(reflecting the origins of the organization culture)
↓
Human Resource Planning
(defining the culture)
↓
Recruitment and Selection
(locating the bearers or holders of the culture)
↓
Training and Development
(instilling the culture)
↓
Target Setting and Appraisal
(enabling the culture)
↓
Reward Management
(reinforcing the culture)
↓
Succession Planning and Exiting
(maintaining the culture)

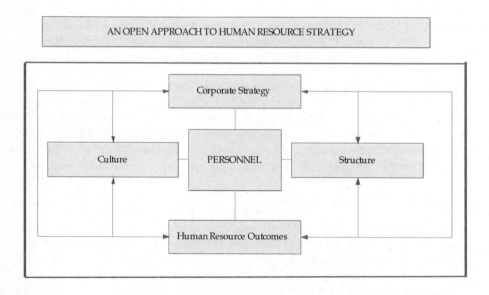

Diagram 6.1 An open approach to HRM

Source: Mabey, C. & Salaman, G. (1995) Strategic Human Resource Management,
Blackwell Business, Oxford.

Although in principle this might be seen as a real implementation of HR strategies, research has shown that today's organizations may not be in a position to simply adopt this approach without taking other issues into account. Hence, the closed approach, seen in the further diagram, proposes that there are a number of other external factors which are putting pressure on the organization, probably to a greater extent than its people.

As a result of the business pressures, organizations generally react by making strategic responses. These in turn have a direct effect in the HR strategies.

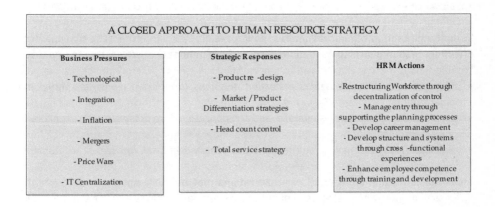

A CLOSED APPROACH TO HUMAN RESOURCE STRATEGY

Business Pressures	Strategic Responses	HRM Actions
- Technological	- Product re -design	- Restructuring Workforce through decentralization of control
- Integration	- Market / Product Differentiation strategies	- Manage entry through supporting the planning processes
- Inflation	- Head count control	- Develop career management
- Mergers	- Total service strategy	- Develop structure and systems through cross -functional experiences
- Price Wars		- Enhance employee competence through training and development
- IT Centralization		

Diagram 6.2 A closed approach to HRM

Source: Mabey, C. & Salaman, G. (1995) Strategic Human Resource Management,
Blackwell Business, Oxford.

Companies do not adopt a total *Open Approach* or alternatively a total *Closed Approach* to the management of human resources. There are a number of internal issues (pertaining to the organization) and external issues (pertaining to the macro and international markets) which generally condition whether companies adopt one approach over the other. So these two approaches are always at least partly present. Companies usually adopt an integrative approach which combines elements of the open and closed approaches.

MODELING HR TO THE ORGANIZATION REQUIREMENTS

In the light of the developments highlighted above it becomes fairly obvious that to ask the simple question – "Does Human Resource Development work?" – would always get the "it depends" reply!

The question could be meaningful if put in the context of a particular type of organization, and if a specific strategy for its introduction and implementation was available. There would also be a need for details regarding both the internal and the external environments of the organization.

The question, therefore, really is - Does HR work in this particular type of organization which happens to operate in this external and internal environment? Furthermore, how does it have to be introduced and implemented so that it has a greater chance of success?

In mechanistic structures, which are characterized by high level of control, human resource strategies are seen in these terms:

- *Management is directly responsible for planning and important decision making;*
- *Management directs people;*
- *Management is directly responsible for managing people;*
- *Management feels that generally it cannot trust employees with important decisions.*

In the other hand in organic structures, which are diffused structures, the management of human resource strategies is more open and are generally characterized in this way:

- *Management usually delegates important decisions to different employees within the organization;*
- *Employees are generally less passive and resistant, and more proactive and supportive of the organization;*
- *Employees are perceived to have the ability to achieve high performance.*

This implies that different types of organizations may be more apt or conducive to the success of modern HR strategies. It should also seem fairly safe to assume that there will be a better chance of success where the objective of their introduction is genuinely in the interest of the employees and not a cover-up for a management with a hidden agenda.

DOUBTS SURROUNDING THE HUMAN RESOURCE MOVEMENT

Needless to say HR and its policies have received their fair share of criticism. First one cannot deny that it has at least one thing in common with all the other theories of management - it is itself another 'Management's' theory of management. This means that although it purports to put employees' interests at par with those of the organization, in the end it is just another attempt by management to get *"more for less"*. Although Human Resource theorists argue that there is evidence that this strategy makes economic sense and that it may be the only weapon with which to confront the competitive challenge of globalization, one may still argue that the ultimate *'raison d'être'* of any organization is to leave a profit for its owners. The fear remains that HR is yet again another management ploy. One may thus argue that HR is an important strategy to create the relationships and environment required to give people the assurance that the organization has some interest in their personal growth and development.

This is done in the hope that employees' loyalty and commitment is won over. In this way it is another attempt by management to harness the ever-elusive element of employees' entrepreneurial spirit which is always reserved for their own private endeavors. One can argue that employees are entrepreneurs in their own right. They all manage their own affairs with imagination and creativity.

The adoption of HR strategies may also be essential and necessary if the organization is to be successful within the labor market. This becomes increasingly critical in situations where there is fierce competition for trained and skilled labor. Thus HR has been criticized as being mainly an internal human relations exercise and external public relations and recruitment strategy. The author concludes that like all other business strategies, it will only be feasible as long as it is affordable and it leaves an economic return to justify it. However, once this return is not so obvious and if hard times come about, owners will demand their pound of flesh and human resource directors will probably be the first to go.

Another conclusion by the author is that HR is trying to get away with adding on further responsibilities to employees without more compensation. The creed is that making employees responsible for the organization and the quality of their work improves their self-esteem and humanizes their job, thus enhancing their self-development and actualization. In turn, this will improve the quality of the product as this is now built-in rather then imposed by inspection.

Critics see this as a strategy to cut down on the company's payroll as it makes the traditional quality control departments obsolete. This has made the trend towards leaner organizations possible. But does it necessarily imply that employees feel more at ease and fulfilled? The evidence is not conclusive. Some cases have shown that the uncertainties caused by the continuous change of processes and organization restructuring have themselves lead to the development of a reign of terror and a feeling of doom amongst employees. Rather then producing employee commitment, it has been argued that HR strategies produce nothing more then a new silent compliance.

The harshest criticism to the Human Resource field has centered on the implications that these developments have had on the issue of industrial relations. One of the most central aspects of HR is to treat each employee as an individual, thus trying to focus on his/her individual potential and aspirations. Thus, this trend has reflected the wider social trends towards individualization and its negative facet – atomism. Critics see this trend away from collectivity as a deliberate management attempt at weakening the trade unions and labor representatives by dividing their ranks.

ALIGNING HR TO BUSINESS STRATEGY

In pursuit of meeting the real HR objectives – in the final analysis – it is important to ensure comprehensive and constant alignment to the overall business strategy of the organization. Several contributors, including Grundy (1998), Hall and Torrington (1998) and Hunt and Boxall (1998) have all led us to understand that good HR Management cannot be separated from the overall business strategy. Several strategy authors (see Mintzberg, 1994; Pedler et al., 1991; Senge, 1990) all propose that strategy cannot be differentiated from Human Resource Management.

Most managers today realize the importance of people in the achievement of organization strategy. In achieving this goal, the following steps are generally taken:

1. Managers define the organization strategy with other stakeholders within the organization;
2. The strategic objectives are then cascaded down to other employees within the organization;
3. Employees at different levels are given clear objectives which can be measured at all times to identify progress.

Torrington et al. (2005) argues that there are three theoretical approaches to strategic human resource management. Guest (1989) bases his model on four HR policy goals, namely strategic integration, commitment, flexibility, and quality. The basic theoretical construct proposed by Guest was that these four qualities are generally seen as one package. A later development of this fit was the Harvard framework for Human Resource Management which was produced by Beer et al. (1984).

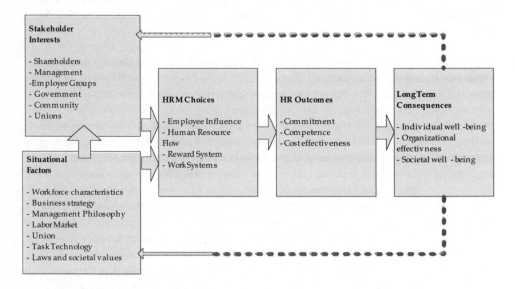

Diagram 6.3 Harvard model of HRM

Source: The Harvard Framework for Human Resource Management
Quoted from Torrington et al. (2005) from Beer, M., Spector, B., Lawrence, P.R., Quinn Mills, D., Walton, R.E., (1984) Managing Human Assets, New York: The Free Press

In addition to the above model, the 'Contingency Model' (also referred to as the 'Fit Model') is also another well-considered and documented approach toward aligning business strategy to the practice of human resource management. The earlier mentioned theoretical construct by Fombrun et al. (1984) proposes that all HR policies and activities fir together so that they make a coherent whole. The strength of this model is in the fact that the various HR systems including selection, appraisal and development as well as reward systems are integrated to produce the desired type of employee. This model has been criticized because of its dependence on a rational strategy formulation rather than on an emergent formation approach (Torrington, 2005, p. 37).

Finally, the 'Resource-based View of the Firm' produced by Boxall (1996) is mostly concerned with the relationships between internal resources, strategy and performance. This approach is based on the promotion of competitive advantage through the development of human resource development. This notion led to the new idea of human capital, whereby employees are considered as important resources in the whole production process.

The 'Economic Model of Human Capital' developed by Monks (1999) states that investment in human capital is dependent upon expectations of future rental rates of it. The greater the increase in expected returns to human capital, the greater the investment in human capital. Employers, fully or partially, fund the development of workers (development of human capital) in the hope of gaining a return in this investment in terms of a more productive, more competitive, and consequently more profitable firm in the future. In practice, however, it is still very difficult to measure this return. More knowledgeable workers receive higher wages which have to be paid out of productivity gains, and therefore provide a lower bound on the likely size of productivity increases. On the other hand, when training has a large firm-specific component and in case labor mobility is effectively restricted, there may be productivity gains from training that are not passed on to the employee in terms of wages, but are only reflected in direct measures of competitiveness, productivity and profitability (De Bono & Van der Heijden, 2007).

Exercise: Consider your own working career and the investment your employers have made in your development as a person and in your ability to do your job effectively. What has been their motivation? To make you more productive and valuable as an employee? To motivate you to work beyond the call of duty? To retain you and stop you leaving to go to another job? Do you think their efforts have been successful? How would you/do you feel about your own employees in this regard?

CONCLUSION

The management of people is a highly dynamic subject which is constantly changing and developing. Organizations are living organisms, so continuous development in the way people are managed across different boundaries and cultures will take place. Employees are individuals, who are actively or passively engaged in their own ideas, influenced and motivated by an array of internal and external factors. Here, we have looked at the evolution of thinking on people management, and how this has influenced the emergence of personnel and then HRM, and we have summarized some of the latest thinking on how HRM plays a part in the formulation of strategy by organizations. To what extent does HR drive strategy, or is it driven by it? This leads into our next chapters, on recruitment, training and development, and performance.

REFERENCES

Appleby, R.C. (1994) *Modern Business Administration.* 6th ed., London: FT/Pitman.
Beaumont, P. (1993) *Human Resource Management.* London: Sage.
Beer, M. et. al. (1984) *Reward Systems in Managing Human Assets.* New York: Free Press.

Daft, R.L. (2003) *Management*. 6th ed. Mason Ohio: Thomson/South Western.

Editorial (1990) *'Human Resource Perspective: An Agenda for the 1990s'*, International Journal of Human Resource Management, 1.

Editorial (1997) 'HRM-ism and the images of re-presentation', *Journal of Management Studies, 4:* 5

Fombrun, C., Tichy, N., Devanna, M (1984) *Strategic Human Resource Management*. New York: Wiley.

Guest, D. (1991) 'Personnel Management: the end of the orthodoxy', *British Journal of Industrial Relations*. Autumn

Guest, D. (1987) 'Human Resource Management and Industrial Relations', *Journal of Management Studies, 25:* 5

Handy, C. (1993) *Understanding Organization*. Harmondsworth: Penguin.

Hellriegel, D. & Slocum, J.W. (2004) *Organizational Behavior*, Mason, Ohio: Thomson/South Western.

Hendry, C. & Pettigrew, A. (1986) 'The Practice of Strategic Human Resource Management', *Personnel Review, 15*

Hunt, J. (1998) 'Are top human resource specialists 'strategic partners' ? Self-perceptions of a corporate elite', *International Journal of Human Resource Management, 2:5*

Keenoy, T. (1990) 'HRM: Rhetoric, Reality and Contradiction', *International Journal of Human Resource Management 1:* 3

Minztberg, H. (1994) 'The Fall and Rise of Strategic Planning', *Harvard Business Review*, February

Pedler, M., Borgonoyne, J., Boydell, T. (1991) *The Learning Company: A Strategy for sustainable development*, London: McGraw-Hill.

Poole. M. (1986) *Industrial Relations, Origins and Patterns of National Diversity*, London: Routledge.

Senge, P. (1990) T*he Fifth Discipline. The Art & Practice of the Learning Organization*, London: Random House.

Storey, J. (1989) 'Introduction: From Personnel Management to Human Resource' Management, in Storey, J. (ed.) *New Perspectives on Human Resource Management, London: Routledge.*

Schuler, R.S. & Jackson, S.E. (1987) *'Linking Competitive Strategies with Human Resource Management Practices',* Academy of Management Executive Journal.

Sisson, K. & Storey, J. (1993) *Human Resources and Industrial Relations*, Buckingham: Open University Press.

Torrington, D. et al (2005) from Beer, M., Spector, B., Lawrence, P.R., Quinn Mills, D., Walton, R.E., (1984) *Managing Human Assets,* New York: The Free Press.

Torrington, D. & Hall, L. (1998) *Human Resource Management,* London: Prentice Hall.

Torrington, D., Hall, L. & Taylor, S. (2005) *Human Resource Management*, 6th ed. London: Prentice Hall.

Towers, B., ed. (1992) 'Human Resource Management in the UK', in the *Handbook of Human Resource Management*, Oxford: Blackwell.

Walton, R.E. (1985) 'From Control to Commitment in the Workplace', *Harvard Business Review, 63.*

Walton, R.E. (1985) 'Towards a strategy of eliciting employee commitment based on principles of mutuality', in eds. Walton, R.E., Lawrence P.R., HRM *Trends and Challenges*, Boston: Harvard Business School Press.

RECOMMENDED FURTHER READING

Armstrong, M. (2003) *A Handbook of Human Resource Mangement Practice*, 8th Ed. London: Kogan Page.

Beer, M. & Spencer, B. (1985) *Human Resource Management: A General Manager's Perspective*, New York: Free Press.

Dessler, G. (2005) Human Resource Management. 10th ed., Upper Saddle River, New Jersey: Prentice Hall.

Flamholtz, E. G. (1985) *Human Resource Accounting*, San Francisco: Jossey-Bass.

Goss, D. (1994) *Principles of Human Resource Management*. London: Routledge.

Handy, C. (1993) *Understanding Organizations*. London: Penguin.

James M. (1999) *The Effect of Uncertain Returns on Human Capital Investment Patterns*, Unpublished Paper, Mount Holyoke College, USA.

Mayo, E. (1949) *The Social Problems of an Industrial Civilization*. London: Routledge.

Molander, C. & Winterton, J. (1994) *Managing Human Resources*. London: Routledge.

Noe, R.A. et. al. (2003) *Human Resource Management*. New York: McGraw Hill.

Peery, N.S. Jr, Salem, M. (1993) 'Strategic Management of Emerging Human Resource Issues', *Human Resource Development Quarterly, 4.1*, 81-95

Purcell , J. & Ahlstrand, B. (1994) *Human Resource Management in the Multi-Divisional Company*. Oxford: Oxford University Press.

Rousseau, D.M. (1995). *Psychological contracts in organizations: Understanding written and unwritten agreements*. London: Sage.

Towers P. (1995) *The People Strategy Benchmark Awareness and Attitude Study*, New York: Towers Perrin.

Van der Heijden, B.I.J.M. (1996) 'Life-long expertise development: the goal of the 1990s', *Proceedings of the 5th Conference on International HRM*, San Diego, USA

Van der Heijde, C.M., & Van der Heijden, B.I.J.M. (2006). 'A competence-based and multidimensional operationalization and measurement of employability', *Human Resource Management, 45:3*, 449-476.

CHAPTER 7

RECRUITING TALENT
SILVIO DE BONO

OPENING CASE:

Global Jewels is a small company dealing in the importation of costume jewelry from Africa and Sri Lanka into Italy. It was set up in the early 1990s as a family business venture. The original owner passed control of the company to his only daughter, a fashion designer with ambitions to put the company on the map – both nationally and possibly internationally. Her strategy as Managing Director is to merge her professional fashion design activity with that of the current business, marked under the brand name 'Star Bright'.

Global Jewels currently has five different outlets which are all positioned in strategic positions, mainly in shopping malls and airports. Each shop is run by a Senior Sales Person and an Assistant Sales Person. They are all answerable to the Sales Manager who in turn answers to the Managing Director who manages the business on a full-time basis. The Financial Controller assists the company on a part-time basis. The general profile of the Senior Sales Persons and the Assistant Sales Persons is as follows: five Senior Sales Persons have been employed with the company since its inception while the others have been employed over the past five years. There has only been one person who left the organization, for personal reasons. The average age is 25, with the oldest employee being 42 and the youngest one in her early 20's. All employees are females with a high flair for fashion and design.

Global Jewels has just acquired a new outlet in another strategic site. However, this outlet is so big that it requires at least four persons to run it. Financial projections show that this could be a very profitable outlet and consequently the recruitment processes needs to be carried out without further delay.

The Managing Director considered hiring the services of a Recruitment Consultant to carry out this recruitment process and get the right people on board. She has been advised that ideally some of the existing personnel could be re-deployed in the new outlet and she could recruit more people as Assistant Sales Persons to the other outlets.

Questions on the opening case: You are asked to carry out the recruitment process for this company. What are the primary factors which you need to consider prior to the recruitment process? Would you deploy some of the most experienced personnel to the new outlets? Would you deploy the new Sales Assistants to the same outlet? What are the immediate advantages and disadvantages of promoting some employees to take the more senior employees in the new outlet? Write a detailed job description and a job advert for the posts which you have identified (see below for more insights into advertisement writing). Prepare the criteria for short-listing and then interviewing (see below for more details).

LEARNING OBJECTIVES FOR THIS CHAPTER

Employee recruitment is a process starting from a thorough job analysis to identifying the exact requirements of the vacant post to actually making the offer and signing the contract. Throughout, managers will carry out a series of activities which may either help or hinder the effectiveness of the process. Although many different scholars and management experts have tried their best to set this process to objective measures, it is hard to measure the success of a recruitment effort until after the employee is recruited – and perhaps some time after.

By the end of this chapter you should be able to:

• Understand that the employee recruiting or resourcing process starts well before the vacant post has been announced;

• Identify the measures that are to be taken by any HR professional in conducting an effective recruitment and selection process;

• Develop practical measures in order to carry out effective recruitment and selection processes in your own workplace.

We start off with an outline of the recruitment process, and go on to try to understand the role of recruitment in organizational strategy. We then look at how recruiting is an ongoing challenge, and how we can master the phases of the recruitment process in detail. We consider practical and best practice approaches, especially as many organizations lose good people, time and money through ineffective recruiting. We look at checklists and guides on how we can keep improving our practical skills, backed up with theory and in-depth academic investigation. This includes particular emphasis on interviewing styles and criteria for selection.

INTRODUCING THE CHALLENGE OF RECRUITING TALENT

Employee recruitment or resourcing is one of the major responsibilities managers have to face in their organization . This exercise seems to be a very plain and straightforward event, but is one of the biggest headaches for many executives, and for HR and line managers. Recruitment and selection is a matching process between the organization requirements and the employee attributes and ambitions.

The variable requirements of the different jobs available in different sectors of industry and the variable capacities and dispositions of human beings pose a general problem of aligning people with jobs appropriate to their personalities and abilities, and that in turn poses problems for both parties, of measuring the differences on each side of the equation. The worker cannot always find a job with the characteristics that he or she demands or considers appropriate. Organizations, on the other hand, cannot always find people with the required skills, dispositions or attitudes considered to be necessary to sustain an efficient and 'stress-free' cooperative relationship.

In principle these problems can be reduced if both parties, individuals and industry, are dedicated to producing a more accurate fit between their several demands and offers. From the standpoint of industry, the need is one of either redesigning jobs to match the demands of people, or selecting people who match the demands of the jobs available. From the standpoint of the individual, the need is one of finding the employment which most closely accords with their abilities and taps into their motivations. In practice, this need is frequently not met (and some form and degree of strain or stress results) because the range of offers on one or both sides of the equation are inadequate to meet the demands made by the other.

RECRUITING TALENT AND ORGANIZATIONAL STRATEGY

Recruitment needs to be carried out in line with the overall strategic business of the organization. In carrying out effective recruitment and selection, managers are responsible to consider a number of internal factors including the structure, culture and overall vision of the organization In addition, managers are also required to look into other external factors including the market supply, demographic developments, diversity of employees as well as the skills and qualifications required for the job.

Torrington et al. (2005), state that one of the main strategic aspects of employee recruitment consists of considering the different levels of organizational flexibility in the current market. They argue that at face value one can look at four main types of flexibilities, namely: numerical flexibility which was primarily developed by Atkinson (1984), temporal flexibility, functional flexibility as well as financial flexibility.

Numerical flexibility (Atkinson, 1984) allows the organization to respond quickly to the environment in terms of the number of people employed. Today's organizations have an array of different contractual agreements with their employees which could vary from the traditional full time employment to part-time employment, from short-term fixed contract to permanent reduced-hour contracts, from outsourcing to sub-contracting. As one may consider, these different employment contractual arrangements enjoy different job security and benefits.

Temporal flexibility (Torrington, 2005) circles round the different patterns of hours worked in pursuit of responding to the business demands and to the employee needs. The realities of the labor market have changed across the globe and today's employees are actively seeking different working patterns in order to meet their social obligation to themselves, their loved ones and their community at large. In addition, the labor market all over the globe has been highly influenced by working mothers, who may wish to enter the labor market once again under reduced or flexible arrangements.

Functional flexibility generally looks into the employability factor of employees. It is a well-known international 'secret', that one of the main factors affecting employment is the employability factor, meaning the increasing potential of the employee for doing more than one job or a set of skills (see also Fugate, Kinicki & Ashforth, 2004; Van der Heijde & Van der Heijden, 2006). Several contributors in this field namely, Blyton (1988) and

Reilly (2001) have all pointed out that although at face value this is beneficial to the organization, some employees may still reject the idea.

Financial flexibility concerns the different payment arrangement the company is willing to make in order to attract and eventually to retain the best employees in the market. Over the years a number of salary arrangements have been developed ranging from fixed salary to payments based on commission(s), profit-sharing schemes and performance bonuses.

The debate on these flexible arrangements has been going on for quite some time. Managers generally have a positive attitude towards adopting flexible arrangements. Legge's (1995) assertion that flexibility is used in a pragmatic and opportunistic way rather than as a strategic HRM initiative seems to hold true today.

Notwithstanding this belief, different managers have considered various flexible arrangements as being advantageous in their drive to increase the organization's productivity. In different ways each type of flexibility arrangement aims to deploy employee time and effort more efficiently so that staff are only at work when they need to be and are wholly focused on achieving organizational objectives throughout that time (Torrington et al., 2005).

The introduction of flexibility may also bring about some disadvantages to the organization. Torrington et al. (2005) argues that as a result of flexibility there is expected to be higher rate of employee turnover and reduced employee commitment towards the organization. Sisson and Storey (2000) further claim that high levels of flexibility have a direct effect on organizational learning and as a result lead to loss of expertise. On a more serious level, Heerey and Salmon (2000) and Burchell (2002) argue that too much flexibility may have damaging economic consequences to the organization in terms of lack of continuity in customer relations and project handling.

Exercise: Discuss your organization's attitude to recruiting in the framework discussed above? To what extent can your organization respond to different employee needs in terms of flexibility of employment arrangements? To what extent is this common in your business environment? Do you encourage part-time working and is your organization able to accommodate returning mothers, for example? How about flexibility concerning job functions? And what about different financial arrangements? Are these driven by your company's attitude, or by the business context in which you work?

THE CONSTANT CHALLENGE OF RECRUITING

One of the most difficult questions manages have to answer is the amount of personnel required in the organization at a point in time. While on one hand, managers must ensure not to have extra human resources on the organization's payroll, on the other hand, they must also ensure to have enough human resources to meet production deadlines and/or service delivery. Macaler & Shannon (2003 p.189) point that the most common personnel planning approaches involve the use of simple techniques like ratio analysis or trend analysis.

Dessler (2005) defines three types of analysis which are generally actively considered by managers in recruitment processes. **Trend analysis** as a study of the firm's past employment needs over a period of years to predict future needs. **Ratio analysis** is a systematic technique used to determine the number of employees required in relation to a determinant factor such as sales. Scatter plot analysis is a graphical method used to help identify the relationships between two variables.

Today's managers have realized that the actual cost of recruitment is extremely high and as a result, it should be carried out professionally and diligently. The actual cost of recruitment is much higher than the direct costs incurred in the recruitment process. These costs start from the commencement date (if it is a new employee) or from the resignation date (in the case of an existing employee who is exiting), and continue irrespective of the gaps in productivity caused by holidays, training, sickness and other planned or unplanned absences.

In addition, there is the recruitment responsibility of getting it right. A hired employee who leaves for whatever reason after a few months inevitably escalates the overall costs to the company.

In view of these difficulties, managers generally consider an array of possible short-term solutions prior to actual recruitment, including amongst others:

a   Overtime possibilities;
b   Promotion possibilities;
c   Development of staff to new positions;
d   Temporary employees;
e   Re-organization;
f   Introduction of shift working;
g   Job sharing;
h   Flexible working hours;
i   Introduction of sub-contractors; and
j   Outsourcing parts of the job.

Sonnerfield et al. (2002) propose a model which relates entry and exit of staff with promotion and development in the organization (see Figure 7.1 on the opposite page).

On the Supply Flow Axis, i.e. the vertical axis of this model, it is proposed that strategically, organizations that focus on internal supply tend to see people as assets with long-term development value, rather than as costs in terms of annual expenditure. Managers favoring this approach would generally look into the development of employees and consequently look at possibilities of how to promote the employees once the right opportunities arise within the organization. The other axis, i.e. the horizontal axis, is labeled as the Assignment flow, which describes the basis on which individuals are assigned new tasks in the organization. The criteria for allocation may be in terms of individual contribution to organizational performance, or on group contribution. Organizations that emphasize individual contribution expect individuals to provide value on a continuous basis, whereas those that emphasize group contribution see employees as having intrinsic value (Torrington et al., 2005, p. 95).

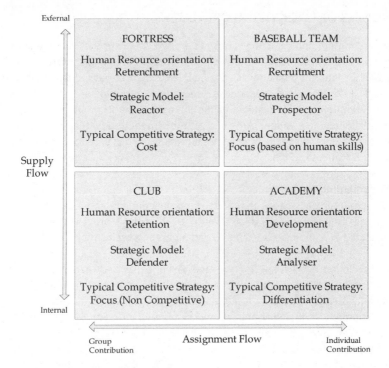

Figure 7.1 A Typology of career systems

Source: (A Typology of Career Systems) Adopted from: Sonnenfield et al (1992) Strategic determinants of managerial labour markets. Human Resource Management, Vol 27, No.4, © 1992 John Wiley and Sons Inc.

The model proposed describes the combination of these two aspects of recruitment – namely, Supply Flow and Assignment Flow – and results in four typical career systems namely:

1. **Fortress** which are characterized with survival and cannot afford to be concerned with individuals in terms of either reward or promotion.
2. **Baseball Team** which uses the external labor sources at all levels to seek higher contribution. There is an emphasis on outside recruitment
3. **Academy** which emphasizes the individual contribution in terms of reward and promotion where many employees remain until retirement.
4. **Club** which puts emphasis on the internal market where promotion is based on loyalty, length of service rather than individual contribution.

Exercise: considering this model, where would you place your organization? Is the Academy model appropriate to describe our company, where people stay for a long time because they are recognized? How about the Club approach, but do the best people get the top jobs? Or is your company more influenced by hiring stars, and getting them from wherever they need to find them? Or, if you consider the matter in terms of the company's current prospects and outlook for the future, does it have a fortress mentality? You may compare a number of companies you know well.

THE PROCESS OF EFFECTIVE RECRUITMENT

Effective recruitment and selection is based on a systematic process Once a decision has been taken that recruitment of new personnel is necessary in order to meet the organization targets, the manager is responsible to ensure that the job is well analyzed and defined. In doing so the manager is generally required to carry out a thorough job analysis to identify the main aspects of the job as well as to be able to determine the personal attributes (knowledge, skills and attitudes) required by the new job holder. Job descriptions and person specifications are still widely used in practice (Brannick & Levine 2002; Pearn & Kandola, 1988).

Step 1 Documenting the job

Effective recruitment envisages that a clear job desctiptions and a person specification are developed. This is generally done through a job analysis process the result of which is also reflected in a good job description and a person specification.

The **job description** gives a summary of the tasks, skills and responsibilities of a job. These can only be realistic if one analyzes the results of an overall job evaluation exercise. This is usually carried out either throughout the entire workforce, or else for a single job within the company. In this way, the job descriptions of all posts can be amended when the tasks of a job change. As a line manager you would already have a good idea of the tasks of the job to be evaluated, but you now have to know everything about the job to make a successful recruitment. This will mean discussion with the total local line supervisor, a visit to the place of work and probably a chat with the person performing the job function. Scientifically the job can be evaluated through a proper Job Evaluation exercise. The Job Description can be useful in many spheres in the personnel area. Two important uses pertain to the evaluation of different jobs in a grading exercise and as background information for pay negotiations. It can also contribute to training and manpower scheduling. During recruitment the job description can be used:

- For drawing up a person specification;
- As a reference aid when writing a staff vacancy advertisement;
- As part of an information pack to send to prospective employees;
- As a ready reference for an interviewer or panel member.

Person specifications define qualifications, experience and personal qualities required by the job holder and any other necessary information on special demands made by the job, such as physical conditions, unusual hours, or travel away from home. The information on qualifications, experience and qualities should be derived from an analysis of the knowledge and skills needed to carry out the job. The biggest danger to be avoided at this stage is that of overstating the qualifications required. Perhaps it is natural to go for the best, but setting an unrealistically high level for candidate requirements increases the problems of attracting applicants, and results in dissatisfaction among recruits when they find their talents are not being used. There may also be unrealistic demands on the pay for the position if the qualifications are set very high.

Step 2 Designing a job advert

Irrespective whether the job will be advertised internally or externally, a good job advert is always necessary. Although there are no hard and fast rules as how to design job adverts, good practices demands that any person responsible in designing the advert should take the following steps into account.

1. Give a clear description of the company and why recruitment is necessary. This geneally avoids unwarranted surprises and helps in enhancing good company image. As much as possible, avoid box item advertising. It will severely reduce the response which could mean losing some of the most promising applicants. It implies that the advertiser has something to hide.

2. Give a brief but clear description of the job and the competencies you are looking for. Be concise, factual and describe the functions of the position realistically. Do not be vague and do not romanticize the job or try to be clever, conveying little or nothing about the job. Otherwise you will invite a large response from a wide audience, and you will find yourself with extra work during pre-selection.

3. State the salary to be paid (if possible). Don't use the word 'negotiable'. This can promote a bad image of a firm keen to get the best from offering the least. If you are uncertain of the salary (which you shouldn't be) don't mention it at all.

4. Be careful you do not inadvertently use discriminatory sentences in any part of the advertisement. The text should be worded so that there is no doubt that the job applies to people of all racial backgrounds and both sexes.

5. Make it clear how the interested applicant should apply for the job and whether he/she should send a résumé. Give a person's name for applicants to contact; this puts each application on a personal level and encourages the applicant to feel he/she is communicating with a person and not a title.

Generally speaking, there are two main types of advertising namely, press advertising and e-advertising.

(a)**Press advertising** is probably one of the most sought-after methods since it reaches a wide range of audience within a relatively short period of time with relatively low costs. The time spent in drawing up and the subsequent cost of publishing the advertisement will depend on the type and level of the job to be offered. For a senior position it is almost as important to promote the company image as it is to describe the job function and a double column display will provide ample space for this. For a junior or general post in the organization a few lines in the classified section may be sufficient.

(b) **e- advertising** has become more and more popular , and has become a must for many organizations. In recruiting, companies do not only advertise vacancies on their own company web-site, but also use third-party job boards. This is a relatively cheap way of advertising, and Frankland (2000) claims that the total cost of setting the company's web-site may be equivalent to the cost of placing a recruitment advertisement in a printed newspaper.

In addition to advertising as described above, specialized recruitment consultants and executive searches are also considered as two important methods for recruitment of candidates.

(c) Recruitment consultants are specialized organizations who will take over virtually all your recruitment chores. They will design and draw up advertisements, place them in suitable publications and handle the recruitment selection down to a shortlist of between 6 and 15 suitable candidates. But you should still be aware of the criteria, especially that the consultants are representing the job and the organization fairly.

(d) Executive search is a special type of consultancy which concentrates on tacking down and recruiting very high caliber executives and high flyers. Often known as headhunters, they are sometimes accused of poaching employees from other companies, but in reality they can be highly efficient in targeting the most relevant employees for a particular position, especially one which is very specialized or quite senior. The use of executive search is also significant in making a strategic search in an objective and transparent fashion.

Exercise: collect a series of job advertisements from your local paper, web-sites and specialist journals, considering a variety of media. Critique these advertisements according to the steps and suggestions outlined above. What is the most common weakness of these ads? What are their strengths? Return to the ad you prepared in the opening exercise and analyze how you could improve your work. Have you ever applied to a job ad? What was attractive about it for you?

INTERNAL RECRUITMENT

Filling a vacancy from within the company either by promotion or lateral transfer is convenient and cost-effective. Even if further training is needed it is a more efficient method than starting to recruit 'cold' from outside the organization. There are a few ways of achieving this:

- By setting up good ongoing communication between departmental managers and supervisors;
- By issuing an internal memo from a section head to other departments announcing an expected vacancy;
- By creating a regular spot in the organization's newsletter or news sheet; and
- By making a section on the main internal notice board and any other departmental display areas.

Although internal recruitment carries along a number of advantages, over external recruitment its process and method of selection is said to be more difficult. Any person who had some working experience can recall that many internal employees who apply for an internal promotion feel that they have the right competencies and the correct attitude for the job. Since generally only one employee is selected, this will often lead to serious problems with the organization. When an applicant is not selected, there can be a decline in performance, cynicism and lower standards of ethical attitudes, which overall reflect in lower levels of organizational citizenship behavior towards the organization.

Step 3 Pre-selection of candidates

Some inexperienced managers, carrying out recruitment for the first time, may think that following the day the advertisement has appeared, there is only a short time before they will make the appointment. Generally, the panic of realizing that a new person is required within the organization means that he or she is needed within the shortest time possible. Yet it is essential that the recruitment process is carried out with highest quality standards since this reflects the cultural values of the organization, and this takes time. The process may take from one month to three months, depending on the seniority of the hire, and candidates coming from the outside will often have to be served within a promised period of time as well.

Step 4 The interview

An interview, like all selection devices, must measure important knowledge, skills and abilities as discovered in the job analysis you previously performed. A structured interview process, designed to assess past behaviors and accomplishments, can be most accurate and reliable.

Managers carrying out interviews for the first time may think that they will get all information required through the interview. This is generally not the case since interviews are structured to test knowledge and attitude, whilst skills can be tested through other means such as skills tests (discussed above). The main 'raison d'etre' of the interview can be summarized as follows:

- To collect information about the job applicants which could not have been identified from the résumé or the job application;
- To assess the suitability of the candidate in relation to the particular position;
- To place the candidates in order of merit in accordance to the criteria which have been set for this position.

Center your questions on some well-defined important knowledge, which is needed to perform the most important duties. If you ask candidates to indicate how and in what way they perform duties that require the knowledge you want to assess, you may also be able to find out about the person's abilities. Ask all candidates the same five to fifteen questions. Follow each of these with follow up questions designed to find out the person's level of knowledge and ability. Dwell on a few questions rather than ask a lot of questions finding out very little. You will find that you will understand the capabilities of a candidate better by finding out a lot about their experience in relation to one or two projects they worked on which are closely associated with the work you will assign.

By the time job applicants reach the selection interview, they have already passed a careful evaluation of their education and experience and are considered to possess at least minimum qualifications for the particular job. The purpose of the interview is to collect additional information on the applicants' job-related skills, knowledge, and abilities, which should be helpful in selecting the individual best qualified for the position. Your goal as the interviewer is to assist each candidate in effectively presenting all pertinent information concerning his or her qualifications.

An interview should be as structured as possible, yet tailored to each particular applicant. As an interviewer, you should evaluate the same general criteria for each applicant and ask each applicant the same set of core questions. An interview that follows a general standard outline will produce more reliable and valid information for selection than an unstructured interview, will allow for valid comparisons among applicants, and is less likely to run afoul of laws and regulations governing the selection process.

1. **Create a relaxed interview setting.** In a job interview, the applicant's apprehensiveness can impede the flow of useful information. The interview setting should be quiet, comfortable, and free from distractions and interruptions. Ask that all phone calls be intercepted. Keep on schedule, as candidates become anxious when asked to wait.
2. **Welcome the candidate.** Research has shown that rapport between the interviewer and the applicant contributes substantially to the effectiveness of the interview. A friendly greeting and a suitable introduction will help establish rapport and create a pleasant atmosphere. If a selection committee is present, introduce the candidate to the rest of the committee. Give the candidate an update on the status of the recruitment, e.g. how many candidates are being interviewed and the expected time frame for filling the position. Tell the candidate what the interview is meant to accomplish and let him or her know what the agenda will be for the interview. Briefly define the job responsibilities.
3. **Let the candidate do the talking.** It is extremely important to listen and concentrate on what the applicant is saying. The applicant should carry 80 to 85 percent of the total conversation. Your input should be limited to asking your prepared questions, probing deeper and asking follow-up questions as needed, and keeping the applicant talking and on track. Allow silence after asking a question so that you don't interrupt the candidate's thinking process. Use facial expressions (i.e. smiling), eye contact, and gestures (i.e. nodding) to assure the candidate that you are interested and listening to what he or she has to say.

   Note taking can be helpful, especially if you have several interviews scheduled, and it helps ensure accuracy. Explain to the candidate ahead of time that you will be taking notes so that you will not have to rely on memory. Make your notes brief by writing down only key words and phrases. Be sure to maintain some eye contact while you are writing. It may be helpful to develop a rating guide before the interview for taking notes.
4. **Close on a proper note.** After you have explored all performance factors, ask the candidate if he or she has any questions, needs clarification, or has anything to add. Well-prepared candidates will want to ask relevant questions about the job. You may also want to introduce the candidate to others in the office and/or give a tour of the work setting. Thank the candidate for coming and explain your notification process - when a decision will be made, whether a second interview will be conducted, and how candidates will be notified.

EFFECTIVE QUESTIONING TECHNIQUES

Well-crafted questions can assist employees in digging deeper for more thoughtful responses. They can allow employees to reflect on their own thought processes and to develop the ability to clearly articulate their thinking. Skillful questioning leads employees to make their own discoveries, create their own learning. If you don't do this already, spend some time anticipating the kinds of questions you want to raise during a discussion and the kinds of questions employees are likely to raise. Think through how you want to respond to these questions and have several illustrative examples ready to explain and enhance more difficult material.

- Give candidates 'thinking time' or 'waiting time' after asking a question.
- Move from simple questions to those that require thought.
- Ask only one question at a time.
- Make sure that you know the exact kind of answer you are looking for in response to your question(s). Probe to make sure you get it.
- Make sure that the candidate heard and understood the question.
- In a panel interview, don't let a few interviewers dominate a discussion.

Step 5 Making the offer

The last step in the whole process is to make the offer. This is done without having any guarantees that the person selected will accept the post. In order to avoid disappointment at the end of the process, the proposed salary and benefits of the post will have been discussed with the candidate during the interview or interviews. The successful applicant's availability may also be known and a provisional start date agreed. However, these facts have only been mentioned verbally and it is necessary to set them down in writing so that the candidate and the company fully understand the terms of employment. This is usually done in a letter offering the job. The letter should contain:

- The offer of the job stating the job title;
- The salary to be paid;
- The conditions of employment pertaining to the job;
- Any probationary period to be worked;
- Any restrictive conditions that apply;
- The reply slip;
- Other contract terms.

Exercise: Consider the process by which you joined your current organization, whether or not you responded to an advertisement or were sourced from another recruitment aid, such as a recruitment agency. In what way was the process managed efficiently and professionally? How could it have been improved? Have you ever changed your mind about a job offer because you felt that the company did not present itself well in trying to recruit you? Do you think that your company could be more pro-active in recruitment, or does it assume that the best people will come along? Are they aware of their image in the market?

THE COST OF RECRUITMENT

The overall cost of recruitment is one of the most expensive 'unwanted' costs that organizations face, usually unplanned in their annual budget. The overall cost of the recruitment process is generally composed from the actual direct costs as well as other indirect costs which have been an integral part of the whole process as the following table (see Table 7.1) shows:

Table 7.1 The cost of recruitment

Cost of advert	Writing Design Publishing	XXXXX XXXXX XXXXX
Employment termination Period		XXXXX
Induction Training	Direct Expense Trainer in terms of hours Recruited employee	XXXXX XXXXX XXXXX
On- the-Job Training	Direct Expense Trainer in terms of hours Recruited employee	XXXXX XXXXX XXXXX
Induction Period	(Executive - Manager 6 months to 1 Year) or (Supervisors 3 months to 6 mnths) or (Others 1 month to 3 mnths)	XXXXXX
Personnel	Preparation (in terms of hours) Interviewing (in terms of hours) Selection (in terms of hours)	XXXXXX XXXXXX XXXXXX
Sub total of recruitment **10 % Contingency**		XXXXXX
Total Cost of Recruitment		XXXXX

In addition to the direct costs mentioned above, managers may also consider other costs including transportation, accommodation costs amongst others.

CONCLUSION

No wonder recruiting is one of the biggest headaches to all managers. The lengthy process of looking to find the right candidate, whether within the organization or from external sources has always posed difficulties, concerns and doubts whether the selected person would ultimately fit with the role and whether this person would perform to the required standards. Here we have looked at attitudes to recruitment, sources of talent, and steps for getting that talent on board. If we accept that human assets are one of the most important pluses of our company, are we really doing the utmost to attract it? And do we really appreciate the costs of getting it wrong?

This review of recruitment implies that although every effort could have been made and correct steps could have been taken to ensure that the right person has been selected, you can only get to know the result a few weeks, at times a few months, following the actual signing of the contract. Selecting the wrong person means that you have to repeat the process, undertaking more time and expense, and having created more problems in the meantime. With a senior person, and with an expatriate, there are even more issues to consider. Obviously, it is one of the most important jobs as well as one of the biggest headaches in HRM.

REFERENCES

Atkinson, J. (1984) 'Manpower strategies for flexible organizations', *Personnel Management*, August.

Brannick, M.T., & Levine, E. L. (2002) *Job Analysis: Methods, research and application for human resource management in the new millennium*. California: Sage.

Blyton, P. (1998) 'Flexibility', in M. Poole and M.Warner (eds.) *The IEBM Handbook of Human Resource Management*. London: Thomson.

Burchell, B., Lapido, D., & Wilkinson, F. (2002) *Job Insecurity and Work Intensificiation*, Routledge, London.

Dessler, G. (2005) *Human Resource Management*, International Edition, Prentice Hall, New Jersey.

Frankland, G. (2002) 'If you built it they will come'. *People Management,* March.

Fugate, M., Kinicki, A.J., & Ashforth, B.E. (2004). Employability A psycho-social construct, its dimensions, and applications. *Journal of Vocational Behavior, 65*, 14-38.

Heerey, E., & Salmon, J. (eds.) (2000). *The Insecure Workforce*. London: Routledge.

Legge, K. (1995) *Human Resource Management: Rhetorics and Realities,* Basingstoke: Macmillan.

Macaler, B., & Shannon, J. (2003) "Does HR Planning Improve Business Performance" Industrial Management, January/February 2003.

Pearn, M. & Kandola, R. (1988) 'Job Analysis: A Practical Guide for Managers', *Institute for Personnel Management.* London: IPM.

Reilly, P. (2001) *Flexibility at Work: Balancing the interest of the employer and employee.* Aldershot: Gower.

Salaman, G. et al. (eds.) *Human Resource Management*. London: Sage.

Sisson, K., & Storey, J. (2000) *The Realities of Human Resource Management: managing the employment relationship.* Buckingham: Open University.

Sonnerfield, J.A. et al (2001) 'Strategic determinants of managerial labour markets', in Torrington, D., Hall, L., & Taylor, S. (2005) *Human Resource Management*, 6th Ed., Prentice Hall, Essex.

Van der Heijde, C.M., & Van der Heijden, B.I.J.M. (2006). A competence-based and multi-dimensional operationalization and measurement of employability. *Human Resource Management*, 45, 449-476.

RECOMMENDED FURTHER READING

Anderson, N. & Shackleton, V. (1990) 'Staff selection decision making into the 1990s', *Management Decision, 28*: 1

Barber, A.E. (1998) *Recruiting Employees: Individual and Organizational Perspectives.* Thousands Oaks, CA: Sage.

Bartol, K.M. (1981) Vocational behavior and career development, *Journal of Vocational Behavior, 19*

Boyatiz, R. (1982) *The Competent Manager.* London: Wiley.

Carrington, L. (2002) 'At the cutting edge' *People Management, 8*:10

Commons. M.L., Sinnott, J., Richards, F.A., & Armon, C. (eds.) (1986) *Beyond Formal Operations: comparisons and applications of adolescent and adult developmental models.* New York: Praeger.

Davidson, M. (1987) 'Women in Employment', in P.B.Warr (ed.), *Psychology at Work*, Pengiun, Harmondsworth.

Dickens, L., Jones. M., Weekes, B. & Hant, M. (1985) *Dismissed: A Study of Unfair Dismissal and the Industrial Tribunal System.* Oxford: Blackwell.

Judkins, P., West, D. & Drew, J. (1985) *Networking in Organizations.* Aldershot: Gower.

Kanter, R.M. (1989) *When Giants Learn to Dance.* New York: Simon and Schuster.

Lewis, C. (1985) *Employee Selection.* London: Hutchinson.

Plumbey, P.R. (1985) *Recruitment and Selection.* 4th Ed, London: IPM.

Rojot, J. (2001) 'Security of employment and employability' in R. Blancpain and C. Engels (eds) *Comparative Labour Law and Industrial Relations in Industrialised Market Economies.* The Hague: Kluwer.

Schein, E. (1978) *Career Dynamics.* Reading, Mass: Addison-Wesley.

Taylor, S. (2002) *People Resourcing.* London: CIPD.

Townley, B. (1991) 'Selection and appraisal; reconstructing social relationships?', in J. Storey (ed.) New Perspectives in *Human Resource Management.* London: Routledge.

Whiddet, S. & Kandola, B. (2000)'Fit for the job?' *People Management*, May

Wood, S. (1986) Personnel Management and Recruitment, *Personnel Review*, 15.

Wright, M. & Storey, J. (1994) 'Recruitment' in I. Beardwell & L. Holden (eds) *Human Resource Management.* London: Pitman.

CHAPTER 8

TRAINING AND DEVELOPMENT
SILVIO DE BONO

OPENING CASE:

Euro Micro Limited is a middle-sized manufacturing company based in Europe. Its main business is the manufacturing of micro chips for the IT industry. Over the past years the organization has developed from a modest family business to a mid-sized company, with high profile investors buying shares. Euro Micro Limited has recently made some very good deals with various other European and Middle East companies, and is set for expansion.

During the last few months, Euro Micro Limited has undergone some important restructuring, and a new Human Resources Department has been formed, with an effort to establish proper HR functions. As a result, the new HR Manager is developing HR policies and is consulting employees to ensure that these new policies would not only reflect good HR practices but also will be designed in line with the current HR Culture. This is generally appreciated by the other managers, who have been employed with the organization since its inception some ten years ago.

During these past years, the company has been training its personnel. Over 120 employees are directly working in manufacturing, and another 45 in other supporting functions. The training has been designed to help them carry out their technical jobs effectively and efficiently. Although no training policy has ever been written, the Company has developed a range of training activities, and some employees have enrolled in Bachelor Degrees in different subjects. A number of MBA Degree courses have attracted members of its managerial cluster.

One day, the new HR Manager receives a note from one of the secretaries working in the Sales Department, which is currently undergoing heavy re-structuring to meet the new deadlines, asking to attend a ten-week development program in a foreign country. In her letter the employee explains that she has been studying Ballet for the past twelve years and has been awarded a 50% paid scholarship from her School to attend this Ballet Symposium. She asks for a ten-week paid leave and possibly a scholarship token to pay for her lessons while attending this symposium. In receiving this letter, the Senior HR Manager looks into her file and finds that she is one of the most diligent employees. She joined the company as a Junior Clerk and has managed to climb the ladder over the years. While in employment she also has successfully completed a Degree Course in Customer Management, and her Manager has nominated her to take the new post of Assistant Manager in the Customer Care Department.

During the same week, the HR Manager receives another request from the Assistant Accountant working in the Finance Department. The employee is asking for company sponsorship to pursue a four-year evening course to obtain an Accounting Qualification which would make him a Professional Accountant. Upon receiving this request, the Senior HR Manager looks into his file and notices that the employee has only been employed for a few months and he is still in his probation period. He asks his immediate Manager for an urgent appraisal which shows that the employee is not an excellent performer, despite a promising interview. However, his Manager points out that his performance has shown some signs of improvement and he is sure that he will make a very good Accountant within a few years time.

The HR Manager has to make some very important decisions here. He is aware that his present training budget has already been exhausted for this year but on the other hand recognizes that he cannot ignore these requests. Being a rather new Senior Employee he calls in the Production Manager, who has been in the organization since its inception and the Sales Manager, who has been employed for the last ten years. These two Senior Managers used to make similar decision in the past, before the HR Manager was appointed.

Questions on the opening case: In view that there is a limited budget which would only accommodate one request for this year, whom would you propose to be given the training and development grant?

a   *Would you prefer to give the training and development grant to the Secretary who is about to be promoted to the post of Assistant Manager? Her development course is not related to company needs and her scholarship would mean that she would be absent for a very important ten weeks.*

b   *Would you prefer to give the training and development grant to the Assistant Accountant who would be pursuing the course in the evenings with very little disruption to his work? This Assistant Accountant is still in his probation period and his full employment status is still not confirmed.*

Explain the reasons in detail to support your choice. In particular, think about the differences between training and development. What is the impact on the person concerned? Relate this case to your own experience – to what extent has your company supported your own training and development? Clearly differentiate between the two interventions, and consider the impact on Return on Investment for the company, and for you.

LEARNING OBJECTIVES FOR THIS CHAPTER

Almost any book which deals with HRD will at some point warn the reader that training and development are not a 'panacea' or cure-all for all HR-related problems. It seems to be a common mistake among the less experienced HR practitioners to regard HR and training and development as synonymous. Clearly, there are different levels of training which correspond to different needs of the organization. Using a training budget wisely and well for maximum effectiveness is a major HR challenge.

By the end of this chapter students should be able to:

- Understand that the training function is a crucial element in the overall human resource management and development function;

- Appreciate that a professional approach to training is based on a well thought-out application of the training cycle;

- Identify how training and development stimulates employees and motivates behaviors towards higher level of performance.

In this chapter, we will look at how to develop a training cycle, how to differentiate between training and development and to understand how they can be applied, and the strategic implications of creating a training and development policy. How can we design and deliver a training event, based on training needs analysis? And how can we evaluate the results? What are the costs involved in providing a training service for employees?

Introduction to training and development The training function is probably one of the most specialized with an HR department, demanding an almost impossible combination of not only knowledge, skill and foresight but also sensitivity and 'political' awareness from the HR practitioner. This is not only because training can be very costly in financial terms but also because training and development raises hopes and fears amongst participants, who are ambitious and seeking opportunities, but who at times feel threatened by training. If the training is not what they expected they can be disillusioned, and there can be conflicts between those who consider themselves deserving of more training and development, but who may not receive it (Mabey & Salaman, 1995).

This means that a mistaken approach to training, or an insensitivity to these aspects may not only cause financial losses and waste, but can leave people de-motivated and can tarnish relationships within the organization. This will inevitably have a spill-over effect in many other HR aspects and future interventions.

So rather than regarding training as a one-off event or a stop-gap solution to individual problems, it should be tackled from a 'holistic' perspective primarily aimed at organizational objectives. Training therefore should be a continuous process or cycle whereby organizational objectives are constantly reviewed and the implications for skills and training needs assessed and acted upon.

The training cycle below (see Figure 8.1.) indicates clearly the major steps which are involved in ensuring that training forms part of the organizational objectives, and helps ensure that any formal training given to employees is targeted at overcoming performance problems. When the training cycle is adequately followed, training is no longer looked upon as a cost but starts to be seen as an investment, as trainees and the managers will start to appreciate the value of the results.

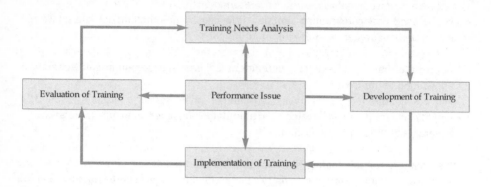

Diagram 8.1 The training cycle

Theoretically speaking ,goals can only be identified if the organization's management has set clear performance objectives. As we have seen in previous chapters, there has been a growing recognition of the importance of linking training and development, and consequently the practice of HRM, to the strategic intent of an organization. Ideally, the human resource function has changed its role from being peripheral or incidental to the organization, to one which is central and vital to corporate planning (Molander & Winterton, 1994).

Definitions

Several authors have given an array of definitions on training, development and learning. The average person would probably not make any clear difference between these different aspects of personal growth, but **training** is generally defined as a planned and systematic effort to modify or develop knowledge, skill and attitude through learning experience. Training is generally very specific and is aimed towards achieving an effective performance in an activity or range of activities. Its purpose in the work situation is to enable an individual acquire a series of competencies to adequately perform a given task at a desired level. (Molander & Winterton, 1994).

Learning or development at the individual level is often defined as being a process whereby individuals acquire knowledge, skills and attitudes through experience, reflection study or instruction. (Molander & Winterton, 1994).

Training is:
       Planned by others;
       Planned for others;
       Planned for a specific reason.
Development is:
       Planned by self;
       Planned for self;
       Planned for more generic reasons.

Taking into account these broad definitions, training can be seen as a systematic modification of behavior through learning, which occurs as a result of education, instruction, development and planned experience. The fundamental aim of training is to help the organization achieve its purpose by adding value to its key resource – the people it employs. Training basically means investing in people to enable them to perform better and to empower them to make the best use of their natural abilities.

The particular **objectives of training** are to:
- Develop the competencies of employees and improve their performance;
- Help people grow within the organization;
- Reduce the learning time for employees starting in new jobs and ensure that they become fully competent as quickly as possible.

Effective training can:
- Minimize learning costs;
- Improve individual, team and corporate performance in terms of output, quality, speed and overall productivity;
- Improve operational flexibility by extending the range of skills possessed by employees (multi-skilling);
- Attract high quality employees;
- Increase the commitment of employees by encouraging them to identify with the mission and objectives of the organization;
- Help to manage change by increasing understanding;
- Help to develop a positive culture in the organization;
- Provide higher levels of service to customers.

Exercise: How is training viewed in your own organization? Is training and development clearly differentiated? Is there an established training cycle? How many training days do most employees receive? Is training related to the overall goals of the organization? Does it reinforce the culture? Is it geared towards different levels of trainees, their functional specialisms, and their individual needs? Reflect on your own experiences of training in the companies where you have worked.

A STRATEGIC APPROACH TO TRAINING: CREATING A TRAINING POLICY

A training strategy should take a long-term view of what skills, knowledge and levels of competence employees of the company need. The company's training philosophy should emphasize that training and development should be an integral part of the management process. Performance management leads to performance development plans and learning agreements or contracts between manager and employee. Basically, in an ideal situation, the training plans of an organization are fully integrated into all its activities.

Since training is undertaken primarily to train, educate, and develop individuals to ensure that they are capable of helping the organization achieve its goals, the people responsible for training within an organization must be aware of the plans of the organization. Training cannot be expected to respond to the needs of the organization if it does not know what these needs are. Like every other business function, training exists to support business strategies. In order to achieve this, training must have a strategy of its own that is developed keeping the organizational needs in mind. The goals of the training department should therefore reflect the corporate strategy, mission, and goals.

In order to be effective, a training strategy must take into account any factors that have an impact on the organization. Such factors include management and supervisory style, the organizational culture, the working environment, the nature of the work, the market place, the size of the training department, and the quality of trainers, as well as the training budget. Therefore, it is important for those responsible for training within the organization to be able to read the signals, and assess what can and cannot be done, given the situation.

The training strategy should, therefore, outline the overall approach to learning adopted by the organization, hence the necessity of understanding the organizational culture. The training strategy should have a clear and defined purpose, so that management and employees alike know what to expect from it. All aspects of training must be taken into account in the training strategy, and therefore, the strategy should not be discarded once training has been carried out (Robinson, 1988).

An organization's training strategy should revolve around three main factors, namely:
- Establishing a training policy;
- Implementing the training policy;
- Achieving the organization's goals.

The training policy spells out the focus of training within the organization. It is the means of communicating to all members of the organization exactly what the organization is prepared to do to develop employee potential. For the training policy to be of any use at all, all members of the organization, from top management to all employees, must accept it.

Effective training is generally communicated to all members within the organization Robinson (1988). A well communicated training policy is like a well oiled-engine, whereby all parts working together optimizes performance. On an organization perspective, employees with higher commitment to training increases their personal and organizational potential

The training policy should not be static; rather, when drawing it up, the people responsible should understand that any factors affecting training so far are likely to change in the future Boydell, T. & Leary, M. (1996). Hence, training policies are to be monitored on regular basis to ensure congruency with business environment. When changes are necessary, all stakeholders are to be equally informed about developments.

THE IMPORTANCE AND BENEFITS OF TRAINING AND DEVELOPMENT

Training is expensive and generally involves hefty sums of money. As yet the result is not always so immediate. In order to ensure effectiveness, all stakeholders are encouraged to pull the same rope, at the same time and in the same direction. Unfortunately, there still prevails the view that this is a waste of valuable time and money. This is mainly because the benefits of training are not viewed in the short-term. Unlike other investment opportunities, there is no immediate and calculable financial gain.

Training success very often depends on perceptions of top management. Management teams with positive attitude towards training are more inclined to invest in training than other management team with a less positive attitude. Furthermore, since top management is the main installer of the organizational culture, if it is skeptical about training, it is highly likely that all other members will adopt the same attitude.

On the other hand, line management view training negatively mainly because this means the absence of the employees involved from the workplace. But the co-operation of line management is also important for training, as they have direct contact with the employees' everyday work performance, and they are most likely to be the ones who identify any obvious indications of training needs. Indeed, the people responsible for training should liaise closely with the line managers all throughout the process.

"The management of that part of the organization must be involved at all stages and be committed to changing organizational structures or practices which conflict with the new practices which are being introduced. In almost every case this will imply that the managers are involved in the design and delivery of the training. They will be responsible for encouraging the new behaviors in the workplace by appraising performance and coaching or supervising as necessary to ensure that the learning becomes incorporated in standard work practices."

(Bramley, 1993, p. 6-7)

Finally, without the co-operation of the employees themselves, training would be a waste of time. If they don't have the will or the interest to undergo training then it will all be in vain. The organization can send employees to training courses, but they cannot make them want to learn. Employees are sometimes reluctant to undergo training as they see in it a message from the organization that they are not deemed good enough in their job. This is why the commitment of management is important; it serves to promote the message that training is a morale booster. Those organizations that provide training will attract the best people to work with, as it shows a commitment on the part of the management to invest in their employees. Opportunities to learn must therefore be presented at all times.

Resistance to training may be overcome by marketing the training function internally. The department responsible for training should constantly seek ways of proving to the rest of the organization that training is an investment in the employees, and not merely spending money for nothing. They should:

"....seize every opportunity to show the management what the training department is doing, what success it is achieving and the ways in which the activity can be developed for the good of the business. If they are not already represented at the business planning stage...they should continually lobby for that representation....."

(Robinson, 1988, pp. 195)

Therefore, it is necessary for the training department to realistically evaluate what the outcomes to training are; to appraise financial investment in training; and, just as importantly, to select the right means of communicating this message to all members of the organization. The training department should also communicate the responsibilities of management, and the training programs currently available (Stout, 1993).

The main issue that smaller organizations face regarding training is finance. Since smaller organizations cannot take advantage of economies of scale, training will be more expensive to provide. They will also find it harder to access the necessary finance. Because they are smaller, they have fewer people working for them and the managers are, more often than not, the owners themselves. Organizations such as these are far less likely to devote the resources towards the setting up of a training department:

> *"Some organizations have a designated training function; others may have a 'trainer' or 'HR' person with responsibilities for anything and everything, which fits under the broad umbrella of training and human resource. In many small and medium sized companies, training is the responsibility of one person, who will carry out this task together with other responsibilities."*
>
> *(Training Manual of the University of Leicester, Module 1: 1, p. 14)*

In the cases of small family-run businesses, it is likely that more attention is focused on the owners and therefore the needs of employees are often neglected. It is also likely that the recruitment strategies adopted will be those of recruiting people who fit in best with management's ideals rather than their suitability to the job in question.

Whatever the size of the organization, whoever is responsible for training faces several challenges. The first challenge is the technical challenge, i.e., keeping up-to-date with new methods of delivering training, as well as any changes in company policy. The next challenge is to monitor and respond to changes in skills requirements by continuing to provide training which provides measurable results. This is the strategic challenge.

Exercise: discuss the attitudes of your company's senior management to training, and whether it is viewed as a cost or an investment. Is there a specific training policy? Do the senior managers regard themselves as needing training too? Do they see it as filling a skills gap, or do they see training as a perk, or benefit, to be enjoyed as a right of their position? As a continuation of the last exercise, discuss how training is viewed in the organization, and the time and money invested in it.

Phase 1 Training needs analysis

A training needs analysis (TNA) is an examination of the organization's present and expected operations and the manpower capabilities necessary to carry them out. This will identify the numbers of categories of staff who need to be trained or re-trained. It may also refer to the training needs of individuals to enable them to reach the required standard of performance in their current or future job. An effective training needs analysis could be described as a scientific method towards identifying the existing knowledge, skills or/and attitude gap between the current and the expected level of performance or output.

This analysis can be carried out at three different levels:
- **Organizational Level,** which measures the training requirements across the whole organization;
- **Occupational Level,** which measures the training requirements across a particular level (hierarchical) within the organization;
- **Individual Level**, which measures the training requirements of the individuals within the organization.

Putting too much emphasis on the needs of either the organization or the individual may not achieve a desirable outcome. The art of a successful training needs analysis is striking a good balance between the two. Nevertheless, it is obvious that within an organization, a training needs analysis may have a more immediate connection with organizational needs. Identifying training needs is particularly important where skills required to perform a job are often subject to change – for example, with the introduction of new technologies, many areas of manufacturing have been revolutionized, and new software is continually developed and replaced. A training intervention will usually aim to improve the performance of both the learner and the organization, and will be triggered by an occurrence, which could be either internal or external to the organization. The following table (see Table 8.1.) gives a clear indication of how performance improvement is reached at these three levels. The training needs analysis involves considering how training needs may occur at these three levels:

Table 8.1 Three levels of training needs

Area of need/level of business benefit	Organizational	Group	Individual
Implementing existing tasks well	Meeting current organizational objectives	Working together to meet existing targets and standards	Being competent at the level of existing requirements
Improving tasks	Setting higher objectives and reaching them	Continuous improvement of teams	Having and using systematic, continuous improvement skills and processes
Innovating	Changing objectives and strategies	Working across boundaries to create new relationships and new products and services	Being able to work differently and more creatively with a shared sense of purpose

Performance benefits at three levels (adapted from Boydell and Leary, 1996)

APPROACHES TO THE TRAINING NEED

In order to assess training at different levels, as explained above, different approaches are employed.

Training assessment at organizational level can be **reactive or proactive**. The former looks into identifying past problems, while the latter looks into present and future plan expectations and then develop training plans to meet identified current and anticipated training needs.

In carrying a training assessment at organizational level a comprehensive analysis is required. This involves a very detailed examination of every aspect of the job until each task has been fully described in terms of its knowledge, skills and (if relevant) attitudes. The task must also be described by reference to its frequency of performance, its standards of performance and ways of measuring that performance. This suggests a very time-consuming and detailed approach, which investigates all aspects of the job, and produces a detailed job description and job training specification. It is to be recommended when the following criteria apply:

- When tasks have to be learnt and performed to a particular standard, but are unfamiliar and difficult for the learner;
- When the content of the job changes infrequently but the job-holder may change fairly frequently;
- When the job is predominantly prescribed and little initiative or discretion is required by the jobholder.

Training assessment at occupational level is achieved through an 'Industry Breakdown Approach'. This is effective when the job involves a number of operations, processes or tasks which may have to be broken down into manageable parts. The trainer goes through the work to identify stages or units and to identify areas where training is imperative to ensure the job is carried out correctly.

Training assessment at individual level is obtained through various documents including, amongst others, the organization chart, job description and dpecification documents. In addition to this information, a comprehensive assessment requires the manager to look for 'hidden' information. Some of the basic considerations include:

- What the job holder does;
- What the job holder believes is being done;
- What the job holder says is done;
- What others think the job holder does; and
- What management wants the job holder to do.

This information can be obtained through various methods such as face-to-face interviews; observations; existing records; questionnaires; group discussions; critical incidents where supervisors are used to generate examples of good and bad performance of key job tasks; as well as through the job element method where groups of key employees usually brainstorm the key elements for the successful job.

Training assessment at individual level can be obtained through other technical means including:

(a) Task analysis, is a systematic study of the behavior, In this technical assessment, tasks are listed and analyzed in order to evaluate the relationship between their importance and their degree of difficulty. Tasks with higher degrees of difficulties generally require higher levels of training.

(b) Skills analysis is used to assess skills deficiencies at non-supervisory jobs. It is commonly referred to as skills' analysis program.

(c) The key task analysis approach concerns the identification and the detailed investigation of key or core tasks within the job. It is a more appropriate process for relatively more senior (e.g. supervisory and managerial) jobs within an organization. At these levels, job descriptions and specifications are usually expressed in general terms, concentrating on objectives, targets, and key result areas, and will often include definitions of responsibilities. At this level, jobs will usually involve complex skills such as problem-solving and decision-making, analysis, creativity, reflection and evaluation as well as a high degree of interpersonal skills. From this perspective, it is more realistic to focus on the knowledge, skills and attitude most appropriate in given situations rather than a breakdown of all the job requirements.

Key task analysis is appropriate for any type of job where:

• Tasks are varied and critical to effective performance;
• The job is likely to change in emphasis or content, resulting in a continuing need to establish priority tasks, standards of performance and the skills and knowledge required.

(d) The competency-based analysis involves identifying a list of competencies (or skills) required to produce effective performance in a role, job or function. The competency-based analysis can appear to be similar in parts to other approaches. However, whilst the competency-based approach concentrates on the specific kinds and levels of skills required, it does not cover procedures and details concerning how the job is performed.

Exercise: discuss your own individual training needs, using some of the tools and processes outlined above. How could you improve your competence at your job? Do your managers appreciate the exact nature of your work? Are you aware of areas in your work where more training could benefit you? What is your own attitude toward training – motivational, useful, OK, a waste of time, boring, takes me away from other, more important issues?

Phase 2 Designing the learning event

There is a reason and purpose for learners being trained – they want or need to learn about something, or how to do it, or how to achieve a certain performance outcome. Learners are dependent on you, the designer, working with line management, colleagues and other trainers to create the sort of learning event where this can happen. At this stage of design you should already have clarified:

- The training need, the intended outcome and objectives to be achieved;
- The entry behavior of learners to establish where learning has to begin.

As the designer, you might not carry out the actual training yourself. This could be done by other trainers, or by other means such as training packages or computer-based training. However, you are responsible for creating a learning event that will enable a learner to achieve the state objectives. The design briefly provides a specification for the training, and an understanding between you and the client about what can realistically be achieved. It is important to recognize that the client is likely to be primarily concerned with the outcome of the training not with the learning process itself. But as the designer of a learning unit and, in particular, the learning event, you may feel that your primary concern is to help the learner develop knowledge and skills. The intention of the design should be to satisfy both client and learner.

The term 'task' is often used in reference to work and training. It has been used in previous units to identify training needs, and to focus the process of helping people learn to acquire competence – the ability to perform a task. Unfortunately, as we have already stated, there is no clear answer to the question 'What is a task?' the important point is that you must have a clear idea of what you are designing the training to achieve.

Relating tasks to design: Consider a situation where you are planning to use a visual aid, for example during a training session. One task to be performed will be to develop a power point presentation and the other will be to install the PC with the projector. Treat these as two separate tasks and examine them in more detail.

- Setting up and using the computer projector in a typical training room requires following a set of procedures – setting up the screen, positioning the projector at a suitable distance from the screen and adjusting it to produce a square, focused image on the screen, etc. This description can be expanded to include further detail but, irrespective of who is doing the task, it will be done more or less the same way.

- Developing the power point presentation requires consideration of the learning point to be illustrated and the style of its presentation, for example, whether it is to be straight text, an illustrative model or a cartoon. Only when this has been decided can the transparency be prepared.

- These tasks are familiar to trainers, but there is an important difference between them which has a significant impact on the design of learning events. The first task, setting up the computer projector, involves following a set procedure, whereas the second task involves making decisions. This distinction can be expanded along a continuum with, at one end, the task that must be done in one way only, and at the other, the highly creative task performance depends on circumstances, experience and creative ability.

- Productive tasks require a person to apply task-related skills in a variety of situations, with the emphasis on planning and decision-making. Learning events' content may need to include concepts and principles.

- Reproductive tasks require a person to apply task-related skills to follow laid-down procedures, involving little planning or decision-making. Just the procedure and associated skills may need to be learnt.

The task of setting the computer projector is a reproductive task. There is a procedure, a series of actions to be taken which will result in the computer projector being set up ready for use. This procedure would apply to anybody doing the task.

The task of developing the power point presentaton is a productive task, because there is no predetermined outcome and set procedure to be followed. Every person performing the task will have their own ideas about how to communicate the learning point – one person may choose to use text, whereas another, with artistic talent, may decide to draw a cartoon. Both decisions may be correct, given a set of circumstances. If these were changed, or a different person was making the decision, then there might be a different outcome, but still a satisfactory performance of the task.

The distinction between the two types of tasks may influence both the training objectives and the design of the learning event. It might not be possible (except at high costs using a simulator) to create, a learning event where a learner can learn productive elements of performance. Realistically, this might be better done on the job with resulting modification of the training objectives.

The performance of a task may include both productive and reproductive elements and each may need to be examined to determine what has to be learnt. You may wish to consider the learning event as a jigsaw, with each piece of the jigsaw representing an element of the task and requiring a distinct learning event. Ideally, each of these elements should have its own enabling objective. The skills' cycle, described earlier, can provide a useful basis for making these decisions because it helps to identify the type of behavior required.

From the analysis of the task, it is possible to identify key elements which the learner will have to learn during the learning event. Some of these elements will be underpinning knowledge, influencing a learner's ability to perform the task; other elements will be specific to a particular task. The skills' cycle enables elements to performance to be considered under the following headings:

Recognition	-	*recognizing the need to take action*
Recall	-	*remembering task-related information*
Planning	-	*deciding how to perform the task*
Performance	-	*actually doing the task*

These four elements, and the sequence in which they are used, describe the actual performance of the task under normal working conditions. In other words, they define competence which is specified by means of the performance objective.

The learning event is the period when the process of systematic training becomes 'live' and the learner is actually learning. The design and development of learning events will vary enormously from a short simple session done on the shop floor, to a highly complex simulation of a major management activity. However, for training to be effective, your design of the learning event has to be related closely to the outcome – and this has to be related as closely as possible to actual performance.

Exercise: Discuss a training program you experienced which you thought was successful. Explain the component parts in view of the outlines above. Did you learn a new skill? Did you gain new insights? Do you still use ideas or methods from that training course? Compare it with other training courses you have attended, and consider why it was better. To what extent was it based on realistic scenarios, to give experiences to the participants? How would you use this training program as a template for others in the future?

Phase 3 Preparation of the training plan
1. **Collate findings:** The first stage in the collation is to sort out the findings which appear to have training implications. This is usually the result of your training needs analysis. Other problems identified through the training needs analysis need particularly careful handling as they are not the trainer's direct responsibility. The response to them will depend partly on the role the trainer decides to play. It is more likely that many of the non-training problems have at some point been raised with line managers in either a formal, or more likely, information context during the identification of training needs processes.

2. **Group the need:** Having identified the possible training needs, the next stage is to group them under more manageable headings. Continued evaluation of training will have identified courses and other activities that are providing an effective service and others where amendments regarding redesigning are required. Then turn your attention to needs that are not met. The following headings are suggested (but others can be used as appropriate).

   Group A – Corporate initiatives
   Group B – Technological change
   Group C – Efficiency problems

3. **The priorities:** The next stage is to examine the benefits of tackling each training need. The trainer may look for those activities which will make Training Program Design and Development the biggest contribution to organizational efficiency and profitability, now and in the time span of the corporate plan as well as long term.

WRITING TRAINING OBJECTIVES

The training objectives should provide a clear, precise and unambiguous statement of what learners will be able to do at three distinct, but very important stages in their training. These three stages are:

- On their return to work, when they are required to perform the task to the same standards as those of an experienced or exemplary worker. The objective used to describe this is called a performance objective;
- On completion of their formal training, typically a course, when they have achieved a satisfactory standard of performance under training conditions. The objective used to describe this is called a training objective;
- On completion of a stage of the learning process when they have acquired certain knowledge or skills. The objective used to describe this is called enabling objectives.

Performance objectives: The ultimate aim of training is to help people to achieve mastery of a task so that they will be able to perform the task to an exemplary standard. However, under training conditions, this may not be possible for the following reasons:

- The amount of time needed to gain experience in all the variations of performing the task. Training often lasts only a few days. However, the complexity of a task, and the variation that can occur over a much longer period, may require an extended time for learning long after training as such has been completed;

- The difficulty in simulating the real working environment for training purposes. Training may be done away from the pressures of the working environment where reality is simulated for learning purposes. This can rarely replace the actual situation involving real people; nor can it take account of fatigue factors and the often unpredictable nature of a person's work;

- The availability of machines and systems for training that truly duplicate the ones actually used. This is likely to be a problem when training is being done off-the-job and therefore away from hands-on learning experiences using actual machinery and systems in the normal working environment. This is especially so when people attend an open, off-the-shelf job course.

The performance objective is an important consideration when designing training although it may set a higher standard of performance than you intend your learners to achieve at the end of training. However, for certain training situations, there can be no compromise between what is required for job performance and what has to be achieved at the end of training.

Training objectives: The trainer should be aware of the existence of a learning curve for trainees, from a low standard of performance representing entry-level behavior to the exemplary standard of a high performance objective. Where the curve flattens out a considerable amount of time is taken up to gain only a small improvement in performance. Moving the training objective up or down has a significant effect on the time taken and costs incurred.

Enabling objectives: The performance of a task requires the application of a repertoire of knowledge and skills, some specific to the performance of the particular task and others providing underpinning knowledge. The training objectives define what learners have to achieve; their entry behavior determines how much training they will need to reach the required standard of performance. The enabling objectives define the discrete elements of knowledge and skills the learner will need to complete.

WRITING OBJECTIVES (S.M.A.R.T.)

An objective is a precise, clear statement of what learners will be able to do at the end of a learning event. This may be an enabling objective because it is aimed at the end of a particular knowledge or skills training session, or it can be the training objective defining the task the learner will be able to do at the end of a learning unit. Examples of performance statements include:

- The learner will be able **to type** a business letter;
- The learner will be able **to name** the component parts in an automatic transmission;
- The learner will be able **to calculate** the amount of income tax to be paid on incomes liable to higher rates.

All the verbs in bold and italics in the examples above clearly indicate the actions required of the learner. The performance part of the objective must be written in this manner. Statements that can be interpreted in more than one way must be avoided.

TYPES OF STANDARDS

Accuracy Standards
- The task must be completed without error;
- All measurements must be correct within a range of ± 0.01 mm.

Speed Standards
- The task must be completed within 10 minutes;
- The learner must produce minimally 20 components per hour.

Phase 4 Evaluation of training
Over the last forty years, several systems or frameworks for evaluation have been developed. These provide training practitioners with a suggested methodology that can be implemented in full, or adapted to meet the trainer's needs.

In general, training evaluation should be carried out within a specific context., The ultimate aim is to identify whether training has been properly assessed and implemented. In financial terms, this phase of the training cycle considers whether the training budget has been an investment or simply an additional cost to the organization.

The person with responsibility for evaluation must gain acceptance from key personnel within the organization. Normally, this should present no problem as long as the proposal gets approval from those who will be asked to contribute. The learners can usually be relied upon to take the time out to provide feedback, on both their reactions to the learning event and the learning outcomes. The quality of the data collected can be improved by building the learner evaluation process into the learning event, rather than asking for feedback from the learners at the last minute, when their main pre-occupation is getting out of the training room.

The trainer should allow sufficient time for a full evaluation of the learning event at the planning stage. This can be extended to include group or individual learning reviews as the final exercise. This type of review can be built in at appropriate points throughout the event. In this way the learner becomes more comfortable with the concept of learning outcomes, learning becomes pivotal, and the quality and quantity of feedback at the end of the course is significantly increased.

In the course of time, several training experts have come up with a number of training evaluation methods. The common denominator across some of the most common training evaluation techniques is that they are all based on three pillars namely, whether there has been the correct assessment, the process of training implementation and the outcome achieved.

- Input Evaluation – an analysis, assessment and identification of the resources necessary to meet the training requirements within the training program. In other words, an assessment of the inputs required to make the training happen. Key questions to ask at this stage include: How much time do we have for training? What training methods are most appropriate? What media are most suitable? What are the results of similar courses? Who should deliver the training? Will the proposed content achieve the learning objectives?

- Reaction Evaluation – the systematic collection of learners' reactions to the training both during and after the event. Information to be gathered would include feedback on course content, environment, trainer performance and learning materials among others.

- Outcome Evaluation – the traditional approach to evaluation that measures the extent to which objectives have been achieved. This assessment proceeds through four states:

  1. Is there a correct definition of training objectives in relation to meeting the identified problems or areas of need?
  2. Are the test instruments providing an accurate measurement of whether or not the training objectives have been achieved?
  3. Are the assessment instruments being applied at the most appropriate time to test learning outcomes?
  4. Results and recommendations for changes to subsequent programs.

KIRKPATRICK APPROACH

One of the earliest approaches was that of Kirkpatrick (1967) who suggested the collection of data at four different levels namelys:

- Level 1: Reaction – the learner's immediate impression about the training event;
- Level 2: Learning – the new knowledge or skills achieved within the program;
- Level 3: Behavior – the change in behavior brought about by the program;
- Level 4: Results – the change in behavior that has been 'embedded' into the results of the organization.

All these measures are recommended for a full and **meaningful** evaluation of learning in organizations, although their application broadly increases in complexity, and usually cost, through the levels from 1 to 4.

Hamblin approach: For effective training and learning evaluation, the principal questions should be:
- To what extent were the identified training needs objectives achieved by the program?
- To what extent were the learners' objectives achieved?
- What specifically did the learners learn or be usefully reminded of?
- What commitment have the learners made about the learning they are going to implement on their return to work?

And back at work:
- How successful were the trainees in implementing their action plans?
- To what extent were they supported in this by their line managers?
- To what extent has the action listed above achieved a Return on Investment for the organization, either in terms of identified objectives satisfaction or, where possible, a monetary assessment.

Organizations commonly fail to perform these evaluation processes, especially where:
- The HR department and trainers, do not have sufficient time to do so, and/or
- The HR department does not have sufficient resources - people and money - to do so.

Obviously the evaluation cloth must be cut according to available resources (and the culture atmosphere), which tend to vary substantially from one organization to another. The fact remains that good methodical evaluation produces a good reliable data; conversely, where little evaluation is performed, little is ever known about the effectiveness of the training.

Traditionally, in the main, any evaluation or other assessment has been left to the trainers because is it largely seen as their job, but arguably it should also reflect the involvement of the trainees, their supervisors, and even customers. Considerable lip service appears to be paid to this, but the actual practice tends to be a lot less.

CIRO approach: The CIRO approach to evaluation covers all four aspects of the training cycle:
C (Context). Evaluation here goes back to the reasons for the training event. How was the training opportunity specified? How were the training needs identified and analyzed.
I (Inputs) Evaluation here looks at the planning and design processes, which led to the selection of the trainers, programs, employees and materials. Determining whether the inputs were appropriate to the training event is critical to its success.

R (Reactions) Evaluation here is aimed to the nature of the training undertaken. How did the learners react to the training and was the training course relevant to their roles.

0 (Outcomes) To what extent has the learning been transferred to the workplace? This is easier where the training is more aimed at 'hard' and specific skills but, on the other hand, more challenging where less quantifiable competencies including behavioral skills are involved.

Exercise: Return to your description of the training event you enjoyed and found useful in the last exercise. Your evaluation of this event was probably quite subjective and may not have been based on any formal evaluation process. Consider it in the light of your insights into training evaluation from the tools and techniques above. Which of these do you find most useful?

THE COST OF TRAINING

Just like any other activity, training and development initiatives include relatively high costs which are generally divided between real and opportunity costs. Real costs include any activity which is directly related to the organisaton and development of the training activity. Included in real costs are such items as learners' wages, staff salaries, cost of materials used, and equipment purchased. Opportunity costs are more difficult to quantify. They are the notional costs incurred by undertaking one activity rather than the other. Thus training incurs an opportunity cost because the learners, trainers, materials and equipment could all be used in alternative ways to benefit the organization. Opportunity costs of training arise from the use of capital and manpower resources in the training activity. Capital is employed through plant, machinery and buildings used for training and the purchase of storage of material. Manpower resources are learners, trainers, the supporting administration, and all whom could be employed in alternative functions. The opportunity cost of capital is the return which could have been achieved by using these resources for productive output. Similarly the opportunity cost of manpower is the output that could have been gained if everyone concerned in training were employed in some directly productive activity.

TYPES OF COSTS

Direct costs are those directly attributable to the activity at stake. In a training program the wages of trainers and learners during training are direct costs. Other direct costs incurred by a training activity, which will be allocated to it as a cost centre, are materials used during training and expenses incurred. Expenses may be travel, accommodation, protective clothing etc.

Indirect costs (supportive) are all those costs which are necessary expenditures for the cost centre to operate but are not directly attributable to its activities. Such expenditures as rates, rent, insurance, heating, lighting, administration etc. have to be paid but are difficult to attribute to specific cost centers.

CONCLUSION

In this chapter we have considered many aspects of the training and development process, and have looked in detail at the issues of how it can be more professional and valuable to individuals, their departments, and to the organization as a whole. This may have been more complex a process than you might have imagined! Many organizations are struggling to meet these standards, which are essential to meet head office requirements (for multinationals), achieve quality awards, and attract and retain the best people. The best approach is to start from the top – the organization's objectives – and work downwards to gain individual employee satisfaction. Every step on the way must be measured and evaluated to keep checking on performance quality.

REFERENCES

Bee, F. & Bee. R. (1994) *Training Needs Analysis and Evaluation*. London: IPD.

Boydell, T. & Leary, M. (1996) *Identifying Training Needs*. London: IPD.

Bramley, P. (1993) *Evaluating Training Effectiveness: Benchmarking Your Training Activity Best Practice*. London: McGraw Hill.

Brettle A., Hulme, C. & Ormandy (2005) 'Evidence to support strategic decision making for health care information services: effective methods of providing patient care' *EMPIRIC Project*.

Kaplan, R.S., & Norton, D. (1996) The Balanced Scorecard. Boston: *Harvard Business School Press*.

Kolb, D.A. (1984) *Experiential Learning*. Englewood Cliffs, NJ: Prentice Hall.

Kirkpatrick, D.L. (1996) 'Evaluating Training Programs: The Four Levels', in Berret Koehler, (2003) *Metropolitan Police review of training*.

Mabey, C., & Salaman G. (1995) *Strategic Human Resource Management*. Oxford: Blackwell.

Molander, C., & Winterton, J. (1994) *Managing Human Resources*. London: Routledge.

Robinson, K. (1988) *A Handbook of Training Management*. London: Kogan Page.

University of Leicester (undated) Certificate in Training Practice. Module 1 Introduction to Training and Development & Module 2 Identification of Training Needs.

University of Leicester (undated) Certificate in Training Practice. Module 3 Individual and Organizational Learning & Module 4 Designing Learning Events.

University of Leicester (undated) Certificate in Training Practice. Module 5 Training Delivery & Module 6 Assessment and Evaluation.

Webb, J. & Powis, C. (2004) Chapter 8: 'Feedback and evaluation In Teaching Information Skills'. *Training Theory & Practice*. London: Facet Publishing.

RECOMMENDED FURTHER READING

Argyris, C. (1985) *Strategy, Change and Defensive Routines*. London: Pitman.

Bentley, T. (1994) *Facilitation: providing opportunities for learning*. London: McGraw-Hill.

Brooks, J. (1995) *Training and Development Competence: A practical guide*. London: Kogan Page.

Buckley, R., & Caple, J. (1995) *The Theory and Practice of Training*, 3rd. Ed.. London: Kogan Page.

Burns, R. (1995) *The Adult Learner at Work*. Sydney: Business and Professional Publishing.

Casey, D. (1987) 'Breaking the shell that encloses your understanding' *Journal of Management Development, 6*: 2.

Cook, A. (1990) *The Adult Learner: A Neglected Species* 2nd Ed. Houston: Gulf Publishing.

Cook, S. (1994) *Training for Empowerment.* Aldershot: Gower.

Clutterback, D. (1991) *Everyone Needs a Mentor: Fostering talent at work.* 2nd Ed., London: IPD.

Editorial (1995) 'Rapid changes require enhancement of adult' *HR Monthly*, June

Eitington, J. E. (2002) *The Winning Trainer. Winning Ways to Involve People in Learning.* 4th Ed., Boston: Butterworth Heinemann.

Honey, P. (1990) 'Confessions of a Learner who is inclined to lapse', *Training and Development Journal,* June.

Kanter, R.M. (1994) 'Future of Workplace Learning and Performance' in *The Past, Present and Future of Workplace Learning,* ASTD, Alexandra, VA.

Knowles, M.S. (1984) *Andragogy in Action, Applying Modern Principles of Adult Learning.* San Francisco: Jossey Bass.

Knowles, M.S. (1993) *Self Directed Learning.* New York: Association Press.

Laird, D. (1985) *Approaches to training and development.* Reading Mass: Addision Wesley.

McGill, I. & Beaty, L. (1995) *Action Learning,. A guide for professionals.* 2nd Ed. London: Kogan Page.

Pedler, M. (1991) *Action Learning in Practice.* 2nd Ed. Aldershot: Gower.

Pogson, P. & Tennant, M (1995) *'Understanding Adults" in Foley, G. ed. Understanding adult Education and Training.* London: Allen & Unwin.

Pont, T. (1998) *Investing in Training and Development,* Turning Interest Into Capital, 2nd Ed. London: Kogan Page.

Rae, L. (1992) *The Skills of Training. A guide for managers and practitioners*, 2nd Ed. Aldershot: Gower.

Stewart, J. (1996) *Managing Change Through Training and Development,* 2nd Ed. London: Kogan Page.

Thijssen, G.J.L. & Van der Heijden, B.I.J.M. 'Evaporated talent? Problems with talent development during the career' (2003) *International Journal of Human Resource Development and Management. 3:* 2, 154-170

Tichy, N. (1994) 'The Future of Workplace Learning and Performance' in T*he Past, Present and Future of workplace Learning*, ASTD, Alexandria, VA.

Van der Heijden, B.I.J.M. 'Age and assessments of professional expertise in SMEs: differences between self-ratings and supervisor ratings' (2002) *International Journal of Human Resource Development and Management, 2:* 3-4, 329-343

Whitmore, J. (1992) *Coaching for Performance.* London: Nicholas Brealey.

CHAPTER 9

MANAGING AND REWARDING PERFORMANCE
SILVIO DE BONO

OPENING CASE:

Flatfoot is a medium-sized manufacturing company based in South America. Its core business activity is the production of footwear, particularly sandals, of various sizes, shapes and colors. Mr. Francis Franks, the Managing Director of Flatfoot, feels that the overall production of the company could be expanded. As the result of a new strategic plan, the company invested in new machinery to ensure that both quality and production are increased. During the past five years, since its inception, the company has been doing well, with Flatfoot sandals selling strongly across many South American countries.

Mr. Franks noticed that, not withstanding the different efforts made, and although the company was reaching its production targets, not every employee was actually performing to the same output and standard. At first he thought that this was due to the fact that some employees were new and their skills were less developed than other employees, who have been there five years. However, on looking into the matter in more detail, it transpired that this was not the case. Some new employees were in fact performing better than other employees who were employed for longer periods.

Mr. Franks thought that one of the immediate solutions to entice employees to work harder was to introduce a performance bonus. After carrying out a time-and-motion study and after taking into account the production requirements of the company for the next year, he concluded that each of the 20 employees on the production line should equally produce the same amount of sandals. Mr. Franks thought that this was rather easy to measure since, contrary to other production companies, each pair of sandals was produced by just one person. However, in order to give the full benefit to all employees he assigned different tasks to employees depending on their training and skills, as well as taking into account the complexity of the type of sandals the employee was producing.

The following table (see Table 9.1) gives details of the planned production as against the actual production reached by the respective employees for one full year of operation. The table also gives the type of sandals the employee is producing and the number of years the employee has been in employment before the one full production year. Other employees who did not work a full year are not included in this table.

Table 9.1 Planned vs actual production table

Employee Number	Planned Performance in units for year 1	Actual Performance in units for year 1	Sandals' Type
0001	50	55	Pointed
0002	50	45	Pointed
0003	50	50	Pointed
0004	45	50	Pointed
0005	45	50	Pointed
0006	45	40	Pointed
0007	40	40	Pointed
0008	40	35	Pointed
0009	35	30	Pointed
0010	35	40	Pointed
0011	80	90	Flat
0012	80	90	Flat
0013	80	65	Flat
0014	70	65	Flat
0015	70	65	Flat
0016	55	60	Rounded
0017	55	55	Rounded
0018	50	45	Rounded
0019	25	15	Rounded
0020	25	15	Rounded

The overall result was as follows:

Table 9.2 Total planned vs. actual output attained

Type of sandals	Planned Output	Actual Output	Variance
Pointed	435	440	+5
Flat	380	375	-5
Rounded	210	190	-20

Mr. Franks was seriously considering whether he should give a bonus to his employees. However, his main concern was whether he should reward on an individual versus a team level.

Looking into the results in more detail he observed that although the production of pointed sandals was reached, not everyone has contributed according to his/her expected and planned level. On the other hand he also noted that not withstanding that the production for flat sandals and rounded sandals was not reached there were employees who contributed much more than what had been expected from them.

Questions on the opening case: Mr. Franks has hired you as his consultant(s) to give advice and to suggest a performance plan which could be used in measuring his employees' performance. He would like you to help in solving this year's problems too.

1. *What would you advise Mr. Franks about the best performance system to be applied in this case?*
2. *Would you recommend rewarding employees individually or as a team?*
3. *Would you agree to set reward systems based on performance and why?*

What other suggestions do you have for improving the levels of motivation of staff, to encourage more workers to exceed their targets? What other issues might be impacting on production outside of the control of the employees? How do you think the employees might feel about Mr. Franks' efforts?

LEARNING OBJECTIVES FOR THIS CHAPTER

Management theorists have proposed that anything which cannot be measured, cannot be managed. This concept also applies to measuring employee performance.. There have been a series of debates between academics and practitioners about how to best measure employee performance and allocate rewards. Changes in business, the effects of globalization as well as labor union pressures have all been determining factors in looking into different ways of how to ensure that organizational objectives are cascaded to all employees as objectively as possible. By the end of this chapter students should be able to:

• Identify how over the years, thinking and discussion of areas of performance and reward management have evolved;

• Identify one of the major hindrances in performance management – the setting of measurement criteria;

• Appreciate different possible methods of how to set performance management systems and apply these in the workplace.

In this chapter, we are looking at the definition and evolution of performance management systems and their relationship with motivation theories. How do you set up a performance management program? How do you measure individual and team-based performance? What are some of the reasons for ineffective performance? How can we implement more effective appraisals, and how can we reward strong performers? This chapter combines theory and practice to help you identify and evaluate performance management and reward systems in different contexts.

DEFINING PERFORMANCE MANAGEMENT

The area of performance management has always been one of the most researched areas in the field of management and HRM. This is probably because managers and researchers in the field of management are still looking for a clearer understanding of what are the main drivers that lead employees to perform. Whether there is a link between people management practices and organizational performance. Can one identify which policies and practices result in high performance? (Torrington et al., 2005).

The essence of performance panagement is establishing a framework in which performance by individuals can be directed, monitored, motivated and modified; and how the links in the performance cycle can be audited and measured. Performance management can be described as a process that consolidates goal setting, performance appraisal, and development into a single, common system, the aim of which is to ensure that employees's performance is supporting the company's strategic aims (Dessler, 2005) Two theories are particularly relevant to discussions of performance management:'goal setting theory', and 'expectancy theory.'

GOAL SETTING THEORY

Goal setting theory was established by Edwin Locke in a paper published in 1968 (see Torrington et al., 2005) in which he argued that goals pursued by employees can play an important role in motivating superior performance. In following these goals people examine the consequences of their behavior. If they surmise that their goals will not be achieved by their current behavior, they will either modify their behavior, or choose more realizable goals. Therefore:

- Goals should be specific, rather than vague or excessively general;
- Goals should be demanding and challenging, but also attainable;
- Feedback performance information should be made available; and
- Goals need to be accepted by employees as desirable.

EXPECTANCY THEORY

Expectancy theory (Vroom, 1964), states that it is the anticipated satisfaction of valued goals which causes individuals to adjust their behavior in a way which is most likely to lead attaining them. The theory can be expressed in these points:

- The person's own assessment whether performing in a certain way will result in measurable result. This factor is labeled the expectancy;

- The perceived likelihood that such a result will lead to attaining a given reward. This factor is known as instrumentality; and

- The person's assessment of the likely satisfaction or value associated with the reward.

The value of organizational performance has been widely discussed. Huselid (1995) and Pfeffer (1998) point that the overall objectives of a good performance management program can be summarized in the following four points:

- Making the correct administrative decisions,
- Looking at the individuals' potential,
- Systems' maintenance, and finally
- Documentation purposes.

Exercise: Revisit any previous studies you may have made on motivation in the workplace and/or consider the impact of goal-setting and expectancy on your own performance. Does the existence of specific goals encourage you to perform more strongly? Do you set goals for yourself, or do you expect the management to set them for you? If this is so, are you involved in setting the organizational goals?

THE PERFORMANCE MANAGEMENT PROGRAM

When the Hawthorne Studies (Roethlisberger & Dickson, 1939; Rice 1982) were completed, motivation experts like Maslow, Herzberg, Aldefer, McClelland, and others particularly specializing in the so-called process theories of motivation, may have thought to have found the answers to why and how people perform. Further more recent studies have shown there is much more to the matter, with two other approaches.

Firstly, employees perform to reach planned targets in order to satisfy their internal needs. MacDuffie, (1995) and Pfeffer (1998) list a number of reasons why employees need to satisfy their internal needs, including attractive HR policies; emphasis on employment security; good remuneration packages; good opportunities for training and development. Secondly, a ten-year study carried out in the United Kingdom (Patterson et al., 1997) has concluded that in addition to these internal organizational issues, there are also other aspects including different elements of culture, supervisory support and employee welfare, as being vital for ensuring employee performance. These approaches have been highly criticized by several authors (Guest 2001), arguing that the statistical conclusion may at best be too simplistic and does not give any conclusive evidence.

Further studies in the field propose that in order to identify the relationship between employee and organizational performance, a longitudinal study is generally required. In order to reach this aim. Becker and Gerhard, 1996 proposes that the relationship between the employee and the organization as a whole is highly determined by its structure and not just a group of HR practices. This approach also proposes that the relationship between employee and organization performance is in the fabric of how organization practices are implemented and how change is managed (Hutchinson et al., 2000).

The essence behind these definitions lies in the fact that they all emphasize that the aim of the performance management program is to improve individual performance by linking objectives with those of the organization (Fowler, 2000). A performance management program has been defined as the organization of work to achieve the best possible results, especially where the program has to be introduced in the context of organizational culture, communication systems, and human resource policies (Fowler, 1990).

In addition to the above definitions, Armstrong and Baron (2000) argued that a performance management program has a strategic dimension since it should be concerned with the broader issues facing the organization as well as integrated vertically and horizontally. It attempts to link vertically the organization's objectives with those of the individual, and to link horizontally the different aspects of human resource management such as training and development, culture, rewards as well as leadership style.

The three main phases of performance management include planning performance, supporting performance, and reviewing performance (Torrington et al., 2000). The planning phase includes the setting of jointly devised objectives by the manager and the employee. Practical experience in the field advocates that more employee input increases success and satisfaction by both parties. Martin (2000) emphasizes the importance of accurate objectives as the key factor toward overall success in the overall process.

Supporting performance circles round the support and coaching offered by the immediate superior (the manager) helps to achieve the agreed objectives by providing the necessary training and resources (Storey & Sisson, 1994). Constructive and continuous coaching is one of the key factors in leading the individual and the team to higher levels of performance (Delbridge & Turnball, 1992).

The third phase includes the actual employee or team assessment which is described in detail in the following parts of this chapter. In general terms, this stage is aimed toward assessing whether the actual objectives have been reached. Management literature suggests that the prerequisites toward the introduction of a performance management program are generally divided in two domains. Organizational (internal) requisites relate to structure, culture and management systems, while environmental (external) relate the different environments within which the organization operates in.

INDIVIDUAL VERSUS TEAM PERFORMANCE

A working definition of what constitutes a team in an organization is a group of employees who are working together, share the same organizational norms and are striving to achieve the same goal. Just like a sports team, the individual members have specific roles to play and are directly responsible for their individual and collective actions. As the opening case suggests, carrying out a team evaluation may not always result in producing the best idea. Up to a certain point, this may seem to contradict the general literature on teams and performance of teams (Bacon & Blyton, 2003) which proposes that the overall team performance is generally higher than the sum of individual performance. Critics of team performance including Applebaum et al. (1999) claim that there are a number of issues which are generally related to team performance: mostly, that team members may not feel comfortable with the idea, and that in some cases the team may not be the most effective unit, for a number of reasons beyond its control including its composition and the task assigned.

Moxon (1993) and Katzenbach (1997) have described differences between teams and working groups and identify teams as comprising individuals with complementary skills, shared leadership roles, mutual accountability, and a specific team purpose. Torrington et al. (2005) further say that in organizations this dedication only happens when individuals are fully committed to the team's goals. This commitment derives from an involvement in defining how the goals will be met, and having the power to make decisions are particularly characteristics of self-managing teams which are generally given higher levels of authority and decision-making.

Contributors who are loyal to team performance propose that although there are individual cases and exceptions to every rule, by and large team performance produces more effective and efficient results. The general claims center around the idea that team performance produces higher performance levels since team members are more flexible, have better communication network with other members of the team, are more committed to the work and the team, and, generally, display higher levels of ownership.

Like individuals, different teams in the organizations ranging from cross-functional teams to self-managed teams, and from top management teams to problem-solving teams, often require some sort of reward and recognition for their effort. Although monetary rewards are still highly common and pragmatic, other companies have tried non-monetary rewards such as team recognition in the company's in-house journal, or possibly external media, and inscribing the team's name on company shields and other trophies.

Exercise: Discuss your own experience with team and individual based performance incentives – what are the advantages and disadvantages of each? This is also partly related to your own personal preferences, toward working in a team or working by yourself. With a team-based system, was real team performance improved, or was it a case of a few people doing all the work? With the individual system, did you feel more competitive against the others and less willing to help them? Reflect on the differences and the outcomes.

MEASURING PERFORMANCE - FROM THEORY TO PRACTICE

In the course of the past years, different performance appraisal systems have been applied to measure employee performance. The major hurdle faced by managers and employees alike is ensuring that the performance appraisal interview reflects a true picture of the performance at a certain point in time. In overcoming this hurdle, appraisal methods are now shifting from subjective to objectives measures, and thus from a qualitative method to a more quantitative method.

Traditionally, appraisal interviews were based more on aspects of the employee's behavior . This created great pains and difficulties for managers since they acknowledged that their performance rating was highly subjective, and different managers in the organization interpreted the scales based on their own personal ideas. Their personal relationship with the employee was also a factor in the overall evaluation. In the process, other measures to align behavior with performance on the job such as Behaviorally Anchored Rating Scales (BARS) ratings and Behavioral Observation Scales (BOS) rating were developed, but it was suggested that these are not always effective (Williams, 2002).

A potentially more accepted objective way of assessing performance is the process of cascading organizational objectives to the department and to the individual. Employees are then measured to identify to which extent these objectives have been achieved. This is called a management by objectives (MBO) system (Howell 1967).

Other possible ways of measuring performance is through external reviewers, generally referred to as 'mystery shoppers' (Newton & Findlay, 1996). The problem with mystery shoppers is that they can be identified by employees after a while, and the employees feel they are being spied on, and monitored. Each organization has to decide which objectives for performance appraisal are to be pursued in relation to the objectives of that organization.

A list of possible aims and objectives of a formalized appraisal system relating to the employer and employee is as follows:

The employer:
1.   To assess current and past performance;
2.   To help improve performance;
3.   To allocate fair and just reward;
4.   To set performance objectives;
5.   To establish an effective two-way communication system;
6.   To assess training and development needs;
7.   To assess career planning decisions;
8.   To identify staff with promotion possibilities;
9.   To aid human resources and succession planning.

The employee:
1.   To let the employee know where he/she stands in terms of performance;
2.   To provide an opportunity for discussion about the performance of the employee during the period under review;
3.   To agree on an action plan to improve the performance of the employee;
4.   To identify training needs and aspirations of the employee.

Exercise: Discuss your attitudes to performance management as both an employer and an employee – is it equally useful to both? Can the same system be of equal benefit to both? If there is no performance management system, who suffers the most – the employer – who does not know who and where and why there is strong or weak performance – or the employee – who has no measure of how he or she is getting on? Reflect on your experiences as a manager having to manage performance, and as an employee who is thinking about his or her own career.

DIFFERENT TYPES AND APPROACHES OF APPRAISAL METHODS

The selection of appraisal method is directly related to what is being measured. Various types of appraisal methods exist and are used by organizations depending on their size, industry, and the experience of the managers. The following are some examples:

Graphic rating scale method. This is the simplest form of appraisal and probably still the most popular technique used. This method, which used numeric rating as its basis, lists personal traits on one side (such as quality and reliability) and a range of performance values (from unsatisfactory to satisfactory). In this case, the supervisor is limited to appraise the qualities listed only.

Alteration ranking method. Dessler (2005) points that ranking employees from best to worst on a trait or traits is another option. In adopting this method, the manager lists all subordinates to be rated, and then cross out the names of any not known well enough to rank. In this method the manager ranks employees from best to worst on a particular trait, choosing highest, then lowest, until all are ranked. This system is slightly more difficult to administer and may propose subjective judgment. Some managers prefer to use the paired comparison method, which helps to make the ranking method more precise. In this method, subordinates are compared on every trait.

Forced distribution method. This method proposes the idea that the manager appraises subordinates across pre-agreed categories such as average, below average, above average ands so on. The proportions in each category need not be symmetrical.

Critical incident method. This method falls under the category of free written reports. In adopting this method, the supervisor, keep a log of positive and negative examples of a subordinate's work related activities. Every so often, the supervisor and the employee meet to discuss the latter's performance using the incidents as examples.

Behaviorally anchored ratings. These methods combines the benefits of narratives, critical incidents and quantified scales, anchoring a rating scale with specific behavioral examples of good or poor performance. Dessler (2005) notes that in adopting this method the following sequence of activities must be adhered to:
- Generate critical incidents.
- Develop performance dimensions.
- Rellocate incidents.
- Scale the incidents.
- Develop a final instrument.

Management by objectives. This method requires the manager to set specific measurable goals with each employee on periodic basis. On regular basis, the manager holds individual meetings with subordinates to assess progress.

The success of any performance system is highly dependant on the commitment of the managers concerned, the willingness of subordinates' to participate in activities freely as well as the abilty to select the best approach or a combination of approaches.

360° feedback: Such an approach refers to the use of a range of sources from which feedback can be collected about an individual. Generally speaking this feedback is collected from managers, peers and subordinates, but can be customers, suppliers and those outside the organization as well.

All these types of appraisal schemes have their advantages and disadvantages and are all used as a framework for performance appraisal in many organizations. So, ideally, based on the most up-to-date research, what is the best way to set up a performance management system?

Table 9.3 List of advantages and disadvantages of appraisal tools

Tool	Advantages	Disadvantages
Graphic rating scale	• Simple to use. • Provides a quantitative rating	• Unclear standards • Personal bias (halo effect). • Central tendency error. • Leniancy error.
BARS	• Highly accurate. • Provides behavioural anchors.	• Difficult and complex to develop.
Alternation Ranking	• Simple to use. • Avoid central tendency.	• Can cause disagreement among employees. • Unfair if all employees are excellent.
Forced distribution	• End up with a pre-determined number of people in each group.	• Employees appraisal results depend on choice of cut-off points.
Critical incident method	• Helps specify what is right and wrong. • Forces supervisor to evaluate subordinates	• Difficult to rank employees relative to one another.
MBO	• Tied to performance objectives.	• Time consuming
360° feedback	• Gives a wider assessment of employee	• Time consuming. • Issues of accuracy.

Adapted from Dessler, G. (2005) Human Resource Management, International Edition. Prentice Hall, New Jersey p. 330

MOST COMMON REASONS FOR INEFFECTIVE APPRAISALS

If performance appraisal systems in an organization are not being effective (or if appraisals do not take place at all) a conscious effort to improve the way in which people are being appraised might be necessary. A look at the following insights might help you understand why an appraisal system may not work:

Attitudes of managers who are responsible for appraising others:

1. A lack of willingness to accept ownership of the responsibility to appraise people - "It is someone else's job";

2. A lack of acceptance of the fact that appraisal should be a natural bi-annual, or annual 'stock-taking' activity;

3. A lack of skills or knowledge with regard to setting a clearly defined standard of performance, against which to appraise;

4. A lack of skills in distinguishing between that which is the job holder's control opposed to that which is controlled by others;

5. A failure to recognize and/or to accept that the manager's own behavior can influence a job holder to perform well or to perform badly;

6. A fear of discussing performance.

7. A fear of confronting people who are not performing and coping with their response, whilst trying to think of ways to improve the situation.

Attitudes of the people being appraised:

1. Suspicion of why they are being appraised;

2. Concern for fair appraisal;

3. Fear of the use of totally subjective measurements of performance;

4. Being appraised against personality traits rather than results;

5. The assumption by the manager that job holders are totally in control of their performance - the more effort needed syndrome;

6. That very little will happen, if anything, as a result of being appraised;

7. That their morale will be reduced and they will fear and distrust the management team:

8. What use is a once a year (or twice a year) event anyway?

These attitudes about performance management are very common in many companies, especially those with a fast pace of work and many pressures, where the appraisal is seen as yet another chore. There is also the tendency to assume that the employee is just the same as last year, so there is nothing new and nothing much to do. Although employees are typically cynical and critical of performance management systems (and fearful and nervous) probably the majority of the problems associated with these relate to the poor performance management skills of their managers.

STAGES IN SETTING UP A PERFORMANCE MANAGEMENT SYSTEM

Step 1 Setting goals. As an instrument of strategic human resource management, a system of performance management requires taking the wider, strategic goals of the organization as a starting-point and translating them into goals for smaller groups of individuals.

Measuring performance: Assuming the organization has been able to identify which dimensions of performance it will choose to include in a performance management system, it faces another set of issues about how the dimensions will be measured. Various theoreticians in the field including Kaplan and Norton (1992) argue that in setting goals organizations should consider a mix of a number of goals including financial measures, customer measures, internal business measures, and innovation and learning measures. Past experience shows that in developing a comprehensive performance measures one needs to take into account attitudinal and behavioral commitment (Walton, 1985), as well as work-related goals.

Objective versus subjective measures: In practice, one of the biggest challenges in setting up a Performance Management Program is determining the performance dimensions. Fowler (1990) has suggested that performance dimensions are sometimes chosen not because they are most valued to the organization but because they are most easily measured. Some guidelines for setting performance standards:

- Clearly identify the individual's main result areas; example finance, staff development.
- Select the vital key tasks, those priority tasks from the result areas which, when performed well, ensure that the required objectives are being achieved.
- Set standards of performance against each of the key tasks which when met, are acceptable to all concerned. Use information from past experience, present conditions and any foreseeable culture changes.
- Standards must be valid in terms of result in the job.
- Agreement between the job holder and the manager will ensure commitment and cooperation.
- Ensure that standards are realistic - and not too easy! - but present a challenge which is within the job holder's capacity.
- Strive for a clear definition at all times. Standards which can be defined clearly minimize doubt and ambiguity.
- Arrange for information regarding the actual performance to be available to allow for the appropriate recording or monitoring.

Step 2 Monitoring of performance. A system of performance management will not succeed in bringing about high performance against objectives unless employees consciously act in ways seen as being most likely to achieve the objectives.

Step 3 Monitoring the performance gap. In this stage, the manager gathers information from various different possible sources about the job holder's performance. A well defined performance gap analysis, which can also be performed independently from the appraisal interview, is also designed to minimize instances of missing out the obvious details related to the performance of the employee.

Step 4 Preparing for an appraisal interview: The objective of an appraisal interview is to establish the true cause(s) of problems which are affecting a plan of action. In order to do this appraising, the manager must ensure that the interview is an interchange of views geared toward problem-solving and planning using a two-way communication approach. The common fault with all of these cases is that they are based upon the traditionally held view of appraisal, which regards appraisal as a one-way method of control and the interview is used solely for the purpose of informing the individual how well, in the opinion of the appraising manager, he or she has performed.

The good appraising manager starts the preparation for the interview as soon as the actual performance is compared with the standard of performance required. Notes will be made highlighting any significant differences, whether positive or negative, as there are the areas where analysis and discussion will be needed.

Reasons for highlighting the positive areas are threefold.
* It is important that managers show satisfaction for performance achieved by subordinates.
* It provides understanding how successful employees have ahieved good results and as a result it may show you how others could improve by a similar approach.
* It could be that better than standard performance in one part of the job is actually responsible for a shortfall in performance in another related area, for example, savings on a safety budget versus increase in accident rate.

Step 5 Appraising the employee: This phase is generally characterized by the formal meeting between the respective supervisor and/or manager and the subordinate. Effective appraisal meetings are:

* Free from distractions.
* The meeting is held in a friendly atmosphere where there are no hidden agendas.
* The supervisor/ managers allows the subordinate to express his/her point of view.
* Results are discussed.
* Proper feedback is given.
* Action plan is agreed.

Step 6 Implementing the action plan. It is completely useless to carry out a performance appraisal scheme just for the sake of identifying the strong sides of the workforce. A systematic approach toward appraisal schemes implies that this exercise has to run concurrently with other human resource strategies.

Action plans which are generate from performance appraisals meetings are generally of two kinds. In the first instance, the respective supervisor/ manager is responsible to identify the training required by the respective subordinate(s).. For those employees who have not met the required standards or goals which have been agreed before by the parties concerned, it would be more beneficial to train the employees concerned in those skills and areas they lack expertise.

In addition, performance appraisals are also used as a basis for rewarding employees for their performance during the year. Rewards can be in monetary forms or in anither forms such as promotion opportunities.

Step 7 Continuous monitoring of employees: In addition to the formal regular appraisal interviews, good managers appraise their employees in regular basis throughout the year. Effective and efficient managers are aware that certain things can be overlooked when the day-to-day business pressure is on, which is why they combine the informal with the more formal approach to minimize occurrence.

There are good reasons therefore to recommend that appraisal should be formalized to some extent within the company; each manager's competence in appraising should be monitored; and effective training in this competence should be provided when necessary. Collectively this will have the result of encouraging all managers to be more uniform in the way they manage their staff, the real problems affecting performance will be tackled, more employees will be able to work more effectively toward specific results, and departments will be more able to work in harmony for the good of the company's future growth and security.

REWARDING PERFORMANCE

The idea behind linking performance to pay is that it is believed that when an individual reaches the performance targets, monetary rewards should be given as a sign of recognition of 'good' performance. This approach, known as performance-related pay, involves awarding the individual variable increments according to individual performance ratings.

Although different contributors in the field have different perspectives on rewarding performance, studies performed by the Institute of Personnel Development (UK) in 1999, stated that performance-related pay is desirable for three main reasons, namely, it delivers a message that performance is important, it motivates employees to perform better and develop their skills, and it is fair and equitable to reward people differently according to their performance, competence or contribution (Armstrong & Baron, 1998).

On the other hand, the limitations of a performance-related pay system also became clear in the results of many other studies. Several authors in the field including Flores (1998) and Bevan (2003) suggest the idea that performance-related pay inhibits teamwork because of its individualistic nature and may not be a guaranteed motivator. Further on, Buchan (1994) argues that performance-related pay may be too subjective. In addition it can also be noted that performance-related pay is generally costly to administer and at the end it is still a dilemma whether performance is really improved having an increase in pay as the driving force (Beecham & Bevan, 2003).

As a result one can safely argue that the studies on performance-related pay are still somewhat inconclusive. The main constraints which are brought forward by sceptics of performance-related pay include amongst others:

- Performance payments tend to be relatively small due to budget constraints.
- There is usually a large time lag between the end of the appraisal period and the payment related to reward.
- Managers appear to be unwilling to differentiate between employees and all receive a similar pay rise.

Exercise: How do you feel about the rewards accompanying performance in your organization? Are they sufficiently motivational? Do any of the above problems apply to your organization? Have rewards been thought through and matched to the individual person, or is the same reward (perhaps varying in quantity or quality) given to everyone? Is it assumed that people are only interested in money? Which are some of the most popular non-monetary rewards in your organization?

CONCLUSION

Notwithstanding the various limitations discussed in this chapter, it is overtly clear that in the course of time companies are adopting performance management programs as part of their effort(s) to achieve the overall business objectives. The common understanding underlying the introduction of any Performance Management Program lies in the fact that the program should be:

- **Participative** where the individual and the manager discuss goals and results;
- **Task-oriented** where the results are measured against pre-defined goals instead of personality traits;
- **Developmental** where the evaluation process should not only rate individuals but also assist them to improve their performance and to identify any training needs.

In this chapter, we have looked at the importance of managing employee performance, why it can be challenging and difficult for the manager, and a worry to employees. We have looked at how performance management has evolved, to some different approaches, and have come up with a step-by-step guide. We have outlined many of the problems related to the important HR task, and asked you to think about your personal experiences in this area. Above all, we suggest, that there is a need for matching the approach to measuring performance with the business needs of the organization. It should be a useful and relevant exercise otherwise there is no point in doing it at all!

REFERENCES

Applebaum, S., Abdallah, C. & Shapiro, B. (1999) 'The Self-directed team: A conflict resolution analysis' *Team Performance Management, 5:* 2

Armstrong, M. & Baron, A. (1998) *Performance Management – The New Realities.* London: IPD.

Becker, B. & Gerhard, B. (1996) 'The Impact of human resource management or organizational progress and prospects' *Academy of Management Journal, 39*: 4

Bacon, N. & Blyton, P. (2003) 'The Impact of teamwork on skills; employee perceptions of who gains and who loses' *Human Resource Management Journal, 13*: 2

Butcher, D. & Bailey, C. (2000) *'Crewed awakenings' People Management.* August

Delbridge, & Turnball, R. (1992) *Reassuring Human Resource Management.* London: Sage.

Dessler, G. (2005) *Human Resource Management*, International Edition, Prentice Hall, New Jersey.

Guest, D. (2001) 'Human Resource Management; when research confronts theory' International *Journal of Human Resource Management, 12*: 7

Huselid, M. (1995) 'The impact of human resource management practices on turnover, productivity and corporate financial performance' *Academy of Management Journal, 38*: 3

Hutchinson, S., Purcell, J. & Kinnie, N. (2000) 'Evolving high commitment management and the experience of the RAC call centre', *Human Resource Management Journal, 10*: 1

Katzenbach, J. (1997) 'The Myth of the Top Management Team' *Harvard Business Review,* November – December

MacDuffie, J. (1995) 'Human resource bundles and manufacturing performance: organizational logic and flexible production systems in the world auto industry, *Industrial and Labor Relations Review, Vol 48*, No. 2.

Moxon, P. (1993) *Building a Better Team, Gower, in association with ITD*, Aldershot.

Newton, T. & Findlay, P. (1996) 'Playing God? – the performance appraisal' *Human Resource Management Journal, 6*: 3

Patterson, J., West, M., Lawthom, R. & Nickell, S. (1997) *The Impact of People Management Practices on Business Performance.* London: IPD.

Pfeffer, J. (1998) *The Human Equation.* Boston: Harvard Business School Press.

Rice, B. (1982) The Hawthorne deficit. Persistence of a flawed theory, *Psychology Today, 16* (2), 70-74.

Roethlisberger, F.J. & Dickson, W.J. (1939) *Management and the workers: An account of a research programme conducted by the Western Electric Corporation*, Hawthorn. Chicago, Cambridge M.A. Harvard University Press.

Storey, J. & Sission, K. (1993) *Human Resources and Industrial Relations.* Buckingham: Open University Press.

Torrington, D., Hall, L., & Taylor, S. (2005) *Human Resource Management.* 6th Ed.. Harlow, Essex: Prentice Hall.

Williams, R. (2002) *Managing Employee Performance.* London: Thompson Learning.

RECOMMENDED FURTHER READING

Anstey, E., Fletcher, C. & Walker, J. (1976) *Staff Appraisal and Development.* London: George Allen & Unwin.

Argyris, C. & Schon, D.A. (1978) *Organization Learning.* Reading, Mass: Addison Wesley.

Armstrong, M. & Baron, A. (1998) 'Out of the box', *People Management*, July

Beaumont, P. & Hunter, L. (2002) *Managing Knowledge Workers: Research Report.* London: IPD.

Bernardin, H.J. & Cardy, R.L. (1982) 'Appraisal accuracy: The ability and motivation to remember the past', *Public Personnel Management, 11*

Belbin, M. (1993) *Team Roles at Work.* London: Butterworth Heinemann.

Drenth, P.J.D. (1984) 'Personnel appraisal', in P.J.D. Drenth, H.Thierry, P.J. Williams and C.J. de Wolf (eds), *Handbook of Work and Organizational Psychology.* Chichester: Wiley.

Ezzamel, M. & Willmott, H. (1998) 'Accounting for teamwork; a critical study of group-based systems of organizational control', *Administrative Science Quarterly, 43*

Fletcher, C. & Williams, R. (1992) *Performance Management in the UK*: Organizational Experience. London: IPM.

Garratt, B. (1990) *Creating a Learning Organization.* Hemel Hempstead: Director Books.

Long, P. (1986) Performance Appraisal Revisited. London: IPM. Longenecker, C. (1997) 'Why managerial performance appraisals are ineffective: causes and lessons' *Career Development International, 3*: 5

Mabey, C. & Salaman, G. (1996) *Strategic Human Resource Management.* Oxford: Blackwell.

McGregor, D. (1957) 'An uneasy look at performance appraisal', *Harvard Business Review 35*

Oliva, L.M. (1992) *Partners not Competitors.* London: Idea Group Publishing.

Van der Heijden, B.I.J.M. (2002) "Age and assessments of professional expertise in SMEs: differences between self-ratings and supervisor ratings" *International Journal of Human Resource Development and Management. 2*: 3-4, 329-343

Van der Heijden (2005) 'No-one has ever promised you a rose garden. On shared responsibility and employability enhancing practices throughout careers', *Inaugural lecture, MSM/OU.* Assen: Van Gorcum.

Ward, P. (1995) 'A 360 degree turn for the better' *People Management*, February.

Williams, R.S., Walker, J. & Fletcher, C. (1977) 'International review of staff appraisal practices: Current trends and issues', *Public Personnel Management*, January – February

CHAPTER 10

INTERNATIONAL HUMAN RESOURCE MANAGEMENT
STEPHANIE JONES AND SILVIO DE BONO

OPENING CASE:

PricewaterhouseCoopers, the international audit firm, can be seen as a useful example of the problem of managing the challenge of international staffing. With over 150,000 auditors, consultants and other staff in over 150 countries, based in nearly 1,000 offices worldwide, the firm provides financial and management consultancy services to a range of clients, both international and local. With knowledge workers as the firm's main asset, recruiting, retaining, developing and deploying talent is a major concern of their HR Consulting division (see diagram below), which serves both external and internal clients. The creation of a pool of internationally mobile consultants and auditors is the function of 'International Mobility.' The pool of people is also rewarded, given benefits and pensions, and deployed as part of the HR plan.

PricewaterhouseCoopers' employees within the 'International Mobility' domain fall into a number of categories, mostly according to the needs of the organization and the size and demands of its operations in different places. These different possibilities for employees are also driven by developmental needs and personal preferences. Thus the firm can maximize its ability to attract talent and use it to the best advantage:

1. International Expatriate – This is one of the most traditional ways of perceiving an international staff member, with he or she being sent to different 'postings' after a certain period of time, especially to newly established offices with a clear need for an experienced executive with a firm grasp of the head office culture.

2. Permanent Transferee – This international executive may have been an international expatriate who has expressed a preference to stay in one place, possibly for personal reasons. This scenario can also take place when the firm has set up a large office in a fast-growing area and can confidently feel that there is a justification for an expatriate who has commonly been sent to several postings to stay in one place.

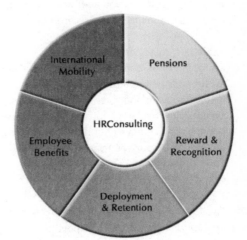

Diagram 10.1:
PricewaterhouseCoopers' HR Model

3. Cross-border Commuter – This is often an international expatriate or permanent transferee who uses one office as a base and then travels to satellite offices which may not yet have the need for a longer-term, constant employee from head office. These may be smaller cities in one country or nearby countries which are still developing a business for the firm. The cross-border commuter may actually move to one of the satellites in due course, or move to new satellites, depending on the demands of the business.

4. Rotational Transferee – This is an alternative arrangement whereby the staff member is moved from one location to another, perhaps 'swapping' with another staff member, especially to gain useful exposure to different markets, as a form of 'job rotation.'

5. International Hire – This executive might be a third-country national (see further explanation, below) who has joined an office of the firm which is not his or her local country; neither is this executive from head office, from where the international expatriate might typically come. They may have been hired for their strong experience in a particular area of specialty or market, and to increase the diversity of executives in a particular office.

6. Local Hire – This is a host country national (see further explanation, below) who has been recruited as a local to work in their own local environment. This person might then become an international hire by going to another country for the firm, and could commute into other markets upon becoming more experienced.

7. Virtual Assignee – This can refer to a number and variety of executives within the firm, with duties in another office – including mentoring and developing colleagues – without necessarily having to be there in person. The use of e-mailing and the telephone has revolutionized the management of employees and the creation of specialized groups of consultants and auditors in certain offices. This is often more cost efficient than the other options listed above.

Why do consultants and auditors at a firm like PricewaterhouseCoopers want to venture overseas to the firm's offices around the world?

There is a clear perception that the firm's international service brings improved pay and living standards, especially to newly hired staff, otherwise why should these executives seek such opportunities? Developing skills and employment opportunities are also attractive features of working overseas, as are improving living standards and experiencing life overseas (particularly important for newly recruited employees). However, lowest on the list is the need to show commitment to the employer. Clearly, PricewaterhouseCoopers does not require employees to accept an overseas posting without an element of choice. There is no obligation to accept an international posting, so it seems unlikely that an employee would lose his or her job if he or she turned down the possibility.

The firm accepts that there are barriers to labor mobility, and that not everyone in the firm is looking for these opportunities. These barriers can be seen as relating to the business of the firm, the individual concerned, and the policy of particular offices in different countries:

Business of the firm

- Greater mobility of executives creates a greater challenge for HRM in different offices, with having to cope with different nationalities and contracts.
- Many problems arise as a result of differences in the firm's own internal policies.
- The terms on which workers are employed are highly inconsistent between countries, and this can cause problems when people are moving around.

The individual concerned

- Lack of employment opportunities for spouse – so one has to make a sacrifice.
- It is increasing difficult to get highly skilled senior managers to accept international assignments, because they can become comfortable in their home base, and they do not want to disrupt their spouse and children.

The policy of particular offices

- Immigration procedures take endless time and are very complex, varying between different countries.
- It is very difficult to find a transferable, standardized pension scheme that can be accepted in many different countries.

Despite these issues, PricewaterhouseCoopers focuses on attracting, retaining, developing and deploying the talent they have, using specific strategies. Employee referral programs are combined with advertisement campaigns aimed at making the firm seem attractive to go-getting and ambitious consultants, managed through a global website. Strategic hiring decisions are often made through executive search, seen as a more accurate, responsive and cost-effective recruitment process for specialist talent. A performance measurement system emphasizing work/life balance (unusual in a consulting firm) is used as part of a Global Capabilities Framework, a competency-based system for managing expatriates of various descriptions. Offering 'world-class learning opportunities' and access to a personal coach/mentor, the firm considers itself as offering 'access to a world of knowledge' for both clients and executives.

HRM acts as the contact point for opportunities and deployment issues, resolving problems in moves of executives between locations, ensuring that the firm's deployment and development needs are met, offering challenging and rewarding careers, providing training and support to encourage competency development and, most importantly, encouraging an environment of respect for people and clear leadership.

Questions on the opening case: Why does this firm find it necessary to make so many different classifications of international staff in the way it operates? Could this be streamlined and be just as effective and easier? What would be the closest to the way that your own firm operates, or to your own personal experience (especially if your firm has international employees)? What are the main advantages and disadvantages of these different expatriate arrangements? Why is it so difficult for this firm (which is quite reputable and well-known) to attract people to work internationally? What would be your own greatest barrier to expatriation in your personal case? On the other hand, what about the reasons that would attract you to venture overseas?

LEARNING OBJECTIVES FOR THIS CHAPTER

In this chapter, we conclude our summary of human resource subjects and applications and their impact on 'Managing Cultural Diversity' by presenting a number of important issues in the area of international human resource management. Most managers working internationally would agree that one of the most critical determinants of organizational success in global ventures is how a company handles its international HR. It has also been suggested that up to 80% of the time of local managers, especially in some of the most challenging postings, is spent dealing with HR issues. So what are the attitudes of different multinationals to international HRM issues? What are the different kinds of expatriates (as discussed in the opening case)? How do multinationals deal with the matter of providing compensation for their expatriates? How frequent is expatriate failure, and how do multinationals cope with this?

In this chapter we are focusing on two particular challenges of the international HR manager: how to recruit staff in an international context, and how to provide incentives to international staff (particularly front-line staff, as in sales positions) for top performance. Finally, we look at a detailed case from China with recommendations for retaining expatriate talent – possibly one of the biggest challenges facing international HRM for the last few decades.

ATTITUDES OF MULTINATIONALS TO INTERNATIONAL HRM

There are as many different ways of managing international HRM as there are multinational companies. What are some of the most important issues? For Siemens, for example, with many large operations overseas, there is a perceived need to send expatriates from the parent company – but Siemens prefers to send a large number of older German 'expats.' The dilemma for them is that younger employees – who may be more mobile and keener to be expatriates – are not seen as experienced and responsible enough. Older employees, with 25 to 30 years of experience, are more likely to be chosen. But many of them are less interested in expatriate opportunities. In their late 40s and 50s, few are as adventurous as they perhaps once were and many are bringing up families. Their spouses are more likely to have senior jobs too, and are unwilling to give these up.

There is also the question of multinationals venturing into new markets preserving their home approach, adopting a local way of operating, or achieving a hybrid of mixed strategy. Intel – when asked this question about their China business – insisted that they aimed to stay American-style wherever they go. That objective, they felt, was part of their differentiating factor. Other companies – especially those serving local markets – were more concerned with localizing as much as possible, in terms of the development of a local culture.

Some large USA multinationals, despite their presence in many countries, insist on centralizing much of their management practices, including international purchasing, for example. Many savings could be made by sourcing locally – but some companies do not do this. Sourcing includes not just things – but people too.

Policies for hiring vary dramatically with different companies – seen as ethnocentric, polycentric or geocentric. The first-named policies are based on sending parent country nationals – for example, a. Dutch company, or a Germany company sending lots of Dutch and German executives overseas. This is in contrast with geocentric policies, of recruiting locals or host country nationals as much as possible. Meanwhile, with polycentric policies, multinationals are looking to create a pool of the best talent from anywhere and put the best person in the right job whenever they can. Despite efforts at localizing and being meritocratic, many multinationals are still predominantly ethnocentric.

Whichever way they recruit, international HRM departments have to face cultural, legal, economic, political, and social factors affecting staff. There are also language issues, and different attitudes to ethics to deal with. Government regulations can be highly variable and appear arbitrary. Joint-ventures, and the local partners they bring with them, can cause endless worry for those dealing with people issues. Overall, the need to identify and develop talent on a global basis is paramount. See Jackson (2002), Adler and Ghadar (1990), and Barnum and Oates (1991) for a further discussion.

Exercise: How would you define the attitude of your own company to these points? Or a multinational company with which you are familiar? What are the advantages and disadvantages of an ethnocentric hiring policy? How about being geocentric or polycentric? How does your company handle the issue of expatriation and localization? Does your company try to blend in with its local environment when operating overseas, or does it behave in a consistent way wherever it goes? Are you aware of some of the people problems of your company in its international dealings?

DIFFERENT KINDS OF EXPATRIATES

As suggested by the opening case, companies operating internationally find themselves with a variety of employees. They can be 'transnationals', 'expats', locals or host country nationals, or home country nationals (which can include international managers, 'expats', technical specialists, and 'occasional parachutists'), as discussed in Brewster (1991). There is also the matter of TCNs (Third Country Nationals), which could relate to a particular group – e.g. Indians working in the oil industry in Yemen – or the term can be used to relate to anyone who is not from the parent company country or the country where they are now based.

The term 'transnational' is fairly new but describes a phenomenon on the increase in recent years, that of the decline of traditional expatriates who move between a succession of career postings – like diplomats – and, by contrast, the rise of the self-managed expatriate. These 'transnationals' are loyal to their own career rather than to a company, are mercenary in terms of looking for opportunities for themselves, and do not expect an employer to offer them a traditional expatriate career path. They clearly have less job security, but they have developed opportunities for employability for themselves through their technical skills and their international experience. Transnationals are mostly task and project-oriented, focused on completing a job and moving on. Employers are adopting this kind of expatriate as they find that offering long-term careers and strategically planning postings is becoming more and more problematic. Many such multinationals find it hard to see so far ahead, and long-term expatriates can be a heavy financial burden. The transnationals are 'hired guns' but can be useful, involve less commitment, and can be cheaper. See Wes Harry (1997, 2002, 2004, 2005).

These attitudes – from the company and the individual – can be used to define types of expatriates. The 'hired gun' is the mercenary and self-motivated locally-hired executive, who can be from anywhere; the 'leave your heart at home' expatriate can be somewhat reluctant – he or she never wanted to go, but needed to help out the company. They spend a lot of time keeping in touch with the head office and wishing they were back at home. The 'dual citizen' has been held up in expatriate literature as an ideal, as a person who apportions their loyalties and concerns equally between the needs of the multinational head office and of the local organization. This can be conflicting, however, and a difficult balance to achieve. Or expatriates can also be defined in terms of their behavior and attitude to the local environment. If they have 'gone local', they emulate the people they live among. Or they could be a 'half-way house', or live in a 'gilded cage' from which they rarely step outside. Transnationals are likely to be 'hired guns' and many have 'gone local', which can be convenient for multinationals facing local problems in the field.

So why would a company hire expatriates or home country nationals (Scullian, 1991)? Maybe there's a scarcity of talent in the particular country. Also, the company wants to control what's going on, so it wants to have its own people in charge. Being an expatriate can offer a temporary niche for foreigners, before a local can be recruited and trained and then the job can be localized. Migration among 'expats' and 'transnationals' around the world, and the spread of globalization generally, has created a bigger pool of foreign talent in countries that is available to be hired on the spot. Some progressive companies are using expatriation to develop their staff, creating a career ladder or fast career track including international postings to develop executive talent. For example, look at the career of Jeff Immelt of GE (General Electric). As part of the process of being groomed as a candidate to be the next CEO, Immelt needed international exposure. This is in considerable contrast with his predecessor, Jack Welch, whose practical experience was almost completely confined to the USA.

Exercise: What are the advantages of being a 'transnational', and do these outweigh the disadvantages for you? Or would you prefer a traditional expatriate approach to being employed overseas, if given the chance? Do you think this relates to personality, lifestyle, and levels of ambition? What might be the ultimate result of different kind of expatriate career options? Should we develop our own personal pension plans in any case?

EXPATRIATE COMPENSATION POLICIES

This can be a major problem area for international HR staff concerned with attracting the quality of talent needed whilst maintaining some form of internal equity. Should they adopt company-wide pay scales or adapt to the local market? Should they make allowances for hardship postings, giving extra pay to work in places with high costs for housing, food and other essentials? It can be hard to access reliable survey data and find the real picture. The

'Balance Sheet Approach' has been adopted by 85% of USA companies operating overseas, offering international staff the same standard of living as at home, with the company paying additional costs if necessary. For example, if an executive is moving from Chicago to Brussels, he or she will find housing and the cost of living around 20 to 30% more expensive. If the executive is to have the same net pay after expenses, the company has to take care of it – otherwise there would be no reason why he/she should go, as it would be a case of being worse off financially. As we have seen from the opening case, this is one of the reasons for seeking overseas' job opportunities (Greene, 1995).

Some executives get non-salary extras too when they are overseas to cope with costs – such as relocation expenses, local mobility costs being covered, housing allowances, overseas travel tickets, education costs of children, and medical and insurance charges. The cost of maintaining expatriates with all these benefits can be several times the cost of their salaries. This is another reason why 'transnationals' – who may have lower expectations in this regard – can be attractive to an employer. Some companies also tend to be more generous with benefits than with salary, where they have less flexibility. The salary can be used for the calculation of an end-of-contract bonus, especially as many overseas jobs are not pensionable. Benefits are sometimes calculated according to needs – thus married couples are allowed a more substantial housing allowance than singles. Or sometimes they are based on seniority, irrespective of needs.

EXPATRIATE FAILURE

The inclusion of expatriate postings by international companies in executive development programs is not always well-run. International experience is not always seen as increasing an executive's value to an organization. Being an expatriate can be a dead end. Of 152 USA companies surveyed in a Conference Board study, it was found that 80% of the USA-originating expatriates working overseas feel that their contribution is not fully valued by the head office. The insular nature of many USA companies means that only around 15% of the top 50 executives in the USA have expatriate experience, whilst 35% of the top 50 European executives have worked overseas, and 27% of the top 50 Japanese executives. More experience of expatriate life, especially in many different countries, tends to reduce the risk of failure. Even if an executive does not enjoy working overseas, at least he or she becomes more used to it over time.

Repatriation back to the home country after a stint as an expatriate can also be a major issue, as many returning executives find it hard to fit into the hierarchy back home at the head office – they may have become used to more autonomy in their offshore postings, and may have missed out on promotions and the career track at home. Meanwhile, their families can have issues readjusting to the home posting. The Conference Board study of 152 USA companies already quoted shows that 15 to 20% of USA executives leave their company within 12 to 18 months of their return from an expatriate posting, due to these relocation difficulties. Forty per cent have left within three years. So much for senior executive development, especially as only 10% of this sample was promoted as a result of their international experience. As many as 50% dislike the new assignment they have been given on their return, and hence the high drop-out rate.

Re-entry culture shock difficulties need to be handled competently by international HR staff, or they will lose these people who have gained valuable experience. Culture shock is well-known – executives can go through the honeymoon period, then suffer irritation, go into the trough of depression, bottom-out, and then, with luck, experience adaptation and adjustment. Eventually, they learn to like it, and some even achieve biculturalism. But less well understood is re-entry culture shock, probably because executives returning to their own countries are not expected to have problems, but they do. How can this be handled? Expatriates should be prepared for their return, kept in the loop with head office so not to be out of touch, or have a mentor or sponsor there to help them readjust. Or, increasingly, companies are considering using 'transnational'; they may be less loyal but they can be effective, and have no problem with returning home as this is not a problem for the multinational!

Expatriate failure rates overall can be as much as 70% in some particularly challenging countries, and are typically 25 to 45% for USA expatriates, with European and Japanese expatriates experiencing a much lower rate, of only around 5%. Again, it would seem that having more experience with being an expatriate can be helpful here.

An inability to adjust to an expatriate posting, problems with the spouse and children, the expatriate's own personal and emotional maturity, and his or her ability to cope with extensive international responsibility and autonomy, in a highly dynamic and fast-moving environment, can be among the reasons for expatriate failure. As we have seen, the executive may be not motivated for the assignment, and not prepared for the job culturally. Most expatriates still have no orientation training, may not even be technically competent for the job to which they are being sent. Now, there is more emphasis on cultural training, using experienced expatriates to coach new ones, with the planning of competencies for certain jobs, more developmental activities, and spouse programs too. But working with expatriates is still a huge cost for companies venturing overseas. For a further discussion of the expatriate failure issue, see Harzing (1995) and Hiltrop and Janssens (1990).

Exercise: What are some of the most important contributing factors to expatriate failure? In your own case, what would be most important for you in ensuring your success in an expatriate assignment? In what ways could companies do a better job with expatriates, in order to keep their people? Do most companies realize the full extent of the cost of expatriate failure – not just monetary but in terms of disruption and the impact on existing staff?

THE RECRUITMENT OF LOCAL TALENT

Hiring locals is usually cheaper (except in the UAE, Kuwait, and many Gulf states, where locals are a small minority, and much more expensive than expatriates), and many multinationals are facing pressure to localize and share the wealth they are generating with the local community. Sometimes it can be difficult for international employers to find enough foreigners willing to go to some countries, and they are thus forced to localize. Meanwhile many companies operating overseas are trying to be 'good corporate citizens', and are localizing for the 'right' reasons. It can be seen as all part of the process of globalizing for companies to try to hire more locals, or at least not be too dominated by parent company nationals. One challenge here is to incentivize expatriates to willingly recruit and train locals to take over their jobs. For them to want to do this, they should be rewarded and encouraged, and given the chance to move on. Too many international companies focus on localizing without another thought for how expatriates may feel about training up another person to take their job, and wonder why this task is not working out. See Harry (1997, 2002).

RECRUITMENT CHALLENGES – 12 REASONS FOR HIRING FAILURE

This case about recruiting in the Middle East can easily be applied to other international environments, and shows how easily good candidates are lost by organizations operating internationally because they fail to think through the implications of their processes, and mishandle this crucial area of recruitment (Jones, 2002):

1. The company carrying out the hiring insists that the candidate should be interviewed by many people, who then cannot agree on the finalist: One major multinational company, based in Saudi Arabia but recruiting a Sales and Marketing Manager for Dubai, actually required ten of its people to be involved in the hiring process. These ten included the HR VP (in Saudi) the HR Manager (in Middle East HQ, in UK), the Country Manager for UAE (in Dubai), the GM (in Jeddah), the business division VP (in Riyadh) and the International HR VP (from the USA). A further difficulty came from the fact that interviewers were traveling constantly and, with vacations and sick leave, interview appointments dragged on for months. And the interviewers gave varying impressions to the short-listed candidates – of the duties of the job, targets and objectives, and the plan of the company in the ME. Confused, the candidates started to waver, especially when they received counter-offers from their existing employers. Was the new company attractive when key managers couldn't give a consistent picture?

2. The company is not available to make time for Interviewers: Another multinational company, this time hiring a senior manager for North Africa, suffered hiring difficulties when the boss was not around to see candidates for interviewing. This domineering GM refused to delegate or to involve others in the hiring process. He had few windows of opportunity for interviews, but candidates could not be interviewed by other managers until they had been screened by the GM.

As a result, star candidates – previously impressed with the dynamic and aggressive management team – lost interest. And feedback on each candidate, to keep them interested and understand which characteristics were most attractive to the client, was not forthcoming.

3. The company is totally inflexible on the package: A company with many operations across ME was hiring a key local manager, but had a fixed idea of how much it was willing to pay, and would only look at people in that salary range. Dissatisfied with the level of experience and competence they were seeing (inevitable because of the low salary they were offering), they demanded to see better candidates. They liked the better candidates very much, but refused to offer them appropriate compensation. When they did finally decide to upgrade their offer, it was still too little, and when the chosen candidate realized that he would have to take a cut in income to join the new company, he changed his mind. When he pulled out, the HQ of the company in Europe instructed the company in the ME to offer him whatever he wanted in order to attract him – but it was too late.

4. The company comes over as unattractive (mean, tough, unsuccessful, not offering promotion prospects, appearing risky, unclear strategy, lays off staff, etc.): Many companies are genuinely surprised when they receive negative market feedback during a recruitment exercise. In trying to hire new staff, perception is reality. A foreign bank in Dubai closed a department on the instructions of HQ, leading to the redundancy of several staff members. Although most of them quickly found new jobs, the damage was done to the bank's reputation and they found it extremely difficult to recruit new staff. Job security is nearly always a high priority.

A confused and unclear strategy, with a lack of transparency over the company's investment and commitment to the region, is also to be avoided when recruiting new people. In an example of a foreign company with an operation in Qatar, when candidates asked about the future strategy for here and the region as a whole, the expatriate manager explained that the company was waiting to see what would happen in the next few years, and then would decide. Candidates were not convinced. Another company, a consulting firm, found recruitment difficult because the culture was too tough. With massive work-loads, staff worked evenings and weekends and traveled in their own time. It was a well-known, reputable company – but people did not stay.

5. There are questions about the legality of the company's operation in the region, relationship with sponsor, etc.: For a foreign company not yet officially set up in the ME, recruiting staff based in offices without local sponsors is, in most cases (except free trade zones) not legal. There are ways around this – the staff can be temporarily hired through a business partner or a consulting firm – but few locally-based candidates feel comfortable with this. Similarly, if a company has an expired business license or has had some legal problems – perhaps publicized by a disgruntled former employee – new would-be recruits may be scared off.

New employers must convince candidates of their legality by showing them documentary evidence, introducing them to the local sponsor if necessary and to other long-term employees, showing them the premises and, in some cases, sending them overseas to HQ.

6. The company takes too long to issue an offer letter/contract: In one example, a company had 'hired' a senior manager – a verbal agreement on salary and duties had been reached, with an approximate start date. The hiring manager, located outside of the ME, assumed that everything was OK and the person was coming on board. The contract would follow. This was now a rubber-stamping exercise.

But this was not the way the candidate saw it. Are they querying my salary? Perhaps they are thinking again about the job description and performance targets? Maybe they are even re-thinking about the need for making a hire altogether?

In reality, the hiring manager was too busy, forgot, was off sick for a few days, and then discovered that his boss was on a business trip and could not make the final approval until the following week. Yet the candidate suffered uncertainty, worry and even trauma as a result of the non-delivery of this vital document. The slow provision of the offer letter and/or job contract can lead to the loss of a star candidate at a late stage in the hiring proceedings. Then the identification of replacement candidates and the eventual completion of the search are even more drawn-out.

7. The company is looking for the perfect candidate who frankly does not exist: In a particular instance, where the hiring manager expected candidates to be more plentiful with 80 to 90% match to the job, he insisted on seeing more and more candidates – and none of them were good enough. In this instance, the company would not compromise on any features of the successful candidate – such as English or Arabic speaking ability, experience, qualifications, background, even age. The pool of candidates to be presented was becoming exhausted. But still the hiring company was not satisfied. And rejected candidates were not interested in being reconsidered, even when the company was forced to accept a degree of compromise.

8. A candidate is hired who does not then stay, because the company does not keep its promises or was not truthful about the nature of the job: In an example of an Abu Dhabi-based foreign company, a successful candidate soon departed due to the company's inability to live up to its promises. The expected relocation, the promised promotion, the scheduled overseas training trip and the destined opportunity to work on the exciting new product just launched – all evaporated within the candidates' first few months in the company. In another case, a candidate was hired after meetings held in the prestigious, down-town sales office only – to then find himself based at a run-down plant in an inaccessible and remote part of the area.

There are many other cases of candidates hired in a sales role who then find themselves spending all their time on the job of collecting their predecessor's debts. Others expected to have a boss they met and liked at the interview, and end up with another. Others were told the company was "doing quite well in the region" and soon discover that the reverse is true.

9. Inability to find anyone in, or willing to move to, an unattractive location: This can be one of the greatest problems in recruitment – the need to find talent for a company established in the middle of nowhere, isolated and with poor transport links, where the standard of living is low, and which is unsuitable for the rest of the family. It may also be perceived as politically unstable or subject to many restrictions.In an unattractive location, companies must make the opportunity as attractive as possible by offering compensating benefits, and must be more flexible than usual about the quality of candidates who will be prepared to consider the opportunity.

10. Inability to find candidates willing to accept a certain salary for a certain position: This is another form of inflexibility on the client side – similar to hiring failure number three, above – the insistence by a company that they should be able to find people for a specific job for a specific salary, without any compromise.For example, a joint-venture in Egypt with a very strict pay policy was looking for a HR manager – at a time when this functional area is in great demand, and where people in similar jobs in other companies were being paid up to three times as much. The company would not – could not – pay any more, but neither would they accept a junior person for this role. Quite simply, the people they wanted expected more money, and the people willing to accept this comparatively low package were not seen as suitable or good enough for the job. In another instance, a European company – which regards itself as financially very conservative' – has a policy of recruiting young, junior people very cheaply then training them and growing them into a more senior role, continuing to pay them as 'conservatively' as possible. It worked in a few cases, and with people recruited from the remote, poorer places and brought to the company's operations in Jeddah and Riyadh.

11. A merger affecting the company, which makes the job less attractive or, after joining, the newly-hired candidate is made redundant by a new boss: In one recent merger, for a long period no one knew who would be leaving and who would be staying, and newly-hired people were infected with the uncertainty, even when assured that they were needed. The successful candidate was worried about potential cost-cutting, even if there were no further redundancies, and how he would cope in the situation of reduced morale. He worried about the company's new image, and how two different cultures would be absorbed and integrated. Maybe his job would not be the same because of changes in strategy which could not now be predicted.

12. Inability of the most desired candidate to leave his previous job (usually when leaving the state sector): Finally, recruitment failure can also occur when candidates find it impossible to resign. They are threatened with the loss of their housing and all benefits which a new employer may not be able to match, the loss of their spouse's job, the loss of all retirement benefits, the loss of their right of residence to live in a certain place – such as being banned and forced to leave the country. For some candidates, it is too much. This situation can happen in many developing countries around the world.

Exercise: Have any of these problems happened in your own experience? Do you think companies operating internationally take the hiring of staff seriously enough? What was most important for you when you were being hired into your current job, especially when you were working for a foreign company? In a local company, do you still face similar problems?

CASE STUDY: THE ROLE OF WASTA IN RECRUITING IN THE BANKING SECTOR IN KUWAIT

Another issue in recruiting which many foreign companies have to contend with is a tradition in many countries (of which the oil-rich Gulf state of Kuwait is a possibly extreme example) of new hires being identified by connections, nepotism, introductions – and not by merit, qualifications or experience (Al-Humayan, 2007; Al-Humayan and Jones, 2007). A foreign-owned organization entering such a country may find the local ways of recruiting rather alien. Such actions may be very worrying and disturbing for multinationals and as a result may feel that their ethical standards are being dangerously compromised.

Although it can be a positive attribute to develop a team who know each other well and trust each other, it can be negative if they are not the best people for the job. A recent study of 'wasta' in Kuwait – a local slang word widely used to describe nepotism and the helping of friends and relatives to find jobs and short-cut other processes – discovered that the widespread nature of this tendency in the banking sector meant that there was serious worry about the qualifications and experience of up to 80% of new hires .

Foreign companies may have decided that this will not be allowed in their organizations, but they may have to take certain steps to prevent it. Another consideration is that without 'wasta' the staff recruited may be less effective, and have no possibility of speeding up procedures and getting things done. 'Wasta' can be seen as a two-edged sword – dangerous to use, but perhaps even worse if you do not have any. Westerners used to life in countries where connections are paramount often adapt to the system and develop their own form of 'wasta.'

INCENTIVES – AND NATIONAL CULTURAL VARIANCES

A very important aspect of international HRM is choosing the right incentive scheme for the type of business you are in, and especially the country in which you are operating. It is not acceptable to assume that the incentive scheme in head office will work everywhere. A considerable amount of adjustment and adaptation will be needed. It may also need to vary in terms of the functional area of your business. This case focuses on sales incentives, one of the most challenging areas to develop reliable performance.

Sales Incentives Schemes can produce amazing results – but for some companies, they may get more than they bargained for. As with many HR tools, it's a case of 'Horses for Courses' – that the impact on behavior and results can be strongly influenced by the incentive programs in place. Some people respond well to certain kinds of incentives, whereas others do not. In managing an incentive program internationally, the HR manager must be concerned with important cultural variances. It may not be clear at first that they are encouraging behaviors identified as positive. This can be another aspect of the learning process for the international HR manager – see Greene (1995) and Smiley (1989).

Top of the range incentive approaches: At the top of the spectrum, some companies offer up to five different elements in terms of remuneration to their sales people. These can include basic salary only; a bonus based on individual performance of up to 50% (or even 100%) of salary; team bonuses paid out on the achievements of the team; commission paid on individual or team-based sales of particular units of a product or service; and company performance bonus, paid on the success or lack thereof of the whole business in a particular country or region. Some companies also offer a form of stock option or bonus, based on the performance of the company worldwide. However, these are not allowed in several countries where nationals are not permitted to own stocks in companies overseas or to keep foreign currency (Jones, 1999).

In some countries known for a high 'uncertainty-avoidance' culture, a guaranteed salary is a must. In such cases, employees generally receive high bonuses for their job which is expected on regular annual basis. If bonuses are not received, employees feel that they have lost money, their salary reduced and most of all suffer loss of face. Attempts to explain that bonuses are 'special' and have to be 'earned' are sometimes not understood, and trust and motivation can be lost as a result.

Incentives can take the form of cash or even team outings or overseas trips. Some training courses are also offered as incentives. It all depends on the way these offerings are packaged, and the tradition and culture of the company concerned. Sometimes training is seen as a right, not an incentive. It is also the right of the most senior person, whether he or she is the most appropriate person to be trained or not. Overseas trips are particularly contentious. Rewards – especially conspicuous ones – must start at the top.

Not known at this address: At the lower end of the range of incentive offerings are the companies offering only basic salaries with no bonuses, except perhaps an annual company-wide share-out based on how the company fared last year – which may not have been great, in which case the share-out is little or nothing. In some countries share-outs are not common, so it may not be noticed if there isn't one. As mentioned above, stock options are, in any case, not allowed in some countries. Those with very strict foreign exchange controls forbid their nationals from owning stock in foreign companies. In this case, 'ghost' or pretend options can be given. Employees can follow the progress of their company and its performance, and 'cash in' their options as if they were real.

A question of seniority: Sales representatives and more junior sales managers can, in some cases, earn a similar pattern of bonuses, commission, and team-based pay-outs – but senior people may want to get more company-performance-based awards, especially if they are senior enough to make an impact on company strategy. Junior people tend to receive their bonuses more frequently – monthly rather than quarterly or annually – as their time frames tend to be shorter, they are less strategically-minded, and more regular efforts must be made by their employers to retain them and keep up their motivation levels. There is also a higher prevalence of more junior sales people being incentivized by commissions paid out on units sold, so they can receive instant cash gratification upon doing a good job.

In some countries the senior staff may want to receive their incentives more often, too, not trusting that they will actually get them. And they may want to do the handing out of rewards themselves to their more junior staff, building allegiance to themselves from the sales team. They want the sales people to be loyal to them, not to the foreign management.

Get it right! Certain problems associated with sales incentive schemes have been identified, each with their cultural ramifications. Ten to watch are:

1. No path to the top
Some sales people have found that they can earn so much money with their incentive scheme that they do not want to be promoted to the position of manager, because then their income will be reduced. Thus, unless they create other bonus systems, companies cannot grow outstanding sales people to be managers – they are not interested in moving from

their front-line sales jobs. In some countries, people want to be managers at any price – but they don't necessarily want to do the work, they just want to the title. So the HR manager must be careful when no one wants to be the manager, or wants to do the work either .

2. Individuals rule OK – not the team

If sales people are primarily incentivized individually, not only will they not be interested in working as a team – they may even try to scupper the attempts of others, stealing their leads and battling each other to take telephone calls which may be customers. This breed of super-sales people will also keep all contacts, methodology, sales tips and insider-info to themselves, refusing to mentor, coach or train others. They will be on the look-out for potential tall poppies around them in the shape of competing sales people – and try to cut them down to size. In countries where there can be a lack of trust between workers, such negative competitiveness can be damaging – including to customers. Creating what might be seen as 'healthy competition' can seriously backfire.

3. Cash or quits

If sales people are only motivated by the opportunity to maximize their cash take-home pay, do not enjoy benefits linked to bonding with fellow team members and do not receive company recognition, they are easy to lure away with promises of a higher salary and bonus possibilities. If the company is not doing well and prospects for more cash are poor, they will be on their way. In many overseas business environments, local staff members feel no loyalty to foreign companies, and will move even for small pay increases. Efforts must be made in each individual context to see how staff can be retained in a proactive way. Motivating people entirely by cash, in a fast-paced business environment, can lead to high levels of turnover with their attendant high costs and disruption.

4. Sales people are kings

In companies where only sales people are rewarded with incentives, other staff can be disempowered and depressed. They may be making an important contribution to the overall result and working in a strong support role to the sales people – but they feel like nobodies. This can result in poor customer service, product quality, and order fulfillment – unless these services are also incentivized. In some countries there is a rigid pecking-order of staff, and these are not necessarily sales people. These 'top' people – with their connections, special experience or the membership of a top family or other elite – need to be carefully rewarded first, to win them onto the side of the management. Assessing equity in these situations is problem-laden but essential.

5. Team-based bonuses – a hiding place

In cases where companies offer a bonus for the team but not for individuals, non-performers can sometimes be carried by the stars – and the stars soon become resentful. They may feel that they are not being adequately rewarded, that they should have more than those who are less successful. In some countries, 'carrying' a person in a team who apparently makes no contribution is acceptable. They may come from a leading family and have important connections, and it's important that they are looked after. Sometimes it can be difficult to work out the results of group bonuses in terms of equity, when people are 'protected' by co-workers.

6. Quantity but not quality

In companies which emphasize unit-sales-based commission, sales people will go to great lengths to get the product out of the door – but it may be to customers who are not going to pay, and there are plenty of these in many parts of the Middle East and China, for example. Collections should also be part of the deal, and factored into the bonus payments, to ensure that the 'customers' are for real. And some companies also encourage the introduction of the product into new outlets, special promotion achievements, and new marketing ideas – and reward these, to offset the obsession on sales volumes alone. Rewarding just one aspect of the sales effort can be dangerous. Many local staff members in foreign companies are only interested in their own personal gains, and have no commitment to the long-term success of the company.

7. Feast or famine

If sales people receive mostly commission earnings and very limited basic salaries then when sales collapse due to no fault of their own, they can suffer a big down-turn in income. In some countries this can be against the local labor law, as basic salaries are mandatory.

8. Not in our backyard

In some cases, incentive systems can be rather ahead of their time in some countries which are still developing basic HR systems. Commissions yes, but anything else might be seen as difficult to administer and relying too much on employee honesty and sincere co-operation. Typically, many sales people in some Middle Eastern countries and China – for example – can be quite cautious and risk averse, and incentives schemes are not always attractive in times of economic slowdown, when bonuses may be much reduced. Many sales people in these regions, when being approached to consider a new job opportunity, express a need to know exactly how much they will earn. Not everyone wants to take the risk of feast or famine.

9. Again, horses for courses

Some products are much easier to sell than others – especially low-end, everyday consumer products supported by huge advertising campaigns and after many years of being sold in a particular market. High-touch, complex, expensive, specialized products are much more challenging to move. So incentives need to be matched to them.

For example, in many countries mass consumer product manufacturers like Pepsi and Coke offer sales representatives only a low monthly basic salary, with a moderate bonus potential. It is not such a tough job – but there are no millionaires here. Conversely, a small, niche software house pays the same basic, but bonuses could be much higher. Incentives must be matched to the job to attract the kind of sales people needed. It depends on the levels of risk aversion in the country concerned.

10. More than the money

Research amongst sales staff – and other employees – shows that more cash, bonuses and junkets are not necessarily the most attractive things in life. They want training, promotion, career development, praise, recognition, quality working relationships with peers and subordinates, and a good working environment. Very important for many can be the concept of 'face' – prestige, status, and how others see them.

Companies need to find out what turns on their people in a particular environment – and not just assume that it must be money. If such tools as employee opinion surveys and needs analysis are used to help develop an incentive plan, companies can develop staff who are more than adherents to the 'greed is good' maxim – even sales people. One company – where outstanding sales people are given the honor of becoming sales trainers – is a case in point, but they will need careful training in the task of training.

Summary and outcomes: your sales incentive plan is working if:
- Your track record in retaining sales staff is good;
- You are able to build a career path for them;
- Your sales turnover is high;
- Prices are maintained;
- Profitability targets are being met;
- Collections are satisfactory and Accounts Receivables are minimal; and
- If the cost of sales is controlled.

You have also got it right if your outstanding sales people are:
- Training and coaching others;
- Sharing contacts; and
- Working well as a team.

If you have been able to create a transparent culture where people can openly discuss how to address such issues as corruption, bribery and kickbacks – this is a strong sign that you are on the right track. If you have specific problems in sales, incentives can be used to address these – as long as you do not create new problems at the same time!

Exercise: How about the use of incentives in your own organization? Which are the most and least effective? Why do attitudes to incentives vary so much between different cultures worldwide? In your particular environment, what are the contrasting attitudes to team-based and individual bonuses? Explain what kind of incentive program would best make the respective employee to work more toward maxizing the firm's revenue and attaintment of goals?

CLOSING CASE

The task of managing expatriates in China – including the attitude of multinational companies and their experiences – has been the subject of many studies of this large and complex market (Jones, 1997). Many studies have considered the importance of preliminary orientation training. This can involve immersing recruits in local culture, and also proving programs for spouses and other family members (Mendenhall & Oddou, 1985).

In particular, a study of European companies (including ABB, Alcatel, BASF, BP, Citroen, Heineken, Lufthansa, Philips, Roche, and Siemens) found that over 25% of expatriates were experiencing difficulties, and for younger ones the figure was as high as 45%. This might be due to frustration and impatience, especially as those expatriates seen as generally effective put it down to an ability to cope with stress, having an adaptable personality, and being able to get on with a wide variety of people (Torbiorn, 1982). These factors were rated more highly than previous experience in Asia, previous job ratings, above-average intelligence or the ability to speak Mandarin fluently. Above all, the study showed that the lack of preparation and training for an expatriate's China posting was a big problem, and the lack of understanding of the challenges of doing business in China by the expatriate's boss also contributed to the problem. China was seen as a hardship posting, not always contributing to success in the expatriate's later career. For more on the China context, see Bjoerkman and Lu (1997).

The recommendations produced by this study included:

- Providing China familiarization training not just for the expatriate but for their bosses;
- Ensuring opportunities to gain feedback on performance and discuss problems faced by the expatriates;
- Taking into account personal attributes when recruiting (see Tung, 1981);
- Especially looking for flexibility and adaptability in personality;
- Involving expatriates' partners in job decisions to a greater extent;
- Providing language and culture training for partners, not just the expatriates themselves.

Questions on the closing case: How would you design an orientation program for your expatriates in China? How would this compare with a program for other countries? What would be some of the main issues to confront? How could you reduce culture shock and encourage a shorter period of adaptation and adjustment?

CONCLUSION

In this chapter we have considered a number of important issues affecting the job of the HR manager operating internationally, especially the varying approaches of different multinationals; the different scenarios involved in international hiring and employment; some issues with pay and benefits; a number of the reasons for expatriate failure; and the challenges of recruiting local staff. We have looked in detail at how the recruitment of staff in different markets can cause problems for both parties involved, and how some of the recruitment processes used in the head office might not work in the field. The same can be true of incentive programs – those successful in a head office environment may not work out in some of the more remote parts of a company's international footprint. Overall, one of the main issues of managing an international business is the importance of HR – and getting it right!

REFERENCES

Adler, N.J. & Ghadar, F. (1990) 'Strategic human resource management: a global perspective', in R. Pieper (ed.) *Human Resource Management: an international comparison.* Berlin: De Gruyter.

Al-Humayan, R. (2007) *A Study of Corruption: Nepotism and Employment in the Banking Sector in Kuwait.* Unpublished MBA thesis.

Al-Humayan, R. & Jones, S. (2007) '"Wasta": nepotism and employment in the banking sector in Kuwait' *International Management Development Conference,* Maastricht.

Barnum, K. & Oates, D. (1991) *The International Manager.* London: The Economist.

Bjoerkman, I. & Lu, Y. (1997) 'Human resource management practices in foreign invested enterprises in China: what has been learned?' in S. Stewart and A. Carver (eds.) *Advances in Chinese Industrial Studies.* Greenwich, CT: JAI Press.

Brewster, C. (1991) *The Management of Expatriates.* London: Kogan Page.

Deller, J. (1997) 'Expatriate selection: possibilities and limitations of using personality scales' in D.M. Saunders and Z. Aycan (eds) *New Approaches to Employee Management. Volume 4, Expatriate Management: Theory and Research.* Greenwich, CT: JAI Press.

Greene R.J. (1995) 'Cultural diversity and reward systems', *ACA Journal,* Spring, 24-33

Hamill, J. (1989) 'Expatriate policies in British multinationals' *Journal of General Management, 14*:1, 18-33

Harry, W.E. (1997) 'Changing terms of conditions of service as nationals replace expatriates'. Paper presented at *Fifth Arab Management Conference* University of Bradford Management Centre, Bradford.

Harry, W.E. (2002) 'Localization: the challenges of developing host country nationals to replace expatriates'. Paper presented at the *International Federation of Training and Development Organizations (IFTDO)* conference, Bahrain.

Harry, W.E. (2004) 'Achieving New Venture Success in the Emerging Arab countries' *Cross-Cultural Management, 2* (4) 3-15

Harry, W.E. & Banai, M. (2005) 'International Itinerants' in Michael, M., Heraty, J. and Collings, D. *International HRM and International Assignments.* Basingstoke: Macmillan.

Harzing, A-W.K. (1995) 'The persistent myth of high expatriate failure rates', International *Journal of Human Resource Management, 6*:2, 458-74

Hiltrop, J.M. & Janssens, M. (1990) 'Expatriation: challenges and recommendations', *European Management Journal, 8*:1, 19-26

Jackson, T. (2002) *International HRM: a cross-cultural approach.* London: Sage.

Jones, S. (1997) *Managing in China: an executive survival guide.* Singapore: Butterworth Heinemann. (Including a European Commission report on the training needs of expatriates in China.)

Jones, S. (1999) 'Sales incentive schemes in China', *China Labor Weekly* online publication

Jones, S. (2002) 'Twelve Reasons for Hiring Failure', *Human Assets Middle East,* Autumn.

Mendenhall, M. & Oddou, G. (1985) 'The dimensions of expatriate acculturation: a review', *Academy of Management Review, 10:* 39-47

PricewaterhouseCoopers survey, based on author interview

Scullian, H. (1991) 'Why companies prefer to use expatriates', *Personnel Management,* 23:32-5

Smiley, T. (1989) 'A challenge to the HR and organizational function in international firms' *European Management Journal, 7*:2, 189-97

Torbiorn, I. (1982) *Living Abroad: personal adjustment and personnel policy in overseas settings.* New York: Wiley.

Tung, R.L. (1981) 'Selection and training of personnel for overseas assignments' *Columbia Journal of World Business, 15*: 68-78

RECOMMENDED FURTHER READING

Adler, N.J. (1991) *International Dimensions of Organizational Behavior,* 2nd ed. Boston: PWS-Kent.

Brewster, C. (1995) 'Towards a "European" model of human resource management', *Journal of International Business Studies, 1*:1-21

Chakravarty, B.S. & Perimutter, H.V. (1985) 'Strategic planning for global business', *Columbia Journal of World Business, Summer:* 5-6

Chen, M. (1995) *Asian Management Systems.* London: Routledge.

Derr, C.B. (1986) *Managing the New Career.* San Francisco: Jossey-Bass.

Derr, C.B. & Laurent A. (1987) *The Internal and External Careers: a theoretical and cross-cultural perspective, working paper,* University of Utah and INSEAD

Desatnick, R.A. & Bennett, M.L. (1978) *Human Resource Management in the Multinational Company.* New York: Nichols.

Dowling, P.J. & Schuler, R.S (1990) *International Dimensions of HRM.* Boston: PWS-Kent.

Doz, Y. & Prahalad, C.K. (1986) 'Controlled variety: a challenge for HRM professions in the MNC', *Human Resource Management, 25*:1, 55-71

England, G.W (1978) 'Managers and their value systems: a five country comparative study', *Columbia Journal of World Business, 13*:2, 33-44

Keep, E. (1989) 'Corporate training strategies: the vital component' in J. Storey, ed. *New Perspectives on Human Resource Management.* Routledge, London.

Laurent, A. (1986) 'The cross-cultural puzzle of international HRM', *Human Resource Management, 25*:1, 91-102

Rosenzweig, P.M. & Nohria, N. (1994) 'Influences on human resource management practices in multinational corporations', *Journal of International Business Studies, 25*:2, 229-51

Storey, J. (1992) *Developments in the Management of Human Resources.* Oxford: Blackwell.

CHAPTER 11

DEFINING CULTURE
STEPHANIE JONES

OPENING CASE:

DHL, a well-known multinational courier and delivery company, now managed by the German Deutsche Post, operates in 135 countries with 111,000 employees. It is famous for its speed, efficiency and supportive, service-driven culture. How can we assess its strengths and weaknesses with regard to its culture, structure and core values? What are the internal and external changes impacting on this multinational? Especially in its branch in Egypt, a large market with a growing population, with 22 million people living in Cairo alone?

Research at the Cairo branch of DHL found, on the positive side, "a family spirit that covers the entire place" and "an open, honest and ethical atmosphere." According to employees, this is partly due to the layout of the company's workplace areas, which take the form of open partitions, not closed offices. The culture is seen as showing "a sense of acknowledgement and respect towards people. No titles are used, there's a pleasant atmosphere, with no borders between employees and managers, which all helps to solve work problems."

Colleagues in the company are seen as friendly, having very good relationships with each other, although "there is a healthy and fair competition among employees." The company is governed by clear systems, policies and procedures, which most people there like. (The culture in Egypt is traditionally risk-averse and characterized by a high uncertainty-avoidance). Part of the way of building the culture has been focused "on spreading the family spirit among its members and their families by organizing a family day gathering on a yearly basis." Another aspect of the culture is being "keen on having close relationships with customers through organizing a yearly ceremony for them." The work is hard, but "there is no stressful culture or fear of loss of jobs," say the employees.

The local corporate structure is seen as following the worldwide company's structure, with no titles or jobs "invented for special people". Chances of promotion are available within the structure to those who are excelling in their duties. The internal structure allows qualified people to be transferred outside their home countries, if they want this. DHL in Egypt is described by employees as having "a learning organizational culture that tries to apply the double-loop learning principle (Fiol and Lyles, 1985) where errors are corrected by modifying the organization's objectives, policies, and standard routines". All of the above shows that DHL Egypt is a "secure culture to work for. The friendship and family-orientation minimizes the sense of work stress and load. Meanwhile, the way the company operates gives a chance for employees' promotions and self-improvement".

Yet there are clear cultural weaknesses. There is "no clear vision and plan for the future, so this causes gossip and rumors, and this affects both the employees' and the company's performance". Frustration and low morale is evident, as a result of low salaries. This also affects both the effectiveness and efficiency of employees, especially as some employees take home much lower salaries than others of the same grade and work experience. This issue is also true of managers. Therefore, "as a result of the double standard culture, many employees are concentrating on getting their rights or looking for another job outside the company, rather than focusing on their duties". At the same time, "the HR department puts much focus on training, but without any employees having insight into developmental plans". The employee turnover rate is increasing year after year, with 8% in the half year ending June 2004, high for a reputable multinational. Offices and furniture "are of bad quality, which affects people's behavior towards the concept of quality".

Only new employees know about DHL's culture and core values through their induction courses, while most of the others who have been there a long time know nothing officially about it. There would seem to be a lack of communication, resulting in low awareness of any decisions and changes. The friendly atmosphere is "only on individual basis, while departments lack co-operational spirit. The managers tend to attribute any success to a department rather to the company as a whole".

The company structure tends to be mechanistic, characterized by departmentalization, formalization, a limited information network, centralization and little participation by low-level members in decision-making. There are "an unjustifiable number of supervisors and managers that makes job specifications and responsibilities overlapping and unclear". The culture tends to be a weak one rather than strong, where sub-cultures (departmental cultures) are very distinctive and there is no dominant overall culture.

Looking at internal and external changes and their affect on the DHL in the Egyptian culture, the most important change that has recently taken place has been the hiring of a new country manager with Egyptian origins. "This step has affected the company's culture, as the DHL dominant corporate culture in the past was influenced by foreign country managers keen on imposing their own culture for years. This was replaced by the new country manager's national and sub-culture outlook", an employee explained. Normally, the DHL culture states that the hiring of new managers must be within the company. "But the individual sub-culture of the new country manager was stronger as he started to hire all new managers from outside the company", he continued. There used to be a corporate cultural habit stating that it is the right of any employee to meet the country manager without any previous appointment. But the new country manager applied the closed door policy, and now employees must talk to their direct line managers only. The impact was such that "the culture of retaining good employees and finding ways to compensate them, in case they have better offers, was replaced by another culture. Now, employees who think of leaving the company are not loyal, and they do not deserve any efforts to keep them".

Another very important change that affected the company culture – from the outside – was the change in the ownership of the company. Deutsche Post of Germany bought all the company's shares, and came with its own culture and values. These confronted the different core values of both the British and the Americans, who were occupying most of the key positions in the organization. The effect was mostly positive and enhanced the learning organization concept. Therefore, the double-loop learning was gradually imposed, where errors are corrected by modifying the organization's objectives, policies, and standard routines. Yet the German culture was seen as increasing the staff workload, through a heavy emphasis on selling campaigns throughout the year, which was not the case before.

Meanwhile, the economic recession and stagnation of 2004 affected many companies locally and internationally, and the floating of the Egyptian pound negatively affected most of the industrial sectors in Egypt. As the Egyptian Pound is linked to the USA Dollar, the value of it dramatically went down and the consequences of that were very dangerous, affecting the economy at large. This made the employees "struggle for salary increases, and made them feel that the company is not dealing with them fairly". But so far, the economic situation is the only external change that is currently leaving an affect on the organization's culture.

Questions on the opening case: What can we learn about both organizational and national culture from the DHL in Egypt case? What can you say about the cultural characteristics highlighted in this case? How would you describe the organizational culture? This company used to be a predominantly American-run multinational and is now German-owned – has its culture changed? What changes did the German company introduce? How about the change in Country Manager – was localization a good or bad move? What about the impact of the internal and external environment on the company? In what ways was there a clash between national and organizational culture, given the differences between the Egyptian and Western ways of doing things? You may have to read the rest of this chapter and the following chapters on organizational and national culture to find out!

LEARNING OBJECTIVES FOR THIS CHAPTER

Defining culture is a very difficult task, as culture is almost impossible to define exactly, a nebulous concept in a very diverse world. Yet it is extremely important if we are to fully understand the organizations in which we work and with which we do business. Another dimension of culture is based on nationality – where we come from, where we were brought up, where we live and work, where we carry out our business. These are defined in the upcoming chapters.

The following chapters include detailed introductions to both organizational and national culture, with the following learning objectives: **Organizational Culture – Chapter 12** introduces you to models of corporate culture and more cases to test your knowledge, so that you can confidently describe, identify and evaluate the cultures of contrasting companies, picking up on some of characteristics and features. **National Culture – Chapter 13** is designed to help you understand the challenges of managing in different countries, also looking at helpful models and classifications, again providing examples from around the world to put the theory into context. **Developing Cultural Awareness – Chapter 14** looks at how you can put these insights into practice, identifying how culture can shape our views of people and organizations.

This chapter, kicking-off the concept of culture with a case revealing both organizational and national culture characteristics, outlines some of the most important issues we need to consider in informing ourselves about 'what is culture?' Firstly, we will look at cultural sensitivity as a management competency, then attempt a definition of organizational culture. How can culture in an organization be built or, in a more difficult task, be changed? What is the job of the culture change agent, and the culture change consolidator? What is the relationship between organizational culture and corporate structure? How do we identify organizational culture at work – its rituals, norms and values? What is the role of the founder and/or current leader in shaping a company's culture? We will also look at other factors affecting culture, such as technology, and how employees working within different cultures feel about factors like organizational culture and employee job satisfaction and dissatisfaction. We then move on to an introduction to national cultures, identifying some of the most important issues and ending with a national cultural case study.

WHAT IS CULTURE?

Culture represents a complex pattern of beliefs, expectations, ideas, values, attitudes and behaviors shared by members of a group or team (Hellriegel and Slocum, 2004) who come from the same village, town, country or region – or from the same work unit, department, division or organization. The beliefs, expectations, and so on, can evolve over time and keep changing, but the main point is that they are recognizable and can be related to this group or team. Aspects of culture can relate to rituals, ceremonies, language, norms, values, philosophy of life, and a 'feeling' that you might have being with people from this group or team, which might be just a few people or a large number.

Some examples of aspects of organizational culture: Describing the company as 'a prison camp' and the employees as 'inmates'; saying hello to everyone in the company on arriving for work in the morning; having a party for staff members who are leaving; the bosses have reserved parking spaces near the office; the offices are open-plan with no walls or doors ; people come and go whenever they want, without clocking-in; the company believes in looking after pensioners; people personalize their workspace and even bring pets to work.

Some examples of aspects of national culture: Describing the country as 'heavenly' or 'paradise'; warmly greeting new arrivals to the country; encouraging people to return when they are leaving; some people are clearly richer and more aristocratic than others; people hang around at street corners rather than staying in their houses; people come and go whenever they want, without locking-up their cars or houses; old people are looked-after by their families, not sent to care homes; people paint their front doors different colors and show ornaments in the windows.

Exercise: to familiarize yourself with the concept of culture, describe your own organization using some of these concepts, terms and ideas, or their opposites. Then do the same for your country – or it may be just your local area, depending on your country's diversity. Discuss these with your friends at work and people you know from your own region. List your points of agreement about the cultural characteristics in both cases. This can be used to further your understanding of these concepts in the coming chapters.

A CULTURE COMPETENCY

Cultural sensitivity is an increasingly important management competency. With managers and employees working for several different organizations and in several different countries, the need to be aware of contrasting attitudes and behaviors has become a business essential. Behavioral indicators of the cultural sensitivity competency can be defined as:

Negative indicators

- Shows arrogance, intolerance of people who are different (nationality, social class, gender, experience);
- Is negatively critical of clothes, food, behavior of people of different background;
- Believes without question own views must be right and others must be wrong;
- Accepts or rejects arguments or ideas based on the person who expressed it, not the idea itself; and
- Takes no trouble to explain anything which a person from a different background would not automatically understand.

Positive indicators

- Gives examples of how people from other cultures etc. would behave, making observations which are not negative in tone;
- Listens attentively to all people equally, asking questions and working hard to understand their background and where they are coming from;
- Can put themselves in 'other people's shoes; and
- Is respectful of the 'face' of another person, even from a different background, not just their own.

Exercise: observe your colleagues in the workplace, and even your fellow students in your business program, identifying attitudes to culture. These could relate to organizations or to nations or social groups. What are the other characteristics of those who seem to be the most culturally aware? Have they traveled and lived in other countries a good deal? Have they changed jobs frequently? Do they study culture? And how about the attributes of those who exhibit intolerance of other cultures – do they have a different background?

DEFINING ORGANIZATIONAL CULTURE

Types of Organizational Culture have been created and classified to help us put companies into convenient boxes - not always fully accurate but broadly helpful. Chapter 12 introduces us to two famous models – by management guru Charles Handy and by textbook authors Hellriegel and Slocum, based on the work of Hooiberg and Petrock (1993). Other authors have created circular charts defining culture – with the outer layer being the general environment, the middle layer the task, and the internal core cited as the location of the culture (Daft, 2006). The external environment defines the existence of adaptive and unadaptive cultures, depending on levels of uncertainty. Visible and invisible aspects of culture include artifacts (dress, office layout, symbols, slogans, ceremonies) discussed more in Chapter 12, contrast with invisible culture (expressed values – such as 'The HP (Hewlett Packard) Way' – and underlying assumptions and deep beliefs, such as a family environment), explained in Daft (2006), George and Jones (2002) and many other popular OB textbooks.

Culture Change is an area of increasing concern, as culture is often seen as a hurdle or barrier as well as an asset to an organization. The Swatch example in Chapter 12 shows how the founder, George Hayek, created a new culture out of the death-throes of an old one. There are many examples of companies changing their cultures again and again to survive and compete – such as Microsoft, Fleet Bank, Siemens – described in Harvard Business Review. cases. How do you change a culture, and how do you consolidate the change once this is complete? Culture change agent and consolidator competencies are required, showing the difficulties of this task, and here we are probably talking about two different people with quite different skills and attitudes:

CULTURE CHANGE AGENT

Risk-taking
- Willingness to make radical changes for big upside, despite downside;
- Not afraid of loss of 'face; and
- Gives feedback on others' mistakes – positively.

Entrepreneurial and innovative
- Takes different view, risk-taking, outspoken, strikes out on own;
- Individual style in dress, manner;
- Embraces newness enthusiastically – "I like this, it's different"; and
- Beyond personal recognition, wants successful business results.

Tough – in hiring and firing
- Able to take tough decisions;
- Good at 'selling' the new vision to motivate people.

Inspirational, with charisma, leadership-oriented
- Immediately wins followers over, even to completely untested ideas; and
- Strong personality, excellent communications and motivation skills.

Thick-skinned – not over-sensitive
- Willing to be unpopular to gain results required;
- Prepared to be ruthless, refuses to withdraw ideas; and
- Not trying to protect 'sacred cows'.

Short-term success-oriented, project-based, change-leading
- Focus on short-term objectives, rejecting those in conflict;
- Talks about overall objectives to be achieved from the start; and
- Will make short-term sacrifices for overall result.

Pushy, aggressive
- Demanding, focused, expecting results from others, pressurizing, willing to fight for results, doesn't give up easily; and
- Not afraid of personal rejection – but will carry on pushing his ideas.

Strong impact and influence skills
- Able to help senior managers to reach decisions, so they feel they thought of it themselves;
- Clear on own understanding, can inspire confidence in others;
- Uses rational arguments, logic, facts and figures, not subjective;
- Builds relationships easily – people want to work with him/her; and
- Is reasonable in approach, but strongly assertive.

Honest and direct to the point of bluntness
- Radical, uncompromising, no whitewash, everything in black and white;
- Willing to force people out if unwilling to support the cause;
- Directly points out strengths and weaknesses in others, no cover-up.

Uncompromising, revolutionary
- Thinks around the problem, not just considering obvious solutions, and challenges all suggested solutions – which could be better?;
- Quickly makes decisions – does not ponder too long; and
- Is confident and assured in decision-making, sticking to his/her decisions and not changing his/her mind later.

Savvy, street-smart, even cynical
- Politically-aware;
- Knows what works; and
- Understands the demands of the marketplace.

Maverick, unconventional
- Willing to change behaviors to achieve organizational change;
- Can put themselves in 'other people's shoes' to convince them; and
- Suggests crazy ideas – some of them good.

CULTURE CONSOLIDATOR

Prudent, careful
- Thinking of long-term results, needing to consolidate and build;
- Responsible; and
- Good at assessing risk and researches a wide range of options.

Committed to the company for the long-term
- Always focused on the future, identifies strongly with the company;
- Committed to the team, tries to inspire long-term loyalty in others;
- Wants the company's success, more than individual achievement; and
- Concerned with the reputation of the company and will not compromise.

Reasonable, perceptive, team-building
- Says "we" or "us" rather than "I";
- Supports others in a meeting even when does not fully agree with them;
- Seeks solutions of overall value not just to self;
- Listens, does not try to speak more than others;
- Encourages weaker/less experienced members of the team to contribute; and
- Refers to comments made by others when making a point.

Focused on managing resources effectively
- Careful, considered, economical, works 'smart';
- Thinks about multiple uses for same task; concerned with resources; and
- Prepared to investigate job sharing, etc.

Sensitive, caring
- Thinks about the feelings and motivations of others in making decisions; and
- Cross-culturally sensitive.

Long-term oriented, focused on steady and secure growth
- Not revolutionary but looking for incremental improvements;
- Considers options and obtains consensus before making changes;
- Sensitive, conservative, building on established strengths; and
- Focused on the benefits in the long term of any new strategy.

Assertive, not passive, but not so aggressive
- Willing to stand up for himself/herself but not alienating others;
- Consensus-oriented, a good communicator, able to lobby effectively for internal support;
- Is seen as the boss and able to inspire respect, but is not feared; and
- A strong personality, but not overwhelming, not charismatic.

More discreet and subtle impact and influencing skills
- Discreetly helps colleagues to come to a decision which is acceptable to them, making them think they thought of it themselves; and
- Uses rational arguments and logic, facts and figures, not just subjective arguments.

Diplomatic, culturally aware, able to play politics
- Considers the agendas of different members of the management team, avoids conflicts;
- Sensitive to protocol and not 'stepping on others' toes';
- Achieves own objectives subtly without being manipulative;
- Strong at building and maintaining relationships, despite changes in respective status; and
- Aware of the many aspects of culture and their implications for role-playing, decision-making, etc.

Flexible according to the needs of the business
- Adaptable, able to 'go with the flow' and
- Understands changes in the economy, customer preferences, activities of competitors – how these affect the company.

Focused on believing in the company, loyal, supporting company policy
- Able to take direction from above for the good of the company;
- Shares values of the company;
- Supports values and policies of the company strongly in public, even if disagrees privately; and
- Can motivate people to stick with the company even when they are wavering.

Fitting-in with company culture
- Understands how people in the company behave and the nature of the company's rewarded behaviors;
- Listens attentively to all people equally, asking questions, working hard to understand their background, where they are coming from; and
- Is respectful of the 'face' of another person.

Exercise: do you think you could fit into either of these categories? Which one most appeals to you? In your own organization, how would you describe your current CEO? Is your company in a state of change and evolution right now? How would you start to describe your company's existing culture, and what could it be moving towards? We will continue this exercise in the next chapter.

CULTURE AND ORGANIZATIONAL STRUCTURE

These frequently influence each other – it can be hard to tell which comes first, when an organization starts to grow and develop and takes on unique characteristics. The way that culture can determine an organizational structure can be seen in the existence of hierarchies and levels of bureaucracy, or the existence of a flat structure with project teams. The Swatch case also shows the symbiotic relationship between these two factors – as discussed in the next chapter. What are the determinants of organizational structure and culture? The organization's environment – including factors affecting supply of resources, such as suppliers, distributors, competitors, customers – is it certain or uncertain? Internal and external influences can affect the structure and culture, as we saw in the DHL Egypt case. This is altogether a complex issue, to be described in more detail as we familiarize ourselves with the concept of organization culture.

Values, norms and behaviors play a big part in organizational culture, enabling us to identify different cultures, getting into the different layers of organizational culture to find out what is really happening. There can be a big contrast between the organizational culture the company wants to create, and that which has grown, organically and inevitably. Organizational ceremonies, rites and corporate language, together with symbols, stories and other expressions of cultural values – such as who are the heroes, and why – are explained more in Chapter 12.

The role of the founder in an organizational culture can be strong – such as in the case of Virgin. Richard Branson is seen as unconventional, creative, colorful and personally very popular amongst his staff, making his company attractive as an employer, especially among young people. Highly ambitious and risk-taking, his venture into airlines was seen as dramatic and pioneering, a powerful anti-establishment message against the traditional flag-carrier British Airways. Fashionable and radical, the Virgin businesses cashed in on the 'cool Britannia' image of Britain in the 1980s, and Branson's eccentric and high-profile style worked well in building up the company's image.

Rather inarticulate in dealing with the media and seeing himself as in many ways 'hands-off', Branson has recruited many able deputies and developed many new businesses, diversifying from the popular record stores and occasionally-troubled airline to consumer brands and rail travel. Train transportation being a highly contentious area of business in Britain, prone to loss-making, there are fears that Virgin's involvement in the railways may have damaged the otherwise successful Virgin brand. Several websites describe Branson's skills as a brand builder, in time management, as a developer of his delegation skills, an encourager of innovation, and able to challenge and motivate people. He spends 80% of his life working. The Virgin Group is still thriving in the United Kingdom and overseas, with Branson strongly personifying its message. What will happen when he steps down or leaves completely?

The role of the leader – even if not the founder – in organizational culture is also powerful, as illustrated by **Lou Gerstner of IBM,** who in his book *"Who Says Elephants Can't Dance?"* (2003) presents the full story about how he led the turn-around of IBM, which included a huge culture change. Gerstner was selected as the CEO of IBM in 1993 as an effective leader who was skilled at generating and managing culture change in big-brand organizations. He came from a background with contrasting organizations, not in the computing field (McKinsey, RJR Nabisco, American Express) but he had learned about changing and building cultures. He overcame a strong individualist tendency within IBM, to build a more teamwork-oriented view. He overhauled the company's strategy, away from building and selling 'boxes' or hardware to a focus on 'solutions' and a variety of value-adding software offerings. Being a strong communicator, the e-mails he sent to staff included in this book show him making a big effort to see the world from the staff members' points of view. He went a long way to restoring pride in the company by arguing that change was not only desirable but essential for survival. Bringing IBM back from the brink was a patriotic duty, as the company was seen as an icon of corporate America and could not be allowed to go under.

Although he was criticized for his 'Neutron Jack' attitude to firing a large number of GE staff, few would dispute the effectiveness of **Jack Welch's** leadership in improving the business performance of **GE General Electric (GE)**, bringing it into the 21st century and radically changing its culture. His style was tough and uncompromising, aimed at making GE number one or number two in all its businesses. He was concerned with the achievement of precise business targets. He was not impressed by flowery descriptions; presentations without numbers were not tolerated.

By introducing stock options, Welch's favored staff (surviving the periodic sweep out of underperforming people) could enjoy the rising share price of GE. He radically changed the strategy of the company, from traditional manufacturing to new cutting-edge businesses in financial services, for example. He encouraged managers of divisions to fight for resources and present their achievements in an atmosphere of challenge and debate. The tough contest for his successor was typical of the Welch approach to justifying and earning each position in the company (Welch, 2005, with additional material from several web-sites).

Roberto Goizueta, as an immigrant from Cuba who decided to seek other opportunties in the USA, rose to the top of the world's leading beverage marketing company by dint of hard work, aggressive ambition and risk-taking. Gaining respectability as a Yale graduate and admired for his approach to strategy, he focused on improving the 'Economic Value-Added' for **Coca-Cola** from the relationships with the independent bottlers who made and sold Coke and its associated products worldwide – in 200 countries.

For many years of Goizueta's period as CEO, the company faced tough competition from arch-rival Pepsi, dominant in many Asian markets. Goizueta led an expansion in the company's brands – now more than 300 – and made an acquisition in the film industry of Columbia Pictures, seen as having strong synergies with a business focused so heavily on marketing. Entrepreneurial, inspirational and aggressive, Goizueta was one of the few Coke executives brave enough to attack the 'sacred cow' of the Coke formula. His disastrous foray into 'New Coke' showed how popular Coke really was to the American public, and he was able to turn a strategic blunder into a new insight into his product (Greising, 1989).

Organizational culture and creativity/innovation also have an important relationship with certain cultures fostering creative thinking, rewarding entrepreneurship and encouraging thinking out of the box, like 3M, with its new product portfolio and 'skunk works'. Bureaucratic cultures, on the other hand, can kill new ideas. Progressive cultures absorb new ideas, and less progressive ones let them go, in the way that Du Pont gave up on W.L. Gore and the fabric that was to become 'Gortex'.

FORMING A CULTURE – HOW CULTURES EMERGE

How are cultures created? This is rarely deliberate. Corporate culture is rarely something founders think about – it just happens. An exception is the Virgin Group, where Richard Branson deliberately set out to target young people and be provocative. He wanted to create a company whose image would 'shock people's grandmothers'. Founders play a big part in forming cultures, especially if they make an effort at **role modeling, teaching and coaching**. Other important factors are the sector of the business, the environment, and the customer focus. **Sustaining a culture – maintaining** the image, values, beliefs and practices – often takes a different kind of person, hence the look at Change Agent and Consolidator competencies listed above. The Consolidator helps to bed down the changes which the Change Agent introduces. It is hard to follow a period of rapid change with another. People need time to settle down. For example, the tenure as CEO of Jack Welch at General Electric is very different from that of his successor, Jeff Immelt.

Reactions to incidents and crises can also be defining moments for corporate cultures. Their survival of strikes, terrorist attacks, booms and slumps help to make them what they are. British Airways will always be affected by its turnaround to a more customer-focused organization, and its ongoing difficulties with labor unrest. Johnson and Johnson after the tampering of its Tylenol product has developed a stronger-than-ever culture as a result.

WHICH CULTURES ARE GOOD FOR EMPLOYEES TO WORK FOR?

In terms of how to create an employee-friendly culture, tips to attract, retain and motivate employees have been identified:

1. Pay employees fairly and well - then get them to forget about money.
2. Treat each and every employee with respect. Show them that you care about them as persons, not just as workers.
3. Praise accomplishments and attempts:
   i. Both large and small;
   ii. At least four times more than you 'criticize';
   iii. Publicly and in private;
   iv. Verbally and in writing;
   v. Promptly (as soon as observed); and
   vi. Sincerely;
4. Clearly communicate goals, responsibilities and expectations. NEVER criticize in public - redirect in private;
5. Recognize performance appropriately and consistently:
   i. Reward outstanding performance (e.g. with promotions and opportunities);
   ii. Do not tolerate sustained poor performance – coach and train or remove!;
6. Involve employees in plans and decisions, especially those that affect them. Solicit their ideas and opinions. Encourage initiative;
7. Create opportunities for employees to learn and grow. Link the goals of the organization with the goals of each individual in it;
8. Actively listen to employees concerns – both work-related and personal;
9. Share information promptly, openly and clearly. Tell the truth... with compassion; and
10. Celebrate successes and milestones reached – organizational and personal. Create an organizational culture that is open, trusting and fun! (US ER-HQ, 2001).

THE IMPORTANCE OF EMPLOYEE SATISFACTION IN CORPORATE CULTURE

Employee commitment, productivity and retention are the most critical workforce management challenges that affect organizations' profitability. "Job satisfaction is important both because of its bearing on the physical and mental well-being of individual employees and because of its demonstrated implications for job-related behaviors and hence for the productivity and profitability of organizations" (Cranny, Smith, and Stone, 1992). There can be a direct relationship between employee satisfaction and culture – and organizational performance.

Several articles, models and researches have shown the importance of increasing employee satisfaction and its results on organizations and individuals, especially the contribution that increasing employee satisfaction can make to an organizations' profitability. Workforce management challenges (i.e. commitment, productivity and retention) are better met by job satisfaction, and they drive profitability. Job dissatisfaction – often caused by a negative or weak culture – also has significant consequences.

EMPLOYEE SATISFACTION, ORGANIZATIONAL PROFITABILITY AND CULTURE

Research at the University of Sheffield showed that 12% of the variation between companies in their profitability can be explained by job satisfaction issues (Lahiri, 2002). These are often strongly related to culture.

Customer satisfaction is a critical component of organizations' sustainable profitability and growth. To make customer service an essential part of organizations' culture and to produce empowered and motivated employees who are committed to ever-higher standards of customer service and satisfaction, organizations must demonstrate continuously that customer service comes before all else, develop systems for collecting customer satisfaction data, relay this information to those responsible for value creation, and develop a system that rewards people for building and maintaining customer relationships. A customer-driven culture requires that organizations don't just respond to what customers say they need and want, but that the organization can apply its own body of knowledge acquired from years of experience and study, in addition to the best knowledge of the customer, to deliver a product or service that will exceed customer expectations, delight customers, and lead to customer success.

EMPLOYEE SATISFACTION AND WORKFORCE MANAGEMENT CHALLENGES (COMMITMENT, PRODUCTIVITY AND RETENTION) AND THE IMPACT OF CULTURE

The Gallup organization researched the impact of employee attitudes on business outcomes on 12 work places. The research showed that businesses where responses indicate high employee satisfaction out-perform rivals on traditional hard measures of: productivity by 22%; employee retention by 22%, customer satisfaction by 38%, and profitability by 27% (US ER-HQ, 2001). The Harvard Business Review reports that a 5% increase in staff retention results in an increase in productivity ranging from 25% to 65%, and a 10% decrease in cost (Mercer, 1998).

Organizational Citizenship Behavior (OCB) is the behavior by an employee intended to help co-workers or the organization (Spector, 1997). OCB-inspired actions are those which are outside the employees' specific assigned tasks, or above and beyond the call of duty. The opposite of OCB is so-called counter-productive behavior that is defined as acts committed by an employee that either intentionally or unintentionally hurt the organization, such as aggression against coworkers, sabotage and theft.

Exercise: Consider the impact of job satisfaction levels on the culture of your organization. Return to your answers to the exercise asking you to describe aspects of your organization's culture. How many of these comments are negative (such as the company being described as 'a prison camp')? Do you think people just like to be cynical and not 'creepy', or do they really believe in these observations? Consider the HR issues below in the light of your own organization.

Other HR issues also have an impact on corporate culture, and are demonstrated in the cases here and in Chapter 12. **Allocation of rewards and status** helps to define culture, because this helps to pin-point the behavior encouraged in the company. **Recruitment, selection, promotion and removal** also help us to put our finger on what is an organization's culture, especially in terms of the kind of people who fit in around the place. Whether a culture **fosters cultural diversity** also makes a difference. How tolerant is it? The **socialization of new employees** is a process used to reinforce a culture – and it can be formal or informal. How long does it take a newcomer to fit in with a new environment? What are the different **steps in socialization**?

DEFINING NATIONAL CULTURES

National cultures are looked at in detail in Chapter 13, and also in Chapter 14. Here, we examine models and theories of national cultures, and especially how and why living and working in different countries can be such a **culture shock**. Why do we get all excited when we arrive in a new country, and then find things increasingly frustrating and difficult? Why do we sometimes grow to like the place again, or find it impossible? It depends on our experience of culture shock, and how many times we have moved to different countries.

Some of the other important issues we need to consider include **national culture and joint-ventures** – why are some mixed-nationality joint-ventures doomed to divorce fairly soon after marriage? Are the differences so great that they cannot be reconciled? Would it help if they understood each other better? An interesting example is featured in a fictitious (but very real) HBR case, named "Oil and Wasser". Are there such things as **global organizational cultures**, encouraging consistent ways of operating all over the world, or is the case of DHL in Egypt (and possibly elsewhere) more likely? If they are **ethnocentric** in style, with leaders from the parent company, this might be the case. If they recruit locally – being polycentric or keen on host country nationals – their operations may be culturally quite different in different countries.

MANAGING CROSS-CULTURALLY – AN EXAMPLE FROM CHINA

Managing Chinese in China can be more complex than first imagined. Chinese employees, as in any other country, vary according to their experience and outlook. In Chapter 13, we will be introduced to the 'Chuppie' – or a Chinese form of 'Yuppie' – or young, upwardly-mobile urban professional. These are especially common in the vibrant fast-growing city of Shanghai. Meanwhile, there are also many Westernized Chinese, who have spent time in the West but do not see themselves as Chuppies – they might be older, more serious and mature, and less influenced by consumerism. Thirdly, the vast majority of Chinese employees – even in Western companies, and especially outside of the big cities – are still traditional in outlook, influenced strongly by the Chinese national culture, and not much affected by factors from outside. These can be regarded as 'Traditionals'. To consider the issues of managing Chinese employees in a business in China, these questions were asked to a large sample of all three of the above 'Chinese types' – Chuppies, Westernized Chinese, and Traditionals: *How do you perceive your job, boss, colleagues, backgrounds, and choice of career area?*

Chuppies regard their jobs as very important. Their careers can be more important than family ties. What they do and the companies they work for define their identities. When introducing themselves, Chuppies may more often say "I work for Motorola" (for example) than refer to their own names. They work long hours, travel in the company time, wear company-branded tee-shirts and enjoy company-organized motivational events. Chuppies admire a boss with their values. Whereas a Chuppie sees a company as the vehicle for his or her ambitions, a more traditional Chinese will see the boss as playing a bigger role in the development of his or her career.

Colleagues are also seen in terms of leveraging the success of the Chuppie's career. By contrast, Traditional Chinese will set great store by relationships with their work mates, protecting them from unwelcome exposure if things go wrong. Chuppies like a boss and colleagues who are also young, ambitious and dynamic, and chose a company for its strong brand name and fast-growth record, so that they can move up the corporate ladder as rapidly as possible. If this is not happening as quickly as they want it to be, they will look for something new. Chuppies like jobs in high-tech industries, in high-profile consumer products, in anything which has a big American brand name, and in new businesses connected with the media and entertainment – such as Public Relations, advertising, and leisure industries. They are also drawn towards the service sector, in financial services and consulting. They like an exciting pace of work, high salaries, and making things happen.

Westernized Chinese also regard their jobs as important, but they can be less obsessive, and many have other money-making interests on the side. Chuppies moonlight as well, but they also appreciate their time for having fun. Westernized Chinese can be prepared to make sacrifices, such as leaving their families in Hong Kong or Canada or back in the USA. Westernized Chinese also identify with their companies, but they can go a lot deeper than just the brand name. If they have visited the head office and spent a lot of time with Westerners working in the company, they are more likely to adopt a strongly Westernized attitude to work. If the company has a culture which includes working long hours, they will work long hours – if it does not, they will not. Some Westernized Chinese make negative comments about company-organized motivational events and in-company training courses, seeing them as rather unsophisticated and beneath them. This attitude can upset foreign bosses, who see the Westernized Chinese as acting in a snobbish and superior manner towards the locals, and also losing the opportunity to bond with them at these events.

Westernized Chinese like a Western boss, and want to act as a bridge between him or her and the locals. He or she must come from the parent company and operate in quite a Western way. However, Westernized Chinese can job hop a good deal, especially if they may lose their prized expatriate status. Westernized Chinese do not feel comfortable working with a Chuppie or a traditional Chinese as their boss – but these Chinese would not hire them anyway. Westernized Chinese are often ineffective as coaches, mentors and trainers – they do not like Chuppies, who can undermine their jobs and status. This has been seen by Westerners as among the greatest shortcomings of the Westernized Chinese.

Westernized Chinese like jobs in large foreign companies, especially in consumer and industrial products, particularly those long-established in China. As Westernized Chinese set greater store by status and money – and may have more expensive lifestyles – they are less risk-oriented than Chuppies, who may be more excited by Internet start-ups and new kinds of businesses.

Westernized Chinese like respect, a big job title, the chance to be able to represent their company in the community, and to work for a well-known organization. They like large diversified conglomerates, pharmaceutical companies and banking. They prefer manufacturing to the service sector, seeing it as more prestigious and reliable. They expect to work hard and take a lot of responsibility, seeing themselves as more like the foreigners, and tend to distance themselves from the locals. They also expect very high salaries – in fact many Westernized Chinese in senior expatriate positions earn a lot more money and enjoy much more generous benefits than foreigners in China.

Traditional Chinese also regard their jobs as very important – but in an entirely different way: it can mean the same as having a career because many traditional Chinese have the same job all their lives, and do not even move up very much in the same organization. For older Chinese, the work unit or *dan wei* was everything – providing meals, medical care, entertainment, even clothes – in an environment designed to encourage solidarity and to discourage individualism, even to the extent of the work unit being more important than family ties. Although this attitude – and the 'iron rice bowl' from which it derives – is now breaking down, it has left a reluctance to make decisions, use initiative or think independently. Thus traditional types like a job which is stable and will not require them to take too many risks.

Like Chuppies, the companies traditional Chinese work for also define their identities, but more in the sense of the community in which one lives. They eat, sleep and breathe their companies, but in a much more literal way that the Chuppies do. The Chuppies may see their jobs and companies as vehicles for their success – but to a traditional Chinese it's more the end result. With the restructuring and even breakdown of many state-owned enterprises and closure of some unsuccessful joint-ventures, the traditional Chinese are far less optimistic about the future than the upwardly-mobile Chuppies.

The traditional Chinese can come to enjoy company-organized motivational events, especially if they are in the tradition and spirit of their own militaristic-type national events, such as those organized for the celebration of the 50th anniversary of the People Republic of China (PRC). Some particularly successful multinational companies in China have created a culture which blends traditional PRC Chinese attitudes to displays of bonding and team building with that of (mostly) American ones.

Traditional Chinese need a strong boss with clear authority as, unlike Chuppies, they cannot separate their boss' personality and their relationship with the boss from the nature of the job they are doing and the organization for which they work. As discussed above, whereas a Chuppie sees a company or job as a more temporary thing, a stepping-stone to their greater ambitions, a more traditional Chinese will see the boss as playing a bigger role in the development of his or her career. Their guanxi or relationship with the boss will be fundamental to their job security as well as to job progression.

Colleagues are, in an extreme sense for some traditional Chinese, more like comrades. When a foreign boss (or he or she may be a Chuppie or Westernised Chinese) wants to discipline or remove a staff member in a traditional Chinese environment, this may imply a closing of ranks and refusal to co-operate in the process. Traditional Chinese like a boss who is tough and takes most of the big decisions, and colleagues who are supportive, similar in outlook to himself or herself, and not showing each other up by working too hard. Traditional Chinese are not always used to having a choice or a say in the company they work for, and are not necessarily looking for fast promotion – this might mean more responsibility and decision-making and other scary things. If the company is not doing well, they do not think about leaving as soon as possible, and may even in extreme cases accept a pay reduction and short-term working than face the challenges of looking for a new position.

Traditional Chinese are more focused on job security and having a reliable position than seeking excitement in brand-new industries. They like status and respect and would like to maximize their pay, but minimizing risks can be more important. Thus jobs in heavy industries, in mass-market consumer products and in more traditional sectors are seen as more reliable than jobs in new businesses. In working for foreign companies, traditional Chinese can be reliable and steady employees, not as grasping for higher pay and benefits, and motivated by job security and status. They can feel uncomfortable when the pace of work speeds up, and things happen too quickly.

Exercise: Can you relate the concepts of Chuppie, Westernized and Traditional to people in your own country? In what ways do they need to be managed differently? In what different ways can they contribute to an organization? Why is it important to develop cross-cultural insights when managing a team of people in a different country – or should they adapt to you? Which category would you see yourself to be in, or none of these? When you travel to a different country, how long does it take you to appreciate the different behaviors of different people? Or do you tend to look for commonalities?

CONCLUSION

In this chapter we have been introduced to culture as a broad concept, influencing people working in different companies and countries, affecting their attitudes towards job security, satisfaction, status and change. Do we have cultural sensitivities? Could we be culture change agents, or are we more suited to be culture consolidators? How could a corporate culture give us what we want in our jobs? Why do we need to understand differences in national cultures? What kind of business situations could we find ourselves in where a grasp of national cultural differences could be of vital help to you? These questions have been posed in this chapter, but need to be explored further in order for you to grasp their full significance and implications.

REFERENCES

Avery, Gayle C. (2004) 'Swatch: leading through emotion' in Avery, Gayle, ed. *Understanding Leadership*. Thousand Oaks, CA: Sage.

Branson, R. (2000) *Losing my Virginity*. London: Virgin Publishing, and see also

Knowledge@Wharton (2005) 'The importance of Being Richard Branson'

http://knowledge.wharton.upenn.edu [Accessed 13 November 2006].

Chesborough, H. (2006) *Connect and Develop Complements Research and Development* at P&G. Boston: Harvard Business School Press.

Cranny, C.J., Smith, P.C. & Stone, E.F. eds.(1992) Job Satisfaction: How *People Feel About Their Jobs and How It Affects Their Performance*. New York: Lexington Books.

Daft, R. (2006) *Management*. 10th ed. Mason, Ohio: Thomson Learning.

DHL – author research and www.dhl.com

Fiol, C.M. & Lyles, M.J. (1985) 'Organisational Learning' in the *Academy of Management Review*, Vol, 10, No 4. p.803-813.

George, J.M. & Jones G.R. (2002) *Organizational Behavior*. 3rd. ed. Upper Saddle River, New Jersey: Prentice Hall.

Gerstner, L. (2002) *Who Says Elephants Can't Dance?* New York: HarperCollins

Greising, D. (1998) *I'd like the world to buy a coke: the life and leadership of Roberto Goizueta*. New York: John Wiley.

Handy, C. (1992) *Understanding Organizations,* 4th ed., Harmondsworth: Penguin.

Hellriegel, D. & Slocum, J.W. (2004) *Organizational Behavior*. Mason, Ohio: Thomson South Western.

Herbold, P. (2002) 'Inside Microsoft: balancing creativity and discipline', *Harvard Business Review*, March.

Hofstede, G. (1984). *Culture's Consequences: International Differences in Work-Related Values*. Beverly Hills, CA: Sage.

Hoojberg R. & Petrock F. (1993) 'On culture change:Using the competing values framework to help leaders execute a transformational strategy. *Human Resource Management, 32*, 29-50.

Jones, S. (1999) *Managing People in China*. Unpublished manuscript.

Jones, S. (2000). Beyond the stereotypes: the changing face of China's workplace, *China Staff, VI:* 9, 19-24.

Lahiri, D. (2002) 'Competing in a global arena: Understanding employee satisfaction' *INSTART management consultants.* (MSM: MBA Program)

Nalbantian, H. & Szostak, A. (2004) 'How Fleet Fought Employee Flight', *Harvard Business Review*, April.

Pierer, H. (2006) 'Transforming an Industrial Giant: Siemens', *Harvard Business Review* March.

Reimus, B. (2004) 'Oil and Wasser' *Harvard Business Review*, May.

Robbins, S. P.(1998) *Organizational Behavior* (8th ed.). Upper Saddle River, NJ: Prentice Hall.

Spector, P. E. (1997) *Job Satisfaction: Application, Assessment, Causes and Consequences.* Thousand Oaks, CA: Sage.

Spector, P. E. (1985) 'Measurement of human service staff satisfaction: Development of the Job Satisfaction Survey', *American Journal of Community Psychology, 13,* 693-713.

Trompenaars, F. & Hampden-Turner, C. (1997). *Riding the Waves of Culture: Understanding Cultural Diversity in Business*. London: Nicholas Brealey.

US ER-HQ (2001). Attracting, retaining and motivating employees: The realities and the options. www.employee-retention-hq.com/

US ER-HQ (2001). Factors impacting job satisfactions. www.employee-retention-hq.com/

US ER-HQ (2001). Grimme's top 10 tips: To attract, retain and motivate employees. www.employee-retention-hq.com/

US ER-HQ (2001). The secret of attracting and retaining key employees on a tight budget. www.employee-retention-hq.com/

Welch, J. (2005) . New York: HarperCollins.

RECOMMENDED FURTHER READING

Aycan, Z., Kanungo, R.N. & Sinha, J.B.P. (1999), 'Organizational culture and human resource management practices: the model of cultural fit' *Journal of Cross-Cultural Psychology, 30*:4:501-26.

Davis, S.M. (1990) *Managing Corporate Culture*. New York: Harper Business

Deal, T.E. & Kennedy, A.A. (1982) *Corporate Cultures: the Rites and Rituals of Corporate Life*. Reading MA: Addison Wesley.

Fiedler, F.E., Mitchell, T. & Triandis, H.C. (1971) 'The culture assimilator: an approach to cross-cultural training', *Journal of Applied Psychology, 55*, 95-102.

Flynn, M.J. Saxton & Roy S. eds., *Gaining Control of the Corporate Culture*. San Francisco: Jossey-Bass.

Graves, D. (1986) *Corporate Culture: diagnosis and change*. New York: St Martin's Press.

Hall, E.T. (1976) *Beyond Culture*. New York: Doubleday.

Hampden-Turner, C. (1990) *Creating Corporate Culture: from discord to harmony*. Reading, MA: Addison Wesley.

Handy, C. (1990) *Inside Organizations*. Harmondsworth: Penguin.

Handy, C. (1978) *The Gods of Management*. London: Souvenir Press.

Handy, C. (1991) *The Age of Unreason*. Boston: Harvard Business School Press.

Harris, R.P. & Moran, R.T. (1989) *Managing Cultural Differences*. Houston, TX: Gulf Publishing.

Hayes, J. & Allinson, C.W. (1988) 'Cultural differences in learning styles of managers', *Management International Review, 28*:3, 75-80.

Hofstede, G. (1991) *Cultures and Organizations: software of the mind*. New York: McGraw Hill.

Hofstede, G. (1989) 'Organizing for Cultural Diversity', *European Management Journal, 7*:4, 390-397.

Mintzberg, H. (1979) *The Structure of Organizations*. Englewood Cliffs, NJ: Prentice Hall.

Oddu, G. & Mendenhall, M. (1998) *Cases in International Organizational Behavior*. Malden, MA: Blackwell.

Schein, E.H. (1985) *Organizational Culture and Leadership*. San Francisco: Jossey-Bass.

Wilkins, A.L. & Ouchi, W.G. 'Efficient Cultures: exploring the relationship between culture and organizational performance', *Administrative Science Quarterly, 28*:3, 1983.

CHAPTER 12

ORGANIZATIONAL CULTURE
STEPHANIE JONES

OPENING CASE:

When introducing himself to new employees, the President of The Ritz-Carlton Hotel Group says "My name is Horst Schulze. I'm the President, and I'm a very important person around here." After a few seconds he continues, "But so are you. In fact, you are more important to customers than I am. If you don't show up, we are in trouble. If I don't show up, hardly anyone would notice."

These comments reflect Mr. Schulze's attitude that employees are the crucial component in quality service. Therefore, to consolidate its corporate culture, the Ritz-Carlton very carefully selects only those applicants with an appropriate caring attitude. Once selected, each employee learns the Ritz-Carlton corporate culture in a two-day orientation, followed by extensive on-the-job training which results in job certification.

Each employee learns The Ritz-Carlton Gold Standards, which include a credo, 20 basics of service, and the three steps of service. The steps include: (1) a warm and sincere greeting; (2) anticipation and compliance with guest needs; and (3) a fond farewell, using the guest's name if possible. Employees may even have to modify their language. They should say "Good morning," or "Good afternoon," not "Hi, how's it going?" When asked to do something, they should respond "Certainly," or "My pleasure." In addition, all employees should learn the 20 Ritz-Carlton basics of quality service, which range from knowledge of one's work area and The Ritz-Carlton Credo to answering the telephone with a smile and wearing immaculate uniforms. At The Ritz-Carlton employees are not servants, they are "ladies and gentlemen serving ladies and gentlemen."

To back up all this training, employees are empowered to handle any customer complaint on the spot and can spend up to $2,000 doing so. And they can demand the immediate assistance of other employees. Twenty minutes later, they should telephone the guest to make sure that the complaint was handled properly. In addition, once employees learn of particular customer wants, such as foam pillows or a desire for a particular newspaper, that information goes into a 240,000 person' database so that the customer will automatically get the desired service the next time he or she stays at a Ritz-Carlton.

This attention to quality is not confined to hotel staff. Mr. Schulze and the other senior executives meet weekly to review measures of product and service quality. They also look at guest satisfaction, market growth and development, and other business indicators. From top management down, Ritz-Carlton's approach to quality management is characterized by detailed planning. Quality teams at all levels set objectives and devise action plans, and each hotel has a quality leader and work area teams responsible for problem solving, strategic planning, and setting quality certification standards for each position.

Each hotel aims to create a two-to-one ratio of internal to external complaints. Internal complaints are made by employees who spot problems in service delivery. By eliminating internal problems, Ritz-Carlton removes the causes of external complaints by customers. Management thinks that solving problems before they arise is cost-effective. Once a problem has occurred, there are additional costs of employee time to fix the problem plus hotel remedies such as complimentary cocktails and a follow-up letter, not to mention the possible cost of losing a customer. Patrick Mene, Vice President of Quality, expresses this as the 1-10-100 rule: "What costs a dollar to fix today will cost $10 to fix tomorrow and $100 to fix downstream."

To ensure that quality standards are maintained, Ritz-Carlton collects daily reports from each of the 720 work areas in each of the 30 hotels it manages. The company tracks measures such as annual guest room-preventive maintenance cycles, percentage of check-ins with no queuing, time spent to achieve industry-best clean room-appearance, and time to service an occupied room.

Not surprisingly, Ritz-Carlton won the prestigious Malcolm Baldrige National Quality Award in 1992. This moved the firm into a very select company – only one service firm had ever won this award. You might think Ritz-Carlton would be satisfied with a customer satisfaction rating of 97 percent and one of the lowest employee turnover rates in the hotel industry (30 percent). But not Ritz-Carlton! Mr. Schulze has set new quality performance standards: a 100% customer satisfaction rating and a reduction of defects to just four for every million customer encounters.

Eliminating virtually all problems, however, is a costly process that can reduce company profits, and some critics believe that Ritz-Carlton is not sensitive enough to its bottom line. For example, to improve customer satisfaction from 97 percent to 98 percent, some would say, is a marginal improvement that could require a great deal of employee effort and expense for a low dollar return. Besides, how can any firm anticipate all possible problems in order to eliminate complaints? Should it even desire to do so?

Questions on the opening case: How would you describe the corporate culture of Ritz-Carlton, based on the two models explained above? Would you feel comfortable in this environment? How would you feel if your boss addressed you as Mr Schulze does to his employees? Which adjustments might you have to make to your behavior if you joined Ritz-Carlton and tried to fit in to the corporate culture? How are Ritz-Carlton staff members trained to understand and embrace the Ritz-Carlton corporate culture? In what ways are Ritz-Carlton employees empowered? To what extent is this training a factor in the creation of the hotel chain's corporate culture? Why is it important for Ritz-Carlton to insist that employees not think of themselves as servants, but rather as ladies and gentlemen? How would you describe the kind of corporate culture created as a result of this ethos? In what ways does the management at Ritz-Carlton support their staff members? Would you describe this as a supportive culture? Why do you think the Ritz-Carlton has the lowest staff turnover in the hotel industry? Has corporate culture anything to do with it? In what ways do the HR and people management policies contribute to promoting a culture of quality at the Ritz-Carlton?

LEARNING OBJECTIVES FOR THIS CHAPTER

In 'Organizational Culture' the aim has been to introduce you to aspects of corporate culture which you can observe and identify, and which can add to your understanding of how organizations function. Drawing off the work of well-known scholars in the field, we explain different types of culture, encouraging you to look at examples of organizations and identify their culture types. We also look in detail at propensity for change, which is an important aspect of defining a culture, and warn that lack of flexibility can cause as many problems as having too much. We then look in detail at a major organizational culture case, inviting you to consider how the culture was created, how it works, and how it affects management, staff and customers.

MODELS OF CORPORATE CULTURE

What is corporate culture? For many, it's hard to define exactly, but it's blamed when people don't 'fit in' to a new company, when two companies merge and have difficulties integrating with each other, and when a company tries to introduce a major change program. Yet culture is seen as intangible, indefinable, woolly and imprecise, described in vague terms of being 'tough', 'soft', 'strong', 'weak' – but is somehow always there.

Many organizational behavior textbooks, in describing strong cultures, refer to the cohesive sets of values and norms binding staff members together and fostering goal-oriented employee commitment. With positive employment practices demonstrating their commitment to employees, these companies gain in return supportive work attitudes and high performance. Companies like Dell, Microsoft, Intel and Motorola are quoted for developing career paths and investing heavily in training and development to increase employees' value to the organization and build a strong culture (Jones, 2003 based on Handy, 1985).

One way of building a strong culture adopted by many companies (some deliberately, some accidentally) is to develop organizational ceremonies, rites and language. These help people to learn about and take on board aspects of an organization's values and norms. Ceremonies celebrating high performing employees, company social gatherings, internal newsletters and publicized promotions all contribute to this culture-building.
Next to that and in combination with it, one sees the cultivation of 'heroes' and 'war-stories'. So, how may this be defined in a more concrete, ABC, 123 sort of way? In culture-building, we can identify:

1. **Rites of passage;**
2. **Integration; and**
3. **Enhancement.**

Rites of passage, such as graduation, determine how individuals enter, move up in, or leave an organization. This also includes the ways that organizations groom people for promotion, such as fast-tracking. Rites of integration, such as office parties and shared announcements of organizational successes, build and reinforce common bonds between organizational members. Annual meetings are used to communicate an organization's values to its managers, employees and shareholders. Thirdly, rites of enhancement, such as awards' dinners, newspaper releases and employee promotions, give an organization the opportunity to publicly acknowledge and reward employees' contributions and thereby to enhance employees' commitment to organizational values.

This may be a way of looking at building cultures, but what sort of culture are you trying to build? And what are some of the influences on the ways that cultures are shaped? Some of the most insightful and valuable work in this field is from the prolific pen of Charles Handy, particularly from the classic *Understanding Organizations* (1976; 1980; 1985). Handy, seeking a suitable metaphor, described a journey driving from Britain across the Channel and through continental Europe and observing the differing cultures and traditions of the different countries and regions passed on the way. They have different habits, ways of enjoying themselves, of organizing work, and of carrying out their daily lives. As Handy remarked, anyone who has spent time in a country other than their own will appreciate how values, beliefs and cherished philosophies affect the way society is organized. They will appreciate too how these values and beliefs are shaped by history and tradition, by the climate, the kinds of work people do, the size of the country and its prosperity.

The same applies to organizations, with their differing atmospheres, ways of doing things, levels of energy, of individual freedom, and of kinds of personality. Their differing values, norms and beliefs are reflected in the different structures and systems they develop. Company cultures are influenced dramatically by their ownership and the personality of their founder, by the current economic environment, by their industry sector, by the technology they use, by their goals and objectives, and by the people they employ to work for them.

Handy (1985) argues that the fact that there are differing cultures is the natural order of things, that this is a desirable state of affairs; *'vive la difference.'* Attempts to force cultural convergence are typically fraught with disaster, like trying to grow the wrong crops in the wrong climate.

Which elements of organizational life reveal cultural differences? As with country differences, organizations reveal their cultures by their deep-set beliefs about the way work should be organized, the way authority should be exercised, the way people should be rewarded and the way they should be controlled. What are the degrees of formalization or in-formalization? How much planning and how far ahead? What combination of obedience and initiative is looked for in subordinates? Do working hours matter, and dress codes, and expense accounts, and stock options, and everyone having their own secretary or not? Does power lie in the hands of individuals, groups, or committees? Are rules more important than results, or the other way around?

More than just these behavioral and managerial differences, there are the physical signs of different cultures, in the appearance of office buildings, shops and factories, both externally and internally. Are they sober and prudent-looking? Or are they 'flashy' and 'glitzy'? Or do they look innovative and futuristic?

Handy's definitions (1976; 1980; 1985) of four varieties of organizational culture are one of the most useful guides to this complex maze of institutional approaches to management theory, especially because he also considers the influencing factors on these cultures:

- **The Power Culture;**

- **The Role Culture;**

- **The Task Culture; and**

- **The Person Culture.**

Handy warns that it must be emphasized that each can be a good and effective culture, yet many observers are culturally blinkered, thinking that a culture that worked well once can be used again. This is not necessarily true at all.

The Power Culture is frequently found in small, entrepreneurial businesses, particularly in finance. There is an all-powerful head of the business around whom a web is woven – the symbol of this culture is the spider's web. This culture depends on a central power source, with rays of power and influence spreading out from that central figure. The web connects the functions and specialties, but the main strands emanate from the center. Communication is through personal conversation and even telepathy as everyone knows what they have to do and thinks the same way. There is little bureaucracy, few rules, and no procedures. Decisions are taken through the central power source. This culture is strong and fast-moving, but cannot grow to a great size, or the web will break trying to span too many activities. Individual power rules, but when the spider dies, so does the web.

The **Role Culture** is often stereotyped as bureaucratic, characterized by the image of a Greek temple, and is highly rational and logical. The role organization rests on its pillars, representing its functions or specialties, all of which are strong and efficient in their own right. Between the functions or pillars, and controlling their interactions, are procedures, rules and guidelines, controlled by a narrow band of senior management, which forms the pediment. The roles themselves are often more important than the people occupying the roles. Exceeding the expected performance of the role is probably not a good idea. Rules and procedures are the major methods of influence. Role cultures are successful in stable environments, particularly if they are monopolies or oligopolies. Government departments, the auto industry and oil companies frequently exhibit role cultures. They're fine in environments where they can capitalize on economies of scale or on sellers' markets, but Greek temples are insecure when the ground shakes.

The **Task Culture** is a job or project-oriented business, which is represented in Handy's characterization as a net, with some strands thicker and stronger than others. Power and influence lies at intersections of the net strands, in what looks like a typical matrix organization. There is no strong individual leader figure here, and influence is widely dispersed. It's a team culture, where individual objectives are subsumed to the needs of the group. Extremely adaptable, the teams in the net culture form and break up and reform in a quick space of time, moving from project to project. Net cultures are found in marketing departments, in management consultancies, in account groups of advertising agencies – especially where creativity and flexibility are in hot demand. Control is difficult here, as people thriving in a task culture dislike any form of restrictions, and cannot survive a lack of resources. They may then metamorphose into a role culture or power culture. As Handy (1985) describes it, it is a culture most in tune with current ideologies of change and adaptation, individual freedom and small differences in status.

Finally, the **Person Culture** is unusual and highly individual, a manifestation of a group of people banding together to follow their interests and do their own thing, sharing some resources but going their own way. These organizations – which are only minimally organizations at all – exist to serve the interests of the lawyers, dentists, architects and small specialized consultancies who need them. They may hardly exist beyond a shared office, secretary and coffee machine. Figuratively, this culture looks like a galaxy of individual stars, temporarily clustering together. Sharing power, these cultures survive whilst they remain small and individual, but quickly break up or evolve into a different culture when the cluster gets too big. They are hard to manage and constantly form new clusters and move to other galaxies if their cherished individual status is threatened.

Exercise: consider the culture type of your own organization. Does it fit into any of these boxes suggested by Handy? Or could it be a combination of types? Is one department a different type than another? Has it changed in recent times? Do you regard it as positive or negative? What do most people in the company think of it? Is it easy to identify, or confusing? Did you find it useful to return to the exercise in Chapter 11? Consider also the points below, about factors also influencing this model of cultures, and an alternative model of cultures also suggested below.

Influencing factors, according to Handy, include various issues influencing these cultures, such as:

* **History and ownership;**

* **Size;**

* **Technology;**

* **Goals and objectives;**

* **The environment; and**

* **The people.**

Yet cultures remain impressionistic and imprecise, something perceived and felt rather than exactly defined. But define it we must, for the important reason that it must match a person's own individual, cultural preference. As Handy (1985) put it, a fit between the two (a person and the organization) should lead to a fulfilled psychological contract, to satisfaction at work. So if you're a task culture person in a role culture, you'll be unfulfilled and hamstrung; if the reverse, you'll be confused and treading water. Maybe that discontent at work that you find it difficult to pin down as a result of that elusive but powerful phenomenon of the cultural mismatch.

A CONTRASTING MODEL OF CORPORATE CULTURE...

Hellriegel and Slocum's popular corporate culture model (2004, based on Hooiberg and Petrock, 1993) should be considered a contrast to Handy's. There are many more – including that of Schein (1985) – which may also be consulted in building up a picture of corporate culture models. They overlap in one respect: the Bureaucratic Culture to which they refer is very similar to Handy's role culture. But the others are quite different. The Clan Culture refers to a corporate environment with a heavy emphasis on socialization, which looks after its members but expects a high degree of loyalty in return. It is tribal, family-oriented, protective and possessive. Employees are like brothers in the same endeavor. Harley-Davidson, BMW and other famous marques tend to be clannish in their cultures. By contrast, Hellriegel and Slocum also identify the Market-Driven Culture, seen in organizations where profitability, market share and other business measures are most important. Here, there is no sentimentality about people who are not performing – they are simply kicked out. Finally, Hellriegel and Slocum identify the Entrepreneurial Culture, where innovation and flexibility are prized. These businesses are outward-looking and practical, but not as much as Market cultures are, and may evolve into these or other forms. Remember, corporate culture is not static, but is potentially highly volatile and can be in a state of flux, depending on the size, leadership, industry sector, and the country where the organization is based. There is a strong connection between organizational cultures and national cultures, as we will see in the next chapter.

CORPORATE CULTURE AND PROPENSITY TO CHANGE

How can a corporate culture be measured in an organization? What questions can be asked to ascertain cultural flexibility or inflexibility? How do we know whether a corporate culture is open to change or not? The following exercise can be used to determine change-orientation or change-resistance.

Managing change and support for change
This questionnaire is designed to help you understand the level of support or opposition to change within your organization.

Exercise: You are asked to respond to each item listed below according to how true you feel it is in terms of an organization with which you are familiar, ideally the company for which you work. Circle the appropriate number on the scale that follows the item. Consider the behavior and attitudes of people in the organization, and make your decision on the scoring according to the behavior and attitudes of the majority with who you have been in contact.

Usually not true	Not true	Somewhat untrue	Neutral true	Somewhat true	Usually	True
1	2	3	4	5	6	7

Values and visions
1. Do people throughout the organization have the same values or visions?

1	2	3	4	5	6	7

History of change
2. Can the organization implement change smoothly, according to its past experience?

1	2	3	4	5	6	7

Co-operation and trust
3. Would you say there is co-operation and trust in the organization (or mostly conflict)?

1	2	3	4	5	6	7

Culture
4. Are people in the organization prepared to take risks and be flexible, and is this rewarded by the organization (or is it bureaucratic and rule bound)?

1	2	3	4	5	6	7

Impact
5. Are people in the organization good at responding to change (or are they showing signs of exhaustion and being unsettled by changes)?

1	2	3	4	5	6	7

Punishments and rewards
6. Does the organization reward people who help achieve change and improvement (or punish those who try but fail)?

1	2	3	4	5	6	7

Respect and status
7. Will people retain their status after change implementation (or risk losing this as a result of the change)?

1	2	3	4	5	6	7

Status quo
8. Will the change be incremental (not causing major disruption)?

1	2	3	4	5	6	7

Interpretation: Scores 1, 2, and 3 are low; 4 and 5 are mid range; and 6 and 7 are high. The value of the scores lies in understanding the meanings that people attach to them. Generally, low to mid range scores should be a cause for concern. Lower scores indicate possible areas of resistance to change.

Values and visions: Low scores may indicate that values may be in conflict and that individuals and groups may not perceive any common ground. This situation is serious and almost guarantees that any major change will be resisted unless people learn how to build a shared set of values. In contrast, low scores may indicate a communication problem. In some organizations, values and visions remain secret, with people not knowing where their organization is headed. Although this communication problem needs to be solved, it may not indicate deeper potential resistance.

History of change: Low scores indicate a strong likelihood that a change will be resisted forcefully. Those who want the change will need to demonstrate repeatedly that they are serious this time. People are likely to be very skeptical, so persistence will be crucial.

Cooperation and trust: Low scores should be taken seriously. Building support for any major change without some degree of trust is difficult, if not impossible. The opposite of trust is fear, so a low score indicates not just the absence of trust but also the presence of fear.

Culture: Mid range to low scores indicate that people may have difficulty carrying out changes even though they support the changes. They are saying that the reward systems and proce¬dures followed in the organization hinder change. The change agents must be willing to examine these issues in depth to determine their causes.

Impact: Low scores probably indicate that people are burned out. Even though they may see the need for change, they may have little strength to give to the effort. Two important questions should be asked: Is this change really necessary at this time? If it is, how can the organizations support people so that the change causes minimal disruption?

Punishments and rewards: Low scores indicate strong potential resistance. Who in their right minds would support something that they knew would harm them? If employees' perceptions are accurate, the change agents must find a way to move forward with the change and find ways to make it rewarding for others. Low scores indicate a misunderstanding about the scope and reasons for change. The change agents must let people know why they are misinformed. This message will likely need to be communicated repeatedly (especially if trust also is low).

Respect and status: Low scores indicate that change agents must find ways to make this a win-win situation.

Status quo: Low scores indicate that people regard the potential change as very disruptive and stressful. The more involved people are in the change process, the less resistance they are likely to experience. Most often, people resist change when they feel out of control.

How were your scores in this exercise? Do you think that your organization could change its culture, if necessary? An organization which can keep changing can be flexible, and entrepreneurial – the opposite to bureaucratic. The kind of organization that can move with the times can be more robust and a longer-term survivor. Or it may lose direction and tend to be controlled by a dominant leader... think about the implications for your own company.

LEADERSHIP AND CULTURE – HOW A LEADER CAN CHANGE A CULTURE

The Swiss watch industry was dominated by highly bureaucratic and old-fashioned organizations for most of the nineteenth and twentieth centuries – until Nicholas Hayek became involved in the industry and saw a lot of things he didn't like. His aim was to create a much more innovative and entrepreneurial organization – which he did with the famous Swatch brand. How did this happen? As Gayle Avery, in her book *Understanding Leadership* (2002) explains:

"...Not only the success of the Swatch Group, but much of the resurgence in the entire Swiss watch industry can be attributed to the vision of the Swatch Group's President and Chief Executive Officer, Nicolas G. Hayek. Hayek told the *Harvard Business* Review that watches are emotional products, not commodities, as much of the Swiss industry used to position them. To Hayek, watches are important facets of self-image. "I thought if we could add genuine emotion ... and attack the low end of the market (Asian quartz watches) we could succeed", he said. In the 1996 Annual Report, Hayek noted that "the company's unique **culture** is made up of emotionalism and realism, of humanism and combativity in the face of formidable competitors." Not only are the pragmatic elements of low cost, high quality and good design important to the Swatch concept, crucial to their success is Swatch laying its **culture** on the line. That is the most difficult element for others to copy, Hayek claimed.

From the early 1970s, the Swiss watch industry had been slowly losing market share to cheap Asian quartz watches, especially from Hong Kong and Japan, but also from Taiwan, China and South Korea. Switzerland's share of the global market dropped from 43 to 15 per cent between 1977 and 1983, and the amount of jobs in the watch industry fell by more than 50 per cent. By the early 1980s, the Swiss share of the low price watch market had become practically zero. Barely better was the Swiss share of the middle segment. However, in the top layer, Switzerland had about 97 per cent of the market. Overall, the Swiss watch industry had slipped from a 30 per cent share of the world watch market to 9 per cent. The decline has largely been attributed to the Swiss watch industry remaining **loyal to its tradition** of mechanical watch movements and not adjusting to changing consumer habits. The banks, becoming increasingly concerned, called on Hayek's consulting firm to assess the future for the flagship companies of Switzerland's watch industry. Hayek's report described a 'chaotic jungle': a lack discipline and strategy, and too many separate small companies. In late 1983, many were amalgamated into one entity and now form the production arm of the Swatch Group, of which Hayek bought 51%.This became the foundation of the Swatch Group.

In 1979, spurred on by Japanese achievements of a 2.5 mm-thick watch, revolutionary technology enabled the Swiss to produce the Delirium watch, the thinnest in the world with a thickness of 1.98 mm. The Delirium's success inspired the creation of a less expensive quality watch made out of plastic. In the late summer of 1981, the **entrepreneurial** Swatch watch was born - a Swiss-made watch using synthetic material, which is shockproof, accurate, suited for mass production, inexpensive and available in a range of colors. Financially, the Swatch Group performed well from the start, outpacing the watch-making sector as a whole, reading sales of over 4 billion Swiss francs in 2000. The Swiss share of the global watch market has recovered to 51 per cent, with Swatch being the world's largest watchmaker at the beginning of the twenty-first century.

Swatch continues to enjoy considerable growth. Hayek identified four major phases in Swatch's development. First came the survival phase, which was achieved largely because of the Swatch watch and an effective international wholesale distribution system. The second phase involved reviving the luxury sector Omega, Rado and Longine brands, plus acquiring additional luxury brands. The third phase was the worldwide distribution phase, when the Swatch Group created a **dynamic**, international distribution network with branches in many countries around the world, also focusing on the middle-price-range segment of the market with brands such as Tissot. Swatch established a new **entrepreneurial** brand - cK Watch Co Ltd - using a young team of managers. Finally, the current phase involves rapid global expansion while keeping the know-how inside the organization - from production to Research and Development.

Continued growth is vital to the Swatch **culture**: "Growth is and always has been the motto of the Swatch Group, but a growth that is progressive and conscious. It must be based on solid foundations such as expanding customer acceptance of our products, continual and permanent improvement of quality, stringent unit cost controls, and the development and launch of innovative products." Hayek added that growth "must be based on improving the qualifications and motivation of our staff, as well as our management's desires to be met by a sea of smiling faces on a Monday morning, belonging to people who are happy to come to work".

Project teams are very common in Swatch, reflecting a **net or flexible project-based** culture. In planning a new product, Swatch assembles a project team as soon as agreement is reached on product performance specifications. Then the team is presented with parameters for its performance. Hayek said, "we present the team with target economics: this is how much the product can sell for ... this is the margin we need to support advertising, promotion and so on. Thus these are the costs we can afford. Now go and design a product and a production system that allows us to build it at these costs in Switzerland. Creative people tackle an issue and then move on to the next one", he insists, revealing the empowering nature of the Swatch culture.

Although many parts of the Swatch Group are in fact highly organized, the aim is to minimize **bureaucracy** in the Group. Hayek has stated that organizational structure is "the most inhuman thing ever invented. It goes against our nature as people". Instead, Swatch works by using 'clear-but-flexible' boundaries and targets, encouraging conflicting targets between different units within the Group. The brands have complete autonomy over design, marketing and communications, but still need to resolve conflicts with the Group's manufacturer, when it comes to production. This means negotiating over factors like quality, style, speed of production and cost. Such differences are resolved with the minimum of **bureaucracy**, without a formal intermediary in the organization, and as directly and quickly as possible. While each unit has its own delineated responsibilities and rules, each unit is required to interact with others in order to get its job done. It is rare for major companies that market-complex products are as vertically integrated as Swatch, which owns and operates every process, from manufacturing to retailing.

Swatch competes on price by automating aggressively, thereby keeping labor costs down, to less than 10% of total manufacturing costs. "Innovation, creativity, imagination, vision and control mean that from Switzerland, one of the most expensive countries in the world in terms of labor costs, over 80% of our products can be exported to the rest of the world, despite fierce competition from other countries, particularly in Asia," Hayek said in 1998. Swatch uses its own distribution network, paying as much attention to the look of its points-of-sale as to the products themselves. By 2001, nearly 600 Swatch stores had been opened around the world.

Global campaigns and unconventional presentations enhance the Swatch brand. Swatch is present at a range of events around the world from sporting to musical, from environmental to United Nations' activities. A flamboyant **marketing** venture was achieved by using a railway tunnel in Switzerland to show Swatch's 1998 30-second "Time is what you make of it" slogan. As trains pass through the tunnel, a series of images on the tunnel wall flashed by, informing passengers about Swatch and reminding them to make the most of their time.

Creativity abounds at Swatch, which executes many of its 'extreme' ideas.
For example, hanging a 150 m-high, 13-tonne working Swatch from Frankfurt's tallest building successfully launched Swatch in Germany. The only words on the face were "Swatch. Swiss. DM 60". That marketing idea was repeated successfully in Tokyo's Ginza, although with a smaller display.

The Swatch Club brings together tens of thousands of fans from all over the world. The club's objective is to promote communication among like-minded people, across the barriers of country, language, race, and age. Members are identified through their club watches. Since 1985, when Swatch entered the world of art with the first Swatch Art Special designed by Kiki Picasso, Swatch has been promoted as a form of wearable art. **Innovation** is at the core of Swatch's activities. Hayek Senior and his son, G. Nicolas Hayek Junior, have been the driving force in terms of innovation, although new ideas come from all levels of the company. Formal research and development is not a major activity at Swatch; very often the President's intuition, or that of other employees, is developed to see if it is marketable. Both Hayeks are available 24 hours a day, seven days a week to provide '**very hands-on**' assistance on many levels.

Many innovations at Swatch, particularly in marketing, are produced from ordinary meetings or **brainstorming** sessions. Swatch seeks to enhance creativity by fostering a **relaxed, chaotic workplace** in which people can **change jobs easily**. It starts with a totally **relaxed attitude to dress**: Hayek Senior dresses in a unique 'casual' style. Hayek Junior wears jeans, although that is not totally unusual in Swiss business. Most others take their cue from these leaders, and those wearing formal work suits and ties stand out. The Hayeks do not believe that there is an ideal company structure. They prefer to encourage **creativity** in employees by emphasizing that employees should be themselves, have fun and not mind what others in the company think or say. As Hayek Senior put it, "We kill too many good ideas by rejecting them without thinking about them, by laughing at them". His strength as a businessman is that he has retained the 'fantasy' of a six-year-old. "If you can keep and use the curiosity of a child, you can only improve everything around you." Individuals exhibiting eccentric behavior can thrive at Swatch, as long as the Hayeks are happy with their creative output. However, some jobs require intense concentration for long periods, leading to early burnout and hence a high turnover in employees.

Hayek Senior provided the vision, cash and style to make Swatch successful. Variously described by the media as egocentric, idiosyncratic, and passionate, Nicolas G. Hayek was born in 1928 in Beirut, Lebanon, with an American father and a Lebanese mother. After primary and secondary education in Beirut, he moved to Switzerland with his family, where he became a citizen in 1964. By 1994, Hayek's company was the biggest management consulting firm in Switzerland, a US$1 billion business. Forbes Magazine listed Hayek Senior among the world's richest people in 1999, with a net worth of about US$1.4 billion. To secure the future leadership of the Swatch Group, Hayek Senior has placed members of his family in significant positions in the Group. His son, G. Nicolas, is head of the company's marketing and communications, and by 2001 he was also the Swatch brand's delegate to the Swatch Group Management Board as well as carrying responsibility for Swatch operations in Germany, Italy and Spain. Hayek's daughter, Nayla, became an administrator of the company and sits on the board of directors. Hayek's wife, Marianne, was appointed an administrator of Hayek Engineering, of which its founder remains Chairman and CEO. Hayek Senior's philosophy is that he "injects himself directly and visibly throughout" Swatch, especially where strategy and new products are concerned.

He works constantly to cut red tape. Most people seem to be aware of the strong influence that both Hayeks exert on the company, and it could be difficult not to let the owners' moods affect company performance, particularly in the head office. This is not only due to the family members holding significant positions of power, but also to the hands-on approach of both senior and junior Hayeks. If the Hayeks dislike a product or idea, company morale is said to decline; morale is high if the Hayeks are behind an idea.

Despite the strong influence of the owners over most major decisions – and there is no doubt who is running the organization – leadership seems to be widely distributed at Swatch. A small number of positions exist to lead different sections, but basically there is **little formal hierarchy** at Swatch. The head positions are predominantly liaison roles between staff and senior management. **Creative** young people with good ideas lead **project teams**, which form around specific ideas. Creativity develops through the informal interactions of people and temporary leaders emerge as projects arise. Communication is spontaneous with no strongly enforced formal communication lines. While there are rules and procedures, people can contact others spontaneously and take the associated risks of 'going around' the system.

Employees describe the Swatch culture using words such as 'spontaneous', 'chaotic', 'cool' (no tie), 'casual' (no business suit), 'simple' (no glamour) and 'unsophisticated' (no company cars!). The **culture** is full of emotion, dancing, music, ski-boarding, laughing and tolerates no rigidity. Offices are open space.

Cultures in some parts of the Swatch Group may be quite different, presenting interesting challenges when Swatch marketing employees interact with staff from manufacturing or other less flamboyant divisions of the Group.

The Swatch Group consistently employs more women than men. Women represented approximately 56 per cent of the Swatch Group workforce in 2000.

People at Swatch are young (average age 30 years), and in 2000 included 27 nationalities using three to four common languages (English, French, German and Italian). Given the fast pace at Swatch and the need for new ideas, relatively high staff turnover is tolerated. Some new employees leave after a three-month trial period because the **culture** does not suit them, but the average length of stay is about three years. Finance and logistics staff tend to stay longer than their colleagues in marketing and the more creative parts of the company. While high turnover is accepted in Swatch's exciting **culture**, the 1999 peak of 45 per cent staff annual turnover was perceived as unacceptably high, even at Swatch.

Staff members are paid a performance bonus on top of their fixed payment. The performance management system focuses on goals, objectives and developing the necessary skills to achieve them. While careers probably cannot be planned within Swatch's turbulent environment, many opportunities arise for people to progress. In recruiting new staff, Swatch seeks "practical, globe-trotting, sporting people, with language skills and university qualifications."

In addition, particular social skills are highly valued, including having a 'Swatchy personality', being committed, open-minded, customer-oriented, flexible, market-oriented, mobile, and a doer rather than a thinker. Swatch employees should communicate well, think globally in systems terms, and be prepared to act fast.

Exercise: Discussing the Swatch case

1. The Swatch Group is an exciting, creative organization. Which types and aspects of corporate culture can you see operating here? How does the leadership affect the culture at Swatch? How dependent is the company on the energy and influence of the Hayeks?
2. How are decisions made and which kinds of decisions can you see?
3. Which culture model is dominant at Swatch? What would it be like to work there, as far as you can tell from the case study?
4. How are the following cultural contradictions resolved? Bureaucracy, vision, emotion, chaos, automated production, decentralized versus hands-on availability of the founders?
5. There is evidence of extensive teamwork, but how do teams seem to operate in Swatch's chaotic environment? If more designing in the future will revolve around virtual and distributed teams, how well equipped is Swatch's culture to adapt to this style of operation?
6. Where is the unique difference between Swatch and other organizations? Can you describe the Swatch experience provided to customers and staff?
7. Is Swatch a learning or teaching organization? How can mentoring work in a climate of rapid staff turnover? Describe how knowledge is shared and managed through the organization. Is this not an issue for Swatch? What happens to mistakes?
8. What would attract people to work at Swatch, and why would they leave on average after three years? Is this attrition a problem in Swatch's culture? If so, how could it be fixed?

Key issues in the Swatch case:
- World's largest watch manufacturer;
- Growth is vital to its success;
- Vision-driven, passionate;

- Heroic leader, who rescued the Swiss watch industry;
- Financially well-performing;
- Values – fun, quality, fashion, design, low cost;
- Core competency is the Swatch culture;
- Decentralized hands-off management, yet hands-on Hayeks available;
- Hayek hates bureaucracy, preferring a flamboyant and creative culture;
- Team-based culture, especially in marketing and innovation;
- Research and Development teams are given parameters within which to work and then autonomy to come up with the solution;
- Highly integrated vertically, ensures that Swatch can retain its strategic independence; produces not only its own products, but also tools, components, chips and machines;
- Competes on price by automating aggressively and keeping labor costs down;
- Can operate in expensive Switzerland because of its level of automation, but has about 50 production centers worldwide;
- Has its own distribution network, with mega stores, and Swatch stores;
- Brands have considerable autonomy but must collaborate with production;
- Automation controls production processes, marketing is uncontrolled and chaotic; technology is highly innovative;
- Pressure to produce two fashion catalogues annually;
- The Swatch 'experience' affects design of their mega stores, employees and customers;
- Tries to relate marketing to current events, with Swatch poking fun or taking a position;
- Hayeks are the driving force in innovation, with employee teams;
- Mistakes – just move on to the next thing, no blame or 'scapegoating';
- Fractal workplace, chaotic, can change jobs easily, creative;
- Heroic, much decorated visionary leader injects self visibly and directly throughout the organization;
- If the leader disapproves, the project is dropped;
- Distributed leadership, with team leaders providing a buffer between staff and senior management; global and highly diverse workforce;
- High staff turnover, average stay is three years, burnout common;
- Swatch people are young, cool, global, practical, sporting and university-qualified;
- Performance bonus is paid on top of salary; and
- Women represented over 56 per cent of the workforce in 2000.

Compare the Swatch case with other organizations of your choice. Many well-known multinationals are well documented, such as IBM, Coca-Cola, the Virgin Group, General Electric – as mentioned in Chapter 11. Another example might be Pepsi (to compare with Coca-Cola) and Apple (to compare with IBM). Both are profiled in detail in the account of the move of one of their major executives (Sculley & Byrne, 1987).

CLOSING CASE – ORGANIZATIONAL CULTURE AND NATIONAL CULTURE

The Sultan Centre [TSC] in Kuwait is led by high-flying Kuwaiti executive Jameel Sultan, who also has interests in real estate, logistics, training and education. Kuwait's largest independent retailer (Global Investment House report, 2006) was incorporated in 1980 as a holding company. TSC was originally a Petroleum Services Company, which was a major provider of hardware, tools, and supplies to the oil industry. TSC has now expanded to become a premier retailer and leading supplier of supermarket items, perishables, and general merchandise in the Middle East. Currently TSC has 27 outlets in its retail business line in Kuwait, Oman and Jordan. Moreover the company has a market share of 15 to 17% in the retail segment in Kuwait. TSC plans for 2007 included expanding aggressively to launch 15 more retail outlets in Kuwait, Oman and Jordan, seen as its major markets.

The Sultan Center has employees of 22 different nationalities, with 1200 employees in its supermarkets in Kuwait alone. The three predominant nationalities employed by TSC here are as follows: Arabs 269, Indians 251, and Filipinos 552. These three nationalities represent almost 84% of the total amount of employees of TSC supermarket division. How is this organization influenced by (a) being owned by Kuwaitis? (B) being managed by expatriate Arabs, mostly Lebanese and Egyptians? and (C) being staffed by Indians and Filipinos? What are the implications for managing such a business in this environment?

The culture is shaped by a bureaucratic and controlling structure, with minimal transparency and a strong belief in the dispensability of most of the employees. The Chairman personally signs all expense claims, a task which takes up about one whole day a week. Promotion is rare, staff turnover is high, job satisfaction is at best neutral and verging on dissatisfaction. The rank-and-file staff members are predominantly collective rather than individualist socially, are risk averse and uncertainty avoiding, and are accepting high power-distant behaviors from management (see the discussion about national cultures in Chapter 13). These employees are attracted by the status value of working at a prestigious store, but behind the scenes are discontented. The culture is thus predominantly bureaucratic and market-driven, with the Chairman like a spider in a web (Handy's power culture). It is influenced by history, geography, and the leader's personality. With staff recruitment from overseas (much poorer countries) not a problem, there are few efforts to obtain staff buy-in and seek to motivate these people. Recruitment of people for the more senior managerial roles is more likely to be handled outside the group than grown from within. Contrast this culture with that of Swatch.

CONCLUSION

This chapter has looked at models of corporate culture – especially those presented by Handy, and by Hellriegel and Slocum – and asks you to apply these to specific organizations – especially in the Swatch case. After reading this chapter, you should be able to identify predominant and subsidiary cultural types. It is also important to be able to explain the relationship between corporate culture and corporate structure, especially in terms of highly bureaucratic organizations, compared with flatter, more flexible structures. There is also a significant link between organizational culture, the business sector in which the company is operating, and business performance. Can you explain the connection? The impact of corporate history on culture is strong, especially in terms of leadership and culture – and culture change. How ready is your company to change? Finally, as discussed below, what is the impact of national cultures on organizational culture? This question leads us into our following chapter, on National Cultures.

REFERENCES

Avery, G.C. (2002) *Understanding Leadership*. Upper Saddle River, New Jersey: Prentice Hall.

Bechari, F. (2007), 'Job Satisfaction Among Retail Sector Employees: a Kuwait case study', *Unpublished MBA thesis*, Kuwait Maastricht Business School.

George, J.M. & Jones, G.R. (2002), Organizational Behavior. Upper Saddle River, New Jersey: Prentice Hall.

Handy, C. (1976; 1980; 1985) *Understanding Organizations*. Harmondsworth: Penguin.

Hellriegel, D. & Slocum, J.W. (2004), *Organizational Behavior*. Mason, Ohio: South-Western/Thomson Learning.

Hoojberg R. & Petrock F. (1993) 'On culture change: using the competing values framework to help leaders execute a transformational strategy. *Human Resource Management, 32*, 29-50.

Jones, S. (2003), 'The ABC, 123 of Corporate Culture', *Human Assets Middle East, 4*, Autumn.

Ritz-Carlton Hotel Group, www.ritz-carlton.com.

Schein, E.H. (1985) *Organizational Culture and Leadership*. San Francisco: Jossey-Bass.

Sculley, J. & Byrne, J.A. (1987) *Odyssey: from Pepsi to Apple*. New York: Harper and Row.

Swatch Group Annual Reports and Facts and Figures.

Taylor, W. (1993), '*Message and muscle: An interview with Swatch titan Nicolas Hayek*', Harvard Business Review, March/April 1993.

www.swatchgroup.com.

RECOMMENDED FURTHER READING

Aycan, Z., Kanungo, R.N. & Sinha, J.B.P. (1999), 'Organizational culture and human resource management practices: the model of cultural fit' *Journal of Cross-Cultural Psychology, 30*:4:501-26.

Davis, S.M. (1990) *Managing Corporate Culture*. New York: Harper Business.

Deal, T.E. & Kennedy, A.A. (1982) *Corporate Cultures: the Rites and Rituals of Corporate Life*. Reading MA: Addison Wesley.

Graves, D. (1986) *Corporate Culture: diagnosis and change*. New York: St Martin's Press.

Hampden-Turner, Charles (1990) *Creating Corporate Culture: from discord to harmony*. Reading, MA: Addison Wesley.

Handy, C. (1990) *Inside Organizations*. Harmondsworth: Penguin.

Handy, C. (1978) *The Gods of Management*. London: Souvenir Press.

Handy, C. (1991) The Age of Unreason. Boston: *Harvard Business School* Press.

Mintzberg, H. (1979) *The Structure of Organizations*. Englewood Cliffs, NJ: Prentice Hall.

Wilkins, A.L. & Ouchi, W.G., 'Efficient Cultures: exploring the relationship between culture and organizational performance', *Administrative Science Quarterly, 28*:3, 1983.

CHAPTER 13

NATIONAL CULTURE
STEPHANIE JONES

OPENING CASE:

KZ, in her late 20s, works as a consultant in a wholly foreign-owned firm in Shanghai, earning a good salary for her age and experience. Although showing elements of being a traditional Chinese, and also being subject to many Western influences – overwhelmingly she is a Chuppie, influenced primarily by the desire for self-improvement, exposure to new things, and a form of hedonism typical of her generation. But this is not Western hedonism – it combines having fun with a sense of responsibility and ability to work hard and make sacrifices. She wants to have fun based on consumerism and with a view to enhancing status.

KZ's friends are mostly like her. They speak English well, are university-educated, also work in foreign companies, are highly-professional and ambitious, sporty and fun-loving. She is still very friendly with her senior school classmates, being members of an elite cadre of young people with outstanding scholastic records who were, as a result, not required to sit the usual examinations to enter the school. Long-term relationships are just as important to Chuppies as to other Chinese, so KZ's best friends have been the same for the last ten years. One exception among KZ's friends is a university room mate whose career has concentrated very much on the public sector, and she currently occupies a senior position with the government tax bureau. This connection helps KZ keep in touch with the wider world and it could be useful to her career progression.

KZ is still single and lives with her parents. If she had a boyfriend – and she is very particular about who he would be and his characteristics – he would have to share her values of professionalism and self-improvement, and would also have to have a career with good prospects in a prestigious foreign company, such as a bank. Having a university degree is perhaps not so important, but he must be someone with whom she can converse and have a good intellectual relationship.

KZ's favorite activity in the evenings after work is spending time with friends in restaurants and hotel coffee shops, and shopping. Longer spells of free time would be spent on outings, traveling around China, also with friends. For lunch KZ has a lunchbox with her colleagues at work, or goes with them to a nearby restaurant – it's always Chinese food, but the timing is often dictated by the European expatriate boss and when he holds meetings. Dinner would be after shopping in the evenings, and being with friends is more important than the food – because the timing may be erratic, it may be at McDonald's or TGI Friday's. 1PM for lunch and 8PM for dinner would be seen as late. Hanging out with friends, shopping and eating are her favorite hobbies.

Living in Shanghai, KZ lives with her parents, and would not want to move because it is difficult to obtain the internal residency for Shanghai city – this is very highly prized. At home, the interior decoration is quite traditional Chinese, reflecting her parents' taste, and when with them she adopts a much more traditional Chinese outlook. KZ travels mostly by bus, but very often gets taxis, especially if these journeys are being paid for by the company.

Art and culture used to be more important to KZ before she began her career – now she only has time for watching movies and attending the odd classical music concert. As a girl, she played the accordion quite well for over 12 years, but not any more. She's too busy making money and spending it. In terms of sports and physical exercise, KZ likes running, swimming and tennis. She used to do them a lot more when she was a student, but now feels there's little time any more, and it's too far to go to the park where the air is fresher for running. Swimming and tennis can be done with friends, so that's OK.

In terms of holidays, KZ wants to travel within China – she is particularly attracted by the possibility of visiting Tibet. She sees the region as mysterious, clean and with people who are more simple and direct, and a completely different culture. But if she had enough money, KZ would like to go overseas – she hasn't been yet, and it's certainly something she would like to do soon.

When feeling ill, KZ usually uses Western medicine – she sees it as more efficient and quick acting, especially if she wants to get well as soon as possible. But otherwise she still uses Chinese medicine, which takes longer but has no side effects and seems a healthier choice.

A lot of KZ's disposable income goes on shopping, particularly buying clothes, cosmetics and beauty products. She also buys books and magazines, and treats herself and friends to meals in Western style restaurants and going to the movies. Buying presents for friends is also high on the list, at festival times and for birthdays.

In terms of ranking six objects (mobile phone, color TV, indoor toilet, shower unit, CD player, carpet on floor), KZ would put having an indoor toilet as top of the list, but closely followed by the color TV and mobile phone, then a shower unit. Having a CD player is more important than a carpet on the floor.

KZ likes working in a foreign company – many Chinese firms are not very professional, she doesn't trust them. She sees herself as very open-minded, comparing herself with traditional Chinese – they are not efficient, they cannot make decisions, they lose chances for personal improvement and business success because they are so closed-minded. She does accept, however, why they are this way – during the Cultural Revolution everyone was more conservative, they were afraid that someone would be cheating on them or spying on them, or using them for their own benefit. It was a period of a complete lack of trust, and there are still a lot of people around who have been heavily influenced by these difficult times.

By way of further explanation, KZ mentioned how her parents still talk about the Cultural Revolution, and watch TV shows and read novels about it – their memories are neither sad nor happy, they understand why it had to happen, and why everyone went along with it. Particularly upsetting, however, was the attack on her grandmother's house by Red Guards, who took away all her Western style possessions (grandmother used to work for a Western company) and her gold, announcing that "people should be poor". Grandmother had had a Western style wedding, and she destroyed the pictures of it before the Red Guards saw it, fearing the kind of ritual humiliations which accompanied the discovery of such items.

In terms of her career and educational background, KZ's parents did not try to influence her choice but allowed her to make her own decisions. Married in 1972 in a Mao suit, with straight hair and without make-up or a ring, KZ's mother has worked as a mathematics teacher in the same middle school for the last 30 years. Her father, when demobilized from the army, was assigned to the railway bureau and although he has been promoted several times he has stayed in this state-owned unit nearly all his life. Her parents don't mind her working in a foreign company, but would not like her to go overseas for long, especially as she is an only child (although born before the beginning of the one-child family policy).

For KZ, the characteristics of a young Chuppie woman are being open-minded, with a high level of education, a creative outlook, wearing fashionable clothes, and trying out new things – e-mail, mobile phones, new software, DVDs. Above all, Chuppies work hard and play hard – having a good time but also working aggressively for their achievements.

Questions on the opening case: What is KZ's attitude to her job, and what does this tell you about her national culture? How important are relationships to KZ? Is this another cultural characteristic? How is modernization and the impact of Western culture transforming the culture of younger generation Chinese? How is Western-style consumerism influencing KZ's lifestyle? Why do young Chinese prefer working in a foreign company? What is the nature of the gap between the culture of young Chinese and the older generation? Given the choice between these six objects (mobile phone, color TV, indoor toilet, shower unit, CD player, carpet on floor), which would you consider most important? What does this tell you about your culture?

LEARNING OBJECTIVES FOR THIS CHAPTER

In "National Culture" we aim to introduce you to a theoretical framework for understanding variations in cultures between countries, especially as this framework is used in some of the most well-known and well-researched studies. This should equip you to better cope with different cultures, appreciating why they may be different, and perhaps give you some ideas of how you might modify your behavior to be more effective (see Chapter 14 too). Based on several in-depth examples from different countries, we explore ways of defining cultural differences, speculating on how these have evolved and continue to change.

MODELS OF NATIONAL CULTURE

The opening case illustrates a number of characteristics including the need for money primarily for enhancing status and consumerism; ambition to succeed; the need for relationships and connections; gender equality and individual decision-making about marriage and career issues; attitude to leisure pursuits, such as art, culture, sports, travel; and feelings about history, tradition, and one's country. How can we define these characteristics more specifically? Which models can help us? Which authors have described national culture and what it means, to give us more specific guidelines?

It is well known that an individual's behavior and attitude are strongly linked to his or her culture, and this helps determine their perception of the world, of business and of their careers. Hofstede (1991) argues that employees of different nationality have different feelings toward their organizations and their daily jobs. Wood et al. (2004) agrees that the culture in which the person grows up, and lives, can have the potential to affect his or her attitude to their job as a whole. Trompenaars and Hampden-Turner (1999) add to the discussion with their own model (see below).

DEFINITIONS

Over 160 definitions of culture were uncovered in the research of Kroeber and Kluckholm (1985), cited by North and Hort, (2002). There is no universally satisfactory definition of the domain of culture (Daniels, 2004). Trompenaars and Hamden-Turner (1999) simply define it as "culture is the way in which a group of people solves problems, and reconciles dilemmas". Harris (2001), cited by Hellriegel and Slocum (2004), states that culture is a dominant pattern of living, thinking, and believing that is developed and transmitted by people consciously, or unconsciously, to subsequent generations. Different nationalities evaluate the world differently, especially through the factor of social influence, or the influence that individuals, or groups have on a person's attitude and behavior (Daniels, 2004).

Culture consists of people with shared attitudes, values and beliefs. People simultaneously belong to national, ethnic, professional, and organizational cultures at the same time, and thereby their individual and group attitudes, values, and beliefs evolve (Daniels, 2004). According to Wood et al. (2004) there are two types of dimensions to each culture: visible and invisible. The visible dimensions of culture include:

- **Language:** that spoken language in different countries, which reveals the existence and non-existence of certain concepts;

- **Time orientation:** different cultural attitude toward time, either short-term thinking and pressure on time, or a more unhurried, longer-term perspective;

- **Use of space:** it varies among different cultures, in terms of comfort in being close physically to strangers or not;

- **Religion:** that most people follow in each country or a group of countries, and it is the most influential part that can affect the society as whole.

The invisible part of culture includes the different value patterns that exist across cultures, and the different assumptions underpinning human behavior across cultures. Hofstede (1984, p.13) sees culture as "the collective programming of the mind, which distinguishes the members of one human group from another ... culture, in this sense, includes systems of values."

CULTURES OF PEOPLE IN ORGANIZATIONS
– THEORETICAL BACKGROUND

There are a number of models of national cultures created by authors such as Trompenaars and Hampden-Turner (1999), and Hall (1976), but by far the most cited model in most of the cross-cultural management literature reviewed for this chapter was that of Hofstede (1980,1984). Harry (2004) described how Hofstede's dimensions have generated a tremendous amount of research and have been highly influential in all the social sciences. Moreover, he referenced Hofstede's work almost 70 times in the 1994 *Handbook of Industrial and Organizational Psychology*. Even though Hofstede's representation of culture has been extensively used in research, Hofstede's models of national culture have been strongly criticized. Williamson (2002) cited by Navarrete (2003) disqualifies Hofstede's work on the basis of explaining national culture depending on only one company culture. Sivakumar (2001) cited by Navarrete (2003) argues that the value of different indices and cultural constructs were developed by Hofstede over two decades ago and these values could have changed by now. Moreover, many researchers have encountered psychometric problems (i.e. as regards the reliability and validity) concerning his measures.

According to Navarrete (2003), Hofstede's (1980) seminal work first identified how culture becomes encased by the notion of a shared set of values within national identity, but according to Westwood and Everett (1987) there are major concerns regarding what has been measured in Hofstede's work. Hofstede's study on work values makes the assumption that these are valid indicators of national culture (North and Hort 2002). Although Hofstede's work has been heavily criticized, he has developed a promising framework to understand the value differences across national cultures (Robbins, 2004; Wood et al., 2004). Until more extensive and more up-to-date research is released, we can feel justified in looking in detail at Hofstede's model to help us achieve a greater understanding of national culture.

Hofstede (1984) has described culture in four dimensions, then later he added a fifth dimension with Michel Bond (Wood et al., 2004). These dimensions are:

- Differences between small and large power-distance countries;
- Differences between collectivist and individualist countries;
- Differences between weak and strong uncertainty-avoidance countries;
- Differences between feminine and masculine countries;
- Differences between long-term and short-term orientation countries

Power-distance (see below) is the degree to which people in a country accept a hierarchical or unequal distribution of power, and this is clearly shown in their attitudes in organizations (Wood et al., 2004). It focuses on the degree of equality or inequality in a power structure. A high power-distance ranking shows that inequality of power or wealth exists in the society, and is tolerated in organizations. A low power-distance country stresses equality and opportunity for everybody, and the extent of power-distance is clearly reflected in the hierarchical organization of companies (Hofstede, 1980, 2001). Employees from high power-distance cultures prefer centralized power structures and hierarchies. While employees from low power-distance cultures mostly favor decentralized power structure, flat organizations, and equal privileges. This dimension helps to describe the relationship between superior and subordinates and how this differs between countries (Daniels, 2004).

Individualism - collectivism is the degree to which people in a country focus on working as individuals more than working together in a group (Wood et al. 2004). A high individualism country encourages personal initiative and the right to having a private life (Hofstede, 1980, 2001). Employees in organizations in these countries have a desire for personal time, freedom and challenge, and self-actualization will be a prime motivator for them (Daniels, 2004). A low individualism country means that the society is characterized by a collective nature. Everybody tends to take responsibility for the members in the group (Hofstede, 1980, 2001). Moreover, employees have loyalty and/or dependence on the organization. The provision of a safe physical and emotional environment (security need) will be a prime motivator for those employees (Daniels, 2004). Furthermore employees from high individualism cultures have loose ties to their organizations, as they prioritize an individual's need and rights. Employees from high collectivism cultures, on the contrary, tend to respect group needs and rights (Fu and Liu, 2005). According to Hofstede's (1980, 2001) study results on Power-Distance and Individualism-Collectivism, Arab countries, the Philippines and India have a large power-distance and low individualism, as well as many other Asian countries. Many African and South American countries also fall into this category.

Uncertainty-avoidance concerns the degree to which people in a country prefer a structured than unstructured situation (Wood et al., 2004). It also focuses on the level of tolerance for uncertainty within the society. High uncertainty avoidance countries tend to create a rule-oriented society for themselves. Laws, rules and controls are used to reduce the uncertainty, and this is also seen in organizations. Low uncertainty-avoidance countries have less concern about uncertainty; the society tolerates changes and takes more risks, and organizations tend to be less structured (Hofstede, 1980, 2001).

Employees from high uncertainty-avoidance cultures dislike uncertainty. They like to have rules, order, and truths. Employees from low uncertainty avoidance culture prefer fewer and more flexible rules (Fu and Liu, 2005). Employees from high uncertainty avoiding cultures prefer set rules, which are not to be broken, even if it in the best interests of the company. Furthermore, these employees plan to work for the company for a long time, preferring the certainty of their present positions over other considerations (Daniels, 2004). According to Hofstede (1980, 2001), his study results on Uncertainty-Avoidance showed that India and the Philippines have a low Uncertainty-Avoidance, while the Arab countries are slightly higher than the mean average. Western countries are more likely to have a stronger tolerance for ambiguity, and this is reflected in the way their organizations operate.

Masculinity-femininity is a further Hofstede dimension, looking at the degree to which people in a country value an emphasis on so-called masculine traits, such as assertiveness, independence, and insensitivity to feelings as a dominant value (Wood et al., 2004) High masculinity countries experience a higher degree of gender discrimination. Males are dominant in the society. In a low masculinity country, females are more equally treated to males in all aspects in the society (Hofstede, 1980, 2001).

Employees from high masculinity cultures value money and material recognition, performance and growth, self-accomplishment and independence. Employees from low masculinity cultures focus on people, life quality, service and interdependence ((Hughes (1999) cited by Fu and Liu (2005)).

According to Hofstede's (1980, 2001) study results on the Masculinity–Femininity dimension, the Arab countries, the Philippines, and India have a high Masculinity degree. These are countries where generally there is a high degree of gender discrimination (despite the contribution to the economy of a large number of Filipina women working in many countries in the world). By contrast, many European countries, including Scandinavia, show opposite characteristics.

Long-term – short-term orientation describes the degree to which people in a country emphasize values associated with the future (Wood et al. 2004). The long-term orientation perspective is typically characterized by traits of persistence and perseverance, with a belief that things will work out well in the end. It also includes a respect for hierarchies of status and of relationships. Observing this order is an important part of long-term thinking cultures, who also are concerned with thrift and making economies. They can also be seen as having a sense of shame, and feeling that they need to protect their family's reputation. Long-term rewards are expected as a result of today's hard work. The task of business in these countries may take longer to develop in this society, particularly for an 'outsider' (Hofstede, 2001).

On the opposite side of this dimension, short-term orientation is marked by a sense of security and stability, a protection of one's reputation, a respect for tradition, and the need to fulfill social obligations and protecting one's 'face' (Hofstede, 2001). In these countries culture changes can occur more rapidly as long-term traditions and commitments are not emphasized.

According to Hofstede's (1980, 2001) study results on Long-Term – Short-Term orientation India, and the Philippines have opposite rankings to each other, for example. Indian people as a whole have a deep respect for traditions, status, order in society, and the image and standing of their family in society: hence the massive expenditure on society weddings, for example. By contrast, Filipinos are known for their opportunism and taking life as it comes.

A CONTRASTING THEORY OF CULTURE

Trompenaars' and Hampden-Turner's dimensions vary slightly from Hofstede's. There are some overlaps, and some commonalties. The former is concerned with exploring seven main parameters. Firstly, universalism and particularism is seen as the observance of laws and rules rather than the placing of relationships as the highest priority. Secondly, individualism and communitarianism explains the contrast between people with a group or individual outlook (similar to one of the Hofstede dimensions). Affective and neutral cultures differentiate countries where people tend to show their emotions, or preserve them. Specific or diffuse cultures either keep business and private life separate, or mix them up. Leadership is gained by either ascription (being born into the job) or by achievement. Time is seen in terms of being past versus present or future-oriented. Finally, do we control nature, or does it take its course?

HOW CHINA 'FITS IN' WITH THE THEORIES

If we return to our opening case study, where can we place our Chuppie in these models? Hofstede's research was carried out in Taiwan and Hong Kong rather than mainland China, but it can be said that People Republic of China is also relatively high power distance-oriented and showing low individualism. But this is changing. Although traditionally Chinese were respectful, even fearful of authority, they are less so now, especially with many Westerners working in China and many Chinese traveling to the West. KZ's Western boss is not at all intimidating, is friendly and joking, and treats everyone as equals. And whilst KZ's parents can be seen every morning at 6AM doing their exercises in the park, with dozens of other older people, and strident music blaring out of loudspeakers, she is not interested in this. She is much more individualistic in her way of life, and avoids big group activities (although her small group is very important).

China is high on uncertainty-avoidance, with its tolerance for rules and structures. The one-child family policy (including the need to gain permission from one's work unit and street committee to start a family) has been widely accepted, although there are many examples of breaking the rules (mostly by traveling to other countries). KZ's country is also less masculine and more feminine these days, although the so-called masculine traits such as assertiveness, independence, and insensitivity to feelings as dominant values are there. But one of the more positive outcomes of many years of Maoist communism is a high degree of gender equality in society. This started off with women and men wearing the same clothes and doing the same jobs and sharing a communal lifestyle – one of the big changes now happening is the feminization of women again. China is traditionally long-term in its thinking – focusing on dynasties rather than years – but members of the younger generation, such as KZ, show more short-term tendencies. China is clearly a melting-pot of national cultural extremes.

In looking at Trompenaars' dimensions, Chinese people clearly value relationships. Their concept of 'guanxi' or connections with people who can help you is similar to the Arab view of 'wasta'. They are used to having a strong sense of community, although this is being broken down by Western influences. They are largely neutral in terms of showing emotions, and being inscrutable in negotiations is one of their trump cards. They are more diffuse than specific, not keeping their lives in compartments but opportunistically looking for business opportunities wherever these are to be had. In many countries Chinese are seen cruising restaurants at night looking for customers for pirate DVDs – not every nationality would have the patience and entrepreneurial flair to attempt this. Although in the old days, Communist party membership often provided senior jobs to people without merit, China is becoming increasingly achievement-oriented. Their perception of time used to be famous for being long-term – thinking in dynasties – but many young people now want short-term gains and change jobs frequently.

Exercise: does your country, and the characteristics of you and your fellow countrymen, fit into the theories? How would you define yourself, first of all? Are you a child of parents of the same nationality, and born in the same place as they were? Were your grandparents also from the same country? Otherwise, are you a 'mix' of cultures? How does this impact on your behaviors and characteristics?

Locate your country, or two or more countries, in the Power Distance and Individualism chart. Compare yourself with people from other countries of whom you have some knowledge and familiarity. Do you think this is accurate? Quote specific examples of behavior which help explain your decisions.

Think about the following questions: Are you respectful of authority and call your boss 'Sir' or 'Madam' or by his or her first name (in private or in a group?) Do you like to live by yourself, or with a group of people? Do you find most rules and regulations irritating, or comforting? Are men occupying most senior jobs in your organization? Is money and getting on in your company highly prized, or helping others? How far into the future do you think or plan ahead? Years or months? What would be your definition of something shameful happening to your family? Are you more concerned with preserving relationships or keeping within the law? If you are very upset about something, would you keep it to yourself, especially at work? When you finish work at night, do you want to get away from anything to do with it? How do you feel about people in leadership positions who were born into the job? Do you focus most upon the past, the present or the future? Do you see yourself as having a high level of control over your life and your destiny?

NATIONAL CULTURE AND THE IMPACT ON BUSINESS AND MANAGEMENT – THE EXAMPLE OF THE GULF STATES

Now for a change of scene. An example of how a national culture provides a context for different leadership and management practices and business results can be seen in the small oil-rich states of the Arabian Gulf. Their context for leadership involves typically collective values and practices, such as a preference for personalized relationships, and the broad and profound influence of 'in-groups' on their members. People value their membership of a specific family, which gives them a specific ranking in society, and therefore in business. A successful joint-venture between a foreign and a local Arab business may predicate upon the extent to which the Arab side comes from a good family, i.e. one that is well-connected with important authorities. The existence of only limited co-operation with other groups, seen as 'out-groups,' is a feature endorsed in the Gulf societies.

Arab leadership/managerial styles have been extremely influenced by the tribal traditions and their collectivistic culture. Therefore, managers may play the role of tribe leaders (Sheiks), and all responsibility and authority is usually carried by the tribe leader. They consider themselves fathers of their employees providing protection and care. "I am a river to my people", said the tribal leader in the movie *Lawrence of Arabia*. These tribal leaders consult in a practical way with their 'in-groups' (the equivalent of kin) (Ali, 1993). However, they might, by contrast, be relatively aggressive and authoritarian with members of other groups or 'out-groups' (rival tribes) (Mahjoub, Ghonaim, and Shareef, 1997). Showing strong loyalty to their 'in-groups,' tribal leaders might be pressured as well to make certain decisions (reward, employment...etc) by their people. Clearly this affects doing business in a significant way.

Arab expatriates in the Gulf States (mostly Egyptians, Lebanese, and Palestinians) have great influence on the work methods and the native managerial styles here. They have introduced their own traditional, bureaucratic, and power-stratified practices. However, recently with the nationalization of jobs with preference for locals of each State in recruitment , rather than expatriates (although the locals remain a minority in most cases), the influence of increasing education, international exposure, and the Gulf War etc., work environments have become more native than they were before. Thus, the present native managerial style is a mixture of bureaucratic and traditional tribal methods. Some of the bureaucratic habits could be a holdover from colonial times, representing not only the legacy of British leaders but also of the Indian subcontinent people – mostly Indians and Pakistanis – whom they brought with them.

According to writers on Arab leadership, people tend to subordinate their goals to those of the 'in-group'. Due to predominantly collectivist values, teamwork skills and values, those outside the in-groups are not well-developed as leaders or subordinates. Favoritism and nepotism ('wasta') are quite common. These values have a serious impact on organizational practices and productivity. Network systems in various Ministries and other significant government (and to a lesser extent, private) organizations are well developed in terms of "in-groups". In order to ensure that their needs are well served, people spend much of their work time nourishing their social networks (Ali and Wahabi, 1995). This can lead to less productivity in the workplace, with long coffee breaks and many visits to each other's offices. Trips to the airport, hospitals, gift purchases and other relationship boosting activities are highly time-consuming, together with extensive family obligations and religious observances.

Also, it can be noticed through observation that newly appointed managers remove, distance, or freeze the 'in-group' of certain expatriate nationalities of their predecessors and appoint their own people (Ali, 1993). Thus, it is not unusual to find in a specific organization a considerable number of people who carry the same surname, tribe name or certain expatriate nationality as that of the senior manager/administrator. For example, Egyptians or Lebanese might predominate in an organization, if this is the nationality of the boss. Or there might be many Arab people with the same surname.

Most of the businesses in the Gulf – Dubai, Abu Dhabi, Oman, Kuwait, Qatar, Bahrain and Saudi Arabia – are owned by a small number of well-established families, and mostly comprise small and a few medium-sized organizations. Mostly the public sector is the leading sector of the economy and is much bigger than the other sectors. The public sector is committed to the government's full-employment policies (a job for life for every national) and at present it is suffering from over-employment in most jobs. Many locals are reluctant to consider the more risky and unknown opportunities in the private sector.

Lack of a competitive business environment, a dependence on imported technologies, the lack of separation between ownership and management control, and active government protection, have contributed to the poor state of research and development activities in Kuwait, and the relative lack of a competitive spirit, innovation and leadership development. In many Gulf countries, only a maximum of 49% of any business established there can be owned by non-natives, according to the business laws.

So, non-natives have to have native business partners willing to own 51%, who may do nothing but take profits. Moreover, an expatriate must be sponsored by a public or private business or native individual to be able to work in many of these countries. Clearly, all these national cultural issues have a heavy impact on the business environment.

NATIONAL CULTURE AND THE CHALLENGES OF GLOBAL BUSINESS – JAPANESE BUSINESSES COME TO BRITAIN

National culture also impacts on companies from countries wanting to do business in other countries. For example, when Japanese companies first came to Britain in the 1980s and 1990s, there was concern about the cultural differences they would bring with them. Sir Peter Parker, a well-known British captain of industry who also chaired Mitsubishi Electric in the UK, spoke of a distinguished industrialist from Japan who was asked how organizations in Japan compare with those of the West. This executive answered that they were 95% the same but differed in all important respects. Parker reflected that it was important to consider that 5% very carefully!

Research on the perceptions of British employees in Japanese companies revealed that this was indeed the case: there were more similarities than differences. Indeed, many observations about British people that the Japanese were doing things in a very different way were revealed to be myths. Based on an extensive survey, it was discovered that:

Myth 1 – the Japanese always plan for the long term – but in Britain they rotated the Japanese bosses, were willing to change direction in a new environment, and gave the British workers mostly short-term contracts.

Myth 2 – the Japanese believe in consensus decision-making – in Britain, sometimes there were only 2 to 3% Japanese staff, so they did not always bring their management methods with them, and their attitude to consensus-gaining was also limited to senior staff.

Myth 3 – the Japanese are very hard-working – in reality the pace of work was slower in Japanese companies in Britain, as the Japanese executives did not have a strong sense of personal time. They were hard-working in terms of putting in long hours and in their attention to detail and quality, but not necessarily in terms of speedy outcomes.

Myth 4 – the Japanese believe in life-time employment – this applied to the Japanese in their own country, but not necessarily to their employment of foreigners, whom they particularly liked to use as an "expert". Meanwhile life-time employment in Japan has been breaking down for several decades.

Myth 5 – Japanese companies pay low salaries – at the beginning, the Japanese in Britain were paying under the market rates, until forced up by market pressures. In Japan, people joined for security and prestige and not money, but people in Britain could not be attracted to Japanese companies for these reasons.

Myth 6 – Working conditions are often bad in Japanese companies – in Japan the Japanese suffer from a shortage of space, and had to squeeze everyone into small places – but in Britain, especially encouraged by local authorities, they expanded into prestigious sites.

Myth 7 – All senior positions in Japanese companies are held by Japanese – but in Britain, especially in the manufacturing sector, the Japanese companies were willing to promote senior and experienced British people.

Myth 8 – All major decisions in Japanese companies in Britain are made in Tokyo – but a remarkable amount of autonomy was given to many Britain executives, especially after they had been to Tokyo and had been checked out by the senior Japanese. Even some non-Japanese were being appointed to Boards in Japan.

Myth 9 – the Japanese feel superior and act accordingly – but the British felt trusted and liked by many Japanese, and the Japanese were willing to admit a lack of knowledge in many areas, and depended on the British for local insights.

Myth 10 – the Japanese distrust all foreigners – but they were willing to invest a good deal of trust in British executives and place them in senior positions, especially in start-ups and when they had earned a degree of trust.

Myth 11 – it is impossible for a foreigner to communicate effectively with a Japanese – the British executives did not speak Japanese, and many of the Japanese spoke English will difficulty, but trips to Tokyo by the British executives improved communication, and with experience of working together they discovered more similarities than differences.

Myth 12 – the Japanese are sexist – but in Britain they hired several women to work in their offices and factories, and treated them no differently than they way they treated the men.

Myth 13 – Japanese companies never fire their staff – but security of tenure in a Japanese company in Britain had to be earned, it didn't come as a matter of course. And there were lay-offs of British workers at factories and offices, but not to the same extent as in USA companies.

Myth 14 – a Japanese company dominates the entire life of its staff – the Japanese workers in Britain were quite obsessive in their work habits, but did not expect the British to be the same, and some Japanese were being influenced by the 'lazier' British people.

Myth 15 – Japanese companies employ as many Japanese and as few foreigners as possible – although in Britain Japanese companies employed a tiny minority of Japanese in many cases, sometimes just as experts rather than managers – especially as they could not find enough speaking English.

Myth 16 – foreigners feel no loyalty to Japanese companies – yet many British executives came to enjoy working in Japanese companies and succeeded there, especially as in many cases the profits were ploughed back into businesses and not repatriated.

Myth 17 – the Japanese always impose their way of doing things – but the Japanese took the trouble to learn that British ways of managing could help increase their success in Britain.

Myth 18 – in Japanese companies, employees wear uniforms, sing the company song, and do exercises in the morning – to the disappointment of the media, this happened rarely in Japanese companies, and only in manufacturing, and rarely in financial houses in the City of London.

Myth 19 – the Japanese are totally different from us – but the British also saw themselves as reserved and remote, especially the more traditional ones, and had a lot in common.

Myth 20 – the Japanese are all the same!

Exercise: can you relate these 'myths' (and realities) about the way that the Japanese do business in Japan and in Britain to the theories and models of national culture? Do you think most people are too ready to judge on limited information without personal experience? Why do you think many British and Japanese workers and managers had few problems working together? What were the Japanese attitudes to time? What was their feeling about specific and diffuse approaches and ways of doing business? What about the Japanese as a 'masculine' country as a cross-cultural management concept?

RELIGION AND NATIONAL CULTURE

In many parts of the world, religion plays little part in business and national culture. In many Western countries, practicing the Christian religion is an activity which rarely impinges on day-to-day activities in the workplace, except in terms of relationships, where people who are also members of the congregation of one's church might be trusted more than strangers. In Buddhist countries, there is a higher level of so-called 'superstition', at least in the building of spirit houses and other religious icons within business premises. In Hong Kong, feng shui is an important part is locating one's office and even one's desk, although it is arguable if this can be defined as a religion.

By contrast, in Moslem countries, religion is all-pervasive, and therefore influences the world of business and management – or does it? Studies of religion and its impact on how national culture influences business have found few links between religion and day-to-day business practices, even in exclusively Moslem societies. The behaviors of Muslim leaders (and therefore businessmen, in strictly Moslem societies) are ideally based upon the Word of God as revealed in their holy book, the Qur'an (or Koran). They believe that the Prophet of Islam, Muhammad, has modeled the way for Muslims for all times. Muhammad's example is what both Muslim leaders and followers seek to emulate. "The leadership position is vital to the welfare of the group and hence should be occupied only by competent people" (Abdulla and Al-Homoud, 2001, p. 508).

In respect to responsibility of people in society, the Prophet Mohammed attests: "Each of you is a guardian, and each of you will be asked about his subjects", so he must be responsible. According to the Prophet Mohammed, depending upon the situation, every person is the 'shepherd' of a flock, and occupies a position of leadership. Justice must be assured by the leader, applying the rule of Islamic law, preaching the good word, dissuading people from evil, and providing a decent livelihood for his people. The leader has a message: the loftiest of his duties is to develop leaders from among his people. He must be moderate, consultative, forgiving, honorable, abiding by his promises, honest, humble, respectable in appearance, patient, and hold non-materialistic and ascetic values (Al-Obiedi, 1987; Hawi, 1982; Khadra, 1985; Mostafa, 1986).

The Islamic administrative theory is based on the social philosophy of the Islamic system, which suggests that individuals' physiological needs must be satisfied to achieve organizational goals and that a balance should be achieved between spiritual and psychological needs. The theory is based on the principles of hierarchical organizational structure, chain and unity of command, obedience and compliance to formal authority, planning of work, consultation among members of the organization, clarification of roles training, and development of employees (Abu-Sin, 1981; Mostafa, 1986; Nusair, 1983; Sharfuddin, 1987).

Despite widespread belief in these tenets of Islam, many Islamic countries are noted for directive rather than consultative leadership and management practices, where high power distance may be a stronger factor. Many of these countries, especially the wealthier ones, are focused on materialism and consumerism, despite these behaviors being decried in the scriptures. Similarly, corrupt practices involving inequalities in society are still practiced, such as the perpetration of 'wasta' or the use of connections as a form of nepotism, despite the equality of all citizens suggested in the holy texts.

Al-Nemri (2002) said in his study on manners, morals and Islam, that good Islamic morals have a strong positive effect on individual and community life. Therefore, Islam is extremely concerned for moral and not corrupt behavior. The Qur'anic Verses and the Prophet's sayings focus on the importance of good moral values: there are more than sixty sayings of the messenger specialized in doctrines and manners. This undoubtedly represents the Prophet's tradition and care for morals and manners: "And Surely Thou Hast Sublime Morals" where Allah Almighty shows the good manners of the Prophet.

Thus, Islam urges the Muslim individual to adhere to the Islamic creed which calls for good morals and forbids mean behaviors and corruption, and suggests that man must behave in the correct and straight way in all life affairs including work manners. The most important and primary two manners related to work that must be presented by the employee and the employer, are: strength, which means determination and will power, as the Qur'an states "take what we have given you with determination". You should seek eagerness, vigor and seriousness in doing work and avoiding weakness and impotence. These traits apply to the powerful employee who pursues work proficiency. The second moral is honesty and trust, on which the Arabs prided themselves even before Islam: "and those who are to their trusts and promises attentive". People's affairs only become straightforward with honesty, good dealing and eagerness to accomplish work. Due to the importance of honesty, the Prophet urged "Faith is trust and whosoever has no trust never possess pious nature." Therefore, if strength and honesty are combined in a certain person, they will be extremely dedicated in their work.

Through considering the above traits, it is shown to us that one of the most important duties of the employee and laborer is feeling responsibility towards work and sincere and honest performance of work away from failure and negligence. As the Prophet said, "Allah likes anyone of you who gains mastery in performance of work". This means that Allah detests default and negligence in work. Among the employees' duties is non-exploitation of their work, position or authority for personal benefit for helping their families, relatives and subordinates as such exploitation is considered an offense. As Allah's Prophet said: "whomever we appoint him to any work and give him earnings from it, so any other thing taken more than this shall be ill-gotten".

However, we note that in some cases that there is a recession in work ethics through committing unacceptable behaviors, whether purposely, inadvertently or even due to life effects contaminating our mind and principles; but Islam advised us to hold ourselves responsible prior to holding others responsible. We should apply the reward and punishment principle along with eagerness to strengthen the meanings of the Islamic creed and make them deep-rooted in the souls of young children since their tender age, as the saying states: "Teaching in the early childhood is like engraving on a stone".

Thus, it is clear that honesty, fairness, responsibility and hard work are amongst the key tenets of Islam, and this supports an attack on corruption, nepotism and 'wasta' in many Islamic societies, although this is not always happening. In most Islamic societies, it is seen as important that all aspects of the teachings of Islam should be followed, and this in theory strongly supports an increased transparency of society. However, it is also widely seen that national culture can be a stronger force than religious feelings, and has a more powerful impact on the way business is conducted. Otherwise, for example, Moslem countries would be heading the global transparency indices (such as www.transparency.org), rather than mostly being seen at the lower end of such lists.

THE CONTINUING EVOLUTION OF NATIONAL CULTURES

Cultures continue to evolve – especially in fast-changing societies such as China and, to a lesser extent, India. Are we seeing a 'convergence' of world cultures as countries compete for economic superpower status? In some cases, with the rise of globalization, the answer can be yes – American fast-food outlets dominate shopping malls all over the world – but in other instances, people cling to their own traditions. A Harvard Business Review article titled The Five Minds of the Manager differentiates between 'global' and 'worldly' mindsets (Gosling and Mintzberg, 2003). Those with the former tend to see the world from a distance, and it looks uniform. Arriving in a new country and driving in from the airport, they see McDonalds and KFC, Applebees and Hardees – looks very much like America. Or is it? Coming in closer, the people are wearing different clothes, mixing in different groups, eating at different times for different occasions. A 'worldly' person will immerse themselves in the culture until they appreciate the differences. Whilst the 'global' manager generalizes and thinks about the global economic performance of his company, the 'worldly' manager makes the most of local differences to appreciate how local conditions can impact on local performance. As an example of a 'worldly' company, the authors cite Shell, itself both Dutch and British owned. For centuries, this multinational has considered social, environmental and economic variations around the world, and has tried to leverage these. It is still a major success as a leading multinational company, when many others of the same vintage have sunk without a trace.

CONCLUSION

In this chapter, we have considered a number of models of national culture and how these help us to classify behaviors, in ourselves and in others. These models have given us a framework to look at particular examples quoted here, of Chinese, Arab, Japanese and British. Although these classifications are useful to a certain agree, we can see that countries and people are evolving, influenced by global phenomenon such as consumerism, teenage culture, the Internet, mass broadcasting such as by CNN and the BBC, and the ease of worldwide travel. We have been fitting ourselves into boxes, but maybe these boxes don't fit exactly.

REFERENCES

Abdulla, I. & Al-Homoud, M. (2001) 'Exploring the implicit leadership theory in the Arabian Gulf states', *Applied Psychology: An International Review, 50*:4, 506-531

Abu Hurairah, *Sahih Muslim,* (hadith no. 4542).

Abu-Sin, A. (1981) *Islamic administration (in Arabic).* Dubai: The Contemporary Press.

Ali, A. (1989) *The Holy Qur'an: Text, Translation and Commentary.* Brentwood, MD: Amana.

Ali, A. (1993) 'Decision-Making Style, Individualism and Attitudes toward Risk of Arab Executives', *International Studies of Management and Organization, 23*:3, 53+.

Al-Humayan, R. (2007) 'A Study of Corruption: Nepotism and Employment in the Banking Sector in Kuwait', *Unpublished MBA thesis,* Kuwait Maastricht Business School.

Al-Humayan, R. & Jones, S. (2007) '"Wasta": nepotism and employment in the banking sector in Kuwait' *International Management Development Conference, Maastricht.*

Al Kandari, O. (2007) 'The Eight Questions of Leadership: a comparison between Kuwaiti and Western Managers', *Unpublished MBA Thesis,* Kuwait Maastricht Business School.

Al Kandari, O. & Jones, S. (2007) 'A Comparison between Arab and Western Managers: the example of Kuwait', *Maastricht School of Management, Partners' Conference.*

Al-Obiedi, A. (1987) 'Management at the beginning of the first Abbasaite era (in Arabic)', *Journal of the Social Sciences, 15,* 3.

Bechari, F. (2007) 'Job Satisfaction Among Retail Sector Employees: a Kuwait case study', *Unpublished MBA thesis,* Kuwait Maastricht Business School.

Beekun R. & Adawi, J. (1999) 'The leadership process in Islam', *Islamic Training Foundation,* USA.

Daniels, J.D., Radebaugh, L.H., and Sullivan, D.P. (2004), *International Business Environment and Operation,* 10th. Edn. Upper Saddle River, New Jersey: Pearson Prentice Hall.

Fu, S. & Liu, H. 2005, *Corporate Culture vs. National Culture – The Role of Human Resource in Managing Cultural Differences in International Hotel Companies,* Master Thesis, School Of Business Economics and Law, Goteborg University, Sweden. http://www.handels.gu.se/epc/archive/004787/01/Fu%5F%2B%5FLiu%5FTHM.pdf

Gosling, J. & Mintzberg, H. (2003), 'The Five Minds of a Manager'. *Harvard Business Review*. November.

Hofstede, G. (1980) 'Motivating, leadership and organization: Do American theories apply abroad', *Organizational Management Association*, 42-63.

Hofstede, G. (1984) *Culture's Consequences: International Differences in Work-Related Values*. Beverley Hills, CA: Sage.

Hofstede, G. (1991) *Cultures and Organizations: Software of the Mind*. London: McGraw-Hill.

Hofstede, G. (1993) 'Cultural Constraints in management theories', *Academic of management executives, 7:1*, 81-94.

Jones, S. (1991) *Working for the Japanese*. London: Macmillan.

Jones, S. (1999) *Managing People in China*. Unpublished manuscript, but see

Jones, S. (2000) Beyond the stereotypes: the changing face of China's workplace, *China Staff, VI*: 9, 19-24.

Mahjoub, M.A., Ghonaim, M.A.R., & Shareef, F.M. (1997), *Studies in Bedouin societies* (in Arabic). Cairo: University Knowledge Press.

Mostafa, N.A. (1986) 'The Prophet's leadership and his governance and the ideal styles of authority of Max Weber: A comparative study (in Arabic)', *Journal of the Social Sciences, 14*, 135-153.

Navarrete, C.J., & Pick, J. (2003), 'Cross-Cultural Telecommuting Evaluation In Mexico And the United States' *The Electronic Journal On Information System In Developing Countries, 15*:5, 1-14.

Nusair, N. (1983)' Human nature and motivation in Islam'. *Islamic Quarterly, 29*, 148-164.

North, R. & Hort, L. (2002), 'Cross-Cultural Influences On Employee Commitment In The Hotel Industry: Some Preliminary Thoughts', *Research and Practice in Human Resource Management, 10*:1, 22-34.

Sharfuddin, I. (1987) 'Toward an Islamic administrative theory', *The American Journal of Islamic Social Science, 4*: 2, 229-244.

Sivakumar,C. (2001) 'The Stamped Toward Hofstede Framework: Avoiding The Sample Design Pit In Cross-Cultural Research', *Journal Of International Business Studies, 32*:.3, 555-574.

Trompenaars, F. & Hampden-Turner, C. (1997) *Riding the waves of culture: understanding cultural diversity in business.* London: Nicholas Brealey.

Wood J, Chapman J, Fromholtz M, Morrison V, Wallace J, Zeffane R.M.,Schermerhorn R, Hunt.G., & Osborn R.N., 2004, *Organizational Behavior A Global Prospective* , 3 ed edn. Milton, Australia: Wiley.

www.transparency.org

RECOMMENDED FURTHER READING

Abegglen, J.C. & Stalk, G. (1985) *Kaisha: the Japanese Corporation.* New York: Basic Books.

Beardwell, I. (1994) *'Human Resource Management in Japan'*, in Beardwell, I and Holden, L. eds. Human Resource Management: a contemporary perspective. London: Pitman.

Blum, K. (1994) 'Managing People in Germany' in T. Garrison and D. Rees eds. *Managing People across Europe.* Oxford: Butterworth-Heinemann.

Child, J. Boisot, M., Ireland J., Li, Z., & Watts, J. (1990) *The Management of Equity Joint Ventures in China.* Beijing: China-EC Management Institute.

Christopher, R.C. (1984) *The Japanese Mind.* New York: Ballantine.

Earley, P. C. (1989) 'Social loafing and collectivism: a comparison of the USA and PRC', *Administrative Science Quarterly, 34*, 565-581.

Fiedler, F.E., Mitchell, T. & Triandis, H. C. (1971) 'The culture assimilator: an approach to cross-cultural training', *Journal of Applied Psychology, 55*, 95-102.

Gregersen, H.B., Morrison, A.J. & J.S. Black. (1998). 'Developing leaders for the global frontier', *Sloan Management Review,* Fall, 21–32.

Hall, E.T. (1976) *Beyond Culture.* New York: Doubleday.

Harris, R.P. & Moran, R.T. (1989) *Managing Cultural Differences.* Houston, TX: Gulf Publishing.

Hayes, J. & Allinson, C.W. (1988) 'Cultural differences in learning styles of managers', *Management International Review, 28*:3, 75-80.

Hofstede, G. (1991) *Cultures and Organizations: software of the mind.* New York: McGraw Hill.

Hofstede, G. (1989) 'Organizing for Cultural Diversity', *European Management Journal, 7*:4, 390-397.

Lawrence, P. (1980) *Managers and Management in West Germany.* London: Croom Helm.

Oddu, G. & Mendenhall, M. (1998) *Cases in International Organizational Behavior.* Malden, MA: Blackwell.

Pascale, R.T. & Athos, A.G. (1981), *The Art of Japanese Management.* New York: Simon and Schuster.

CHAPTER 14

DEVELOPING CULTURAL AWARENESS
STEPHANIE JONES

OPENING CASE:

The following informal test will help you rate your 'cultural awareness business etiquette'. See how many of the following you can answer correctly. (Answers follow the last question).

1   You are in a business meeting in an Arabian Gulf country. You are offered a small cup of bitter cardamom coffee. After your cup has been refilled several times, you decide you would rather not have anymore. How do you decline the next cup offered to you?

a   Place your palm over the top of the cup when the coffeepot is passed.
b   Turn your empty cup upside down on the table.
c   Hold the cup and twist your wrist from side to side.

2   In which of the following countries are you expected to be punctual for business meetings?

a   Peru
b   Hong Kong
c   Japan
d   China
e   Morocco

3.   Gift giving is prevalent in Japanese society. A business acquaintance presents you with a small wrapped package. Do you:

a   Open the present immediately and thank the giver
b   Thank the giver and open the present later
c   Suggest that the giver opens the present for you

4.   In which of the following countries is tipping considered an insult?

a   Great Britain
b   Iceland
c   Canada

5.   What is the normal workweek in Saudi Arabia?

a   Monday through Friday
b   Friday through Tuesday
c   Saturday through Wednesday

6. You are in a business meeting in Seoul. Your Korean business associate hands you his calling card, which states his name in the traditional Korean order: Park Chul Su. How do you address him?

a   Mr. Park
b   Mr. Chul
c   Mr. Su

7. In general, which of the following would be good topics of conversation in Latin American countries?

a   Sports
b   Religion
c   Local politics
d   The weather
e   Travel

8. In many countries, visitors often are entertained in the homes of the clients. Taking flowers as a gift to the hostess is usually a safe way to express thanks for the hospitality. However, both the type and the color of the flower can have amorous, negative, or even ominous implications. Match the country where presenting them would be a social faux pas (a blunder).

a. Brazil   1 Red Roses
b. France   2 Purple Flowers
c. Switzerland 3 Chrysanthemums

9. In most Middle Eastern countries, which hand does one use to accept or pass food?

a   Right hand
b   Left hand
c   Either hand

10. Body language is just as important as the spoken word in many countries. For example, in most countries, the thumbs up sign means 'OK'. But in which of the following countries is the sign of a rude gesture?

a   Germany
b   Italy
c   Australia

Answers:

1 – c. It is also appropriate to leave the cup full.
2 – a, b, c, d, and e. Even in countries where local custom does not stress promptness, overseas visitors should be prompt.

3 – b.

4 – b.

5 – c.

6 – a. The traditional Korean pattern is surname, followed by two given names.

7 – a, d, and e.

8 – a and 2. Purple flowers are a sign of death in Brazil, as are chrysanthemums in France (b and 3). In Switzerland (c and 1), as well as in many other north European countries, red roses suggest romantic intentions.

9 – a. using the left hand would be a social gaffe.

10 – b, c.

How's your business etiquette? Add up your correct answers:

8 – 10 Congratulations, you have obviously done your homework when it comes to doing business overseas.

5 – 7 Although you have some sensitivity to the nuances of other cultures, you still might make some social errors that could cost you sales abroad.

1 – 4 Look out! You could be headed for trouble if you leave home without consulting the experts.

LEARNING OBJECTIVES FOR THIS CHAPTER

In the task of identifying your own cultural awareness levels, we need to examine our ability to be culturally aware in both organizational and national settings, consolidating our learning from the previous chapters. Here, in 'Developing Cultural Awareness', we ask ourselves the question – which is stronger, organizational or national culture? We then look at national stereotypes – how these have emerged over time and are still strong. We also consider the role of building cultural awareness in becoming an expatriate, as a form of orientation training, looking at some important training themes, especially comparing Asian and Western managers (one of the most popular combinations for cross-cultural training). We also need to ensure that you can use your cultural identification skills in an organizational context, too.

ORGANIZATIONAL CULTURE OR NATIONAL CULTURE?

Which has the strongest impact on most people? Consider these two examples:

A bank in a Middle Eastern city – in the United Arab Emirates – keen on building a reputation for being entrepreneurial and competitive, with outstanding customer service, was seeking to empower its employees. The bank usually spends six months and substantial cash investments' training around a hundred young national recruits each year, with these aims in mind. Yet on completing their training and moving to a front-line interaction with the customers, the recruits revert to their cultural norms of uncertainty-avoidance and risk-aversion, looking for a more senior and experienced staff member for the purpose of looking after their customers, especially those with difficult requirements. They also go back to their bargaining, compromising and deal-making tendencies, offering discounts and undermining the bank's fixed rates and policies.

Another Middle Eastern organization – this time a wealthy and successful energy company – wants to build efficiency and is investing heavily in managing its large and growing workforce with a state-of-the-art Human Resources Information Systems. It is dedicated to offering training opportunities to enable employees to reach their full capabilities, as well as maintaining high quality practices in its oil extraction, refining, distribution and retailing. It has the chance to adopt a tailor-made software package to maximize its efficiency and effectiveness in developing a job analysis, competency-based training and on-the-job training system. But this requires transparency, trust, co-operation and long-term commitment. So it is delayed time and time again and finally rejected. It needs too much of a culture mind set change to take it all on board.

Exercise: What is going on in these examples? Which factor is presenting the most potent force: organizational or national culture? Where does one start and the other end? Why are these decisions being taken – what is the thinking behind them? Considering your own organization – would it be different? Overall, what are the most important cultural factors behind decision-making in your company? Explain with examples of at least three decisions.

NATIONAL STEREOTYPES – BUILDING AWARENESS

The first step in being able to live and work successfully with different nationalities and cultures is to understand that there are differences. To do that, we have to understand our own culture. Another step is to understand how different nationalities perceive us – through the colored vision of their **stereotypes** (and we all have them!). An anonymous and confidential survey was recently designed and conducted to analyze what people think about their own stereotypes of other nationalities, and how they saw themselves. The author collected more than 2,000 responses from and about ten nationalities, all living in a highly diverse environment – the Emirate of Dubai in the Middle East. Dubai is unique in terms of its mixed population: only 10% are nationals, over 80% are from the Indian subcontinent, there are over 100,000 British people, and many thousands of other Westerners, Japanese and Chinese.

Respondents were asked to think carefully about three words or short phrases to describe each national culture below. The responses may contain both negative and positive traits, but survey participants were asked to list just the first three descriptors that came to their minds first. They were asked ten statements, starting off with "I believe that most Chinese people are:" and then were asked to decide on three descriptors:

Comments: (things that may inspire or annoy you,
you wish they would do more/less of)

1.

2.

3.

This was followed by the same question about British people, Arabs, Indians, Americans, French, Pakistani, Australian, Filipino and Japanese. At the end of the survey this chart was included:

Exercise: Try *completing this exercise yourself, about each of these ten nationalities. You may then compare your own thinking with the results of the survey below.*

I am _____(nationality)

I think other nationalities would describe my people as:

1._____

2._____

3._____

The results of the original survey (for you to compare your own results) were as follows:

Table 14: Based on local research in Dubai during late 2004 and early 2005 of around 2,000 respondents

Nationality	Descriptors
Chinese	Hardworking Business-minded Intelligent
British	Arrogant Cold Snobbish
Arab	Religious Lazy Arrogant
Indian	Hardworking Intelligent Unhygienic
American	Friendly Ignorant Arrogant
French	Stylish Arrogant Rude

Pakistani	Untrustworthy
	Religious
	Hardworking
Australian	Friendly
	Easygoing
	Sporty
Filipino	Hardworking
	Friendly
	Hygienic
Japanese	Hardworking
	Intelligent
	Disciplined

Source: Hills, Rodney (2005) Research on National Stereotypes. Ongoing research

This exercise has been conducted by the author of this chapter many times in many different environments, and the results have been around 90% similar to the above. How about your own stereotypical views?

CULTURAL AWARENESS TRAINING AND ITS ROLE IN THE PREPARATION FOR EXPATRIATION PROCESS

With increasing globalization and the presence of many multinational companies in emerging markets, there is a need for cross-cultural management programs designed for the newly-arrived (mostly Western) managers working in multinational companies overseas. These multinationals might be employing local nationals and doing business in non-Western countries, or working in joint-ventures and strategic alliances with companies from and in these countries, employing local nationals.

There is also a need for familiarization training for the local nationals joining multinational companies, working in business relationships with them, or preparing for business trips to (mostly Western) countries to develop business partnerships. One of the most common combinations might be Western managers (from UK, much of Europe, and the US) doing business in China, India, Japan, and other parts of Asia, and in Arab and African countries. Increasingly, nationals from these countries are also traveling to the West to pursue business interests.

A quick look at the chart based on Hofstede in the previous chapter shows us that the emerging markets to which most multinational companies are headed fall into the category of high power distance and low individualism – China (or at least Hong Kong and Taiwan), parts of Africa, India and Pakistan, and Arab countries. By contrast, the source countries of many multinationals – such as UK, much of Europe, the US and Australia, are exactly the opposite – with low power distance and high individualism. Spain, France, Belgium and Italy are regarded by Hofstede as high power distant yet still highly individualistic. How does this translate into leader/manager and team behaviors? How can we become more aware of the possible behaviors we might encounter when we work in a national culture opposite to our own? Orientation and familiarization training courses can help. The behavioral tendencies described below are generalizations, but can be broadly helpful – forewarned is forearmed!

The behavioral tendencies have been grouped into training themes listed here, and these have been segmented to target four levels of manager – CEO or President, General Manager, Division or Department or Operations Manager, and Supervisor – and revolves around their attitude to, and behavior towards, their followers.

Exercise: apply these questions to your own attitudes towards expatriation - either as an expatriate now or as someone interested in becoming an expatriate in the future...

TRAINING THEMES IN EXPATRIATION TRAINING MIGHT INCLUDE:

1. Motivation for leadership and management roles, and perceptions of the role of the leader/manager – the thinking of different managers in different countries
2. Attitude towards technical expertise and knowledge of the business – how important is this factor in the management of a business and therefore successful expatriation?
3. Attitude to being visible or operating behind the scenes – the role of the leader and manager – how important is this issue?
4. Attitude towards work/life balance – differences in perspective
5. The role of teamwork – and the relationship between the team and the leader and manager
6. The relationship between leadership and management – how does it work?
7. Attitude towards followers – their roles vis a vis the leader
8. Longer-term leadership objectives – what do leaders want to leave behind them? For themselves or for their organizations?

MOTIVATION FOR LEADERSHIP

At the highest level, such as President or CEO of a multinational, there may be very few obvious national cultural differences between the top leaders. There is obviously a long traditional of leadership (some from colonial times) in many Western countries. In many emerging markets, there is a long history of leadership and ambition in many aristocratic families, especially those from famous families who saw it as a duty to lead their people and provide for them. Many leaders of emerging markets appreciate the traditions of Westerners providing leadership around the world, even now. Expatriate careers in many continents have been common for many Westerners over the centuries. Meanwhile, many senior leaders in emerging countries have spent many years overseas, are highly educated in top institutions in the West, and feel quite comfortable with any other CEOs.

At a slightly lower level, perhaps in the role of General Manager, we may see more contrasts. Whilst a Western manager might be primarily task-oriented, holding a group of people together to complete a task, keeping "the show on the road", getting on with the job in a practical way, the leader from China, India and Arab countries might be more relationship-oriented, and may also be more concerned about the broader picture of the vision of the business and the job of being a leader. The Western manager might be more short-term oriented, thinking on a day-to-day basis, whereas the Chinese, Indian or Arab manager may emphasize his commitment, drive and a calling to be a leader. He must answer this calling, and satisfy this internal desire. These countries produce leaders in contrast with Westerners, as explained by Hofstede in the chart provided in the previous chapter.

At an operational level, the tendency of Western managers to be more task-oriented, and these contrasting managers to be more relationship-oriented, increases. Whilst the Western manager takes charge, for the purposes of getting the job done, the manager from Asia and the Far East is more likely to be a father-figure, with a unique role of building and nurturing a harmonious culture. Western managers might make their own individual choices in how to prioritize tasks, whilst leaders from the East (as a broad concept) may consciously follow a role model.

At the supervisory level, when many Western managers might be experiencing their first time as a manager, perhaps now in charge of their previous colleagues, there is some ambiguity in their feelings. Some may not be convinced that they want the responsibility of leadership, and some deliberately do not want to be leaders at all. As a result, some Western managers at this level may be as empowering of others as possible, because of their reluctance. By contrast, being a leader is often a strong ambition for Asian executives. On promotion to a supervisory role, even with relatively few staff, their need to be a leader and to be seen to be the leader is the strongest factor here. As a result it is possible that they will have a highly responsible and even controlling attitude to their staff members.

ATTITUDE TOWARDS TECHNICAL EXPERTISE AND KNOWLEDGE

At the CEO level, most top executives tend to see technical expertise as a stepping-stone to a higher level of leadership. Once they have reached a senior position the issue of technical expertise becomes less important. Very high level leaders of any nationality tend to move between CEO roles of companies in different industries with comparative ease. They recognize that now and in the future they will need to manage people whose jobs they don't completely understand, but that human relationship management skills have become much more important.

For the senior Asian manager - Chinese, Indian, Arab, etc. – the issue of trust becomes more and more important. This is because his (and it usually is his, rather than her) span of command is getting larger and larger. His ability to monitor people closely can be limited. He may surround himself with a small number of trusted acolytes whom he has known for many years. They may not be especially well-qualified or intelligent but they are intensely loyal, and can be used by the Asian CEO to head up departments for him and report back. These acolytes will follow this leader between jobs. The Asian CEO is likely to retain close personal control of a key function of his business, such as high-level deal-making and strategy. By contrast, the Western leader may be happy to move between companies and find a new inner management team in a new company.

At the General Management level, both Western and Asian managers seem to be focused on the vision of their organizations and need to mobilize people as part of the leadership drive, and they don't need to be experts to do this. Some Western managers have been

GMs of a wide range of businesses, from banking to healthcare to manufacturing to oil and gas, whereas it is more likely that Asian managers have worked in a narrower range of sectors. The simple reason may be that the economies in many of these countries are less diversified than in the West, although this is changing.

The Western GM is more likely to see himself as an expert in motivating people, and one of his most important tasks is getting the right people in the right jobs. The Asian GM is concerned with his personal progress as a leader, possibly moving up to CEO from here. He will have a strong internal drive and commitment to being a leader, and sees his job as carrying others with him. His followers will see his star as in the ascendant and will go where he is going. Many of them may be chosen for their useful connections. The Western GM might find himself trying to bring together people with different agendas, whereas the Asian's team might be more united.

Lower down the management tree, both Western and Eastern operational people consider they need both expertise in their fields and expert leadership skills. They have to know very well what they are talking about to gain credibility, and also need some basic people management skills. Both of these abilities take time to develop, and Westerners believe that you can't suddenly come in at the top level. In the West, in the majority of cases, managers need to climb the managerial tree branch by branch, gaining promotions over the years (described by Trompenaars as Achieved, as opposed to Ascribed leadership, as discussed in the previous chapter).

In many Asian countries, many young executives start work at this operational level, as a result of family relationships and overseas education, and have no experience of ever being managed. They have always been managers, even giving instructions to family domestic staff at a young age. Many come from leading families in their societies. They express a need for expert knowledge to gain credibility with their staff (as with Westerners) but possibly to prevent the subordinates from "fooling" them and taking advantage of their lack of knowledge rather than to win support for their leadership.

At the supervisory level, frequently a Western manager feels that knowing the basics is enough, as his job is to surround himself with experts and encourage them to do the job. He needs to be an overall supervisor and be available to help with problems, but the team gets on with the job. The Asian supervisor is concerned with a higher level of control, and sees expert knowledge as an essential requirement of leadership. Without it, he cannot manage the team effectively. He must be the best at being the expert of his team, and he must be able to answer any and all questions that come up, to maintain his position as leader. He believes he will lose the respect of his team if he has to admit he doesn't know.

ATTITUDE TO BEING VISIBLE OR OPERATING BEHIND THE SCENES

At CEO level, both Western and Asian leaders are likely to both be clearly visible in their leadership styles, but it could be for different reasons. The Western leader may be slightly reluctant but feels he must be seen, whether he likes it or not (although this clearly depends on personality). He may recognize that quiet leadership is impossible, and he must publicly live the values of the organization, and is on duty more or less all the time.

The Asian CEO, with his strong leadership calling and overwhelming commitment to being a leader, is always visible, and wants to be so. He walks around, informally building relationships, which is part of his approach to making friends and inspiring his staff. He is quite happy to do this and sees it as a key part of his job.

The Western GM is visible because he can find out what's really happening that way. He can engage everyone, build trust, and help people feel they belong. The Asian GM is more likely to want to be seen as proactively leading from the front and to set an example. He believes that somehow he is not a real leader if he leads from the back, or no-one notices him and no one remembers him. There may be a hint of lack of trust here, as he has to lead from the front to be sure of the outcomes. He is monitoring action to make sure there is nothing untoward going on, rather than just to find out the important issues.

At supervisory level both Western and Asian managers are front-leaders too, but the Westerner because he thinks that in dangerous, difficult and risky work the leader must be there and must give directions, and the Asian manager needs to be there to show concern and support and keep building relationships. They can be seen as in considerable contrast, with the Western leader making himself available for help but encouraging staff to solve their own problems and discuss matters with their own immediate supervisors, and the Asian manager being concerned with knowing what's going on, solving problems to stop them from going higher up and keeping personal control.

ATTITUDE TOWARDS WORK/LIFE BALANCE

In the CEO's job, this is always a challenge. Western CEOs are more prepared to take long vacations and be out of contact with the office, whilst many Asian leaders like to keep in contact at all times, whatever they are doing, spending short snatches of time with the family and doing social things. Whilst the Western leader may be prepared to delegate and empower others to take responsibility in his absence, in many cases the Asian leader is happier keeping in closer touch.

A Western manager is likely to focus on work when at work but enjoy his evenings and weekends, and concentrate entirely on relaxing when on vacation. The Asian manager generally also sees balance as important, and knows this is an opportunity for delegation, but he may delegate reluctantly when this is urgently required, and then this delegation is restricted to a couple of people he trusts and knows well. Their long-term relationship with him seems to be more important than their qualifications or experience.

At the operational level, and as expatriates, Western managers lack the opportunity to go home on a daily basis, and often work harder as a result. Asian managers – especially if we count Arabs in this category – know and respect the strength of family obligations and try to fit these in with their daily job. Some Western managers feel that they are not productive anymore after a full day at work and the job should be done in the normal hours, especially if they use good time management skills. Some junior but highly ambitious Asian managers (especially from Japan) want to work 24 hours a day if they can, seeing the need for balance as less important. At the supervisory level, the Asian manager is likely to be highly serious and completely driven.

THE ROLE OF TEAMWORK

Most CEOs believe strongly in teamwork, but may be at different stages in the development of their teams. It is possible that the Western CEO's team may be stronger, as he may have put more effort into team development, although he will often insist on the importance of the role of the leader to gain results and exploit the value of the team. If the companies are well-developed and stable, they will have more mature teams. It depends on the situation of the organizations. For new fast-growing businesses, both CEOs will be forming their teams, which can be challenging due to the variety of cultures. However, it has been observed that Western CEOs put more emphasis on teamwork as a way to get things done in an organization, whilst many Asian CEOs, more concerned with the concentration of authority in their own hands, may build less strong teams, although they still need those teams around them. It might also be true that the Asian CEOs team emphasizes loyalty and the provision of support to the CEO, in preference to independent talent.

At GM level, many Western managers believe that people work together to be effective, that the whole is greater than the sum of the parts. They do not want to do other people's jobs for them. This is in contrast with a typical Asian GM, who although he likes the idea of being a team player, his team members are followers, not equals, except for one or two with whom he shares a degree of trust. Centralization is the easy way out, because he's avoiding trusting others, and he must trust before he can delegate; so full delegation is difficult and may not be possible.

At operational levels, Westerners want to work in a team to delegate tasks to able team members, which can be contrasted with Asian-style relationship building and the use of connections. Although less senior and experienced Asian managers can be happy to work in a team and learn from others, any coaching and advice needs to be received in private, so as not to undermine their authority in front of his team.

At the supervisory level, Western managers see teamwork as the norm, with only an exceptional need to step outside the team and make decisions. An Asian supervisor may insist that he is very much the leader, although he would like his team to be strong. He may think he works in a collaborative way, but he may show reluctance to delegate and share leadership, and wants to keep personal control.

THE RELATIONSHIP BETWEEN LEADERSHIP AND MANAGEMENT

Most CEOs see both roles as important, and feel close to their people by doing both, but have different views about the relationship between the two. Whilst Western CEOs think that leadership includes management, and expect to get help and support from their organizations with the latter (but not the former), many high level Asian leaders see leadership as an outcome and management as a methodology or process. The two functions together are respected in the West, but many senior Eastern executives see leadership as their job, whilst others around them 'do' management.

Western and Eastern GMs also tend to contrast these functions. Whilst Westerners think that management skills need to be developed before a person can be a leader, enabling him to see detail before understanding the big picture, many Asian executives see management as a day-to-day function which others can help with, and leadership is their job, especially as it is more strategic, involving planning and goal-setting, and has a lot more status and "face". A Western perspective can be that it is more likely for a good leader to be a manager – but not the other way around – and Asians tend to see management as the formal job, with leadership as an informal add-on, something extra. For the Westerner, delegating and inspiring others is most important, but for the Asian executive, he needs to make sure he's doing his formal job, for which he was appointed. If he is a good leader too, that would be a plus.

The Western manager often emphasizes the similarities in the two roles and feels that the distinction between the two is not always clear or even needed; it depends on the situation. For the Asian leader, it depends on his personal perspective, his knowledge and experience, and his official job, which he feels obliged to fulfill, which may or may not have a detailed description.

ATTITUDE TOWARDS FOLLOWERS

The CEOs from both the West and the East tend to hold similar views here, realizing that people will follow them due to their positions, but wanting breakthroughs and real commitment from people rather than just going through the motions. They are both concerned with having conversations and listening to their followers; with showing them their own personal commitment, vision and values; and with discovering the followers' needs and goals, and providing for these. Recent thinking in this area has emphasized this way of operating, and Western CEOs – in many cases – have been doing this for some time.

For Asian CEOs, this is a newer concept. When the followers have been social inferiors, or expatriates from poorer countries coming in as contract labor – such as workers from the Indian Subcontinent facing a glass ceiling in Arab countries – this need for follower empowerment and buy-in has been seen as less important.

Typical Western GMs think people will follow them if they look after their welfare and benefits, provide authority and win their respect. They can be prepared to adapt their leadership style to what seems to be effective with their followers. Asian followers are often influenced by fear and their need for rewards, according to many of their executives, who sometimes show a lack of belief in the possibility of integrity in business. The followers will rip them off and cheat them if they are not carefully watching them. There can be a lack of trust because of the low status and pay of followers and the fact that they have little to lose.

Western managers often think that more must be done now to win followers, as people no longer follow authority blindly. Asian leaders often think that people follow them because there are, simply, leaders and followers, and this is a fact of life. People in follower roles generally are becoming more selective and expect more, but in many countries in Asia many subordinates have fewer chances of improving their position, and many are almost captive in their roles. Culturally they may be seen as born into a specific level of society, as in India.

Western managers feel that people make up their own minds why they should follow a leader, and a leader should actively encourage them to follow him. Asian managers are more likely to see people as following the rules in their organization, and they follow their leader because he exemplifies these rules and procedures, he sets an example in this area, and the question of whether to follow him or not does not necessarily arise.

LONGER-TERM LEADERSHIP OBJECTIVES

Both Western and Asian CEOs tend to have clear ideas about their legacies, and have thought these through already. Both also tend to have both organizational and personal goals. Both are likely to be interested in achieving lasting cultural transformations in their companies. On the personal level, Western managers at this seniority have often developed more holistic societal goals, to help improve people's lives, the environment, etc. whereas Asian CEOs tend to be more interested in the pursuit of their own careers. Although the concept of the patriotic businessman with a conscience and need to be a good citizen is there in the Asian world, it is the exception rather than the norm. It is not exactly the norm in the West either, but there is a longer tradition of corporate social responsibility (as discussed in other textbooks in this series).

Most General Managers also want to leave behind a legacy of both culture change and the development of new values, but many of them are also concerned with achieving the financial numbers on a shorter-term basis. Westerners can be very matter-of-fact here, and focused on these highly specific goals. Asian managers at this level also emphasize vision and integrity, but can be most concerned about the need for control if the situation is changing rapidly.

Western managers at an operational level are generally interested in being known for doing a good job in a general sort of way, but are not necessarily ambitious to leave a dramatic legacy. An Asian operations manager is more likely to want to be known not just for his achievements in the company, but for his personal attributes. He won't move away when he retires (unlike an expatriate) so he'll be living amongst the same people, and he wants them to like him. Whilst the Westerner is doing a job, the Asian is more likely to be concerned about personal relationships.

At the supervisory level, there are more similarities between Western and Asian managers. Both want to be known for doing a solid and competent job , and want people to admire and respect them, especially the Asian managers. The latter especially wants to be known for working beyond the call of duty and going the extra mile without complaint and without wanting more money. At the lower levels of management, executives seem to have less sense of overall purpose and lack a grand design, as they are more involved in day-to-day work and others are making the major decisions.

The following summary lists the main points suggested above:

SUMMARY OF CROSS-CULTURAL LEADERSHIP AWARENESS ISSUES

These are generalizations based on extensive research findings, but of course they will not apply to all Western and all Asian managers. They are also likely to be moderated by the different personalities of the leaders and managers, and by issues such as age, gender, and the situation of the companies (such as growth or stagnation). But they do reflect some aspects of culture and expectations of society, and how these can influence leadership style and behavior towards followers.

If there is a clash of styles and misunderstanding of the objectives of two different managers from contrasting cultures, there is likely to be a breakdown of communication between the two. The two styles working together can be more effective than the styles working separately, and this is especially important in the local office of the multinational. If the local managers see the Western style as having some advantages, this can help them to be more effective, and the same is true vice-versa. Both leadership styles working on their own have negative implications for people development, innovation, entrepreneurship and growth. A heterogenous mix of cultures in leadership and management and appreciation of the value of all of them can lead to business and management success, much more than a homogenous approach.

Exercise: in each case, consider which approach is most like you. You may find that your preferences are predominantly on one side or the other, but are likely to include a mix of both, as these possibilities reflect personality as well as national cultural outlook and way of operating...

Western leaders	Asian leaders
A top job with fame and fortune	A duty to protect my people
Someone has to do it, it can be me	A calling, no argument, no choice
For excitement, challenge, adventure	It is what I have been brought up for
Task-oriented	Relationship-oriented
Short-term thinking, opportunist	Longer-term thinking, committed
Practical, focused on doing daily job	Visionary, looking to the future
The man on the spot at the time	A father-figure, building harmony
Making own choices and decisions	Consciously following a role model
A reluctant leader, happy to delegate	Strong ambition to be a leader
Empowering, hands-off	Controlling, responsible
Large span of command – need trust	Manage through group of acolytes
Managed many different businesses	Managed smaller range of businesses
See self as expert in motivating people	Concern with own leadership progress
Climbing the ladder of leadership	Coming in at a high managerial level
Know the business to gain credibility	Know business to avoid being fooled
Supervising experts to do the job	Supervising for control/gaining respect

Finding a new team in a new job	Team follows him from job to job
Has to be visible, his duty to be seen	Wants to be visible, main part of job
Visible to engage people, build trust	Visible to monitor and control
Must proactively help in tough job	Must show concern in tough job
The team must solve own problems	Problems must not go any higher up
Vacations mean long break from work	Vacations short, work contact is kept
Delegation during vacation is a plus	Reluctance to delegate during vacations
Delegation helps to develop leaders	Delegation is limited to a trusted few
Work is for work time only	Work is all the time
The job is a job, other things exist	The job is everything
Time management is important skill	Time management is impossible
Away from home so work is priority	Family obligations are a priority too
Teamwork gets things done	Teamwork provides help in monitoring
Wants strong teams of able people	Wants teams to be loyal and supportive
Whole must be more than sum parts	The team's job is to strengthen boss
The leader is the first among equals	The leader has followers
Culturally low power distance	Culturally high power distance
Decentralized leadership	Centralized leadership
Build trust and then delegate	Lack of trust is barrier to delegation
Delegation is based on ability/merit	Delegation based on close relationships
Feedback can be public, it happens	Feedback must be private, saving face
The team is the norm in doing work	Leader is the norm and team follows
Bosses do leadership/management	Boss is leader, others manage
Try to be a good leader and manager	Do your job exactly – as Manager
Act according to demands of situation	Act according knowledge/experience
Appreciate followers' needs and goals	Followers exist to support the leader
The leader provides for followers	Followers may try to exploit the leader
Followers have to be won/convinced	There will always be followers
People will follow a leader	People will follow the rules/guidelines
Followers can cope with uncertainty	Followers avoid uncertainty
Leaders leave something for society	Leaders achieve things for themselves
Managers must achieve financial goals	Managers must keep control
Leaders do the job and move on	Leaders build reputation in community
Leaders are one-off individuals	Leaders represent their families

BUILDING ORGANIZATIONAL CULTURAL AWARENESS

This chapter has concentrated predominantly on building national cultural awareness. How about the need to develop awareness of organizational culture? This is also important. We can research national cultural norms, and relate these to different countries. But how can we identify which corporate culture we are working in right now? There are no handy reference works to look up – in most cases we have to work this out for ourselves.

We also need to ask whether the organizational culture where we work fulfills our needs, or whether there more that we would like to do, in a different environment. If we are thinking of joining a new organization, we need to define its culture, because it may or may not suit our personality. Think about the questions posed in the next exercise, below:

Exercise: Is there one dominant person leading your organization? How are decisions taken – in formal meetings, or in the corridor? Which is most important – you or the position/job in the company which you currently occupy? Would you still have a job in your company if you stopped performing? Do you regularly change bosses as you move from project to project? Do you feel like an important person, or are you easily dispensable? Do people in the company relate strongly to their workplace, or don't care? Do most people in the company base their lives around it, or is what they like doing best outside the company? Do people willingly work extra hours, or do they watch the clock? Are new ideas welcomed in the company, or rejected out of hand? Do people feel they take part in the successes of the company, or these are just for the bosses? Does the company exist for the benefit of the people working there, for the bosses, for the customers, or no-one knows? How fast or slow is decision-making in the company? How responsive or not to outside pressures?

Check your answers against the organizational culture models discussed in Chapter 12. In which culture do you feel most comfortable? Which is best suited to your personality and style of working?

UNDERSTANDING INDIVIDUAL DIFFERENCES VS. CULTURAL DIFFERENCES

How do you know when your feelings of comfort (or uncertainty) with your cultural environment – your workplace and your country – are due to you and your personality, or the environment in which you were brought up? Is your personality a more significant factor than the context in which you find yourself? You might be an extrovert in a country dominated by introverts. You might be a person who needs structure and guidelines in an environment which is typically ambiguous. You might be gregarious and seeking lots of friends in an individualist culture. Which is most important for you? Do you think you are typical of your fellow nationals, or not? Do you think you are typical of the employees in the company where you work, or not?

CONCLUSION

This chapter attempts to pull together some of the learning opportunities in the preceding culture chapters, to help you apply your insights in a practical way. We have looked at avoiding cross-cultural blunders and being a good citizen of the world; understanding the views of stereotype we may hold, and how stereotypically people may view us; and we have looked in detail at contrasting national cultural behaviors of managers and followers around the world. We are now much more prepared for working and learning from fellow world citizens, if we take the trouble to develop our awareness further. We also may have more insights into the corporate culture in which we work, and whether or not it suits our personality. So now we are able to appreciate the factor of culture in everything we do and the world around us...

REFERENCES

Al Kandari, O. (2007) 'The Eight Questions of Leadership: a comparison between Kuwaiti and Western Managers', *Unpublished MBA Thesis*, Kuwait Maastricht Business School.

Al Kandari, O. & Jones, S. (2007) *'A Comparison between Arab and Western Managers: the example of Kuwait'*, Maastricht School of Management, Partners' Conference.

Ball, D.A. et.al (2002) *International Business.* Mason, Ohio: South Western/Thomson.

Bechari, F. (2007) 'Job Satisfaction Among Retail Sector Employees: a Kuwait case study', *Unpublished MBA thesis*, Kuwait Maastricht Business School.

Hills, R. (2005) *Research on National Stereotypes.* Ongoing research.

Hofstede, G. (1980) 'Motivating, leadership and organization: Do American theories apply abroad', *Organizational Management Association, 42-63.*

Hofstede, G. (1984) *Culture's Consequences: International Differences in Work-Related Values.* Beverley Hills, CA: Sage.

Hofstede, G. (1991) *Cultures and Organizations: Software of the Mind.* London: McGraw-Hill.

Hofstede, G. (1993) 'Cultural Constraints in management theories', *Academic of management executives, 7:1,* 81-94.

Jones, S. (2008) 'The Impact of Socio-Political Context on Preferred Conflict Mode Styles of Business Trainees: a UAE Case Study' *Employment Relations* January (forthcoming).

Jones, S. (2007) 'Managing Training and Development in a Large Organization: an integrated database system' *unpublished article, in preparation.*

Jones, S. & Gosling, J. (2005) *Nelson's Way: leadership lessons from the great commander.* London: Nicholas Brealey.

RECOMMENDED FURTHER READING

Aycan, Z., Kanungo, R.N. & Sinha, J.B.P. (1999), 'Organizational culture and human resource management practices: the model of cultural fit' *Journal of Cross-Cultural Psychology, 30:4:501-26.*

Davis, S.M. (1990) *Managing Corporate Culture.* New York: Harper Business.

Deal, T.E. & Kennedy, A.A. (1982) *Corporate Cultures: the Rites and Rituals of Corporate Life. Reading,* MA: Addison Wesley.

Fiedler, F.E., Mitchell, T. & Triandis, H.C. (1971) 'The culture assimilator: an approach to cross-cultural training', *Journal of Applied Psychology, 55,* 95-102.

Flynn, M.J. Saxton & Roy S. eds., Gaining Control of the Corporate Culture. San Francisco: Jossey-Bass.

Graves, D. (1986) Corporate Culture: diagnosis and change. New York: St Martin's Press.

Gregersen, H.B., Morrison, A.J. & J.S. Black. (1998). 'Developing leaders for the global frontier', *Sloan Management Review*, Fall, 21–32.

Hall, E.T. (1976) *Beyond Culture*. New York: Doubleday.

Harris, R.P. & Moran, R.T. (1989) *Managing Cultural Differences*. Houston, TX: Gulf Publishing.

Hayes, J. & Allinson, C.W. (1988) 'Cultural differences in learning styles of managers', *Management International Review, 28*:3, 75-80.

Hampden-Turner, C. (1990) *Creating Corporate Culture: from discord to harmony*. Reading, MA: Addison Wesley.

Handy, C. (1990) *Inside Organizations*. Harmondsworth: Penguin.

Handy, C. (1978) *The Gods of Management*. London: Souvenir Press.

Handy, C. (1991) *The Age of Unreason*. Boston: Harvard Business School Press.

Mintzberg, H. (1979) *The Structure of Organizations*. Englewood Cliffs, NJ: Prentice Hall.

Oddu, G. & Mendenhall, M. (1998) *Cases in International Organizational Behavior*. Malden, MA: Blackwell.

Wilkins, A.L. & Ouchi, W.G., 'Efficient Cultures: exploring the relationship between culture and organizational performance', *Administrative Science Quarterly, 28*:3, 1983.

CHAPTER 15

CONCLUSION
SILVIO DE BONO AND STEPHANIE JONES

MANAGING HUMAN CAPITAL IN A MULTI-CULTURAL ENVIRONMENT

Throughout this book we have shown that people working in organizations, as individuals and in teams, and wherever they come from and wherever they are working, have become 'free agents' of labor. Employees have the ability to move from one organization to the other without any commitment. In return, companies have become responsible for creating the necessary environment to ensure the best return on human capital. Why else would we want to manage cultural diversity, if it were not to get the best out of people, to make the most (and sustainable) profit for our business, wherever in the world we are operating?

The world has become one global village and employees who are now working around the globe and in different cultures. As citizens of the world, employees are not bound to one company, one country or one culture. Successful organizations are adopting an international multi-cultural approach toward managing their human resources by considering employees as the organizations' most precious assets.

THE EMPLOYEE AS A PERSON

In the course of the past hundred years there has been major shift in management thinking. Early management theorists regarded working organizations as 'machinery' in which the human element was just an extra complication, and indeed a potentially de-stabilizing factor. As organizations grew in size and complexity, and through early experiments with improving productivity, it became evident that greater concern would need to be given to the human element (Torrington et al., 1995).

As a result of the Hawthorne Studies at General Electric in Massachusetts, (Carey, 1967), many managers realized they had to undertake the added task of managing communication strategies in order to create and maintain the social environment needed to optimize working performance. These strategies would have to be designed in such a way that workers would experience a feeling of belonging or participation. Various theorists including Maslow, McClelland, Herzberg and McGregor (Handy, 1993) suggested an array of human needs, which motivate people to work and to realize their full potential.

During the years, there has been a shift from traditional reactive personnel management to a more proactive human resource management. New HRM and HRD principles are based on the realization of self-fulfillment and self-actualization. In addition, the existence of a multi-cultural environment, proved to be an essential element in recognizing employees as the organizaton 'human' assets, even though these are not shown in the company's balance sheet. This is a long way from thinking of a century ago.

THE DRIVE TOWARD HUMAN CAPITAL MANAGEMENT

We are starting to see management of cultural diversity to maximize business performance as revolving around the recognition of people as assets. Where does this concept come from? The term 'human capital' first appeared in a 1961 American Economic Review article "Investment in Human Capital" by Nobel Prize winning economist Theodore W. Shultz. The emphasis on treating labor as human capital has been a reply to the post-war over-emphasis on investment in material capital as the key to economic development, especially in over-populated poor countries. In the late 1980s and 1990s, workers had not yet ascended to asset status in the minds of most senior managers. On the contrary, managers viewed workers as a cost whenever economic pressures forced an expense reduction.

During the last fifty years, an elaborate discussion took place as to what actually constitutes human capital. For this purpose, Davenport (1999) refined the various definitions by breaking them into various elements being ability, behavior, and effort. These three along with the fourth element, time, are visualized below:

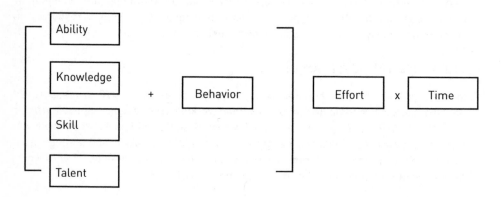

Figure 15: Elements of Ability and Behavior in Human Capital

Source: Davenport, T. (1999) Human Capital, hat It Is and Why People Invest in It. San Francisco: Jossey Bass.

According to Davenport (1999), the ability function includes knowledge and skills as well as talents. In his definition, Davenport (1999) described knowledge as the command of a body of facts required to do a job. On the other hand, skill was explained as a facility for accomplishing a particular task. As a result, skills may thus range from physical strength and dexterity to specialized learning. In addition, talent is interpreted to be the inborn faculty for performing a specific task. Consider the specific aspects of ability. Skills combine knowledge and talent (and sometimes behavior) and are often specific to a particular job or set of tasks (see also Van der Heijden, 1998).

Davenport (1999) further defines behavior as observable ways of action that contribute to the full (complete) accomplishment of tasks. Consequently, he posits that behaviors combine inherent and acquired responses and situational stimuli. In other words, individual behavior is a result of past experiences which can manifest itself in values, ethics, beliefs and reactions. Davenport pointed that in order to assess the value of human capital, the total value of ability (composed of knowledge, skill and talent) is added to behavior. This cluster (within square brackets) is then conditioned by effort and time

Personal effort requires skills, knowledge and talent, which in turn also harnesses behavior. Effort is thus the locomotive personal energy which drives organizations forward. Without personal effort organizations fail to reach their pre-set goals. Finally, but not least, time refers to the chronological element of human capital. Davenport (1999) claims that time it a critical element in the equation since even the most talented, skilled, knowledgeable and dedicated workers will produce nothing without investing time in the job.

MANAGING HUMAN CAPITAL FOR HIGHER ORGANIZATIONAL COMMITMENT

Organizational commitment arises from an emotional or intellectual bond linking the individual with the organization (Perrin, 1995). Employee devotion towards the organization is demonstrated by acceptance to the organizational goals as well as high degree of personal affection to the organization. It is also demonstrated by an implicit agreement to put aside other investment tracks. (Litschka, Markom & Schunder, 2006). It comes in several forms, each with different implications for the relationship between individual and organization. Research on organizational commitment demonstrated three distinct categories being attitudinal, programmatic and loyalty-based (Flamholtz, 1985). While attitudinal commitment implies that employees feel motivated to work for a particular organization rather than any other, programmatic commitment is more reactive and thus leads people to work in the organization because they cannot afford to leave.

Although there are a number of issues which influence human capital investment, organizational commitment and job engagement can be considered as the two main pillars which contribute to higher levels of organizational performance.. When researchers study the two, they find that low levels of organizational commitment tend to increase organizational turnover, whereas a paucity of job engagement is related to higher absenteeism (US Bureau of Census Statistical Abstract USA, 1996). This may explain the reason why generally speaking highly committed and engaged employed are more task-oriented and their primary interest is to get the job done effectively and efficiently. . After all, they identify with their work, care about its outcome, and consider it as a part of the definition of themselves (Caulkin, 1997).

While it is not always easy to demonstrate the investment in human resources pays off, managers are realizing that development of human assets in activities like knowledge and skills training is mandatory. The dilemma if whether such investment is to be made generally circles round the justification of how short-term investment in human capital will contribute to long term organizational goals.

The economic model of human capital developed by Monks (1999) states that investment in human capital is dependent upon expectations of future rental rates of it. Monks states that the greater the increase in expected returns to human capital, the greater the investment in human capital. In addition, employers' decision to pay for the development of their employees is generally based on the assumption that such investment will pay back in a more productive, competitive and as a result more profitable firm. The correlation between investment in training as an independent variable and higher levels of profit as a depending variable is still highly debated. So far, researchers, have noticed that there are a number of mediating and intervening variables which very often conditions the final result. Investment in human capital is also highly beneficial to employees. More knowledgeable workers have higher opportunities for higher wages and are much less bound to the organization than less knowledgeable employees.

In the 1990s several empirical studies have confirmed a direct link between the employment of graduates and the adoption as well as the use of high-level technologies in the firm, and between the extent of investment in employee training, and the speed and successful adaptation of new technology (Bosworth and Wilson, 1993). In fact, education and training have been found to substantially increase a worker's ability to be innovative on the job (Bishop, 1994).

DISCUSSION

It is clear that since the early theories of management up to the most recent developments in the field, there has been a constant drive to identify what could possibly be the best form for the relationship between the owners of capital, very often represented by appointed and salaried managers, and their employees. In order to seriously support both organizational and employees' career growth, both parties must share a common understanding that goes beyond what has been formally specified in employment agreements (see Rousseau (1995) on the concept of the psychological contract).

In order to enable both sustained competitive advantage at the firm level and career success at the individual level, employability is a critical requirement (van der Heijde and Van der Heijden, 2006). Employability can be defined as "the continuous fulfilling, acquiring or creating of work through the optimal use of competences" (Van der Heijde and Van der Heijden, 2006, p. 453) and enables employees to cope with fast-changing job requirements. Stimulating occupational expertise and employability of employees appears to be advantageous for both organizational and employee outcomes (Fugate, Kinicki and Ashforth, 2004; Van Dam, 2004). As such they support the psychological contract framework in that both parties' growth is fostered.

OVERALL CONCLUSION: "MANAGING CULTURAL DIVERSITY": PEOPLE, TEAMS AND CULTURE

The overall purpose of this textbook, and the course on which it is based, is on one level accepting that we have a culturally diverse workforce, and on the next level trying to make the best of it. *'Vive la difference!'*

Let us summarize how we have developed this theme, leading into our conclusion of the importance of our culturally diverse individuals and teams as 'human assets' for companies and other organizations to manage with skill and resourcefulness, as much as they need to manage other resources.

Our **Part One: 'Managing Team Dynamics'** looked at how we can make the most of people working together. The people individually are diverse, and together they make unique teams with their own challenges and ability to contribute.

1. Defining Teams – looked at the nature of teams and how they operate.
2. Leading Teams – examined the challenge of leaders winning over team members to gain their commitment.
3. Communicating in Teams – saw some of the techniques for communicating, and some of the barriers which can stop teams from being effective.
4. Fostering Teams – considered how teams can work productively, especially in their interactions with each other.
5. Conflict in Teams – developed this theme further and analyzed why and how conflict arises, and how it can be managed.

Our **Part Two: 'Managing Human Resources'** was aimed at helping you to understand the processes organizations can use to manage their culturally diverse workforces most effectively. People are different, in personality, attitudes and background – so they need to be recruited, trained and managed to tap into their individual talents:

1. Introduction to Strategic HR – laid the foundations for our study with an appraisal of the evolution of the attitudes towards people in organizations.
2. Recruiting Talent – looked at the most effective and professional ways to identify and attract talent to an organization.
3. Training and Development – examined how organizations can grow and nurture their human assets, for the benefit of both parties.
4. Managing and Rewarding Performance – considered how these human assets can be motivated and engaged to be successful to add value to all involved.
5. International HR – gave a global perspective to the multiplicity of challenges facing organizations wanting to use their human capital to advantage.

Part Three: 'Managing Intercultural Diversity' dealt with the following issues:

1. Defining Culture – considered definitions to the nebulous concept of what makes people different, in behaviors, attitudes and outlook.
2. Organizational Culture – looked at how and why organizations and the people in them have evolved substantially different styles and ways of operating.
3. National Culture – examined how people in regions, countries, cities and even villages develop their unique characteristics, bringing these with them to work.
4. Developing Cultural Awareness – considers how we can learn about cultural diversity, appreciating its richness and added value.

So 'Managing Cultural Diversity', and its investigation into people, teams and culture, has tried to help you feel more confident about developing your career and managing your business in a world without frontiers – or perhaps the frontiers are different from what you first thought!

REFERENCES

Bishop. J.H. (1994) 'The impact of previous training on productivity and wages' in L. Lynch (ed.), *Training and the Private Sector – International Comparisons*. Chicago: University of Chicago Press.

Bosworth & Wilson (1993) 'Qualified Scientists and Engineers and Economic Performance' in P. Swann (ed.) *New Technologies and the Firm: Innovation and Competition*. London: Routledge.

Carey, A. (1967) 'The Howthorne Studies: A Radical Criticism', *American Sociological Review, 32*: 3, 403-416.

Cualkin, S. (1997) 'Skills, Not Loyalty, Now are Key If You Want Job Security', *San Francisco Examiner*, September 7, J-3.

Davenport, T. (1999) *Human Capital, What It is and Why People Invest In It*. San Francisco: Jossey Bass.

De Bono, S. & Van der Heijden B.I.J.M (2007) '*Converging Economic Growth and Human Capital*', Partners' Conference, Maastricht School of Management, Maastricht.

Flamholtz, E. G. (1985) *Human Resource Accounting*. San Francisco: Jossey-Bass.

Fugate, M., Kinicki, A.J. & Ashforth, B.E. (2004). 'Employability: A psycho-social construct, its dimensions, and applications'. *Journal of Vocational Behavior, 65*: 14-38.

Gaspersz, J. & Ott, M. (1996). *Management van employability. Nieuwe kansen in arbeidsrelaties* [Management of employability. New opportunities in labour relations]. Assen: Van Gorcum/Stichting Management Studies.

Handy, C. (1993) *Understanding Organisations*. Penguin, Harmondsworth

Rousseau, D.M. (1995). *Psychological contracts in organizations: Understanding written and unwritten agreements*. London: Sage.

Litschka, M., Markom, A. & Schunder, S. (2006) *Journal of Intelleuctual Capital* Vol. 7 No 2, 2006 pp 160-173

Tekleab, A.G. & Taylor, M.S. (2003). 'Aren't there two parties in an employment relationship? Antecedents and consequences of organization-employee agreement on contract obligations and violations'. *Journal of Organizational Behavior, 24*: 585-608.

Torrington, D. & Hall, L. (1995) Personnel Management: HRM in Action. London: Prentice Hall.

Towers P. (1995) *The People Strategy Benchmark Awareness and Attitude Study*. New York: Towers Perrin.

US Bureau of the Census, *Statistical Abstract of the United States*, 1996 (Washington Government, D.C.: U.S. Government Printing Office, 1996, pp 159, 192,193.

Van Dam, K. (2004) 'Antecedents and consequences of employability orientation'. *European Journal of Work and Organizational Psychology, 13*: 29-51.

Van der Heijden, B.I.J.M. (1998). *The measurement and development of professional expertise throughout the career. A retrospective study among higher level Dutch professionals*. PhD-thesis. University of Twente, Enschede, the Netherlands. Enschede: PrintPartners Ipskamp.

Van der Heijde, C.M., & Van der Heijden, B.I.J.M. (2006). 'A competence-based and multidimensional operationalization and measurement of employability', Human Resource Management, 45:3, 449-476.

RECOMMENDED FURTHER READING

Bartel, A.P. (1991) 'Productivity gains from the implementation of employee training programmes', *National Bureau of Economic Research*, Working Paper, 3893.

Bartel, A.P. (1995) 'Training, wage growth and job performance: evidence from a company database', *Journal of Labour Economics, 13*, 401-25.

De Koning, J. (1994) 'Evaluating training at the company level' in R.McNabb and K.Whitfield (eds.) *The Market for Training* Aldershot: Avebury.

Fombrun, C. & Tichy, N.M. and Devanna, M. (1984) *Strategic Human Resource Management.* New York: Wiley.

Gemmell (1997) 'Externalities to Higher Education; A Review of the New Growth Literature in National Committee of Inquiry into Higher Education (Dearing Committee)', *Higher Education in the Learning Society.* London: HMSO.

Goss, D. (1994) *Principles of Human Recourse Management.* London: Routledge.

James M. (1999) *'The Effect of Uncertain Returns on Human Capital Investment Patterns',* Unpublished Paper, Mount Holyoke College, USA.

Mayo, E. (1949) *The Social Problems of an Industrial Civilisation.* London: Routledge.

Molander, C. & Winterton, J.(1994) *Managing Human Resources.* London: Routledge.

Peery, N. S. Jr & Salem, M. (1993) 'Strategic Management of Emerging Human Resource Issues', *Human Resource Development Quarterly*, 4.1: 81-95.

Purcell , J. & Ahlstrand, B. (1994) *Human Resource Management in the Multi-Divisional Company.* Oxford: Oxford University Press.

Senge, P. M. (1990) *The Fifth Discipline: The Art and Practice of The Learning Organisation,* New York: Doubleday.

Smith, A. (1776) *The Wealth of Nations.* New York: Collier and Son 1937, 103 (originally published 1776).

Maastricht School of Management

The Series

This series makes excellent, affordable textbooks for students worldwide. By emphasizing the international, multicultural, sustainability, and social responsibility dimensions of management, and by giving special attention to change issues in transitional economies, these volumes aim to define the way management subjects should be taught to multicultural audiences. It provides students all over the world with essential advice for successful studies.

Each book is a concise but complete treatment of the topics covered in a core course, based on the philosophy of the Maastricht School of Management's MBA program. Targeted readers are students enrolled in other universities, and practicing managers in countries worldwide, as well as MBA students in MSM's overseas outreach programs.

For more than a half century Maastricht School of Management (MSM) has focused on international cooperation. As a key player in the global education field, MSM is one of the few management schools that systematically combine education, technical assistance and research in its professional services. Every year, millions of students graduate successfully from management courses at universities all over the world. Among them, more than 2,000 students at the MSM branches in nearly thirty countries.

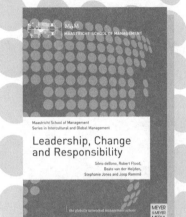

Maastricht School of Management
Vol. 1
Jones, Wahba & Van der Heijden
How to Write Your MBA Thesis

Students of MBA programs who are preparing for the research, writing and defense of their MBA thesis will find this book especially useful. Nine chapters give detailed examples of how students all over the world have managed the problems that the MBA thesis project has thrown at them. The appendices include examples of everything one needs to complete the thesis – proposal, abstract, contents page, introduction, literature review, research methodology, data analysis, conclusions and recommendations, and suggested areas for future research.

320 pages
11 illustrations, 15 charts
Paperback, 6¹/2" x 9¹/4"
ISBN: 978-1-84126-231-4
$ 34.00 US
£ 16.95 UK/€ 24.95

Maastricht School of Management
Vol. 2
DeBono, Flood, Van der Heijden, Jones & Remmé
Leadership, Change and Responsibility

Leadership is an increasingly important subject because of the challenges which require management of some sort. Those challenges are more often characterized by change or the need for change. Strategy and operations are increasingly expected to be formed from a sense of responsibility. Increasingly, various elements in society call for such responsibility, while issues have also arisen which involve management in far reaching challenges, even to life itself. This book addresses the need for a type of leadership not commonly found before.

240 pages
30 illustrations
Paperback, 6¹/2" x 9¹/4"
ISBN: 978-1-84126-238-3
$ 34.00 US
£ 16.95 UK/€ 24.95

The Business of Sports

The Series

This Sport Management Book Series aims to incorporate cutting edge work which is designed to transcend the boundaries between business and sport.

The series will be used as a forum for research and scholarly insight surrounding the major issues of importance for those concerned with sport management and sport marketing.

The series will provide an opportunity to illustrate and highlight the ways in which the business of sport has expanded to become a global industry.

Editors of the Series:
Dr. James Skinner, Griffith University, Queensland, Australia
Prof. Paul De Knop, Free University Brussels, Belgium

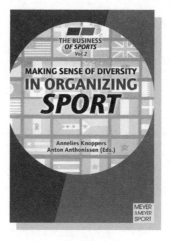

The Business of Sports
Vol. 1
James Skinner/Allan Edwards
The Sport Empire

The book critizises the globalisation of sport from a Autonomist Marxist perspective. This analysis is supported by numerous international sport examples that highlight how sport is being governed by a select group of sport organisations, multinational companies and media conglomerates. This domination of the sport industry is marginalising disadvantaged groups and is subsequently being challenged by new methods of protest and resistance. "The Sport Empire" provides compelling reading for those interested in the effects of globalisation of sport.

192 pages, 3 charts
Paperback, $6^1/2$" x $9^1/4$"
ISBN: 978-1-84126-168-3
$ 19.95 US
£ 14.95 UK/€ 18.95

The Business of Sports
Vol. 2
Annelies Knoppers/
Anton Anthonissen (Eds.)
Making Sense of Diversity in Organizing Sport

This book is about the way otherness can be suppressed by dominant meanings. The purpose of the book is to focus on organizational consequences of processes of sense making and assigning meanings to diversity in sport organizations. There is a dominant European perspective on sense making of diversity and a more American approach. The conclusion is that scholars and researchers who work in the area of diversity need to pay attention to both ways of looking at diversity.

120 pages, 2 charts
Paperback, $6^1/2$" x $9^1/4$"
ISBN: 978-1-84126-203-1
$ 19.95 US
£ 14.95 UK/€ 18.95